Frank Lloyd Wright versus America:

The 1930s

**Ocotillo Camp, 1929. Courtesy and © the
Frank Lloyd Wright Foundation.**

Frank Lloyd Wright versus America:

The 1930s

Donald Leslie Johnson

The MIT Press
Cambridge, Massachusetts
London, England

This book was set in Univers and Galliard by DEKR Corporation and printed and bound in the United States of America.

Library of Congress Cataloging-in-Publication Data

Johnson, Donald Leslie.
    Frank Lloyd Wright versus America : the 1930s / Donald Leslie Johnson.
        p.   cm.
    Includes bibliographical references.
    ISBN 0-262-10044-4
    1. Wright, Frank Lloyd, 1867–1959. 2. Architects—United States—Biography. I. Title.
NA737.W7J6 1990
720′ .92—dc20
    [B]   90-30650
                                                                CIP

This book is dedicated to Paul Hasselberg

Contents

The second flowering of Frank Lloyd Wright's extraordinary career began in 1928 when he was sixty-one. In that year he married his mistress Olga Lazovich. Together they planned a future that, if it was to be successful, required the re-creation of Wright the active man, not the legend. With only a few architectural commissions since the early 1920s, Wright's image had to be reconstructed and revitalized. The fabled life of his first golden age had to be reevaluated and the nightmare of the recent past put behind. All was exposed in an autobiography.

The second life of the newly active man was anticipated in a number of ways but primarily by the formation of an institute for young people. Here the Wrights practiced their notions of *paideia*, work, and thought united in a community of apprentices they called the Taliesin Fellows. The Wrights had developed a holism that revolved about their idea of an organic architecture. They vigorously promoted both the idea and the fact that their daily lives, in concert with the Fellows', were devoted to its practice. Their concerns were not just for buildings in cities but for new villages in and on the North American landscape; not just villages but an organically complete life; not just complete personal lives but a healthier, refurbished, and philosophically unified America. The means to these ends were focused on Wright's talent and life as paradigms incorporating an interpretation of the great American dream of individual liberty. The Wrights therefore argued against the doctrines that supported European hegemony, against traditional prejudice, and against the political left.

As lord and lady they broadcast their ideas from a manor, a modern castle moated by grain fields and psychological privacy. The word also went forth from lecture platforms, in exhibitions, and onto the pages of magazines and books. The Europeans, the English, and the Soviets were impressed and intrigued, but fellow Americans soon became confused. In emphasizing his philosophy Wright's rhetoric seemed to damn everything American—history, cities, home, and nearly all else. Wright could not be ignored.

Finally he acquired two architectural commissions. For them he composed two seemingly opposite concepts of architecture for dissimilar sites. When the buildings were complete, the world again took note. The first commission became one of the most beautiful houses of any century, the Kaufmann country home Fallingwater on Bear Run Creek in Pennsylvania; the second was the Johnson's Wax Administration Building at Racine in Wisconsin. Both were theoretically brilliant. So too was Wright's second solitary castle Taliesin West, built on a pediment overlooking the Arizona desert, a place in the West: the frontier. Wright's new summer lasted from the late thirties until his death in 1959.

The 1930s was a period of turmoil in the Soviet Union and rising political tensions and threats of physical conflict in Europe. The Wrights became involved in those social fractures only parenthetically and with no meaningful satisfaction. During difficult and often blood-letting times in the USSR, he was invited to a convention of Soviet architects held in Moscow and gave a speech to those gathered. During the tension-filled months at the end of 1938 and before the British entered what became World War II, he was invited by the prestigious Sulgrave Manor Board to give a series of lectures in London. Almost immediately thereafter, during the early years of the war, British architects presented him with their highest honor, a Gold Medal. He was honored at other places at other times but these three occasions were unique and therefore intriguing. The evidence revealed by this research justifies that fascination.

If we accept art historian Norris Kelly Smith's observation that our perceptions of Wright have been determined by his "evaluation of himself," determined from his perspective, with his formulations of biographical and artistic truth, and without "reference to the shape of the American world at large," then this series of essays will go some way toward balancing evaluations as well as exposing myths and correcting legends.

The only way to appreciate the greatness of an artist and his products—of Wright's architecture—is not by blind adulation or by intolerance but by seeking a fuller critical knowledge of the person and his work. It is important to know that Wright's architecture was a manifest expression of his philosophy, which when matured linked the man to his country, to his place, to his family.

I have asked only a few basic questions. To paraphrase Leonard Eaton, until 1936 it took intelligence to hire Wright but only money thereafter. Correct? and if so, why? Or, to repeat Reyner Banham's question and emphasis, why did Wright "change from simply a very good architect to the Greatest American Genius?" Wright's son John once said that his father "was an American idea that pressed irresistibly toward fulfillment": was this correct? Why were the Soviets so interested in Wright? Why the British? Why did his architecture of the 1930s appear so different from his previous work?

Like most answers to simple questions, responses are complex and interdependent. In this instance they involve ideas like utopia, urbanism, transcendentalism, education, socialism, service . . . war; and particular things like a speech, a medal, a book, a letter . . . a visitor.

Though it pays close attention to the architect's life and thought, this book is not a eulogy but a critical study of Frank Lloyd Wright's architectural career in the 1930s.

D. L. J.
Kangarilla/Seattle

Architecture is beginning, always beginning. It was not made by the Greeks nor by the Romans. It wasn't even made in the Georgian Period. It is something that has to be made afresh all the time, as life, as opportunity, as growth changes.

FLW, 1940

Not only do I intend to be the greatest architect who has yet lived, but the greatest who will ever live. Yes, I intend to be the greatest architect of all time, and I do hereunto affix "the red square" and sign my name to this warning.

FLW, 1928

Frank Lloyd Wright versus America:

The 1930s

Frank Lloyd Wright's career in the 1930s was dramatic, vacillating sometimes violently through extremes of introspection, notoriety, self-adulation, and national and international curiosity. Social interactions activating his life fit those extremes with confrontation at one pole and quiescence at the other. Outwardly, Wright's presentation of himself before the public seems to have been paramount at all points during his career, regardless of the motivation. So it was in the decade of the thirties. In the beginning there was a desperate necessity to regain the attention required to attract clients; at the end there were rather frantic attempts to influence national attitudes and official policies, even those related to the impending war. During the 1930s he was promoted by people of influence; by institution of and participation in a series of major exhibitions; by giving speeches or "talks" to any and all who would pay; and by writing at first about himself (beginning with his autobiography) and then about architecture and cities, but mainly about American culture, politics, and economics. As a result of all of this activity he successfully secured not only national but international attention to his words and works.

A second realm of activity concerned his architectural production, either realized or projected. Few works were built until mid-decade, so proposals, ideas, and notions dominated the first six years or so. Theoretical and critical works defined a third realm; his Kahn lectures at Princeton University and the proposal of Broadacre City dominated his production in this area. Wright's professional engagements in London and Moscow resulted largely from recent publication of his theoretical works, though the underlying causes were his historical position as a founder of modern architecture and his obvious architectural genius. A fourth realm of activity was education. There can be no doubt that if all had gone well and his practice of architecture had been continuous and full, there would have been no need to create the Taliesin Fellowship. But all had not gone well. For almost two decades the emotion and toil of domestic strife had challenged his attention to his architectural practice. Somewhat related to those problems but more to his extravagences, during most of the late 1920s and into the 1930s he was desperate for money; the creation of a private school was one practical response.

While it is necessary to concentrate on the period 1930 to 1939 in Wright's biography, and while obvious publicly motivated productivities started in 1930, a vital spark had occurred in

1.1 Probably the most popular with Wright, the portrait was published often from 1931 until the 1940s, for instance in the 1932 autobiography and in 1937 in *Pravda*.

1927 and a release in 1928. Evidence of that release was found in one grand exposition executed in 1929. The decade of the 1930s was approached, therefore, with much optimism after a winter of domestic hell and near professional oblivion.

1 Olga Milan Lazovich

The spark was a divorce in 1927 from his second wife, Miriam. Their relationship and marriage had not been in any sense typical; their divorce even less so. Wright and Maud Miriam Noel, a divorcee from Bristol, Tennessee, had met in late 1914 or early 1915 more or less as a result of her overtures. From that moment until 1927 they dominated one another's social and domestic life with a constant and depressing irritation. It needs to be remembered that from 1916 to 1922 Wright resided for nearly half his time in Tokyo, sometimes with his mother and/or Miriam, while supervising the construction of the Imperial Hotel and other smaller commissions in Japan. His American professional practice did not recover from gross inattention until 1936, a period of two full decades. True, there were some interesting architectural highlights, especially in California around 1922 to 1924. They were exciting works if somewhat aberrant in the grand view of his career. The notoriety of proceedings over the divorce did not help Wright's professional practice or Miriam's health. With a troubled and unstable nine-year relationship it is not clear why Wright and Miriam decided to marry in November 1923. When five months later in April 1924 she left him it was probably not unexpected. In July 1925 it was Wright who filed for divorce, but only after he had met and won the affection of another divorcee, Olgivanna Hinzenberg.

There has been some uneasy speculation about early years in the life of Mrs. Hinzenberg, the bright young woman who became the third Mrs. Wright. It is necessary therefore, to briefly outline her relatively peculiar career for it reveals much of the character of the woman who was to play a decisive role in Wright's life and therefore his profession as it evolved during the critical decade of the 1930s.

Wright did not describe her in his 1932 autobiography, perhaps because he was still too close to and emotionally involved with the harrowing events of the divorce and his affair with Olgivanna. He only perfunctorily introduced Olgivanna and vaguely referred to her familial lineage (something important to both of them). After it was clear to Wright that the marriage was consolidated he impressionistically described Olgivanna; that was in the expanded autobiography of 1943. Impressions of their first meeting were vivid in his memory even at that date. Olgivanna was "a dark, slender gentlewoman . . . . Unobtrusive but lovely, I secretly observed her aristocratic bearing, no hat, her dark hair parted in the middle and smoothed down over her ears, a light small shawl over her shoulders, little or no makeup, very simply dressed. . . . perhaps Russian? . . . I instantly liked her looks. . . . sensitive feminine brow and dark eyes. . . . a strange elation stole over me. Suddenly in my unhappy state something cleared up—what had been the matter with me came to look me in the face—it was, simply too much passion without poetry. . . . This strange chance meeting. . . . I was a hungry man."[1] She was thirty years Wright's junior, apparently born in 1898 in Cetinje, Montenegro, a town slightly inland from the Adriatic and about thirty-five miles from the Albanian border to the south.[2]

Montenegro was a proud but hapless and poor country before World War I, unable to support itself agriculturally and dependent for fifty percent of its economy on direct grants from Czarist Russia. It did not exist after the war. In the summer of 1918 the Ottoman Empire in the Balkans was defeated and the last remains of the Hapsburg Empire disintegrated into national components. Independent but vulnerable Montenegro was absorbed into Serbia as the Serbs, Croats, and Slovenes formed a kingdom later united as Yugoslavia, in which Montenegro became a "republic" or province.

Olga Ivanovna Milan Lazovich, or as she preferred, Olgivanna, was born to Iovan (sometimes Ivan) and Militze Lazovich. Of her father little is revealed other than that he may have been a judge or chief justice. Of her mother it is often suggested that she was related to General Marcos Milan who organized the successful defense of Montenegro and helped retain its independence from the Hapsburgs. In any event, her family was wealthy and if not of the aristocracy well placed socially. As a young girl and as was correct for the family's social station, she was sent to school in Belgrade, the capital of Serbia. Probably as a result of the outbreak of war and threats to Serbia, she was again sent away, this time to the city of Batumi in Georgia south of the Caucasus. She lived with her married sister and obtained the Slavic education believed proper by her family. Olgivanna's recollection was vivid: "I lived a sheltered and protected life among the Russian aristocracy at that time; everything was done for me." In fact she "had very little idea where the kitchens were even located in our villa on the Black Sea."[3]

With the defeat of Montenegro in 1918 she became an expatriate. Her parents moved to Belgrade where they remained, while her brother Vladimir emigrated to the United States. In 1916 Olgivanna had married Vlademar Hinzenberg, an architectural draftsman and family friend, ten years her senior. She left Hinzenberg probably in 1918. Around 1922 the daughter of their union, Svetlana, was sent to Hollis, a section of Queens in New York City, to live with brother Vladimir, affectionately called Vlado. (Later she was adopted by Wright but died in an automobile accident in 1946.)[4]

In search of education Olgivanna was separated from her family; her native country literally disappeared; her family dispersed to three continents; her attempt at a permanent new home through marriage with an older man failed. All this extracted an emotional toll and induced her to seek social dependence in a new and atypical family, an artificial one created by Georgi Ivanovitch Gurdjieff.

In 1915 in Petrograd (before St. Petersburg, now Leningrad) Gurdjieff began discussion sessions for some intellectually curious urbanites. Achieving relative success he instituted more formal classes which were about the importance and character of knowledge, the Orient, art, civilization, immortality, "psychic centers," and his method for the reconstruction of the human machine. Worried about a series of murderous revolutionary events in Petrograd in 1917, he and his small group of followers moved south to the town of Essentuki in the Russian Caucasus. There in 1918 Gurdjieff more carefully defined the essentials of his training system and initiated a formal program that he called the Institute for the Harmonious Development of Man. War in the northern Caucasus again forced him and his students to move, this time over the mountains to Tiflis, capital of what was then Georgia, 150 miles east of Batumi. New apostles joined the twelve people who trekked over the mountains; among the neophytes was Olgivanna. After only a few months in Tiflis Gurdjieff was again on the move, this time before the red banners of the oncoming Bolshevik army. The Institute band left Georgia in 1919 for Constantinople where they remained for about a year until, for unexplained reasons, they hurriedly decided to move operations yet again, this time to a more central European location, settling in Berlin. They operated in Germany for about another year, or from spring 1921 to summer 1922. Olgivanna's travels with her new "family," therefore, proved as significant as those of her childhood, and they were to continue.

One of the more intellectually endowed of Gurdjieff's clan and a fervent follower, P. D. Ouspensky, had written a book supportive of and parallel to Gurdjieff's teachings, *Tertium Organum.* When translated into English it met with great success, especially in America's New England states and in old England. As a result Ouspensky and Gurdjieff were invited to give a series of lectures in England. Their endeavors were greeted most favorably and they managed to develop a prominent London circle. With financing from this supportive group and encouraged by the prospect of receiving students from Britain, France, and the United States, Gurdjieff moved the Institute to Paris in July 1922. He soon purchased the Chateau du Prieuré in Avon near Fontainebleau. By then Olgivanna's position in the Institute had become that of Assistant Instructor. Indeed, many Americans,

Europeans, and British did attend the Institute at Avon as did the New Zealand expatriate author Katherine Mansfield. She died at the Institute in 1923 in what were thought to be mysterious circumstances but in fact of tuberculosis. Her death created quite an international stir and did a great deal to focus public attention on what had been a rather obscure society.

Performances of dance, "movements," recitation, and "demonstrations" by Gurdjieff's people were quite unique and usually well attended. He presented these shows both to gain public attention for recruitment to the Institute and to gain money from the box office. He began offering rather modest public performances and demonstrations as early as the first months in Tiflis. By the 1920s they were rather grand affairs employing full string orchestras. It should not be surprising that a tour of New York, Boston, and Philadelphia was undertaken in early 1924, for which the company numbered forty people from the Institute plus full orchestra. These were Gurdjieff's best and most popular years; another tour was never attempted. While in the eastern states Gurdjieff acquired a booking at a theater in Chicago for the end of March. Fortuitously, in 1924 Hinzenberg apparently was living in Chicago and the Gurdjieff tour afforded him and Olgivanna an opportunity to resolve mutual problems and arrange a proper divorce. In early April 1924 the flock's last American show and demonstration, lasting nearly four hours, was held at New York's prestigious Carnegie Hall. A long trip back to France followed immediately thereafter.

When Olgivanna returned to Avon she continued to teach dervish dances, "obligatories," initiations, or whatever. American expatriate and English resident Stanley Nott began attending during that summer. He has recalled Olgivanna's story of her initial meeting with Gurdjieff in Tiflis.

G. Do you have a wish?

O. I wish for immortality.

G. What you do now?

O. I look after my house and servants.

G. You work yourself? Cook, look after baby?

O. No, my servants do that for me.

G. You do nothing, and you wish for immortality!

Nott and Olgivanna were pulling a long saw, cutting wood, when she offered her recollections.[5] In October 1924 Gurdjieff became ill and many of his staff, including Olgivanna, and all his pupils (now reduced to eight young Americans) left Avon. Resolving to attend to her own future, with her daughter Svetlana she returned to Hollis. She then traveled alone to Chicago where her fate and that of her daughter were with a divorce court. She settled final matters with Hinzenberg and planned to return to Hollis.

Wright met Olgivanna in late November 1924 at a matinee performance of the Petrograd Ballet Company; she sat two places away from him in a box. They were introduced, they talked, and he took her on a visit to Taliesin that November; he won her love, and in February 1925— approximately—they began living together in Wright's Spring Green, Wisconsin, home. In April 1925 her divorce from Hinzenberg became final. A daughter, Iovanna, was born to Wright and the young Olgivanna at the end of that same year.[6]

From Cetinje to Spring Green had been a long, arduous journey, one full of diverse experiences, farewells, and temporary families. But Olgivanna's familial struggles, now knitted to Wright's ego and career, were not over. When Miriam Noel learned about Wright's new mistress the situation quickly escalated to one of vengeful proportions. To the public press it became an epic soap opera. Based on substantial evidence one of Wright's biographers, Robert Twombly, has described the details of various proceedings, combats with courts, the involvement of a state governor and the U.S. Congress, machinations of banks, pursuit by federal marshals, flights to safe places as fugitives, and so forth, in combination with the loss of Wright's home Taliesin to a bank acting for creditors. The tragedy of the situation was compounded when his home was partially gutted by fire in April 1925. Suffice it to say that the affair consumed all energies, monies, and emotions. Finally, after a preliminary divorce decree in 1927 Wright was allowed to return to Taliesin so that he might work to pay his accumulated and substantial debts. "Denied work," Wright had said, "and what Freedom have you?"[7] In August of that year, after people began to realize that Miriam's protestations and contestations were spiteful and prompted by revenge—and that she may have been ill—Wright obtained a divorce. However, he was by then incapable of paying his debts of $43,000 or so; so his "personal effects, art pieces, and farm machinery were sold at public auction." The bank took possession of Taliesin and the farm. But all was not lost. After the marriage in 1928 Taliesin was redeemed in the name of the corporation and the "remainder of the architect's debts paid" by stockholders of Frank Lloyd Wright Incorporated. Among them was a good friend Ferdinand Shevill; the writer and critic Alexander Woollcott; designer Joseph Urban; playwright Charles MacArthur; the architect's sisters Jane and Maginel and his first wife Catherine; and his attorney Philip La Follette who became secretary of Wright Inc. and later governor of Wisconsin. Wright personally contacted many of his former clients, some of whom had remained friends,

1.2 Maud Miriam Noel Wright around 1920, perhaps on return from Japan.

stating frankly that he was in financial difficulties and urging them to buy into Wright Inc. Among those former clients who helped were Mrs. Avery Coonley, Harold McCormick, and Darwin C. Martin. As Twombly noted, legally, Wright Inc. "owned Taliesin and everything in it. Its hopes for financial return were based on the architect's ability to design buildings for profit."[8] In October 1928 the Wrights were able to return to Taliesin.

Wright's ability to immediately raise money was limited. His liquid assets were land, buildings, equipment, his artifacts, and an art collection. To help support his various private activities he sold a significant portion of his Japanese art works. On one occasion in 1932 he offered 223 prints and a number of albums (one of eight Hiroshige "Views of Yedo" was sold for a mere $30), manuals, folios, drawings, and sketch books for $2,820.[9] Clearly his major source of income was to be from fees for architectural services; but that depended on people coming to him, not on his own volition.

The extent of Wright's attempts to secure commissions so he might repay those who supported him cannot be fully known, but a measure can be implied by two examples. First, in 1929 he tried to establish a series of partnerships with architects in Chicago, New York, Phoenix, Los Angeles, and perhaps other locations. Although he may have believed they were not partnerships by using his preferred word "association," they were effectively the former. Indeed, his partner-to-be in Chicago, Charles Morgan, was exhorted to devote all of his "energies . . . to the duties and opportunities" of Wright, and he was to seek commissions. All contract documents were to be in the name of Frank Lloyd Wright Incorporated: Charles Morgan, Chicago, Associate.[10] The other example was his attempt in 1930 to obtain a job as consultant or critic to those planning the Chicago "Century of Progress" exposition in 1933. He said he was thinking not of designing a building but of acting as "a good umpire."[11] These various cooperative plans were of no avail: more personal and direct involvement was necessary.

Perhaps in an attempt to understand the recent shattering events that controlled his life, Wright has said he began to write his autobiography while in a safe place—hiding—in a cottage on Lake Minnetonka near Minneapolis. Little was done autobiographically after that initial effort until 1927. Also in that year, after a decade when he built barely a dozen architectural commissions and prepared few other projects, a former employee contacted Wright. Architect Albert C. McArthur asked his former boss to help document the Arizona Biltmore Hotel to be built near Phoenix. This project was financed by the Los Angeles Biltmore people, and Warren and Charles McArthur were

1.3 Mr. and Mrs. Wright sometime in the 1940s.

on the board of the Arizona Biltmore Corporation. Warren had built a house in Chicago designed by Wright in 1892, and Charles was Albert McArthur's father. While in Phoenix in 1928 Wright met Dr. Alexander Chandler and they discussed a proposed desert hotel and resort to be located near the doctor's own town of Chandler, Arizona. One year after the preliminary divorce as required by Wisconsin law, Wright and Olgivanna were free to marry. On 25 August 1928 the ceremony was held at La Jolla, California, one of a number of places of refuge during the preceding few years. Moreover, the rebuilding of Taliesin that had begun in 1927 was not complete, so Wright had to work at La Jolla. Almost immediately after the wedding the Wrights were able to return to Spring Green, where he completed detailed designs for McArthur and began on the ill-fated designs for what became known as San Marcos in The Desert. Chandler approved the preliminary drawings in December 1928 and preparation of the final plans and construction documents began almost immediately. Already things were looking much brighter for the newlyweds.

The legal and emotional permanence of the divorce after years of harassment followed by a long twelve-month waiting period, or "probation" as Wright called it, was sealed and celebrated by the wedding. The woman who had entered his life four years earlier when in her mid-twenties not only became the matriarchal strength he needed after the death in 1923 of his mother, known as Anna, but pragmatically bonded shared ideals of individualism and holism. The evidence of their agreement, her strength, and particularly of his liberation was first evidenced at a small camp on a high plateau of the central Arizona desert.

2 Ocotillo Camp

Across the mesa from the camp are great low-lying mounds of black, burnt rock covered with picture writing scratched on the surface by the Indians who came there at sunrise to worship the sun, the greatest evidence of the Great Spirit they knew.

The desert is prostrate to the sun.

All life here is sun-life: and died a sun-death. Evidence is everywhere.

FLW, An Autobiography, 1932

Dr. Chandler envisaged San Marcos in The Desert as a large winter resort for wealthy tourists. The original San Marcos Hotel, or Desert Lodge, in the town of Chandler served a similar function and was Arizona's first resort hotel. Designed by California architect Arthur Benton and constructed in 1912–13,[1] it was the center of tourism in central Arizona in the 1920s. Dr. Chandler wished to create

2.1 The Wright suite of cabins at Ocotillo Camp under construction in 1929. Courtesy and © the Frank Lloyd Wright Foundation.

a facility that would compete with the newly constructed Arizona Biltmore in the hope of maintaining his dominance of tourism through his enterprises in and around Chandler. The new resort was not to be in Chandler (a few miles southeast of present-day metropolitan Phoenix) but ten miles west. Because of its unique location in rough, jagged, uninhabited desert, and as a matter of urgency, the doctor invited the architect to Arizona to complete the design and prepare other documents. San Marcos in The Desert was a large commission—some $40,000 in fees was in the offering—so it was an invitation easy to accept. Wright and his entourage of servants, architectural staff, and family arrived in Chandler in early January 1929.

Wright could hardly contain his ambition in anticipation of finishing the San Marcos in The Desert commission. "Yes, at last," he exclaimed, "creation long denied, here came opportunity," and for an "ideal site." Nearly in the same breath he repeated, "Having been held off so long from active creation, I could scarcely wait to begin." The cost of hoteling his family and staff in Chandler was in Wright's reckoning too high and the summer would become too hot in typical hotel cubicles. "Why not camp?" he wondered. He approached Dr. Chandler, who responded by offering a site "by a low, spreading, rocky mound rising from the great floor of the desert—well away from everywhere, from which the site of the new [proposed] resort itself might be seen." To the offer Wright asked, "This—do you mean it—can I have this to build on?" Chandler nodded. "Marvellous!," Wright replied. He found it "all too good, but it was true."[2] The knoll top selected for the Camp had a clear view of the site for the proposed San Marcos in The Desert resort and of the Salt River Mountains in the near distance.

Ocotillo Camp was fresh and clear in Wright's memory when he wrote about it for his autobiography, perhaps because it was such a recent adventure; surely because it occurred at a terribly important moment in his new life.[3] In fact much of the text, some of it quoted below, is written in a manner that suggests he was making notes in his camp cabin, or writing almost immediately after its abandonment. As well, like almost all of his writing (including that immediately above) it is in a somewhat journalistic style perhaps hoping to capture the attention of a nonarchitectural audience. The valuable descriptions follow.

Now the architect and his helpers working away to build an architect's "compound," we will call it, in this unmitigated quotidian wilderness unchangeably changing.

We need fifteen [sic] cabins in all. Since they will be temporary, call them ephemera. You will soon see them all like a group of gigantic butterflies—say—conforming to the crown

of the outcropping of splintered rock gently rising from the desert floor. This rock mound itself decorated by cacti, grease wood and palosverdes [sic] will rise between the fleet of surrounding cabins to give a *measure* of privacy to all. . . .

The cabins themselves will be connected together by a low staggered box board wall ["Boxboards (unlucky green) and two-inch battens"],[4] its horizontal zig zag lines completing the enclosure. . . .

The necessary openings in the canvas-topped box buildings? We will close them with canvas-covered wood frames or "wings" hinged with rubber belting to open and shut tight instead of doors and windows, which, of course, there will be none.

And when these white canvas wings, like sails, are spread, the buildings—the butterflys simile aside—will look like "desert ships." The group will look like some kind of desert fleet, so it seems to me as I work at it.

And with cold-water paid we paint the horizontal board walls continuing around and connecting the buildings about the mound the color of dry rose to match the light on the desert floor. The one-two triangles seen made by the mountain ranges around about the site will be seen reflected in the gables of the camp. We will paint the triangles scarlet, make the cabins bloom . . . the one-two triangles of the ocotillo itself.[5]

Henry Klumb was working in the camp and probably did some of the painting. When he wrote to a colleague he described the colors: the timberwork including the wall was pink, the gable triangles were red, "the canvas white, the ground of greyish-yellow sand; the greyish-green vegetation and the blue skies."[6] Design began immediately and it would be safe to say that it was completed in only a few days.

Assisted by a local carpenter, Wright and the draftsmen then began construction of what they knew was a temporary work place. Construction costs ran to about $3500 all up.[7] A temporary place, Wright had said, "'Ocotillo'—the camp—is ephemera. To drop a seed or two, itself? Who knows?" He and his draftsmen "put it together with nails, screws, hinges, and rigged it with ship cord, designed as carefully as any 'permanent' building."[8]

The canvas windows and doors like ship-sails when open may be shut against the dust or may open to deflect the desert breezes into the interiors. Screened openings for cross ventilation are everywhere at the floor levels to be used during the heat of the day; closed at night. The long sides of the canvas slopes lie toward the sun to aid in warming the interiors in winter.

2.2 Ocotillo Camp, plan of 1929. This plan contains a scale (not on other publications) from which it can be seen that the camp was about 200 feet long (and the cars less than 10 feet in length). Some differences between this plan and the camp as built are worth a mention (compare with Figure 2.3). The outermost sleeping room of the Wright suite was not built, possibly to preserve an ancient saguaro cactus. Wright's office next to the experimental block yard was slightly larger than shown. The flag always proudly flown was on a pole immediately to the left inside the entrance opening in the boundary wall. Some but not all of the bracing pilasters (triangular bumps in the wall) were built. A few walls met the cabins differently than shown, no doubt in response to site conditions. The garage—more like a carport—was roofed but did not cover all the cars indicated. Bath houses were off the dining, guest, and servants' courts. The concrete vault was not built nor was housing for the lighting plant; however, after a few weeks a portable plant was installed (in favor of kerosene) but at an unknown location. The three fireplaces were not built, rather wood stoves eventually served most cabins. The "model" was in fact not of, but for the San Marcos in The Desert project and composed of full-sized concrete blocks that could be arranged for study of juxtapositions, geometry, shadow patterns, and form. All in all the plan has proven fairly accurate.

Based on a plan published in *Architectural Record*, August 1930, with modifications interpolated mainly from evidence contained in a series of photographs held by the Frank Lloyd Wright Archives (most may have been by George Kastner) and from an archaeological survey undertaken in 1982 (Green 1983). Collection of the author. © 1990 the Frank Lloyd Wright Foundation.

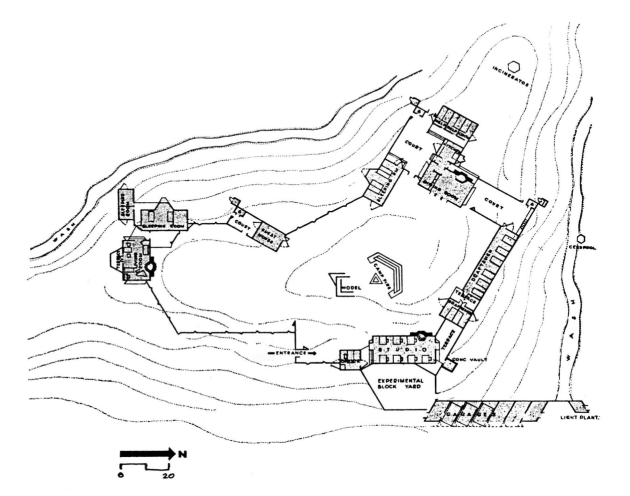

2.3 Ocotillo Camp viewed from the east. Identification of cabins is based on evidence noted in caption to Figure 2.2.

This long side is to have additional cover of canvas, air blowing between the two sheets of canvas, if the camp is occupied in summer.[9]

Within three days the assistants had a place to sleep; a few days later the Wright family quarters were complete. The rest of the twelve cabins followed, each with a stove, not a fireplace as shown in plan. Those who camped in the cabins were Wright, his wife and their two daughters and a nanny (practically speaking), six draftsmen (Klumb, Donald Walker, Vladimir Heifitz, Cy Tomblins, George Kastner, and the Canadian architect Francis Sullivan), and an old employee and friend, William West—a carpenter by trade—whose wife was the cook.[10] In two weeks they had made "the architect's camp a transient liveliness," as Wright put it; "it is living now in the Arizona desert."[11] Wright's autobiographical description reveals an honest excitement not contained in discussions of other projects or buildings. He was creating architecture again in an environment new to his experiences.

Wright often reused his own designs, but in doing so he did not just repeat the older scheme. Rather and to varying degrees he tried to improve and usually elaborated it, although not always successfully, for often the original scheme did not fit the new and different program. With few exceptions during the first decade of his own practice (that was through the 1890s) he often borrowed ideas from his mentor Louis Sullivan or from other well-known architects, more as a familiar eclectic response than anything else, certainly not as plagiarism—at least in the strict sense of the term. But Ocotillo Camp is interesting on another count. Wright borrowed a vernacular idea that he had seen and perhaps experienced in Montana.

Wright had been employed to prepare master plans and buildings for three projects during 1909, each for the Bitter Root Valley Irrigation Company. The first was University Heights (often erroneously called Como Orchards, even by Wright), the second a new city to have been called Bitter Root, and the third a proposed village also called Bitter Root.[12] In order to prepare proper site and master plans for University Heights, the first of the three projects, he was taken along with other company officers and financiers from the Chicago area to the Bitter Root Valley via Missoula during February 1909. They traveled the length of the valley, viewed its magnificent natural beauties and the hundreds of orchards, and arrived at its southern end west of Darby on a high bench overlooking the valley and the Sapphire Mountains. The fruit, including that from an orchard called Como, was picked by itinerant and part-time workers who lived in camps. These small communities were usually composed of housing made of temporary structures called "tent frame," although some tar paper buildings were also used.

Wright family cabins
(living space shown)

Guest cabin

Mr & Mrs Weston's cabin

Dining "room"

Acropolis

Entrance

FLW's study

drafting office (studio)

Experimental Block Yard

Carport

123850

The construction technique for a tent box frame was almost exactly that later used by Wright at Ocotillo. Wood floors of the Montana buildings were joined on the lower half to siding of horizontal board and batten or sometimes lapped siding.[13] The top half of each wall and the roof were of canvas; the roof was doubled canvas with an insulating air space between. The proportional relationship between siding and canvas at Ocotillo was not similar to that in Montana, for Wright wished to emphasize the boundary wall. He certainly saw the Montana houses for they were in their hundreds about the valley. During his week in the valley he may have conducted business or slept in one while on site visits away from Darby on the high Lake Como bench; but that is conjectural. Not dissimilar were the many minuscule, fragile, and very temporary tent bungalows built elsewhere in America around the turn of the century and published from time to time. Constructed of a box frame with canvas stretched over walls and a gable roof, they usually had large canvas flaps for fenestration and almost always wood floors.[14]

In 1927 Wright designed a set of cabins, called Ras-el-Bar, for a site at Damietta, Egypt. Wright planned six seasonal "Tents on the Beach" for a low sandy island off the coast that was frequently washed by Mediterranean winter tides. Therefore, the cabins were not permanent but demountable from their concrete floor slab. They were "tentlike" and strangely complex with a combination of wood and canvas for the roof, canvas fenestration flaps, and wood (appearing similar to horizontal board-and-batten siding) for the single-width walls. Apparently some were built and used at least for one season.[15] Each cabin's plan and three-dimensional form was derived from a geometry related to a square, a continuation of Wright's persistent use of the square as a design generator.[16] The scheme's architecture and stylistic independence from the past generally, and from Wright's own oeuvre particularly, were remarkable. A somewhat awkward design that, nonetheless, was the immediate structural and constructional predecessor to Ocotillo Camp.

While working in Ocotillo Camp on designs for San Marcos in The Desert Wright and Chandler realized that people would need accommodation during construction of the resort which was to be located a good distance from town. Therefore Wright planned a workers' "Camp" in February 1929. His constructional experiences with Ocotillo were carried into the Chandler Camp as was the general character. There were to be wood board-and-batten walls and cabin surrounds to wainscot height, box frame for the cabins with canvas above to facilitate fenestration flaps and act as the roof. The overall plan of the camp was taken to a preliminary stage only and contained a

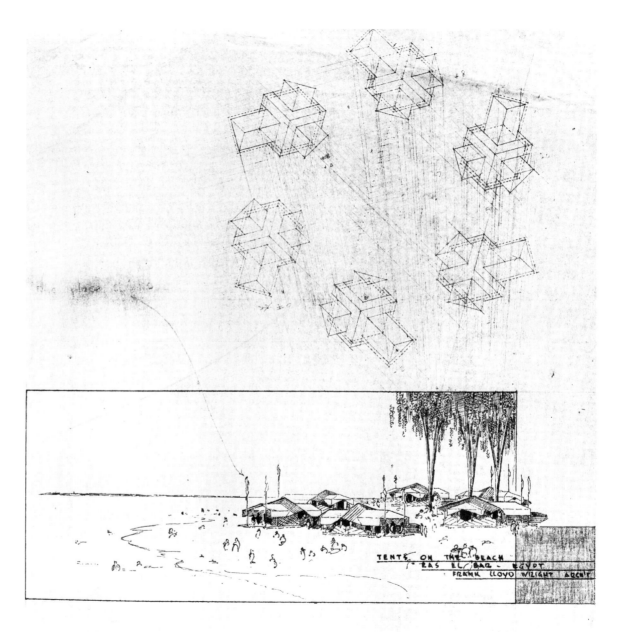

2.5 "Tents on the Beach" at Ras-el-Bar, Damietta, Egypt, 1927, plan of tent grouping with construction lines for the perspective underneath. Another scheme was similar but each cabin plan was more strictly based on the geometry of the square. It is not known which scheme was built. Courtesy and © 1985 the Frank Lloyd Wright Foundation.

bunkhouse, dining room, construction site office, a "pavilion," and other functions. With gambrel-shaped roofs the cabins were, however, more symmetrical than Ocotillo and except for some angled flaps more formal.

The Ras-el-Bar construction method was again employed in 1929 on another project, this time for a site in Chandler, Arizona, to be called San Marcos Water Gardens. Sometimes referred to as the first planned motel, it contained cabins (which mimicked Ras-el-Bar), an adjacent parking lot, recreational area, dining room, and entertainment building. The most complete contemporary presentation of the Water Gardens was in the September 1931 Berlin magazine *Die Form* which described it as "a tent town for weekends." The fact that the high ceilings of the larger rooms were practically impossible to detail did not deter the architect, but that is a practical aside. (The hexagonal scheme for spanning the larger room was reused directly on the Valley National Bank proposed for Tucson, Arizona, in 1947. There it was a "crystal-like" roof over the banking floor.) More importantly, the general layout of the site plan together with the inclusion of "bachelors' quarters" indicates that the idea of a "motor court"—effectively a motel—was an elaboration of the previously designed workmen's camp for Chandler. The Water Gardens were obviously done at Chandler's request, so the motel concept was not Wright's alone. In the late 1930s a slightly modified Water Gardens site plan was placed within the theoretical plan of Broadacre City.

The 1929 plans of the Gardens employed canvas for the roof and concrete block for walls instead of wood siding. The construction method, the potential for different shapes, and the quality of filtered sunlight through the canvas inherent in tents were architectural aspects that intrigued Wright for many years. They are felt, for instance, in the first temporary office buildings at the site of his future Arizona home, Taliesin West, in 1937. With boards but without batten for the lower wall, and with canvas roof, the temporary shelter appeared very much like Wright's design for a "Floating Cabin" at Lake Tahoe of 1922–23.

The positive, joyous events in Wright's personal life during late 1927 and 1928 allowed—perhaps more correctly they induced—the creative impulse that produced Ocotillo.[17] This fact enhances the Camp's position in architectural history and within his biography. Wright entitled the third section of his autobiography "Book Three: Freedom." It was about events that had commenced late in 1927 but it began with Ocotillo Camp. It is doubtful if the Camp could have been conceived by Wright before 1928. Later he dramatically rewrote that section in a manner that suggests he came to more fully comprehend the Camp's importance in relation to later events. Further, although Ocotillo was an immediate ideal physical and social environment for what became the Fellowship,

2.6 Ocotillo Camp, detail of vents and canvas, as published in the 1930s.

there was no *architectural* relationship to Taliesin West, as sometimes suggested. The campus outside Scottsdale was begun nearly ten years later and, although canvas and wood were used here or there, it was quite obviously a different scheme in purpose, plan, construction, and permanency—and in appearance.

Quite simply, at Ocotillo Wright wished people to gather and share dream-planning in the primitive and intellectually stimulating high desert country of the walled enclave. The center of the Camp was a fire near which was a special place for Wright to sit and face his entourage. The place of fire was slightly higher than its surroundings, in a setting rather like an acropolis, for the central space imprecisely followed a bent ridge. About that large and loosely defined center were places for experimentation, gardening, dining and attendant kitchen, electrical plant, garage, studio, bunkroom for draftsmen, guest room, and for the Wrights a suite of rooms. All rooms, or more correctly cabins, were roofed with canvas and were otherwise *part* of the surrounding wood wall. The rose-colored wall prohibited undesirable animals—and nonconforming ideas—entry to the compound and its sacred campfire. A primitive community place. The rationalization of form, material, and site was extraordinarily simple yet conceptually profound. It was liberated from all past and current hegemonies. The Camp was open and expandable; the internal and external spaces were accessibly and aesthetically free. Rooms were graced with sunlight filtered and tinted by the canvas. The wall moved in and out, up and down, as earth, rock, and necessity allowed. Built of wooden board, its strong horizontal lines were exaggerated by a batten's deep shadow. Angular tent roofs and coral-colored ventilators mimicked nearby hills and their boulder outcrops. Tall saguaro cactus, upright and noble, provided vertical counterpoints shared with an American flag unfurled on a straight pole. It was a place starkly different from Spring Green, Wisconsin.

People gathered about their acropolis with nature immediate and unyielding as the desert will demand, with bushy greasewood, sharp-spined cholla (or jumping cactus), whispy palo verde, and erect saguaro; and not an ocotillo in sight. For the cover of his book *Modern Architecture* of 1931 Wright designed an abstraction of saguaro cacti in pale warm desert colors. It was a very personal recollection, for it was there, with nights clear and air fresh in that dry, jagged high desert, that Frank and Olgivanna give birth to their vision of the future. If not materially free, they might have reasoned, at least independent of the old fears, shibboleths, and quarrels.

It was a place of optimism and joy, not of melancholy; but at one moment great sadness attended the flock. A man who had worked with Wright on many occasions, the Canadian architect

Francis Conroy Sullivan had been invited to join Wright at Ocotillo. The two architects had collaborated on a park shelter at Banff, Alberta, in 1913 (demolished 1939) and on at least three other projects they acted as "associate architects." During 1927–28 Sullivan had been ill with cancer and accepted Wright's invitation in the hope that the desert air would help in recuperation. But in March 1929 Sullivan collapsed. Wright attended to finding doctors and hospitals and sanatorium nearby and all else. On 4 April Sullivan died, only 47 years of age. A tragic death, and the end of a friendly and professional relationship of nearly 20 years.

Yet that optimistic statement of individual renaissance, of rejuvanescence, lasted barely five months. During the last week of May 1929 all people had left Ocotillo Camp except a caretaker, perhaps Donald Walker.[18] The documents for San Marcos in The Desert had been completed;[19] only Dr. Chandler's signature was needed when the stock market crashed.

With Chandler's approval, it had been intended that the Wright team would return after the hot summer, around the first of September, to effect design alterations and begin supervision of construction, but that was abandoned as were the tent cabins. About $8,500 had been paid to Wright, but after the crash the doctor's contribution to Wright's fee came to only $2,500.[20] Rather than receiving a full fee of $40,000, Wright faced a deficit of over $15,000. The cost to build Ocotillo was $3,500, or $700 a month for 13 people, or $24 a night plus gasoline, food, etc. Not a bad investment *if* there was also some income; and certainly more fun than hotel rooms. But in fact Wright was now further in debt.

San Marcos was an interesting scheme even if the textile block system was always difficult to construct and much too expensive. The Arizona Biltmore looks more or less like a large prairie-style building combined with the aesthetic of the California block houses of the early twenties. As pictured, the San Marcos resort hotel was to have the character of a pueblo and was, therefore, more in keeping with Wright's search for an American architecture somehow derived from native Americans, an idea he first explored in the Barnsdall house of 1919–21 for a Hollywood site. The hotel resort remained a possibility in Chandler's mind for many years. In 1936 he asked Wright to design another version that became slightly smaller than the first and that the architect called Little San Marcos.

Unprotected, Ocotillo Camp fell prey to thieves, the elements, and neglect. It was an unjust end. Eight years later Wright selected a site for a permanent winter home only a few miles north of Chandler; he initially called it Taliesin in the Desert.

Ephemera? Wright has said of Ocotillo: "I never grieve long now that some work of mine has met its end; *has had short life* [he emphasized], even though it happens that a better one cannot take its place, consoled by the thought that any *design* has far-reaching effect, today, because our machine so easily gives it, as a design, to the mind's eye of all." In his autobiography Wright noted incorrectly that Ocotillo "was published in German magazines two months after it was finished" (he saw it in the magazine *Die Form* of Berlin, not two months after but in July 1930).[21] And so he was pleased that the Camp would prevail "in some graphic thought-form"—a nice terminology. "It will be gone soon," he said, "modest illustration of a great theme, in passing."[22]

In keeping with European practice Wright prepared a manifesto to accompany the text of the article on Ocotillo in *Die Form,* which he sent to its author H. de Fries, who had been editor of a book on Wright published in 1926 entitled *Frank Lloyd Wright.* Perhaps it was written at de Fries's request; anyway the manifesto followed the style of its European predecessors with short, punchy, one-line statements, usually a paragraph each. Some of Wright's were nice truisms or explosive challenges to orthodoxy, which, of course, was one purpose of such manifestos. For instance, in Wright's case:

A good word in architecture is "clean." Another is "integral," still another "plastic"—one more, "quiet."

Architecture is the scientific-art of making structure express ideas.

Architecture is the triumph of human imagination over materials and methods and men. Man in possession of his earth.[23]

Many of these truisms were printed on the endsheets of his book *Modern Architecture* of 1931.

Ocotillo Camp's spiritual revelations and architectural form were immediate and *catalytic* predecessors to the Fellowship and therefore to his ideas for Broadacre City. Wright, his wife and daughters, his six or seven draftsmen,[24] and visitors on occasion would sit about the fire on their acropolis where Wright would play the role of sage, mentor, even guru—if not priest. Perhaps his draftsmen were not too different from students? he similar to a master? And nearby, in contrast to the brown ragged Arizona desert, Wright noticed a long green field of alfalfa that defined one edge of a large cattle ranch. It was called Broad Acre.[25]

3 Trilogy: Wright, Gutheim, Hitchcock

In retrospect Wright very publicly said that "having nothing to build at a very bad time in my life, I did put a good deal of myself, too much probably, in AN AUTOBIOGRAPHY."[1] Events related to his marriages were frankly presented, at least to his reckoning, as were his views about other matters and issues including architecture of course. There seem to have been a number of reasons for embarking on his autobiography. Among them were those that prompt other autobiographers: an ego that believes other people would be interested in oneself; an attempt to set records straight; a need to explain past actions and responses; a desire to philosophize; a belief that one's views are correct; and in Wright's case, as previously suggested, an attempt to sort events of the twenties so he might come to better understand them. (In late 1929 he learned that Miriam Wright was "utterly insane," to use his words, and had but a few weeks to live.)[2] As well, if there was to be a renaissance of the Wright career then it was important to remind his public that he had rebounded and was ready to accept any and all invitations.

In his autobiography Wright thanked Olgivanna for suggesting he begin the work; that he said was back in 1925. He wrote eagerly for a few months, more or less, then set it aside as a result of the continuing harassments accompanying his divorce from Miriam Noel. Wright said that he began writing again in 1927, but it seems more likely that he began his autobiography sometime in 1928. Anyway, he wrote sporadically until sometime in 1931 when the manuscript went to the printers, to be published as *An Autobiography* in 1932. It proved to be his most popular book and, perhaps, one of the most popular autobiographies published in America. It was produced by Longmans, Green and Company, the New York office of the Longmans publishing house of London. Why Wright approached Longmans, Green is not apparent but coincidence and collaboration offer one suggestion. During 1929 and 1930 Sheldon Cheney and Wright corresponded principally about Cheney's book *The New World Architecture.* Wright was impressed by Cheney and helped and counseled as he might. When published in 1930 by Longmans, Green, Wright told Cheney that the book was "a fine work"—that he was "a good craftsman."[3] Perhaps the production of this book persuaded Wright to approach the publisher. While the suggestion is somewhat an aside, the relationship of Cheney and Wright is not.

The first printing of the autobiography was as a "limited autograph edition" (at $10.00) and a trade edition ($6.00) released 30 March. It was reprinted in 1933 in a limp cloth edition and again with boards in 1938. These last two were trade editions. Interestingly, records suggest that Wright published the book at his own expense.[4] Conversely, Wright told a client Dr. Norman Gutherie, that he received a "substantial cash-advance" for two parts or sections of the book as early as February 1931.[5] (These were then called "Generation to Generation" and "Family, Fraternity, Freedom," but in final form became part of other sections.) It is not difficult to accept either proposition; in any case the Longmans imprint was secured mainly for advertising and distribution purposes.[6]

His protracted and rather extraordinarily public divorce always made headlines. That may be another reason why he included so much of the affair—it had a certain soap-opera attraction of which he was well aware—beyond the personal value of writing as a catharsis. Shortly after his return from Moscow Wright approved a dramatically pruned version of the Longmans, Green edition that appeared in the September 1937 issue of the *Readers' Digest* entitled "Building against Doomsday." That condensation and the 1938 reprint, surely not financed by Wright, indicate the successful renewal of popular interest in him. They corresponded with the publication of his documents about Broadacres (1935 through 1938), his buildings for Johnson Wax in Racine, Wisconsin (beginning 1938), the Kaufmann Fallingwater house (also beginning in 1938), a full issue of the January 1938 *Architectural Forum* devoted to Wright's life and current work, as well as many promotions for the Taliesin Fellowship (1933 onward), and bits and pieces extracted from his autobiography and published from time to time in all variety of press.

On its release the autobiography received some special attention. The following appeared in part of an article in *Publishers Weekly*: "Not only did Mr. Wright write the book, and design it, but he has drawn architectural scale drawings for a series of window displays to feature it. The displays are worked out in accordance with Mr. Wright's architectural theories. There are plans for four different displays, some large and complex, some small and simple." A large red square dominated the schemes. The drawings were to be furnished to certain book shops throughout America. So far as the *Weekly* knew these were the "first 'signed' window displays to have been used in the book business."[7] The displays were copyright by Longmans, Green and it was said that they were to be shown in Philadelphia, Boston, New York, Los Angeles, and Chicago. (Probably because Longmans holds the copyright, the designs do not appear in any chronologies of Wright's work.) The article illustrated the design of one of the three-dimensional displays, one face of which contained a boldy lettered advertisement: FIRST EDITION SIX DOLLARS. AUTOGRAPHED . . . SEVENTY ILLUSTRATIONS.

Soon after the release of the 1938 reprint, around mid-1939, Wright began negotiating with Charles Duell of the newly formed publishing house of Duell, Sloan and Pearce. Apparently the idea for a second edition was Wright's, and to the suggestion Duell wrote, "tell me what you think and what you wish."[8] By October 1939 Duell and Wright had agreed to a publication. Why Wright did not continue with Longmans, Green is unknown but rights were transferred from the previous to the new publisher by November. One of Duell's editors, Max Putzel, was charged with making Wright's text, old and new, comprehensible. Wright wanted the 1932 version slightly revised, or

**3.1 Graphics possibly by Wright for Book
1 of the 1932 autobiography. The buckram
cover had a similar design. The interpretation might be as follows. From childhood
and over the years leading to maturity
there were many diversions (temptations?)
each explored then put aside, while other
influences were absorbed; the child
reached adulthood by maintaining a single
philosophy (ambition?) symbolized by the
straight dark single line, which always
controlled psychology and reactions. Personal success and professionalism were
finally attained, symbolized by the red
square in the highest position. Reproduction courtesy and © 1932 the Frank Lloyd
Wright Foundation.**

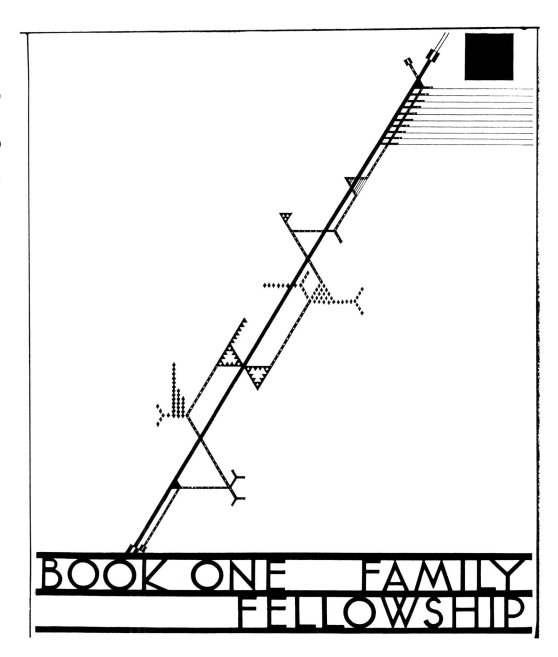

edited by himself. He also wanted to add about seventy thousand words supposedly to cover developments since 1932. The two parties also agreed that maybe two or three years after initial publication the book might be given to a reprint publisher for a cheap edition ($1.00 a copy retail was mentioned) and Blue Ribbon Books was suggested by Duell.[9] Such an edition never eventuated, probably because it was unnecessary for book sales were quite adequate. The contract between Duell and Wright was signed in January 1940.[10]

Putzel labored studiously editing Wright's old text, attempting to put it into acceptable language. He questioned words and meanings, offered thoughts on structure and content, and much more. In general Wright was not too cooperative and usually refused cuts; and the architect was very slow in supplying Putzel with material. By mid-1941 only portions of the manuscript were finalized. However, the autobiography was not the only book being orchestrated by Wright and Duell: there were two others and their enterprise ran parallel with the autobiography.

In March 1940 Frederick Gutheim confessed to Wright that one of his fondest hopes was to see the architect's wisdom, as the New Englander put it, "made available to the thousands of readers who would otherwise be put off by the technical nature of some of the material, or the difficulty of laying on hands" (presumably he meant visiting the buildings). He believed that a compilation of Wright's writings would make a "suitable companion volume to the Autobiography," a belief perhaps engendered by Duell. In fact Duell mentioned to Wright that Gutheim had spoken to him about such a compilation. For reasons not explained Wright had shown Gutheim some manuscript material as early as 1930.[11] Gutheim's proposal appealed to Wright and discussions began during the spring of 1940.[12] But as to Gutheim's participation in the book Wright was not sure. He told Duell that he had given no encouragement to Gutheim, who took "too much for granted." Wright believed that Gutheim was associated with "the left wingers" and would like the credit of a fling in the master's own house in order to promote "his own views which are decidedly to the left." Further, Wright did not consider Gutheim "of sufficient calibre" to write about the architect's work or verbalized thoughts, in an introduction or preface: Wright was, however, willing to "wait and see."[13] Duell neutrally professed to understand both men, Gutheim defended his liberality, and soon Wright acquiesced.

Gutheim began studying the Wright documents and related material in the summer of 1940 in preparation for a book to be called "Frank Lloyd Wright on Architecture."[14] As might be expected things did not proceed smoothly; the final denouement was the book's preface by Gutheim that incensed Wright. In February 1941 the "master" sent the publisher a telegram demanding that book production stop immediately or that Duell "strike out" Gutheim's preface.[15] A follow-up letter put the case: Gutheim's preface *"firmly,"* asserted Wright, stated that "The New Architecture proceeded from Gropius and Le Corbusier and that I have been influenced by it." If this assertion was within Gutheim's original preface then he most certainly did not present facts that were available for all to read in works by, for instance, Douglas Haskell or Lewis Mumford in the late 1920s. Wright found Gutheim's statement "gratuitous, false, and confusing" and he could see no reason why his "granary should have that rat in it." And then Wright wanted to know why prefaces seemed to be a place to air some "meanly controversial opinion" at the author's expense.[16] In the event, Gutheim changed the preface. (His original letter to Wright proposing the book stated that his manuscript "would naturally" need Wright's approval.) The book was released during 1941. The fact that much of the material reprinted in the book had been tampered with in one manner or another probably can be attributed to both Gutheim and Wright.

Gutheim's idea for a companion to the autobiography, one that placed before Wright's public his writings on all kinds of subjects in letters, articles, reviews—previously published or not—may have suggested to Wright the desirability of yet another companion, one about his architecture—photographs, drawings, dates, or whatever. Apparently this proposal was also put to Duell, who agreed to publish this book also. In 1940 and apparently out of the blue, so to speak, Wright asked Henry-Russell Hitchcock to prepare such a book. Hitchcock's close relationship with academia and northeastern society (partially a result of his training at Harvard University's Fogg Museum) and his ability to publish widely in what might be described as the important magazines of his society may have swayed Wright's decision. Or perhaps Wright was attempting to get the influential young art historian on side after a decade of confrontation. Certainly eight years earlier, in 1932, Wright was not happy with Hitchcock's views nor those of most other historians and critics; exceptions were Haskell and Mumford.

It must be conceded that in the late 1920s and throughout the 1930s many historians and observers had difficulty evaluating Wright's architecture and its historical position. There was, for instance, Fiske Kimball's analysis in 1928 in what was one of the first monographic histories of American architecture (a fact that fairly measures the extent of Europhilism even then dominant). Kimball placed Wright in a chapter nearly alone, called "Counter-Currents," more or less as a midwest aberration linked to Sullivan: "A single figure of genius emerged in the generation after Sullivan: Frank Lloyd Wright. . . ." Kimball supplied some erroneous information and introduced Wright's now-familiar works and his followers and persuasion in Europe, only to conclude that "the influence of his ideas here [in America] is indirect."[17] Wright's response was as might be expected. "I am heartily sick of the historical falsifying of the real course of ideas in the Architecture of our Country. . . . I am still smarting from Fiske Kimball's well-meant obituary."[18]

Also in 1928 Hitchcock had given Wright a historical position, if in a somewhat back-handed manner and without substantiation: "the next generation after H. H. Richardson were more important," wrote Hitchcock, listing Louis Sullivan, Charles Eiffel in France, P. J. H. Cuypers in Holland, and Otto Wagner in Austria. It was from those men that "definite lines of artistic descent" could be traced to "the first great masters of the New Tradition." One master was Wright, "a prophet no longer quite without honor in his own country."[19] However, much as Kimball had done, in 1932 Hitchcock cast Wright aside in notes to the New York Museum of Modern Art's "Modern Architects" exhibition. Hitchcock said quite simply that the "day of the lone pioneer is past," that there were "others besides Wright to lead the way toward the future."[20]

Heresy.

Wright responded by asserting that he was obviously still present and producing, if not much architecture at least many provocative theories and ideas. He also outspokenly disassociated himself from the internationalists. Hitchcock was not finding favor with the Wright camp.

Then again in 1934 Hitchcock said it was a "time for quiet assimilation and thoughtful development of the International Style," which he thought "a boon for American architecture."[21] This model was rationalized in the 1920s, defined by Gropius in 1925, Hilberseimer in 1927 (and others), acknowledged by Cheney in 1930, and codified with much pomp by Alfred H. Barr, Jr., Hitchcock, and Philip Johnson in the Museum of Modern Art's 1932 catalogue and in Hitchcock and Johnson's book of the same year, *The International Style,* where their points of codification read much like chapter titles for Heinrich Wölfflin's book *The Sense of Form in Art.* Why Wright was included in the exhibition is not clear. His designs tended to jar with what was to have been a concise presentation of the European model. Perhaps Lewis Mumford (who organized the housing section of the exhibition) suggested, even urged Wright's inclusion.

Mumford's own views of Wright's importance to the cause of American architecture were both sensitive and historically correct at all times, but especially during those transitional years around 1930. His book *The Brown Decades* perceptively analyzed Wright's role in American historical terms as well as European. Mumford defined one aspect of that role: "At the very time when the archaic note of colonialism was being emphasized by the fashionable architect [in post–World War I America] Wright was showing his respect for the actual landscape and the actual problems of his day and locality."[22] Earlier, Mumford had challenged Hitchcock's analysis of Wright in a 1929 review of a pamphlet by Hitchcock published by Cahiers d'Art. Mumford's review (see Appendix A) was a most revealing, carefully structured, and perceptive document that set out problems of objectivity, Europhilism, and precision.

Over the years Wright needled Hitchcock about his too academic stance (New England connoisseurship), too art-historical notions and, within Wright's understanding, distorted views from the political left. In fact, in a letter of 1937 Wright told Hitchcock that his movement in "the direction of an organic architecture has suffered a terrible set back from the exploitations of the left wing of which you are a camp follower."[23] Wright did not say Hitchcock was a "member" or "fellow traveller," but selected the term a "camp follower." In June 1938, after accepting an invitation to visit Hitchcock, Wright confessed that his letter of 1937 was perhaps hasty and "unnecessarily unkind."[24] A month later Wright was recommended for an honorary Master of Arts degree from Wesleyan University for which Wright thanked Hitchcock.[25] When it was finally published, Hitchcock dedicated the book *In the Nature of Materials* to Wesleyan University as the "first American institution to recognize the genius of Frank Lloyd Wright with academic honors." During 1938 Hitchcock was a professor at the Connecticut university. It was all very tidy, and Hitchcock was apparently already on side.

Wright's idea in 1941 for the new book illustrating his architectural works, as put to Hitchcock, "was to record and explain the Museum of Modern Art Exhibit" of Wright's work that had been mounted the previous year.[26] In March 1941 Hitchcock formally agreed to the proposal and by return mail Wright said that he was "delighted" with Hitchcock's enthusiasm for the "opus." Wright believed the book would be "worthy" of them both. "I knew you could do it," said Wright, "as no one also could."[27] They met in May to prepare notes and sort drawings and photographs. Apprentice Edgar Tafel remembered that he and fellow Fellow Bob Mosher "were detailed to find drawings from the files." Tafel's next comment is important, at least for architectural historians and biographers: "Mr. Wright constantly changed the dates on drawings."[28] By June Hitchcock wanted a much larger and more comprehensive book. He also wanted to break away from the proposed trilogy. Wright blamed Duell in part for Hitchcock's notions, which Wright interpreted as an attempt at personal aggrandizement. He wrote to the publisher saying in part that "Russell" ignored the job Wright had given him, that he had gone "his way regardless," that he wanted a "horse-face format," all in all destroying—and that was his word—the idea of the "triptych" volumes. "To hell with that," said Wright; Hitchcock should follow the agreement "or get out." Wright added that he was "more suspicious of this young academic whiskers than I was of 'Polly' Fritz" (i.e., Gutheim).[29] Wright made the point that the visual material for the book preempted another volume he was planning, "the writing already writ."[30] Format, photograph selection, and layout were other difficulties never adequately resolved to Wright's liking. As late as December 1941 Wright's concern was expressed about the photographs: "the buildings should wear their natural dress and countenance, not be left naked to shiver in the cold and dreary." As far as he was concerned "a hash" had been made of his material and some "of the best" had been omitted.[31] Royalties were another problem finally satisfied by Hitchcock, Wright, and Duell after some hassles in the months of 1941. *In the Nature of Materials* was released in 1942.

It is obvious from the text and various captions, as from the history of the book outlined here, that Wright was equally involved. Hitchcock recognized this fact not on the title page but in the acknowledgments where he admitted that Wright was "almost" a coauthor: it was also close to a disclaimer.

From 24 January to 3 March 1940 an exhibition of Wright's architecture had been held at the Institute of Modern Art in Boston. A supplement to that exhibition was the Institute's publication *Frank Lloyd Wright: A Pictorial Record of Architectural Progress.* It is obvious that this show was increased in size to form the Museum of Modern Art exhibition of 1940–41. It is also obvious that the Boston Institute's book was the predecessor to and inspiration for *In the Nature of Materials.* In early 1941 Hitchcock reviewed the Wright exhibition at MoMA in a style typical of his pendantic wanderings. As well, he mentioned that the book *In the Nature* was under way and apologized for the inadequate presentation of Wright in MoMA's 1932 exhibition for which Hitchcock wrote the catalogue text related to Wright. (Hitchcock's excuse for the inadequacies suggest it was probably his own text for which he was apologetic.)[32]

Openly and publicly, in fact on the back of the dust jacket to the 1943 edition of his autobiography, Wright made two points. First, that the "writings gathered by Fritz Gutheim for ON ARCHITECTURE" formed the "first book in the three-volume series, on my work." And second, that the exhibition at the Museum of Modern Art in New York contained "the best I've built from 1893 to 1940 and at last it was put in order by able Henry-Russell Hitchcock. His opinions on architecture I have distrusted as being far too academic, but since it is safer to trust one's point of view to one's enemies than to one's friends, I asked him to record the show." Wright seems still to have been irritated by Hitchcock's rather pristine nonarchitectural view of architecture and his distortion if not misunderstanding of Wright's historical role. Having committed himself to the two books that were to be prepared by others, Wright found it difficult to extract himself from obligations not only to

Duell but to himself. In spite of the fact that he did not get his way on many issues or disagreed with much that had been inserted or ignored by Gutheim and Hitchcock, he could see the value of these books to his career; to the spread of his philosophy concerning architecture, cities, and America; and to his immortality, so to speak.

Through all the problems of the books edited by Gutheim and Hitchcock, the *first* proposal put by Wright to Duell, that of the autobiography, remained in pieces in galley or manuscript form for a year after *In the Nature of Materials* was released. Finally the anticipated second and enlarged edition of *An Autobiography* was launched in 1943. A chapter about Broadacre City had been rejected by Duell who probably sensed that Wright might never stop writing about himself. The first edition was self-aggrandizing; this second edition tended to be hubristic. It exposed the culmination of Wright's personality during the 1930s.

Of the many reviews of both the 1932 and 1943 editions perhaps the most perceptive yet charming, if there is such a criteria for a book review, was that by Sheldon Cheney in *The Saturday Review of Literature* in 1932. Here are some extracts:

America's most creative rebel sets down, somewhere within the confused beauty of this book, the comment that "man's struggle to illumine creation is another tragedy." . . . But the undercurrent of tragedy is not in any failure of the writer to illumine creation, it is revealed in the situation of an original and prophetic artist—and a man attempting to be truly free—struggling against the drag of orthodoxy and ignorance in a shopkeeping and belly-filling civilization. . . . It is the vague "they" of the architectural profession and of the conformist public: the cultured importers of alien architectural knick-knacks, actively hostile to creative innovation, and the "moral" public that feeds its passion for a standard respectability upon sensational "news" reports of non-conformist living. "They" have made for tragedy in Wright's life. . . . But there is hope for mankind in this: the creative rebel rises in the end, with indomitable spirit, with sense of humor about his own wayside failures, with integrity unimpaired, painting a clear picture of the Utopian society that may yet be, if Truth prevail. . . . It not only is the story of a man, bravely and beautifully told; rather it illumines an art in an incomparable way, from the creator's consciousness. It also is a revelation of the sicknesses of civilization.[33]

The autobiography had a good longevity. The first printing of the first edition was probably of about 500 copies; the 1933 and 1938 reprints of no more than 2,000 each. The first printing of the 1943 edition was a run of probably 3,000, but by September 1962 it had gone through an eighth printing. By far the largest printing was that of March 1957 which was selected by the

United States Information Service as "one of a collection of 350 books about the United States of America" sent to many city, state, or public libraries in many countries of the world. For example, almost all copies in Australian libraries are of the 1943 edition donated by the Carnegie Corporation in 1957 through the USIS.

Interestingly a far more useful reset production of the second edition was published in London by Faber and Faber with a contract signed as early as November 1943. The first printing of 3,000 copies was in September 1945 (with Hyperion Press), a second impression in 1946, and a third of 2,000 copies on 20 March 1947 (without Hyperion). It was more useful because of size (octavo), format, the type selected, and especially for the inclusion of many photographs of family and buildings. (These illustrations may have been allowed, so to speak, since the book *In the Nature of Materials* with its many pictures was not published in Britain.) The Faber edition did not go out of print until May 1959.[34] Perhaps 30,000 copies of the various editions of the autobiography had been sold by about 1960. A new edition of *In the Nature of Materials* was planned as early as 1951 and in that year Wright gave Bruno Zevi "full authority" for an Italian translation of the autobiography of 1943.[35] If one includes French and Italian (*Io e L'Architettura*) editions of 1955, another 4,000 or so might be added by 1970. Indeed, Wright's second coming can be declared successful if measured only by the sales of his autobiography.

All of the above emphasizes that beginning around 1930, in Wright's mind it was important to gain some good, solid public attention of virtually any sort. If his friends had not bailed him out with Wright Inc. he would have been nearly destitute save for the farm (actually inherited from his mother's family) that he called Taliesin. Their financial assistance had to be repaid; he needed work. But architectural commissions were not forthcoming, at least not immediately. Therefore he had to find other means to obtain money. Royalties earned from writing were important and continued to be so for two decades; so too giving speeches. Since he charged for the loan of his artifacts, there was good publicity if little money in exhibitions. And there was the Taliesin Fellowship.

4 Fellowship

For decades Wright had thought about establishing a school presumably under his guidance and tutelage. In 1900 he spoke of the need for an "experiment station," inferring some kind of crafts school. In 1908 and 1910 he wrote that a design center was needed, and now and then the idea inserted itself into a text at the proper moment. Finally in 1928, free of a rather hateful ex-wife, able to work again at Taliesin, and in the quietude of a slow professional practice, he and Olgivanna proposed an art school to be located on part of his grandfather's farm on which he had built his home. He would provide the land and buildings (then near ruin) if others would become patrons.

He wrote a few letters soliciting comments on the idea; most recipients did not reply. Most knew he was in desperate need of money and realized this was an effort, perhaps sincere, to obtain cash flow. Of course its pedagogical foundation was not related to coarse practical necessities; Wright's rhetoric on the subject was quite sophisticated. It was to be a constructive step "to save the soul of man himself, from further atrophy, from greater degradation at his own hands." He believed the "creative-instinct" was dead in most people, that it had "ceased to exist." Yet optimistically he was certain that that "quality or faculty" could be reborn. The seed was in the force that would induce revival: imagination. The method was his school, where "this thing might be wooed and won" (see Appendix F). But he wrote little of how in practical terms it would be achieved except for one tantalizing piece of information. Beginning in 1928 and through 1929 he attempted to enlist "the help" of a university, left unspecified but no doubt the University of Wisconsin. Wright had good relations with the Madison campus and "occasionally" professors visited Taliesin. Probably the most influential of his contacts at the university was the amazingly popular poet, dramatist, and novelist Zona Gale, who at that time was a regent. Wright's and Gale's families were old friends. Before meeting Olgivanna, Wright had a serious love for Zona that was politely rejected. ("I just didn't know how to make love to Zona Gale.") As well, Wright was enchanted by Gale's stories and novels about Wisconsin, its people and places, and shared her loathing of war and conscription, her press for women's rights, and her liberal politics. Her dramatization of her own novel *Miss Lulu Bett* won a Pulitzer Prize "amid universal approval" and was made into a movie by Paramount. During the mid-1920s the University of Wisconsin was quite progressive and among other indicators was committed to a new experimental college. Many young, left-wing students in the creative arts had enrolled in the new college. It may be that Gale and the college's founder Alexander Meiklejohn considered that the administrative location of Wright's own experimental school of the arts could have been within the college. In the event, at the request of the university Wright prepared what he described as a "university-prospectus."

Without consultation or prompting and for inexplicable reasons, in December 1928 Wright proposed one of his staunch supporters in Holland, Henrik T. Wijdeveld, "to be the director" of his school. Even more amazing, he did not personally inform Wijdeveld of his proposal but did so casually in a letter to P. M. Cochius, Director of the Leerdam Glass Works outside Amsterdam with whom Wright had just begun designing some domestic decorative items. A copy of the prospectus was enclosed to be passed on to Wijdeveld. Just as casually Wright learned from Cochius via an offhand comment in a February 1929 letter that Wijdeveld was not interested in Wright's proposal; rather he was starting his own "school of architects."[1]

At this crucial juncture in his musing Wright was offered the series of jobs with Dr. Chandler in Arizona from which emerged only the poetically splendid Ocotillo Camp. Almost immediately on returning to Wisconsin from the Arizona desert in June 1929 the Wrights began more serious planning for something like an "Art School," formulating at least its generalities as well as preliminary architectural plans. Beyond floating the idea verbally to a few people (including Lewis Mumford, Douglas Haskell, and Jens Jensen),[2] until the end of 1930 little was done in a practical way—like financing—to see the school realized. It was then that correspondence was renewed with Wijdeveld, who was editor and publisher of *Wendingen* magazine in the 1920s and of a book on Wright in 1925. During 1930 John Lloyd Wright visited Wijdeveld; in August the elder Wright thanked the Dutchman for his hospitality and asked him to assist two of Wright's young acquaintances who were to visit Holland.[3] In about October 1930 Wright asked Wijdeveld to participate in the new school: "to have you join me in Wisconsin to work in the proposed school would be a dream realized." The role of Wright's son John is not clear, but in any event Wright briefly outlined the school, which by then was to include the crafts, named its initial cost (around $300,000), and then mentioned his desire for an exhibition of his work in Europe.[4] Wijdeveld happily agreed to arrange the exhibition's tour. The invitation to travel to America and "take the lead of the Hillside-school of Arts" (as Wright was then calling it) Wijdeveld found "very tempting indeed" but his own plans "in Holland [were] already so far advanced, that I [Wijdeveld] intend to try very hard to realize them in . . . 1931"[5] (his ellipses).

The vital contribution of Wijdeveld to Wright's life, including the wilderness years of the 1920s—and indeed the roles of Berlage, Mendelsohn, and Wils—is explored in detail elsewhere in a new study by Donald Langmead and myself. Here it is necessary to extract an outline of the critical episodes of the second phase of Wijdeveld's lively contribution during the transitional years around 1930, and especially his contribution to the Fellowship.

With Wijdeveld taking charge of the exhibition in Europe, in April 1931 Wright made an extraordinary revelation accompanied by yet another offer to Wijdeveld that was only superficially explained. He informed the Dutchman that a school was forming in Chicago to be known as the Allied Arts and Industries School, that it was to be along lines similar to Wright's proposed private school with an additional and major consideration: the Chicago school was to be endowed with "2½ Million Dollars." Wright had been asked to be director but, he said to Wijdeveld, "I suggested you—with me as Chairman of the board." Wright added that the salary was $10,000 per annum to fit a ten-year contract and that the school was to begin the following September or October.[6] (There was a suggestion that the Chicago school was to be a breakaway from the Art Institute of Chicago, where Wright had useful contacts, but he left this allusion ill-defined.[7]) At this more promising offer Wijdeveld was overwhelmed: in fact he "overwhelmingly" accepted the directorship by return cable; he left all matters with Wright.[8] And then silence from Wisconsin.

In anticipation, Wijdeveld wrote what he unashamedly described as "a curious letter of introduction" presenting individually his family and their accomplishments, and his dreams. It was a very long letter filled with hope. He referred to Wright's "Hillside-home School of Art" as an International Guild and encouraged Wright: "We both see International understanding one day coming. Why not, in the difficulties of our attainment, join our work and make the way free" since the mission required their "united power." He and Wright would "keep a strong mind and a strong hand and lead our plans towards the Happiness in Taliesin," The International Work Community. There was in the letter much delightfully effusive language so typical of Wijdeveld. He mentioned that he had $10,000 to $15,000 to invest.[9] Surprisingly, still no response.

Understandably worried by the lack of communication, two months later on 10 June Wijdeveld wrote Wright a long, handwritten, rather philosophical yet emotional letter that expressed a deep concern about the future course of his life; a concern not wholly rhetorical when one considers the Depression and the aggressive rise of Nazism in Germany. He tried to clarify his own intentions about the relationship between Wright and himself. He believed his efforts always had been directed not to the promotion of Wright personally but to nurturing "the growth of an idea" they shared.[10] A reply to this unhappy, very personal letter came not from Wright but his secretary. Somewhat callously Wright had delegated Karl Jensen, who wrote that he understood there must be some "suspense of not knowing about the school." While not reassuring, Jensen's few lines mentioned that Wright was to travel to Chicago in a few weeks to look into the matter.[11] Again silence.

Finally a note: Wright found Wijdeveld's letter quite "remarkable" but was reluctant to encourage the Dutchman until he was more certain of affairs. Wright had continued negotiations that included the enlistment, to borrow his word, and cooperation of a woman (no name mentioned) who was in some unexplained way "responsible" for the proposed Chicago Allied Arts school, and who was in some unexplained way to help develop Wright's own school at Taliesin. Apparently

Wright was no longer involved in the Chicago venture, yet, rather confusingly, he would become chairman of the board of his own school, a task he would reluctantly assume. He wanted to concentrate on the practice of architecture "for fifteen years more," implying that he found the task of administering a school too distracting, but he would be the "deciding voice." He informed Wijdeveld of these vaguely structured ideas and warned that "times are bad here," the school would take many years to develop; all would "not go smooth."[12]

Wijdeveld did in fact travel to the United States late in 1931 but surely with uncertainty and only a modicum of optimism. He visited Boston and Chicago before traveling to Madison and Taliesin in November. The two men talked; Wijdeveld spoke of his ideas for a fellowship; Wright even prepared a draft contract between himself and Wijdeveld as the nominated director of what *they* decided would be a Taliesin Fellowship. Wright was described as founder, Wijdeveld as "leader," and there were other conditions (including an investment of $10,000 by Wijdeveld) that remained only in draft form, for the contract was never signed.[13] On returning to Holland Wijdeveld wrote a thank-you for Wright's hospitality that contained a "longing" to join Wright; "I hope we'll find agreement."[14] A month later, in February 1932 Wright wrote his friend and colleague:

My dear Dutchy:

Much as I like you and hard up for help as I am, perhaps chiefly because of both, I am going to say no to your coming to join me in America.

He told Wijdeveld that the personal responsibility Wright would need to assume if the Dutch architect and his family made such a permanent change of life was "too great," that it was based on "the slender basis of hope." He closed the door firmly by saying the "leader should, I am now sure, be an American." He said Wijdeveld should begin a school of his own, his own fellowship, free to give it direction and character. With Amadée Ozenfant, Erich Mendelsohn, Serge Chermayeff, Paul Hindemith, and others, Wijdeveld did create and build the Académie Européenne Méditerranée in France. Soon after construction the original buildings were consumed by fire, but the academy was revived on a site in Holland.[15] (On Wright's death in 1959 Wijdeveld was again seriously considered to head the Wright Foundation.)

What happened to the proposed Chicago school dedicated to the Allied Arts is anyone's guess as are the names of the players; extant evidence is mute. However, the unhappy affair with Wijdeveld emphasizes some interesting aspects of the development of the Taliesin Fellowship. The initial idea of a Hillside Home School was not well calculated. Wright and Olgivanna were not certain of its purpose or course. In part this was due to frustration over an incomplete professional life; in part to a lack of funds; and in part to the ambiguities of their life and to an unclear future. Events claimed attention simply because they appeared desirable, not because of their intrinsic value or natural fit into a grand scheme. So Wright could abandon his own school for another; he could give away the directorship to someone else; he could give an inevitable committee great persuasion. In other words he could halve all his dreams just to be involved in the Chicago School or see his own school to reality. However, so little is known of the byplay behind the scenes in Madison or Chicago that accurate analysis is difficult.

Sadly, the Wijdeveld affair must be seen as somewhat malicious. Wright put the proposition of the school only after Wijdeveld agreed to organize and conduct the exhibition around Europe; no easy task. Wright was silent or imprecise about the school and related matters at critical moments in their correspondence to an extent implying tactical delays. Thanks to Wijdeveld the exhibition ran in various European cities from April 1931 to January 1932. The letter to "dear Dutchy" withdrawing the offer to join Wright in America was written *within days* after the exhibition items had returned to Taliesin.

In retrospect, it can be reasoned that at least one other purpose for considering Wijdeveld as "leader" was clear: to unite the philosophies of Europe and America through a Wrightian center where Wijdeveld (a fellow believer and, it should be noted, one outspokenly full of adulation of Wright) and Wright would openly and harmoniously work together. Because of the Hollander's work on Wright's behalf in Europe during the 1920s, this view would hopefully gain greater credibility. The impression Wright wished to convey in 1932 was that Wijdeveld had abandoned the cause they shared.

One other aspect of Wright's and Wijdeveld's relationship is revealed by a much later exchange of correspondence. In October 1947 Wijdeveld wrote Wright a fairly long and typically elaborate letter that said at one point, in mid-letter and mid-paragraph: "Dear Wright; . . . what has happened that you don't answer me in my distress? I wrote you September 1945, telling you our grief during war, the loss of family and my school of arts . . . find a form for my joining you . . . at Taliesin or Arizona. INVITE ME!!" (Ellipses were his.) The distress he refers to stemmed from the fact that after the war and based on flimsy, hastily drawn evidence, he had been briefly blacklisted (and no more than that) by official professional bodies. A zealously idealistic man, he was firmly apolitical.[16] Anyway, to this appeal Wright responded almost immediately, but it proved to be a difficult letter to compose for a number of drafts are extant. He appeared to be forthright when he said Wijdeveld was "one of the occasions" that weighed on his conscience. "I have not known," said Wright, "just how to square myself with myself where you are concerned, so not knowing what to write I did not write." Nonetheless, he believed the Hollander was "right, when, faced with a part in my enterprise (was it more than twenty years ago?) you said, 'he is difficult to work with. It will take many years to build up this place. I have only ten thousand dollars. I do not know what to do.' . . . In fact I am impossible to work with . . . [I am] a solo creative worker," he said. "I would like to be of help to you and yours—your appreciation reached me when my fortunes were at a low ebb and I am not ungrateful." However, "you could not ('nor any older man I fear') *work with me*" (the last three words Wright underlined).

That is what Wijdeveld received. The letter drafts were more revealing and included some sharp words. Wright wrote that America was "over-filled with left wing modernists," among whom he included Gropius, Mies, Mendelsohn, Breuer, Saarinen, Chermayeff, and Lescaze. He (quite incorrectly) set Wijdeveld in their camp. He thought Wijdeveld "a man of deeper feeling and greater vision" than the others listed. But in the Dutch architect's buildings Wright (incorrectly) saw "much the same character" as theirs. He wrote of a widening breach between himself and those men, that their "apostasy" had "betrayed the cause of an organic architecture in the nature of materials which I believe to be the architecture of Democracy." Wright believed that their architecture was "distinctly Nazi." However, that draft was *not* sent. Rather, Wright said less pointedly that "no good ever came or will come of temporizing with one's ideals just to be kind to a friend." The letter as received closed with an invitation to visit Taliesin West and said that, ideals aside, Wright would do everything he could "for you as a friend." Taken together, they are strange but revealing documents.[17]

But Wright knew full well Wijdeveld's political views and their manifestation in architecture. They were discussed while Wijdeveld was at Taliesin in 1931, and in a letter of 1 January 1932 he reminded Wright of their talks. He also said that his work was then in an exhibition in Moscow and that he had been invited to give a lecture there, among other capital cities. The invitation from Moscow was tempting for he saw it as an opportunity to convince himself of the "sovjet experiment and its growth" so that he might have his "own opinion" when he lectured "at Taliesin."[18]

In the light of the 1947 letter and its drafts, the more obvious reasons for Wright's distasteful act of reneging on his offer to Wijdeveld in 1932 become clear. It was not, as he seemed to say, that Wijdeveld was one of the European "left wing modernists" and that the breach between those architects and Wright had widened to a point where, by 1932, he was not just irritated or mad but intolerant. Although that may be true generally, in the case of Wijdeveld he quite simply had nothing to offer but promises too difficult to keep.

5 Apprenticeship

The idea of molding—perhaps a better word is creating—young architects not narrowly or traditionally trained who would act as apostles became evermore urgent as did the need for a monetary
income. Wright became frustrated by the lack of results from both the university enquiry and contacts
with people in Chicago and the Art Institute. Indeed their interest, more verbal that real, seems to
have just lapsed. Therefore, without outside financial support he began his private apprenticeship
program (one always hesitates to use the word "school").

Young people had always worked with Wright for experience. "Not so much as students,"
he said, confessing "I am no teacher. No, they came more as apprentices, beginning with no pay—
except their living at Taliesin—or with small pay if more competent to help. As they grew helpful
they received a small salary in keeping with the work done, or to be done in the office or in the
garden, over and above their living."[1] This arrangement inherited ideas from many sources but not,
as historian Norris Kelly Smith believes, from various communitarian societies of the nineteenth
century. The basic inheritance, Smith has suggested, was the "tendency of romantic thought to exalt
the virtues of a quasi-monastic brotherhood of craftsmen."[2] To Wright, however, collectivism was
abhorrent as were the barracks of last century's communitarians. The inspiration for his apprenticeship program came from an accumulation of experiences, practical needs, and examples. There was
his own dissatisfaction with formal schooling and his success under his mother's teaching with the
at-home Froebel kindergarten system. There was general unhappiness in a formal high school, his
lack of success at university, and then his accomplishments under private, perhaps privileged
tutelage, so to speak, with those employers who had the greatest influence, Joseph Silsbee followed
by Dankmar Adler and Louis Sullivan.

As well, there was his aunts' former Hillside Home School, near his own home Taliesin
and his grandparents' house; all of which were on the family's Wisconsin estate. The private school
had been rather progressive and attended by children of the upper middle class. Joseph Silsbee
designed one of the buildings in 1887 and Wright observed its construction. A former student and
later professor at Smith College, Mary Ellen Chase described her experiences at the school in the
book *A Goodly Fellowship* (1939). By all accounts the school was quite successful until it closed
with the retirement of his aunts around 1915. The buildings remained deserted until October 1932.
When formed, the Wright Fellowship moved into and renovated the abandoned but fortuitously
available buildings. Wright's attachment to that part of his childhood before his parents were
divorced seemed to remain memorably intimate and vital throughout his life and was particularly

5.1 Plan and site for the Hillside Home School of the Allied Arts, 1928. This is probably the first architectural plan for the school. Buildings by Wright for the old Hillside School are at the bottom, although proposed revisions are shown. The farm and barn complex, again with suggested revisions, are on the far right. Other architectural plans of the school and Taliesin at Spring Green have been published, but none adequately portray what was actually built after 1929. In Wright's *An Organic Architecture*, for instance, the plan is fictitious, or more correctly a dream.
A site plan of the entire Taliesin farm and residential complex drawn from memory by John Howe has been published in Creese (1985) and Tafel (1979).
Collection of the author. © 1985 the Frank Lloyd Wright Foundation.

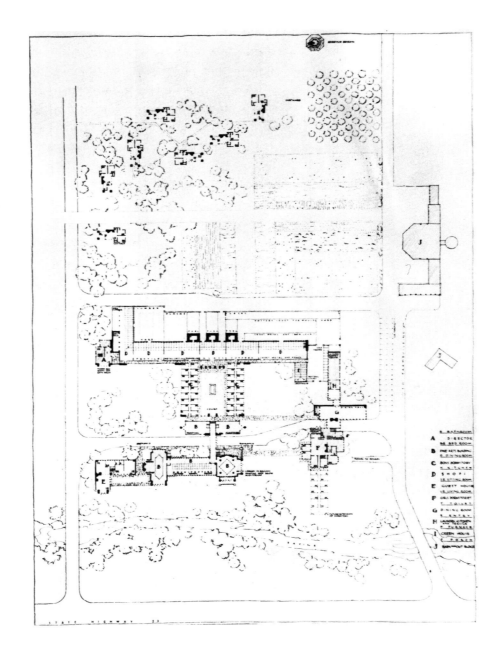

so during the rejuvenescent years immediately after 1928. When Olgivanna and Wright were planning their program in 1929 they called it The Hillside Home School of the Allied Arts. The implications of that title are many: the binding of Wright to a childhood place; the old school becoming a new school; an alliance of the arts in a place dedicated to their being.

The new program was conceived as a school (a prospectus of October 1931 forcefully stated "Why We Want This School"); therefore initially it was not necessarily an apprenticeship system alone. The October brochure, written by the two Wrights, stated that music would "have to mean the fundamental study of sound and rhythm as emotional reaction both as to original character and present nature. Tone weaving in general . . . dancing in this school would be the actual cultivation of rhythms in the co-relations of body and mind to make of both a perfect instrument." Music belonged to Wright; dance to Olgivanna. If the other allied arts were to be as expressionistically experienced as music and dance, it would be difficult to characterize the school as a place where the techniques of the crafts were taught. Yet in preparing his 1928 architectural plan, apparently part of the "prospectus" for the university, great care had been taken to ensure that studios for the crafts and more fine arts were fully equipped. The old Hillside School rooms were to be reused: art and science rooms, for instance, were to become painting and sculpture studios and the classrooms were to continue as such. Plans indicate studios for textiles, metal casting, enamel, and glass; there was a sheet metal shop and forge, greenhouse, lumber room, sheet metal and pottery yards, three furnaces, etc. To build such a school would have been costly; it is no wonder that Wright sought financial help either directly or by some form of collaboration. Progressing up the hillside were to be a number of "Working Man's Cottages" or just "Cottages for Taliesin," and this housing had been developed through preliminary design. At the top of the hill sat a tall windmill that had serviced his aunts' school that Wright had designed and seen built in 1896. By early 1932 and after Wijdeveld's visit the architectural plans had become considerably less grandiose, more general, as had the title settled upon: The Taliesin Fellowship. It was a title almost wholly the result of his talks with Wijdeveld. There were, therefore, Wright's familial, childhood, adolescent, and early professional experiences that were knitted to other, equally profound influences not excluding Olgivanna's.

One of the more practical influences was Elbert Green Hubbard and his Roycroft Shops and Press in East Aurora near Buffalo, New York. Wright's mother and her sisters visited Roycroft in 1913, Wright many times before 1915 (the year Hubbard died aboard the torpedoed *Lusitania*), and he and his wife Olgivanna in May 1930 shortly after the Hillside Home School of Allied Arts was conceived.[3] Hubbard had been a founder with his brother-in-law John Larkin of the soap,

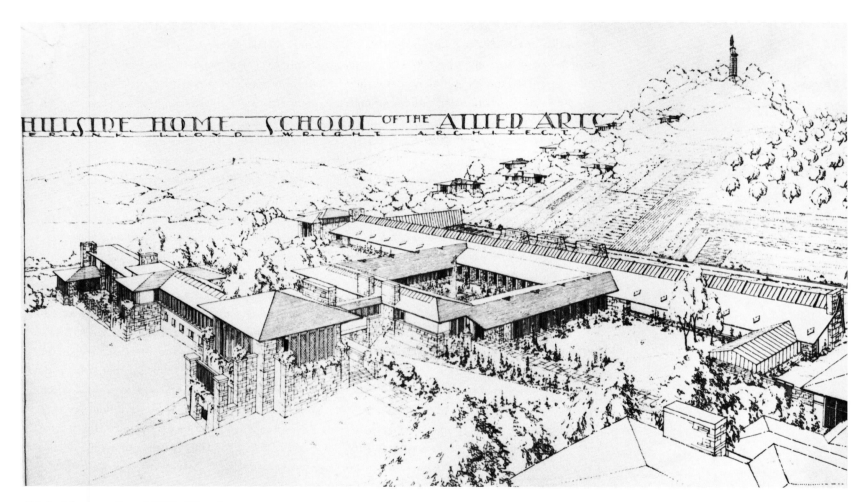

5.2 Aerial perspective of 1928 of the plan shown in Figure 5.1. The old Hillside School of Wright's aunts was located in the large buildings in the bottom left and in the two classrooms immediately to the rear. It is doubtful that Wright drew the plan (Figure 5.1) or this perspective. Collection of the author. © 1985 the Frank Lloyd Wright Foundation.

wholesale, and mail order firm The Larkin Company. The Larkin Building in Buffalo of 1903 was one of Wright's most inspired and prophetic architectural works. Other people associated with the company were also clients of Wright, including Hubbard's sister and the Martin family. When Hubbard traveled to Chicago or Wright visited Buffalo to supervise the construction of his buildings they often visited. Wright's son John remembered Hubbard well: he "was almost as picturesque as was Father—they talked arts, crafts and philosophy by the hour. Said Elbert the Hubbard to the Papa one night, Modesty being egotism turned wrong side out, let me say here that I am an orator, a great orator! I have wealth, gesture, imagination, voice, vocabulary, taste, ideas—I acknowledge it myself. What I lack in shape I make up in nerve."[4] Whitmanesque, yes; but how very Wrightian as well. Hubbard sold his share of The Larkin Company and began Roycroft. He soon became known as the American heir—if not equivalent—of William Morris. Roycroft (king's craft) was a corporation, while its operation has been described as a simplified scheme of capitalism, modified socialism, and practical paternalism. Indeed, all activity was generated by and focused on Hubbard; a similar phenomenon followed at Taliesin.

Like Morris's Kelmscott Press, Hubbard's main activity was the Roycroft Press. It produced works mainly by Hubbard, including pamphlets, broadsides, magazines, and books, and was incredibly successful. So too was his school, if that is a proper term. A long-time Roycrofter, Felix Shay, identified Hubbard's place as "a kind of school—a practical work-a-day school" that responded to Hubbard's work ethic: "to be healthy and sane and well and happy, you must do real work with your hands as well as with your head. The cure for grief is motion. The recipe for strength is action. Love . . . that finds form in music, sculpture, painting, poetry and work is divine and beneficent."[5] A visitor to the East Aurora campus in 1912 observed that the Roycroft School pupils "are taught to work in the open. They are brought in touch with life in the fields. They groom horses, shear the sheep, feed the hogs, milk the cows, plant potatoes, pick currants. . . . They do the toil that fills the larder of the Roycroft Inn. And they pay Elbert Hubbard for the privilege of doing it. Isn't that lovely?"[6] It was obviously a loveliness attractive to Wright. Further, historian Wayne Andrews suggested that the beguiling Hubbard influenced Wright's mode of dress. "After all," said Andrews, "the nation listened when the editor [Hubbard] of The Philistine preached: 'Wear thy hair long: it is a sign that thou art free'"; and a billowing tie too.[7]

A personality the converse of the East Aurora supersalesman was the English architect and designer Charles R. Ashbee, surely another influence on the Taliesin Fellowship. Ashbee's close association with the Art Workers Guild, and more particularly his own Campden School of Arts and

5.3 Elbert Hubbard about the time he started The Roycroft Shops, from Shay (1926), frontispiece.

Crafts in the village of Campden, were familiar to Wright.[8] Not only were crafts taught there in the manner of the Guild but students (apprentices of Guildsmen) engaged in gardening and organized exercise classes and participated in plays produced by the Campden School, and lectures were presented to the proteges on all subjects. Wright and Ashbee met on the Englishman's visit in 1900 to Chicago's Hull House Settlement, center of the arts and crafts movement in the Midwest, and thereafter they had long talks at Wright's home. Wright was active in all manner of things related to the arts and crafts, and quite familiar with relevant historical events and contemporary developments in England. After visiting Chicago Ashbee toured Elbert Hubbard's Roycroft. Beyond these contacts the two architects visited the English Guild and the Campden School during Wright's brief tour of England in September 1909. Then Ashbee was a five-day guest at Taliesin in the summer of 1916. The two men had much in common and an unusually close friendship. Clearly, a place such as the Hillside Home School of the Allied Arts had an affinity with Ashbee's Campden School. The benevolent paternalism motivating the Englishman was at no time present in Wright's and Olgivanna's plans, but the practice of work and self-sustenance as well as intellectual succor through reading, acting, and music most assuredly was.

It would be fair to argue that the arts and crafts movement generally was an influence on Wright at all stages of his career, at least through the 1930s: the physical evidence is plentiful. Another specific influence was the work of Gustav Stickley, furniture manufacturer and publisher also based in New York. He too was inspired by the English Art Workers Guild (in 1888 renamed the Arts and Crafts Society), among whose members were William Lethaby, Ashbee, William Morris, Edwin Luytens, and C.F.A. Voysey. Stickley shared his English mentors' moralism toward labor, their craftsmanship, their antiurban—and later Garden City—notions. Those ideas and their practical results in architecture and the decorative arts were described and well illustrated in Stickley's *Craftsman* magazine. His promotions had a much closer relationship to architecture than Hubbard's. The designs for Stickley's furniture and other home furnishings were based on English counterparts (the famous Morris chair, for instance) and Wright's designs have shown a similar relationship, at least through the 1920s.[9]

More desperate, less part of nineteenth-century ideals of paternalism, yet closely aligned to communal sufficiency and community integration was Ralph Borsodi's well-known "Experiment in Creative Living on the Land" of the 1920s—described in his 1933 *Flight from the City*. Wright would have been interested in how Borsodi's family was self-sufficient through an elaborate household industry (livestock, weaving, food preserving, building construction, etc.) and in Borsodi's idea of the fundamental need to decentralize cities. Indeed, Borsodi's reflections about his own creative experiment more clearly and succinctly outlined the case for Broadacre City than Wright could manage in many writings on the subject. Decentralization, said Borsodi,

means the shifting of people from congested cities to the country; still more important is the decentralization of owner-ship, which means the distribution of property in lands, buildings and other forms of "capital" among the people generally in opposition to concentrating ownership in big businesses. And most important of all is the decentralization of production, which means the shifting of manufacturing from factories where things are made to be sold, to the home and farm where they are made to be used. If decentralization proceeds along these lines, we can look forward to the restoration of some of the security which was destroyed when industrialism shattered the old equilibrium between city and country.[10]

Finally there was the philosophical influence of a book by the German historian Werner Wilhelm Jaeger, later at Harvard University, called *Paideia*. Olgivanna quoted from this book at length in her *Roots of Life* (1963), with special attention to the ancient Greek connection of education in its broadest sense (*paideia*) to aristocracy.[11] (Though Wright never mentioned Jaeger's book himself, he was clearly interested in similar connections and often commented on the nature of aristocracy within a democracy. See for example his somewhat elliptical enunciation of the philosophical foundation of his "school" in a 1928 letter to Jens Jensen; Appendix F.) The word *paideia*, she wrote, "in its most elementary expression [means] child-rearing, but in its wider application its meaning embraces man's entire education. . . . Another Greek word, *areté* . . . is untranslatable because it belongs so completely to [ancient] Greek culture that our language can give only an approximation of the word: nobility, integrity, aristocracy—everything fine is *areté*. The Greeks thought *areté* to be the highest qualification of aristocracy, an ideal toward which the individual should strive." She quoted Jaeger:

The presuppositions of aristocratic civilizations are fixed residence in one place, ownership of land and respect for tradition. These are the factors which allow a sector of life to be transmitted unaltered from one generation to another. But to them has been added good breeding, a conscious education of the young towards the aristocratic ideal under the severe discipline of courtly manners and morals. . . . Aristocracy in all ages and all nations is marked by discipline. It is the only class which can claim to produce the complete man.

To this she added her rather more personal interpretation. "Today the most important factor, discipline, is lacking in hereditary aristocracy, and aristocrats too often take their privilege as due them without having to merit it. Mr. Wright maintained that true aristocracy can exist only in a democracy. . . . Democracy presents the opportunity to earn aristocracy through merit and discipline—a true aristocracy available to everyone without the formation of a privileged class." (Both the Wrights would in some way criticize English society not too differently from this interpretation.) Quoting Jaeger again:

It is not enough for the young to grow as gently as a tree into the social and moral code of their ancestors. The superior rank and worth of the aristocracy implies an obligation to shape its members during their malleable youth into the accepted ideal of nobility. In this process education becomes culture for the first time, that is, it becomes a process by which the whole personality is *modeled on a fixed pattern* [my emphasis].

She went on to say that her, and Wright's, understanding of these ideas is intimated, even clarified, by Jaeger's statement that they represent "a new and deeper view of the relation of education to natural ability . . . that mere teaching has little to do with the formation of heroic *areté*. That is the principle the Taliesin Fellowship has been based upon . . . a pure idea is never lost. The present reaches back into the past and the idea returns in a new form. Mr. Wright and I always believed that teaching in the ordinary sense has little to do with the formation of what is here called *areté*. We believe . . . in the importance of discipline and striving for *areté*."

However clear the Wrights' understanding of Greek civilization, the implications for their own practice were clear. Taliesin was rather like a place of intellectual and landed gentry: a concept that would have appealed to the British. Norris Kelly Smith attempted an analogy: a place like Camelot for Arthur and his Round Table.[12] Yet that is not sufficient. Wright was both Arthur and Galahad, symbol and prosecutor. The Grail was individualism: to work and act "as I think as I am."[13] But not the knights, the apprentices. Theirs was an act of loyalty. Wright was always sensitive to "trouble" and "treachery" from his staff or apprentices, "unless goodnaturedly I will let [them] trade on me. Or in me," as he put it.[14] His over-sensitivity to the potential of staff treachery (to use his word), in whatever form, was no doubt a reaction reflective of his own conduct and extracurricular activities while a staff member with Chicago architects Dankmar Adler and Louis Sullivan back in the late 1880s and early 1890s.

Practice for the Fellowship therefore was found in toil: in the fields at Taliesin farm; in constructing buildings at both Taliesin (and the old Hillside School) and later also at Taliesin West outside Scottsdale, Arizona; in helping cook and serve meals and in cleaning and scrubbing buildings, as well as performing drafting and filing; and finally in listening to Mr. Wright. He needed not only an audience but adoring, malleable young minds who would be their "master's comrade," to use his words.[15] As Mrs. Wright said, "A man takes inspiration from one in whom he has faith; and in the same way he takes advice from one he believes in and who understands his natural ability." Further, she and her husband "confirm that the only real aristocracy is one based on merit, in which freedom and the sovereignty of the individual are held above all else. Advice and direction of this mind are a high form of education. All great societies were built by powerful individuals who created new patterns of education, of civilization and culture."[16] It was not a wholly altruistic endeavor. Theory and practice were motivated as much by Wright's "need for money and for something to do in the depths of the depression" as by lofty ideals;[17] the Fellows, or apprentices as they should be more correctly characterized, became a labor force. "The same formula was impressed upon all," said Wright, "not to imagine they were coming to school." They joined the Fellowship "to make themselves as useful to me as they could."[18] This frank assessment comes from his 1943 autobiography; but the point was made even in the promotional literature of the 1930s. For example, in *The Architectural Record,* a magazine that favored Wright over many years, a handsome spread was given to an article by Wright accompanied by photographs captioned "Students at Taliesin work with materials and builders' tools." He made it clear that "Fellows (young men and young women—all volunteers) have comprised the working group of apprentices to myself at Taliesin." This labor force was intended to help make Taliesin self-sustaining. The young people paid cash to become Fellows. Their farm, construction, and drawing labor together with their money supported Taliesin for many years. Supposedly this was to be an interim arrangement until sufficient architectural commissions arrived, as they finally did in 1936. But even after 1936 apprentices still paid to work.[19]

Olgivanna's conceptual role is not fully understood. It would be silly to assume too much, but also remiss to suppose that she played no role at all. Certainly her experiences at Georgi Gurdjieff's Institute for the Harmonious Development of Man must have been persuasive to the overall character and working aspects of the Fellowship. As early as 1931, before the Fellowship was announced, she described Gurdjieff's philosophy and applied routines, if briefly. "There were men and woman from various countries, several from Russia. There were doctors, painters, dancers, writers, musicians. All believed that the possibilities of development, knowledge, and achievement are much greater than those already achieved; that interior life—through non-identification with the ever-changing states of one's being; through sacrifices, through never-tiring efforts to understand more and do more, through willingness to suffer more when needed—can be made real, can be made even immortal." The notion of immortality is dramatically conveyed in the 1930 statement of Wright's: "I fully intend to be the greatest . . . who will ever live," and in 1949 he said to Elizabeth Kassler, "After me, it will be five hundred years before there is another" architect.[20] For all eternity he would be the measure. It was a promise not spoken, probably secretly believed as early as the decade 1900–1910.

Olgivanna continued her description of routines with Gurdjieff: "Just to be a completely developed human being, to have our mind, emotions, movement, body, mechanism, in well-proportioned order is a difficult task." She believed that they were reaching their development by way of an "ordinary life: in the gardens, in the kitchen, doing housekeeping, farming, until the day's work to keep up the Institute was done. In the evening we worked in movement, exercises, memorizing, concentration." And "some evenings were spent in building the study-house; we were all anxious to finish it soon."[21] The parallel—minus the emphasis on movement and meditation—between these practices and those of the Fellowship is remarkable.[22]

Author Sinclair Lewis described Gurdjieff's place as a "notorious establishment" and said "it must be a hell of a place to live—they sleep only four hours a night, and eat almost nothing, with occasional fasts for six or eight or ten days."[23] Perhaps a slight overreaction, yet typical of comments from many observers. The Russian and his Institute were controversial throughout their existence together. Gurdjieff's philosophy has been concisely and fairly outlined by Robert Twombly: "Gurdjieff taught that civilization had corrupted the primordial harmony among man's intellectual, physical, and emotional faculties or centers'; his followers tried to reunify themselves through work, contemplation, fasting, 'self-observation,' and other coordinated activities."[24]

Wright learned the Gurdjieff ways and means from Olgivanna, but he must have learned something of "the Gurdjieff idea" from Zona Gale. The American literary world, to which Gale was closely associated, came to know of Gurdjieff's experiment through the writing of the New Zealand expatriate Katherine Mansfield in the early 1920s. A colony of Gurdjieff followers developed around Gale at her home town of Portage, only forty miles northeast of Spring Green. A vocal and active promoter of Gurdjieff, A. R. Orage, the English critic and editor, visited Wisconsin in the mid-1920s, perhaps while Gurdjieff's troupe performed in Chicago in 1924. In spite of his many associations with Gurdjieff and his followers, Wright was always confused about the mystic. In 1939 he remarked to Kenneth Bayes at the Royal Institute of British Architects in London: "No. Gurdjieff has had no influence what ever upon me or my work." The two first met sometime around 1924, and Wright discovered common ground with "his philosophy and my own practices which I recognize as proof of the universal validity of both." As for Ouspensky, Wright took "very little interest in him. Gurdjieff seems to me to be his master."[25] The mystic visited Taliesin on a few occasions and during World War II Wright offered Gurdjieff refuge in Wisconsin but the Russian stayed in Paris. (The apprentices' most lasting memory of Gurdjieff was his recipe for sauerkraut.)[26] Edgar Tafel, one of Wright's apprentices from 1932 until 1941, believed that Olgivanna "learned the patterns of living in a closed society run on strict routine by a master with a powerful philosophy." Tafel's experience confirmed that "her experience with Gurdjieff did influence the form of the Fellowship and some of the activities envisioned from the beginning," and that she was "the force that kept the Fellowship in working order."[27] (By 1981, more than twenty years after Wright's death, in *Who's Who in America* she proclaimed herself a "co-founder" of the Fellowship, a term probably close to the truth.) Yet Tafel conceded that Gurdjieff's "transcendental philosophy was never one of the major currents of our life. Spiritual leanings attracted a few people to the Fellowship but the architectural core had neither time nor inclination for an outside philosophy,"[28] at least in the 1930s.

However, the influence of Gurdjieff on the Wrights and their daughter Iovanna must have been more than casual as further evidenced by the following. In 1953 under the sponsorship of the Art Institute of Chicago and Taliesin, members of the Fellowship presented what a program described as "Music, Ritual Exercises, and Temple Dances by Georges Gurdjieff." The program introduction was by Wright, oddly, not Olgivanna. This was preceded by a "demonstration" at Taliesin in October 1950 of movement exercises based on Gurdjieff's teachings; during Easter 1951 there were further demonstrations of "Gurdjieff's Movements" at Spring Green; and "Ritual Exercises of Gurdjieff" were presented by the Fellowship at a Unitarian Church in Madison during November 1951. (Wright designed the church in 1946 and it was opened in August 1951.) The latent influence of Gurdjieff over so many years seems clear.

The Taliesin Fellowship more closely approximated Olgivanna's pedagogical beliefs and experiences than any of Wright's. In application his philosophy was the more pragmatic. One suspects he gladly tolerated her prosaic management. Yet according to Olgivanna they shared a broader philosophy, one that was linked to those more practical applications such as the Fellowship. Tafel summed up the practicalities: in the 1930s "we were a small, well-knit group who felt it would serve our careers best to help Mr. Wright implement his designs. To accomplish this, we often acted as contractors, subcontracting each portion to bring the building within a realistic budget." He found Wright to be "charming, witty, hard, sometimes cruel (often openly), a bold Midwestern Yankee who loved to confuse his critics."[29]

Attempts to entice students were of a wide variety: articles, letters, brochures and other means of more subtlety. He dedicated his book of Princeton University lectures, called *Modern Architecture,* "To the young man in architecture"; one of his lectures at the Art Institute of Chicago in 1930 was entitled "To the young men in architecture," and that title was to appear in articles that published portions of the lectures. (The title was borrowed from Louis Sullivan's paper read to the Architectural League of America, Chicago, 1900.) From 1932 to 1980 well over 460 people became apprentices, an average of about 10 per year. Some stayed a few weeks, most a few months, a small number became permanent employees, and a number came as husband and wife.

Attempts to enlist professional and financial support for his venture were less subtle. When the Fellowship was announced in late 1932 Wright sent a letter to "ten worthwhile architects" that he considered "leaders whom the others follow." He asked for their approval of his venture in writing so he might use their endorsement to obtain financial support elsewhere. There was an implication that they might wish to send some money too. The architects contacted were R. Buckminster Fuller, Joseph Urban, Albert Kahn, Ely Kahn, Thomas Lamb, John Wellborn Root, John Holabird, Eliel Saarinen, and interestingly William Lescaze and George Howe. Of lesser architects (an evaluation made by Wright), such as Walter Willcox at the University of Oregon, in his case two years after the letters to those prestigious people, Wright requested moral and material support in a friendly but serious manner.[30] The extent of Wright's requests for support was quite extraordinary. Replies were supportive but short on finance. Only Ely Kahn made the effort to visit Taliesin so he might learn first-hand about the Fellowship. He was even willing to approach the Carnegie Foundation on Wright's behalf, but Wright said no thank you. "We are not even a school. . . . We are Frank Wright's atelier." (That seems quite clear: it was not a school.) And "no 'foundation' for us."[31]

Those ten special people plus all others who supported the Fellowship—in a variety of unknown ways—were listed and the list was made available. By 1933 the number of Friends was about 150 and included most of his and Olgivanna's friends as well as his family (and her sister in the Caucasus), clients past and present, employees past and present, well-known celebrities (of one kind or another), from Japan, Europe, India, China, Central and South America, and many of the American states. Of more value to this discussion are the views of those who answered Wright's advertisements and became Fellows.

Elizabeth Kassler (formerly E. Mock) became an apprentice and settled in at Taliesin in 1932 but left a few months later. Her account characterizes the experiences of many Fellows, then and now.

That winter was very strange, very uncomfortable. Physical austerities became acceptable, perhaps because they were shared by Mr. and Mrs. Wright. The lasting discomfort was simply that I understood nothing, nothing at all. Why was there no instruction, and no work in the drafting room other than when a hungry Chinese friend would accept my desserts in exchange for setting up a tracing job? If architecture is indeed the mother art, why was the execution of menial chores held equally important and subject to the same demand for attention? What was the unfamiliar quality of that attention, directed to every detail of living? Why the distrust of intellectuals? What was behind the strange compelling beauty of the place? Why did I feel so disturbed, so inadequate, and why couldn't I get my mind around it?[32]

For reasons outlined rather emotionally, yet with some vigor, she left for more certain ground at the Museum of Modern Art in New York. She eventually found some answers to those perplexities when as a mature woman she returned for a short fulfilling visitation during 1948–49.

One of the most interesting accounts was written by a German immigrant from Cologne, Heinrich Klumb, in 1933. He and his wife had spent five years with Wright before he began working for the Los Angeles City Planning Department and then moving to Puerto Rico to pursue a full architectural practice. Klumb had been introduced to Wright by Wijdeveld and was not a "fellow" but was employed at Chicago and Spring Green during the critical years 1928 to late 1933. He wrote to Wijdeveld in an attempt to persuade the Dutchman to become the "leader" of the Taliesin Fellowship. In his letter Klumb related experiences that help explain why some people, including Kassler, hurriedly departed. Klumb noted that there were great difficulties and hardships but some achievement in the preceding twelve months. Old buildings were altered and extended, a drawing room newly built, and work continued on accommodations, dining room, and kitchen. There were twenty-five students accommodated within incomplete facilities being built with credit or by "grants (according to Mr. Wright)," and a small theater was complete. But all the "fellows" were often close to despair for there had been much labor but no creative work. They did not want to dig ditches, chase tradesmen, clean up after them, or "cut timber just to get warm." They wanted "to create," and they made Wright understand this. Education and apprenticeship had been ignored. It was all in such turmoil, but there were signs of improvement. Klumb believed Wijdeveld might prove their savior; but in the end the Dutchman refused.[33]

the studio

5.4 Interior perspective of the drafting
room at Taliesin, Spring Green, of 1932,
perhaps drawn by Wright. The room was
built much as shown but the trusses had
to be beefed up. Courtesy and © 1985 the
Frank Lloyd Wright Foundation.

The late art historian Edgar Kaufmann, Jr., became an apprentice, of sorts, and his recollections have been sporadically and unevenly presented over many years and in many forums. Kaufmann's latest all-too-brief reminiscences can be found in his new book about Fallingwater, the country house designed by Wright for his mother and father. As a "would-be painter of twenty-four, I felt disconnected from the thoughts and ways of America after long study in Europe." Then a friend recommended *An Autobiography;* "reading it I believed Wright saw what I was missing. I went out to Spring Green in Wisconsin, and Wright agreed to let me join the Taliesin Fellowship in October, 1934, though I had no plan to become an architect." His parents visited Wright's Taliesin and they were "moved by the extraordinary beauty of Wright's home and its landscape, and impressed by the devoted enthusiasm of the apprentices." Kaufmann thought Wright and his father were "both outgoing, winning, venturesome men," and that his father "quickly felt the power of Wright's genius. Mrs. Wright and my mother were cosmopolitan and romantic in their taste for poetry; mother responded to Mrs. Wright's courageous character." Of the Fellowship Kaufmann writes that it was "the most important event" in his life, and that

that marvelous place still seems one of my most profound experiences. . . . Without aiming to practice architecture I could benefit from his encompassing view of the art. Every day at teatime Wright would talk informally to the apprentices, often about ideas stimulated by Broadacre. On Sunday at breakfast he would speak more deliberately on general themes. . . . There were hard edges to his teaching balanced by exceptional charm and humor, and quick sympathy for the efforts of those less experienced. So strong and convincing were Wright's principles that after a while—since I was not attuned to the Fellowship routine—it was time for me to leave. . . . By then being a painter had lost its significance for me, and I went to work at the family department store.[34]

Others who apprenticed in the 1930s have commented. Abrom Dombar was a graduate architect: when his "opportunity came to go to Taliesin," he said, "my great longing was satisfied." He then went "cut of Taliesin as a disciple and spread the gospel of an organic Architecture." William B. Fyfe was indebted to the Wrights for scholarships "accorded at a time when they were so needed." On reflection Klumb felt that his experience and Wright's influence had "and still is greatly affecting and guiding me with always renewed vigour, I admit proudly." Noverre Musson believed that "far from realising any profit from my presence at Taliesin, he [Wright] was actually supporting me, giving me a home, and priceless education in addition."[35] Wright's own biased accounting prepared for the 1943 edition of his autobiography, scattered about book five entitled "Form," was probably written after America became involved in World War II. And there are other testimonials, most of them praising but not detailed enough for a reader to gain insight into practices, events, and purposes. There are exceptions: Tafel's writings and illustrations in his *Apprentice to Genius* are one, Kassler's another. There are even fewer useful commentaries by visitors.

Ayn Rand was a visitor, one with great interest in Wright's philosophy but not always understanding of Wright's actions during the 1930s, or later. Rand visited Wright at Spring Green in August 1945 and Taliesin West in the winter of 1947. In the 1930s she had studied architecture, the profession, and Wright's philosophy in preparation for her book *The Fountainhead* which was eventually published in 1943. Her general appraisal was concise: "It was like a feudal establishment." She found the buildings "magnificent, and thrilling," obviously better than mere photographs had explained, but "terribly neglected" and in a sad state of disrepair. As for the Fellowship, Rand was unforgiving. "They were like medieval serfs." The menu for the Wrights and guests ("fancy delicacies") was different from that for the Fellows ("fried eggs"). The Wrights and their guests "sat on a raised platform high above the others," not dissimilar, it should be added, to public (private) schools and university colleges in Britain and Australia. Rand was stunned by the situation: "a real caste system"; Wright "the deity," a "spirit"; Olgivanna the "practical manager." Even more frightening, at least to Rand's reckoning, was that the students, to use her word, moved in an "atmosphere of worshipful, awed obedience." They "seemed like emotional, out-of-focus hero-worshippers." Anything Wright said "was right." Rand supplied a generalized example: "When he and I began to argue about something, the students were against me instantly; they bared their teeth that I was disagreeing with the master." Perhaps more than anything else Rand was saddened by the tragic reality of Wright's Fellowship. The students' own work "was badly imitative" of their guru. Rand knew that Wright "didn't want any of that; he was trying to get intellectual independence from them during general discussions," but Rand noted "he didn't get anything except 'Yes, sir' or 'No, sir,'" usually accompanied by "recitals of formulas from his writing." Rand believed that she and Wright wanted the same response from people: "independent understanding; but he didn't know how to stimulate it. I felt sorry for him."[36]

Indeed, the promise of Wright's words knitted to his individualized life and architectural products were the magnet that drew Rand to Wright in the mid-1930s. Wright was the archetype for her hero and paragon, Howard Roark, in *The Fountainhead.* Her disappointment with Taliesin was real and, perhaps, too close to her own experience. When her philosophy of "Objectivism" became popular, she too gathered around her the same kind of admiring people who stimulated in her a set of emotional needs not dissimilar to Wright's: worship and agreement were two. Yet, after she observed the Fellowship at work, so to speak, and found it wanting, Rand commissioned Wright to design a house for herself and her husband Frank. However nice the preliminary design, it was abandoned in 1947. Cost was a critical factor, at least so said Rand, but in fact she abandoned the idea of a country estate for central New York City.[37]

Another observer was Stanley Nott, who with his family was invited to stay at the Spring Green Taliesin for the summer of 1940. Nott was a religious man unsatisfied with institutional religion, and a wanderer. He had lived in Tasmania, was a sheep farmer in New Zealand, briefly lived in most places in Europe, traveled the world, and studied in Gurdjieff's oriental rug-and-pillow-strewn Study House at Avon where he met Olgivanna in 1924. It was she who invited the Notts in 1940. (Gurdjieff had briefly visited Olgivanna the year before.) Nott has described his impressions of the Fellowship and Taliesin. He had high admiration for Wright the architect as well as a long friendship with Olgivanna begun at Avon. His observations and recollections (written in 1969) should be compared to Tafel's. The Fellowship's aim was to create organic architecture through an "organic life," and Nott believed this was achieved by "living a three-fold life," one of "instincts" simulta-neously with "feelings and the mind." People must "use their hands" and then must appreciate the "things of the feelings" like poetry, music, painting. The Fellows he found to be a "delightful and intelligent group" who were "courteous, helpful, and efficient." Their "youngness" did not have the "outer sophistication with which 'educated' Americans in town so often cover their adolescence." Routine at Taliesin began with a "rising bell" at 6:30, breakfast then at seven, 7:30 to work, a picnic lunch at midday when, before his feet, all listened to Wright talk. On wet days there was a luncheon theater or music or singing. Tea at five and then choir or orchestra or practice at piano (there were many about the manor). Supper was at seven. Visitors arrived on Saturday afternoon, usually "well-known" people from various walks, "or 'runs' of life." Evening clothes for supper and then cocktails with the Wrights sitting on "large chairs, rather like a king and queen on their thrones."

To Nott, Taliesin "represented the highest culture that could be found in America and with it went the feeling of freedom." The words were put together much as by Wright. Gurdjieff's Institute was of course on a "higher level," but nonetheless life at Taliesin "that summer was as full a life as it is possible to have on this planet. It was a three-centered life: the hot weather and beautiful country and the good food and physical work [and the Notts had to work]; the harmony of the buildings, the music, good films and singing; the discussion at [high] table"—which was served by the apprentices—and Wright's "stimulating" informal lectures to the apprentices; it "was about as rich as ordinary life can be." Ordinary?

In Nott's view Olgivanna "inspired the life of the community"; it was she who "received inspiration" from Gurdjieff. With a knowledge of Nott's bias to Olgivanna and in respect of his long stay on Taliesin ground and in the manor house, some further observations are valuable. Nott liked the "patriarchal quality" of life at Spring Green and he noted with sadness that "patriarchality" had been "gradually disappearing from American life" since the South lost the Civil War. Nott had again exposed one of the British diseases: a belief in the superiority of a hereditary aristocracy. In Russia patriarchality was "swept away by the revolution and in Germany by Nazism. It is disappearing in England too, and in China it is regarded as 'bourgeois imperialistic.'" (Nott also found Wright to be very antagonistic to the British government, concerned that it was going to "drag America into a war which did not concern her.") In regard to "being and understanding" it was Nott's opinion that Wright "was a child compared with Gurdjieff," and that he was intensely vain "like all geniuses," and naive. He would "believe anyone who was nice to him and flattered him; he could not see through people." As with so many people "of genius, his personality had been developed at the expense of his essence"—whatever that meant—but still his personality and genius were "fascinating and stimulating."[38] With the arrival of autumn the Wright entourage prepared for their winter campaign in Arizona. The Notts were invited along but decided to return to another temporary place in New York, and to visit Ouspensky who was then in or near Manhattan.

From the evidence both Rand and Nott would seem right.

A view that most of the apprentices who worked under Wright would probably agree with was expressed by one of Wright's granddaughters, the actress Anne Baxter. Although never an apprentice, grandfather had taught her "to mistrust facades and always to observe life beneath its surfaces; to find excitement in a seed pod or beauty in a carpenter's hammer." He gave her "other inner eyes."[39]

Regardless of Olgivanna's role and all the sources, influences, and inspirations, it is abundantly clear that, as Tafel asserted and emphasized, "Mr. Wright *was* the Fellowship." Wright's various summaries were more distinct. His entry in the 1938 *International Who's Who* was short and merely stated he was "founder and conductor Taliesin Fellowship." By the 1950s he tried to invoke a wider context. In *Who's Who in America* during the decade he referred to himself as the "Founder and coordinator of 'The Taliesin Fellowship,' a cultural experiment in the arts."

In the mid-1930s the many contradictions of purpose, fact, practice, philosophy, and all else were almost of no substantial concern. The Fellowship was touted as a self-sustaining workshop. (Parenthetically it should be obvious that the differences between the German Bauhaus and the Fellowship are such that discussion is unnecessary.) It was not meant even to approximate a socialist or communitarian experiment. In its semiisolation in farming country it was to be a means of achieving freedom from "fashion," from "sham," from the "vile gods of trade," and freedom from the old bugaboo of European cultural imperialism, "the old human expressions already dead or dying around us."[40] This alone would have been attractive to those who had defeated the czars. In its most fundamental organization and ideas as promoted not only in circulars but in the press from 1932 to 1936, the Fellowship might have been seen as the beginning of something loosely akin to a soviet, a cadre for similarly modeled people: soviet and cadre not in title but type. Or more reasonably it might have been seen as a kind of *kolkhoz,* a collective farm community, or a kibbutz. But the reality was otherwise. It was closer to an English manor house.

The Fellowship and autobiography did not occur as isolated phenomena. They must be seen as part of a stream of events that flowed together to compose Wright's career in the 1930s—personal promotions, polemical presentations, and architectural designs—all diverse to say the least. In architecture they were not without observable trends and historical consistency if often obscured by astonishing newness. Because his buildings appeared new (and this was usually construed to mean that they did not fit traditional or fashionable modes) and because of their obvious architectural excellence, they attracted attention, appreciation, and analysis, all of which was too often uncritical in favor of either derogation or adulation. To fully understand the trends and historical links in and of his architecture it is best in these relatively short essays to isolate and clarify particular aspects: communities, buildings, ideas, forums.

6 Architecture

While it may not seem the most obvious, Wright's exploration of old ideas with new structural techniques sometimes generated unique aesthetic responses in the 1920s and 1930s that were more daring, so to speak, than the Prairie School years. The core and cantilever structure, an adaption of the National Life Insurance Company "skyscraper" of 1924 that he refined for the St. Mark's Towers of 1929, was rhythmically connected to form a group of apartment buildings in Chicago in 1930. Still connected, it became the high-rise wall of a large complex called Crystal Heights Towers of 1940 for a site in Washington, D.C. None of these tall structures was built, although one of the St. Mark's buildings was modified to become the Price Tower in Bartlesville, Oklahoma, in 1952.

He also explored a concrete masonry system for a series of designs in the early 1920s and used it on houses for Millard, Storer, Freeman, and Ennis. Wright derived his "textile" masonry system from a more sophisticated product called "Knitlock" that had been designed and produced in 1917 by a former Studio employee and confidant, Walter Burley Griffin, while the latter was residing in Australia.[1] Although Wright apparently thought of using some form of concrete block in 1906 on the Harry Brown house project for Geneseo, Illinois, it was to be something like a long, narrow, rectangular masonry log. It should not be confused with the constructional developments of Griffin and Wright. With assistance from Wright, Charles McArthur used one modification of textile blocks to construct the Arizona Biltmore Hotel. Dr. Chandler was attracted to the constructional/structural scheme enough to believe it should be used on his San Marcos in The Desert tourist

6.1 Ground-floor plans in c. 1950 of Johnson Wax buildings, Racine, Wisconsin,
1936–39 (right) and 1944–46 (left quadrangle). The tower completed in 1946 is in
the center of the left quadrangle. Drawing
by Gerald Wilson. Reproduced from Lipman (1986), courtesy Jonathan Lipman.

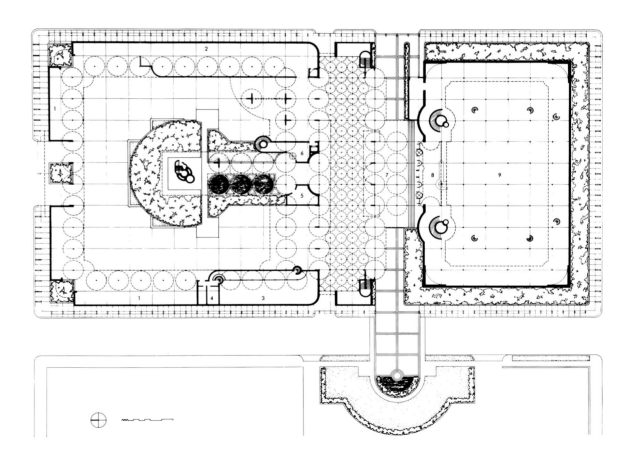

facility project of 1928–29. The block faces designed for San Marcos (and the related Cudney house) had deeply cut surfaces which, when collectively set in a vertical position, gave the impression of the outer structural ribs so obvious on the stately saguaro cactus. (Wright also proposed to use massive amounts of Leerdam glass blocks of his own design.) A few other houses by Wright related to the Doctor's schemes also used concrete masonry. Sometimes Wright's strict adherence to a system got him in aesthetic as well as plan and constructional difficulties. The house for his nephew Richard Lloyd Jones in Tulsa, Oklahoma, of 1929 was such a case, as was the Young house project for Chandler of 1927. The Tulsa block house was trapped by a three-dimensional constructional module that made for ill-fitting volumes. The Young house used plain, square-faced concrete blocks turned forty-five degrees to normal, seemingly to satisfy only whim for they ultimately had to meet plumb walls and doors and the like.

Not typical was one of Wright's better-known structural innovations, the "lily-pad-like tops" to columns for the Johnson Wax Building of 1937–39. The structural columns, first proposed in 1931–32 for a building for the *Capital Journal* in Salem, Oregon, were capped by a great spreading "pad" at the top. Among other rationalizations to be discussed later, each pad was meant to eliminate roof girders and beams. It did so while adding many interior columns reminiscent of great columnar halls found in ancient Near Eastern civilizations.[2] The interior space thereby took on an exciting experiential and aesthetic meaning, one not expected from Wright's previous oeuvre and one that, perhaps with the exception of the expressionists, the Central European aesthetic could not conceive, or more exactly would not allow. The overall impression of the exterior, in spite of different materials, was somewhat similar in both buildings.

Wright had said that an "organic form grows its own structure out of conditions as a plant grows out of the soil: both unfold similarly from within."[3] Historian and contemporary observer Walter Curt Behrendt elaborated the analogy in support of Wright's cause: "In this sense, the laws of organic planning find their continuation and completion in the external structure; and the manifold arrangement of the parts, the lively grouping of building masses, are to be viewed as a result of the inner logic of design, and not as a brilliant show-piece of a deliberately picturesque composition." As for Wright's buildings one should "avoid speaking of 'composition' at all, since no less a man than Goethe has condemned this expression, in nature as well as in art, as degrading." Behrendt reminded readers that Goethe had said that "organs do not compose themselves as if already previously finished, they develop themselves together and out of one another, to an existence which necessarily takes part in the whole." The logical result of such a growth is that Wright's buildings

**6.2 Bird's-eye perspective of Johnson Wax
building, Racine, Wisconsin, 1936–39, as
published in the 1930s. © 1961 the Frank
Lloyd Wright Foundation.**

6.3 Photograph c. 1939 of entry foyer, Johnson Wax building, Racine, Wisconsin, 1936–39. Courtesy of S. C. Johnson and Son, Inc.

6.4 Photograph c. 1939 of exterior detail, Johnson Wax building, Racine, Wisconsin, 1936–39. Courtesy of S. C. Johnson and Son, Inc.

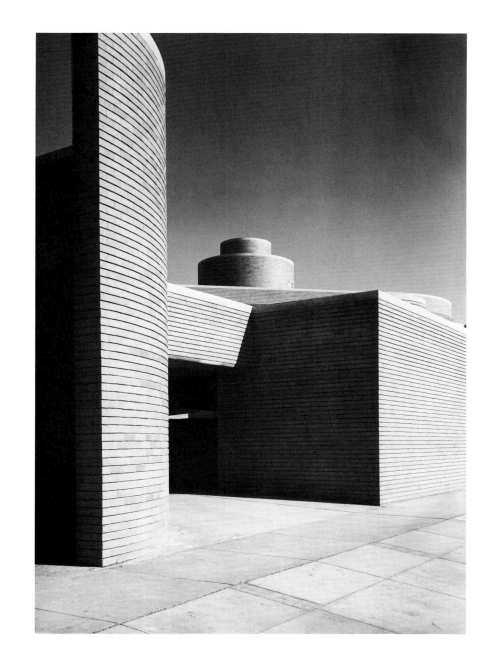

were not exteriorly composed in the traditional sense. This can be seen in the expression of the inherent functional—or more exactly, organic—differences of those buildings built in the period 1929 to 1938: "They are built and created in three dimensions as coherent organisms." Of the structure and like a plant, "a building grows up from the earth to the light."[4]

The necessity of *structure* was natural, of nature, and therefore contained no extrarational—or mystical—imperative in Wright's mind as it did in the thinking of other modernists of the 1920s and 1930s (or 1950s). The proposition that the machine was the primary tool of the new age was adequately put by Wright many times (much to the alarm of the English arts and crafts people), especially from the 1890s to 1915. Science and technology were expressively epitomized in architecture through structure but they were not the only decisive generatives of the new artistic era born in the twentieth century. In Wright's view perhaps they were more critical since the mid-nineteenth century. They were however only one factor to shape an architecture responsive to its own being within Wright's holistic concept of an "organic life." In the 1930s, however, his protagonists (as he saw them) were enamored by the Central Europeans' architecture and the philosophy of the political left. They were convinced by and passionately committed to the implications of the new technologies that would decisively define modern man; or more narrowly, modernism in all design fields. They chose to use rationalism to define architecture through a building's structure and constructional techniques. For Wright structure was a means, not an end; this was a measurable aspect differentiating him from the American protagonists of the European style while uniting him with the traditionalists; a unity both parties refused to acknowledge.

Architectural materials used in construction, whether structural or not, extended his vocabulary well beyond that of his earlier work. Steel was now used more directly, sometimes structurally, often exposed, sometimes the result of a client's request such as the All-steel house project of 1937 for a Los Angeles steel merchant. There was also a farm complex of sheet steel in 1932, another project more properly discussed later. Apparently there were three typical plans for the All-steel houses, each to have been dramatically sited in the Los Angeles hills without the usual and obnoxious land terracing. The project envisaged the use of channeled steel sheets of the barest depth, meant to give the impression of ultra-thin planes.[5] The vertically or horizontally jointed steel sheets expressed compressive support or the dynamics of cantilever; all was to have been viewed through large areas of glass.

More commonly than in previous years, Wright used concrete *in situ* as an exposed material, primarily for walls, roofs, and balconies, especially as the decade proceeded. Brick and

6.5 All-steel house project for a site in Los Angeles, California, 1938, a drawing presumably by Wright. Courtesy British Architectural Library, RIBA, London. © 1990 the Frank Lloyd Wright Foundation.

wood continued to be applied in manners similar to the prairie years, enabling heightened horizontality or massing. In the 1930s as in earlier years brick was sometimes deeply struck on the horizontal joint. Herbert Johnson's Wingspread mansion of 1937 or the Johnson's Wax Building at Racine are good examples. The deep strike was one means, together with glass tubes and continuous concrete trim, to express the sleek curved lines (a streamlining effect associated with the 1930s but introduced in dramatic sketch designs by Erich Mendelsohn in the early 1920s). Stucco was also a favorite material from the past. While Wright used it more rationally in the early years of the century (then as a rough texture in conjunction with darkly stained wood), in the 1930s it tended to be relatively smooth and cover large rather plain areas over masonry or concrete with no apparent expansion joints. It was also applied to exterior volumes or to deep ribbons such as balcony rails.

Stone became a favorite material in the 1930s. In the early years of his practice it was used in a refined manner such as on the exterior wall base of the Williams house of 1895, a nod to typical pseudo-medieval detailing of the period. Only occasionally was it coarse ashlar stone such as on his Taliesin home. Its new use in the 1930s was as rubble and began with the too prosaic and ill-proportioned (and unsupervised) Darwin Martin summer house in 1927. It reached its ultimate application on the Kaufmann Fallingwater house (1935–37) and emphatically at Taliesin West in 1938. As used on Fallingwater it defined natural horizontal surfaces, fireplaces, retaining wall surfaces, or the vertical and ancillary spaces that seem to grow out of the earth's soil or from the great stones on the site. The main spaces seem both to nestle within the stone and to reach out for the exterior. Edgar Kaufmann, Jr.'s *Fallingwater: A Frank Lloyd Wright Country House* is beautifully produced, eloquent with full color illustrations, charmingly reminiscent if imprecise and impressionistic. It includes excellent drawings to explain the house's architectonics, its natural and intimate relatedness to the site, the use of great rocks *in situ,* and the application of stone. (He also mentions that the site with its boulders and waterfall was selected by the Kaufmanns, not by Wright, and that they wished to sit on the rocks, not merely look at them.) In contrast, the masonry at Taliesin West is so coarsely and randomly employed and of such large stones that it all appears to erupt in neat rows from the encompassing desert floor to provide rough edges and cool chambers. That effect was reused with the Pauson sisters' house in 1939 where on the shady side of the masonry wall spaces were defined in wood and glass. It was very much like the wood and masonry spaces created by the Zuni on the high desert plains.

For the most part the Fellows built Taliesin West, or the camp as it was called while they labored. The design was completed in late 1937 and a winter campaign on the pediment site began

6.6 Kaufmann House, Fallingwater on Bear Run, Pennsylvania, 1935–37, "plot plan" showing main-floor bearing walls; dated May 1936. The four boulders on the left remained in place, the house designed in and around three of them. The road was existing and as it passes behind the house the top boulder rises above it by about 12 feet. Courtesy and © 1990 the Frank Lloyd Wright Foundation.

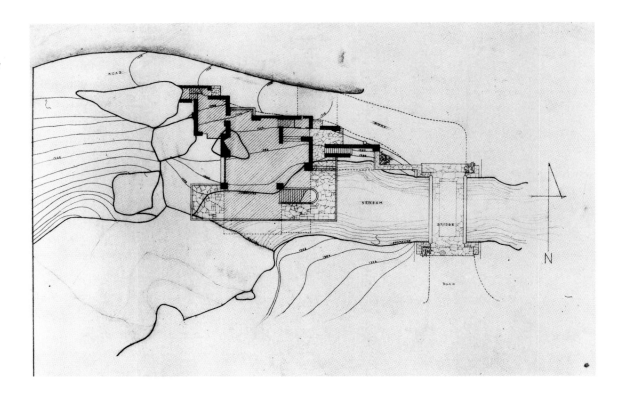

6.7 Plans of the Kaufmann House, Falling-water on Bear Run, Pennsylvania, 1935–37. Based on Zevi and Kaufmann (1962) and *Architectural Forum*, January 1938.

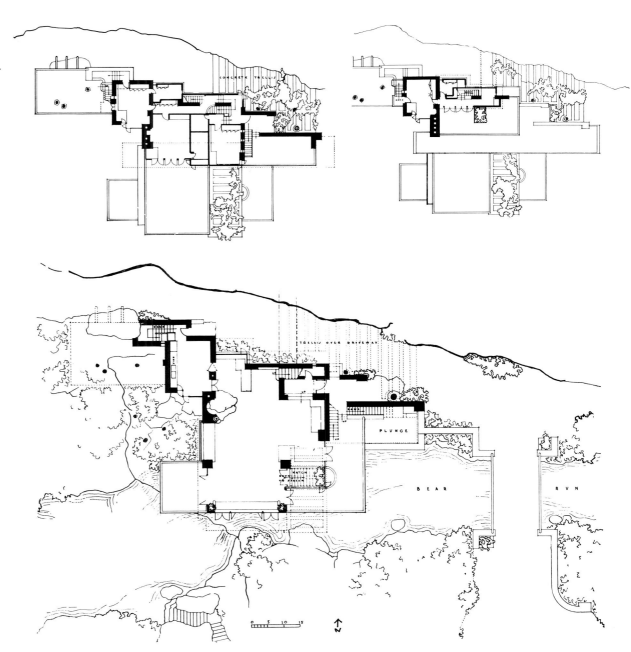

6.8 Kaufmann House, Fallingwater on Bear Run, Pennsylvania, 1935–37, exterior photograph of November 1937 by Hedrich Blessing, probably the most widely published photograph of the house. From *Architectural Forum*, January 1938, and widely published in the 1930s.

6.9 Section of Kaufman House, Fallingwater on Bear Run, Pennsylvania, 1935–37. Based on Zevi and Kaufmann (1962).

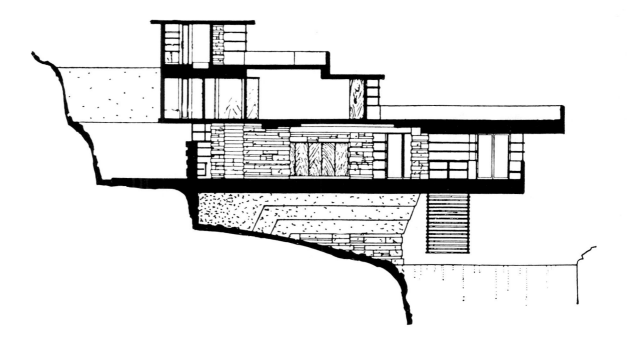

6.10 Detailed interior photograph of living room in Kaufmann House, Fallingwater on Bear Run, Pennsylvania, 1935–37, widely published in the 1930s.

6.11 Ground-floor plan of Taliesin West, c. 1937. It is not known if this is based on the original design because the buildings have been in a constant state of alteration and enlargement. For the most part this plan agrees with Figure 6.12. Courtesy and © 1986 the Frank Lloyd Wright Foundation.

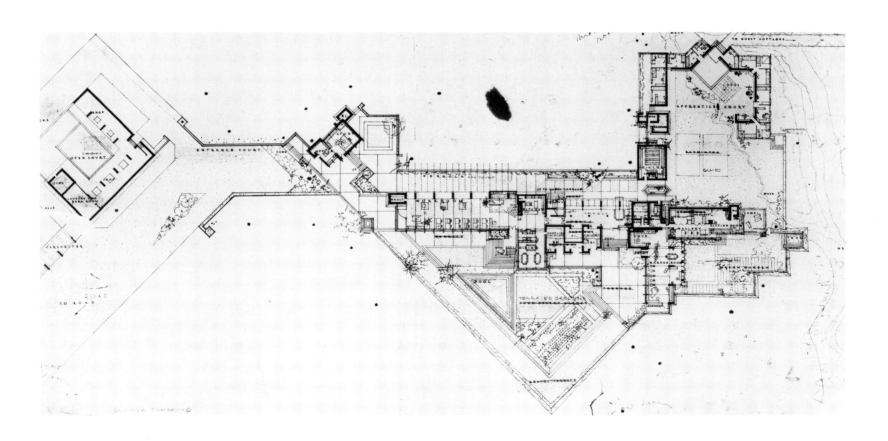

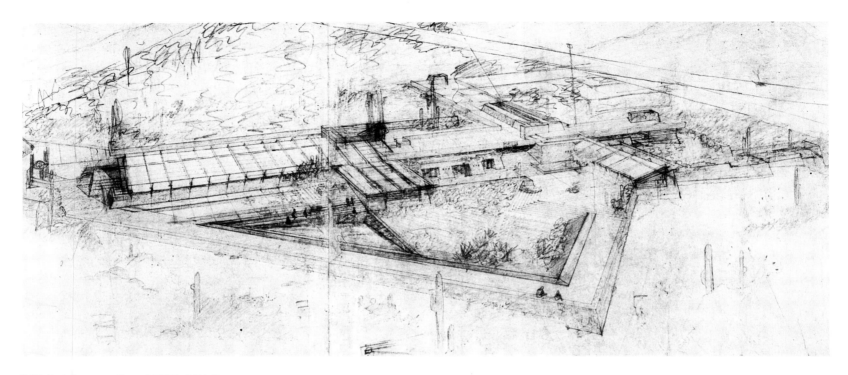

6.12 Aerial perspective of 1937 of "Taliesin in the Desert," also called the "Arizona Compound." A study presumably by
Wright; only the right half of the drawing
is illustrated here. Courtesy and © 1962
the Frank Lloyd Wright Foundation.

shortly after Christmas 1937.[6] From January through March 1938 the young apprentices together with professional builders determined levels, graded, and finished most of the rugged masonry walls, heaving great stones—some weighing tons—into place, then binding them with a surround of concrete. While working they lived in tents and hauled potable water from five miles distant.

The extension externally of horizontal space was new. In his previous houses, with only few exceptions, internal space was contained within the building's interior. A band of windows invariably rested on the top line of a wainscot on the interior or the exterior sill line. The exterior, usually a patio for houses, was reached by a door. When on the patio, a person was in another but exterior room, so to speak. Sometimes but not always the roof and therefore the ceiling extended beyond the window line, partially or wholly over the exterior space. The ceiling may have visually linked the interior and exterior but the high windowsill prohibited its full exploitation.

In the 1930s, by employing glass to the floor or by a series of glazed French doors, Wright created a transparent wall. The horizontal *surface* was thereby extended as a continuous plane into the exterior and across a terrace or to a balcony edge. It is difficult to find a Wright house or apartment of the 1930s that does not employ this spatial manipulation. It was noticed by Wright's contemporary, the historian Behrendt, but in another related manner: take "the horizontal slabs boldly projected, that new motive which has been the most imitated in modern building: in these widely overhanging eaves, spreading themselves canopylike over terraces and balconies, there seems to be plantlike existence translated into architectural form."[7] One of Wright's most prophetic houses of the prairie years was the Gale house of 1909, whose balcony/living room relationship would be as close as he would come during the period to realizing the potential of the extension of space just described. Note that the Gale house also possessed a cantilevered second-floor balcony not in concrete but with wood joists. Wright was emphatic: the Gale house was the "progenitor for Fallingwater," therefore by implication paradigmatic of much of the theoretical stuff presented in Europe after 1918 and of his post-1932 work, at least to c. 1940.

There were two other dramatic changes in Wright's domestic architecture that quite naturally were intimately related; one was plan and the other the influence of the Central European aesthetic, created principally by de Stijl, Le Corbusier, van Doesburg, Walter Gropius and the Bauhaus buildings, Erich Mendelsohn, and related movements and people. In America in the 1930s the house of the average income earner had become slightly larger and single-story. Most if not all of Wright's famous Prairie School houses were two-story. In the 1930s his houses were, with notable exceptions, single-story. The exceptions Wright treated similarly to his single-story house, both on the ground floor with terraces and usually on the upper floor with balconies. The house plan was much more open about the entertaining spaces, which remained the focus of home life in a Wright house. The "work space," as he called the kitchen (with attendant storage and/or furnace) was tucked into an open but cupped space. Juxtaposed to the kitchen space and in a *single* large—and it could be an amorphous—space were dining, sitting or living, and sometimes a reading nook or a music alcove. As previously described, this room was often extended horizontally to an adjacent terrace. This general plan configuration was true even for the great Fallingwater. A corridor usually led away from the kitchen or away from a corner of the central entertaining space to the necessarily private bedrooms with their attendant bathrooms. If a second floor was used, it contained private rooms reached via stairs usually located near the entry and kitchen.

The evolution of Wright's house plan can be described visually in diagrammatic form (Figure 13). On the left is a typical plan of the 1880s that persisted well into the 1900s. Then slowly the strictly defined and formally arranged rooms gave way to spaces informally defined until even the kitchen became an alcove off the entertaining area. Wright's new plan reflected not only a change from two- to one-story houses but the new and more relaxed, less formal lifestyle of the 1930s. One of his major contributions to that lifestyle was to include the kitchen (work space or work room or laboratory in his nomenclature) as an intimate part of family social life in the home. In so doing he also improved its physical conditions. In all manners, his domestic architecture transformed the typical suburban house to a more livable, responsive place, at least in North America.

It is understandable if a little surprising, therefore, that around 1930 Frederick J. Kiesler invited Wright to become a member of the American Union of Decorative Artists and Craftsmen, or AUDAC. Its members were a formidable and impressive group who were individually influential throughout the 1930s and included interior and furnishing designers such as Walter D. Teague, Norman Bel Geddes, and Russel Wright. (It was around 1952 that Russel Wright spent a summer weekend at Taliesin, Spring Green. Frank Wright offered some advice about Russel Wright's naturalesque and somewhat Japanese-inspired house he called "Dragon Rock" in upstate New York. But there was little to sustain a private friendship.) Wright gave a talk to his AUDAC colleagues in New York City in 1931 during the run of an exhibition of his work.

Typical plans for Wright's detached houses can be simply diagrammed. A typical two-story plan (Figure 14A) is not only a familiar functional diagram of the 1930s but of his first prairie houses. From an entry one can proceed to the living room, or upstairs to bedrooms, or in some

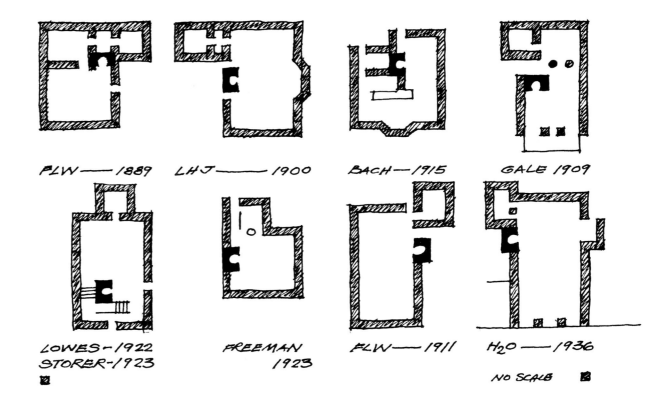

FLW——1889 LHJ——1900 BACH—1915 GALE 1909

LOWES~1922 FREEMAN FLW——1911 H₂O——1936
STORER~1923 1923

NO SCALE

6.13 Schematics of typical kitchen/dining/
living relationships for two-story houses,
1889 to 1936.

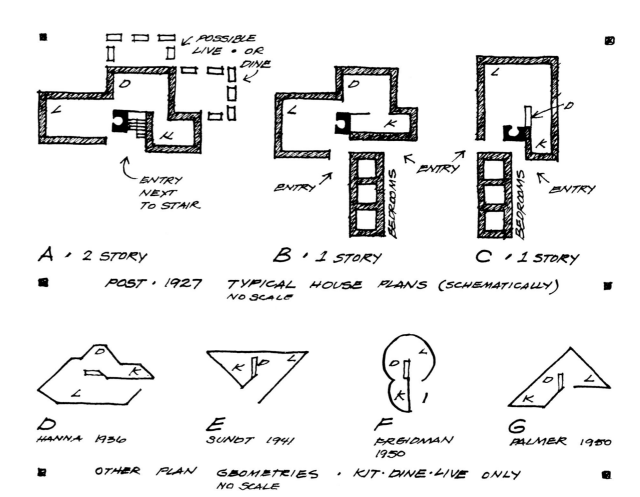

A · 2 STORY   B · 1 STORY   C · 1 STORY

POST · 1927   TYPICAL HOUSE PLANS (SCHEMATICALLY)
NO SCALE

D   E   F   G
HANNA 1936 SUNDT 1941 FREIDMAN   PALMER 1950
                        1950

OTHER PLAN GEOMETRIES · KIT·DINE·LIVE ONLY
NO SCALE

6.14 Outlines of typical house ground-floor plans, post-1927.

cases to the kitchen, an open space serving the dining space, or sometimes just a fixed dining table located at the kitchen side of the living room. Upstairs, the private spaces of bedrooms and baths were arranged similar to the prairie years with variances only for clients' wishes. The diagrammatic plan shown here is like the Pew house of 1940 or the Gridley house of 1906, and very similar to, as examples only, the *Ladies' Home Journal* project (1900) and the Bradley (1900), Henderson (1901), Willits (1902), and Ross (1902) houses. Examples from the 1930s include Fallingwater, the Rebhuhn (1937) and Schwartz (1939) houses, and to a lesser degree the first design for the Willey house (1932) where the bedrooms are below the entertaining floor.

The typical single-story house diagrams (Figure 14B, C) were first articulated in designs for the Little Farm Unit house in 1932 and later became the plan for a typical Usonian house. Critical circulation and functional disposition of the main spaces (kitchen, dining, living) were similar to those of the two-story plan. Circulation to the private rooms remains immediately off the entry sequence, and those rooms are isolated in a wing or at the opposite end of the entertaining spaces rather than on a floor above. Architect Harwell Hamilton Harris understood the simplicity and functional clarity of this scheme (B) and applied it to a design for a "House in California" of c. 1948, which was built and was in plan almost a duplicate, if opposite-hand reversed, of his and Carl Anderson's design of the Lowe house, Altadona, California, of 1933. Gregory Ain also understood the scheme for he used it in a projected house for J. F. Henderson in 1932. Both Ain and Harris were apprentices to Richard Neutra, who had worked for Wright during 1924 and was greatly influenced by his elder.[8]

The Farm Unit plan was a more in-line plan (Figure 14C) than its Usonian successors, with the exception of the dramatically sited and cantilevered Sturges houses of 1939 and the magnificently robust Pauson sisters' house (1940). A sampling of those 1930s houses that are quite similar to Figure 14B are Jacobs (1936), Hanna (1937; geometrical contrivances could not hide the underlying design), the elegant Rosenbaum (1939), and Winkler-Goetsch (also 1939). (For his non-professional audience Wright referred to these plans as shaped like a "polliwog" with shorter or longer tails.) Most of the remaining single-story dwellings of the period directly reflect the diagram. Note that the fireplace acts as a pivot in most plans and therefore in the diagrams.

Perhaps it is obvious, but not to mention the following would be a dereliction. Larger houses for families requiring—for whatever reason—formal lifestyles necessitated architectural plans that were somewhat different from those outlined above. They responded to the need for increased entertaining areas, both in size and in type, including dining rooms for pomp and ceremony.

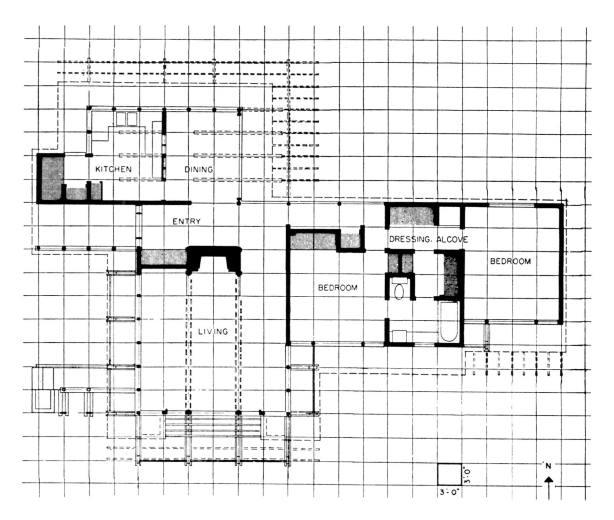

6.15 Ground-floor plan for a "House in California" by Harwell Hamilton Harris, architect, 1940s.

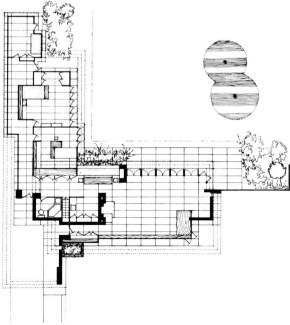

6.16 Perspectives of the Herbert Jacobs house, Madison, Wisconsin, 1936, artist unknown. From *Architectural Forum*, January 1938. © 1961 the Frank Lloyd Wright Foundation.

6.17 Plan of the Herbert Jacobs house, Madison, Wisconsin, 1936. Reproduced from Sergeant (1976).

6.18 Plan of the Winkler and Goetsch house, Lansing, Michigan, 1939. Reproduced from Sergeant (1976).

6.19 Plans of the Clarence Pew house, Madison, Wisconsin, 1940. Reproduced from Sergeant (1976).

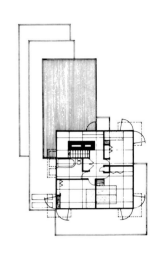

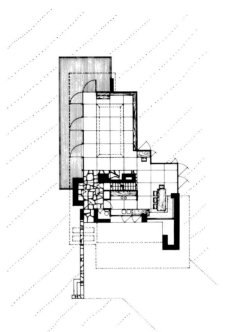

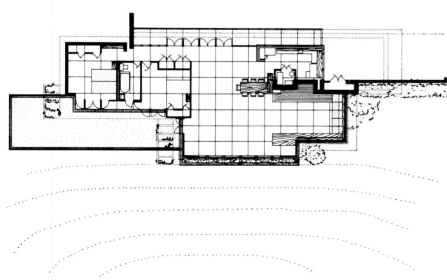

Increased kitchen arrangements with attendant serving staff were a necessity. Examples of the few prior to the 1940s include the Coonley (1908), Barnsdall (1919), and Herbert Johnson (1937–38) mansions, the latter located north of Racine.

In 1927 Ernst May was collecting essays for an article about the flat roof in domestic architecture and called upon his colleagues in Europe to support its use. The subject may appear almost trivial now, but then it teased the intellect and was a test of theoretical liberality. For unkown reasons he asked Wright to participate in the debate. The American's contribution in the seventh issue of *Das neue Frankfurt* was to declare that there must be sound reasons for its use beyond mere aesthetics, or even concrete technology, and preferably reasons more architectonic than politically symbolic. Wright had, of course, used the flat roof on many domestic buildings in America's northern climes. He attached to his essay, however, three perspective drawings (surely not executed by himself) of a house with a gable roof, an inverted gable or butterfly roof, and a flat roof, each covering the same plan and exterior walls. They were published in the July 1930 issue of *L'Architecture vivante*.[9] The sketches hint that the plan of the house is the same as that of Figure 14B or C, so perhaps it was applied as early as 1927.

It would be tempting to argue that Wright's multiphased reaction to the Central Europeans was defensive, that he was not motivated by his own attempt to resolve a philosophical problem but acting negatively to something he disliked. Such an argument would be wrong. Wright knew that the old Prairie School aesthetic (not its plans) would not last beyond its natural life or acceptance. "Art is always beginning" was his truism. Out of the prairie years he evolved a new aesthetic in the second decade of this century exemplified by the Barnsdall house, Hollywood (1919–21), and applied less obviously to the Pauson sisters' house as late as 1939–40. He had always believed that within indigenous sources might be discovered an American architecture devoid of Europhile influences. So he explored the plain architectural volumes of the southwestern native American cultures. The Barnsdall house was the most direct reference that Wright would create to the villages of the Hopi and Pueblo on high mesas. Many designs to follow were less dependent on Indian forms while becoming more abstract as witness the Sachse and Ennis houses (1920 and 1923). At odd moments between 1913 and 1920 Wright did use ornament that had a character something like Mesoamerican cultures, but those flirtations had no lasting effect.

However, without ornament the elemental volumes of those earlier civilizations were primal and to myopic Western eyes void of at least their cultural impedimenta. Such rudimentary forms prompted Wright to use cubic and parallelepiped volumes for his nondomestic architecture at the turn of the century—his own studio additions in 1898 and then the Larkin building and Unity Temple. The application of elemental geometric volumes was also one of the foundations of the cubic white box of the Central Europeans in the 1920s. Wright was firmly convinced they got the notion from him and recent research has confirmed his belief.[10] Wright provided the architectural *rationalization and material wherewithal* that allowed, so to speak, the Europeans to make their break from historicism to direct plans, clean planes, simple volumes, and plain forms. In any event in the 1930s Wright was, therefore, returning to the fundamentals he had resolved thirty years earlier. The *lineage* was clear to him and should be to historians: the Oak Park studio (1898); Yahara Boat Club (1902); Unity Temple (1904); Gale house and a hotel at Mason City (1909); Midway Gardens (1913–14); Sachse house project, Mojave Desert (1920); Storrer house (1923); Chandler block house project (1927); Noble apartment house project (1930); and so forth.

On 11 March 1930 Wright mailed preliminary plans for a proposed apartment block for mother and daughter Elizabeth and Elizabeth Noble. (The project is not of 1929 as previously believed.) Wright described his design as a scheme of "overhanging Terraces" and they were to be sheathed on the exterior with "verdigris copper"; each apartment was to be a "large studio room" and indeed only Murphy beds were suggested; and there was a tenants' "roof-garden" for entertaining before a fireplace.[11] The plan had a long central spine with apartments vertically staggered on each side. But the overall plan was terribly cramped, the circulation tedious—one apartment (no. 6) was only accessible by three and one half stories of stair—and one egress stair from above was open through the office. Mother Noble, apparently the financer, was not impressed, noting inadequate parking and sleeping arrangements.[12] By 1933 the Nobles had built a house not to Wright's design and he was still trying to get his drawings from them. In any event the overall appearance of the Noble building had a more private lineage than might first have been believed.

It would be remiss, however, to suggest that there was no reciprocity. The central European aesthetic did influence Wright in many ways as his designs reveal, but it was a result not of mimicry but of a thorough reexamination of his own ideas—such as plain volumes or the proposition that within the problem lies the answer—and then rigorously applying them. There were, therefore and naturally, changes between the earlier and later works that began with the Noble project. At the beginning of the 1930s his buildings related as much to the constructional fetish of the Central Europeans (prefabrication, light and slender construction, repetitive parts, etc.) as to the way the Europeans explored space, plane, and line *beyond* the inspiration given by Wright. But very soon the American's own response matured; it was more individual while at the same

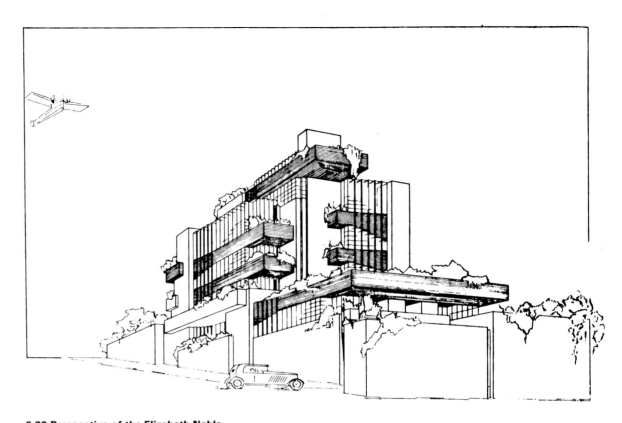

6.20 Perspective of the Elizabeth Noble apartment house building, Los Angeles, California, a project of 1929. From *Trend*, 1934. © 1990 the Frank Lloyd Wright Foundation.

moment more respectful of the needs of each individual client and building site. If Wright was true to his stated beliefs about an organic unfolding, an "inner logic of design," then individuation was natural, it could not be otherwise. The obviousness of that philosophic promise, and respect, can be seen by comparing each of his works with one another. Then of course it is necessary to compare them with what Wright believed were the Central European formulae.

Wright had done such an exercise and reached certain conclusions that he put as a series of dictums much as Europeans had in the past composed their manisfestos. These he called Principles of Design. They show both a dislike of the plain Central European proposals and of designers with a cleverness unsupported by natural reason. For instance.

• **The insensate, characterless flat-surface, cut sheer, has geometric possibilities—but it has, also, the limitations of bare Geometry. Such negation in itself is sometimes restful and continually useful—as a foil.**

• **The sense of rhythm—how deep it is planted in human-sensibility. How far above other consideration in Art!**

• **Human-sensibilities are interwoven with organic-growths of every kind, emotionally susceptible to their living rhythms and opulent textures.**

• **Human-sensibilities are the strings of the instrument upon which the true artist plays—"abstract"—but why not avoid the "symbol," as such? It is too literal.**

• **But the box idea of a building is childish (not childlike)—because when holes are cut in the box the beauty of the box is gone. It is no longer simple.**

• **Emulation shows itself as a Mode.**

• **The box is divorced by nature from Nature.**

• **Decoration asserts the whole to be greater than any part and succeeds to the degree that it helps make this good.**[13]

And so forth. And like those earlier European examples he too was more clever than clear. Nonetheless his principles seem to be a reiteration of the fundamental concepts he cherished in early manhood, redefined as a result of the threat, as he reasoned, of the un-American "modernism" to which he had become so intolerant.

The general trends in his work are clear. His architecture was inclined to become more internally open, more cubic, rather more volumetric, and considerably more simple through a reductive process. The examples previously mentioned display the evolution of reductivity and abstraction while those of the 1930s reveal the refinement of that process: the *Capital Journal* building (1931), Johnson Wax (1937), and the Jacobs (1937) and Rosenbaum (1939) houses, for instance. As well, Wright seemed to become *more* sensitive to the potential of glass, not only for transparency but for effects of parallax, than in previous decades. Glass and steel were often combined in a manner implying volume but exploiting transparency; this occured both internally and externally. There were the open corners of the Freeman house of 1924; the transparent surface of the 1930 Noble and *Capital Journal* projects; then the transparent surfaces between the canti-levered slats and corners of Fallingwater; ceiling corners at Taliesin West; and these are only samples. (Taliesin East, by the way, was an apartment in the Plaza Hotel, New York City.)[14] While the extension of space horizontally was vigorously explored, parallax was achieved across corners, or from lower levels to upper, or more ineffectually through translucent tubes on the Johnson administration building or wood cutouts on walls of the Jacobs house.

Another conspicuous trend was not only the use of a flat roof rather than some form of gable, but an exploitation of line and plane and their unity with horizontality. An examination of both the interior and exterior of most buildings of the 1930s, especially the mid to late years, reveals how boldly or delicately and how differently this was applied. Related to this exploitation was the structural cantilever. By definition, unless a post (or high-rise building), it more than likely gave further horizontal emphasis. The use of cantilever was relatively new to Wright's experience. It was only subtly used before, for instance in the Gale house of 1909 and the Gladney house of 1925. Beginning more or less with the Noble apartment house project it became a relatively standard feature and usually followed the style of that used in the two-story Willey house project of 1932: a heavy mass on the exterior, horizontal boards sometimes corbeled out and overlapped, or stucco or concrete, a deep projection (or long cantilever) that carried a wide balcony that was an extension of the interior floor. A direct descendant of the cantilevered balcony of the Willey project was the dramatic horizontal thrust of the Sturgis house built on the side of a hill in 1939. Between the two were a host of projects or buildings, many related to his Usonian concept for housing, something amply discussed by historian John Sergeant.

Consider only these works of the decade 1929–39: Ocotillo; the Fallingwater house on Bear Run; the Johnson Wax Building at Racine; "Taliesin in the Desert," and the Pauson sisters' house. They rank with the most important architectural works of the twentieth century, each *remark-ably different* from the others. Comparison was (and is) inevitable: as far as Wright was concerned the white boxes of the European modernists appeared naive, except the milestones by Mies van

6.21 Plans of the Pauson sisters' house, Phoenix, Arizona, 1939–40. From Hitchcock (1942). © 1942 the Frank Lloyd Wright Foundation.

6.22 Photograph c. 1940 of the Pauson sisters' house, Phoenix, Arizona, 1939–40. Courtesy and © the Frank Lloyd Wright Foundation.

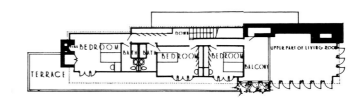

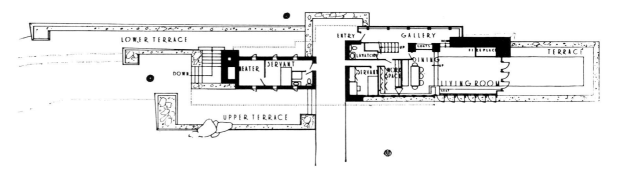

der Rohe—the German Pavilion at Barcelona (1927–28) and later at Plano the Farnsworth House (1946–51).[15] But then Mies never did fit comfortably with his German confederates after 1928.

Wright knew the significance of his own singular works: "The spiritual cathartic that was the desert worked—[it] swept the spirit clean of stagnant ways and habitual forms ready for fresh adventure."[16] The late historian Reyner Banham noticed the change too. It was in the desert, he said, "the true wilderness, that Wright was ultimately to achieve freedom in planning; freedom from axial symmetry, from right angles, from centralised spaces, which had persisted in the geometry of all his earlier works, even when the functional relations and human use of the spaces were at variance with the formal plans."[17] Wright knew the value of that wilderness at the time of his Ocotillo Camp, yet it was medical advice that urged him to return to the high desert country. For the winter of 1934 he planned "to take it easier with a group of some fifteen I will take with me to the grand scale of Arizona. A complete change."[18] After two winters quartered in a "pseudo-rancho complex," as Tafel described it, Wright decided to build a new camp. It was begun in 1937 and became Taliesin West.[19]

Then almost suddenly, perhaps as a reaction to the strict right-angle aesthetic of the Central Europeans, in 1938 Wright began to explore volume, form, and plan disposition wrought by compass. Such a geometry had been preceded by the functionally responsive aberration for Sugar Loaf in 1925; applied rationally if conservatively in the *Capital Journal* and Johnson Wax buildings; and then emphatically employed on the Jester house project of 1938. Rooms were to be circles or segments of circles and walled by plywood bent to shape, structurally sound. The circle teased his creative mind from then on. The scheme was rejected by Ralph Jester, offered to Martin Pence the same year and rejected, and then became part of a number of other houses including the ill-fated Loeb house of 1944–49,[20] and was finally built in stuccoed concrete block to a slightly modified plan in 1971 at a site near to Taliesin West for Arthur and Bruce Pfeiffer. The house is now owned by the Taliesin Foundation. The concept is a circular modification of Wright's theoretical project of a "zoned house" for the country, designed as early as 1934 and revised for one of the All-steel house projects in 1937. It was a spatially extravagant concept of little practical value but full of potential only partially realized in the Jester, Loeb, and Pfeiffer houses.[21]

Wright also wrought aberrations with the T-square, triangle, or compass. These included drawings for "skyscrapers" in 1926; in many respects the cramped San Marcos in The Desert of 1928–29 and most of the housing related to the proposal; the Rosenwald School of 1929; the monumental pavilion he sketched in 1931 for the Chicago Century of Progress exhibition (which admittedly was not presented too clearly); a chapel project in southern Wisconsin in 1937; and the Monona Terrace Civil Center—the scheme of 1938. Monona was an impractical and unresolved dream, but some of the concrete structural ideas reappeared from time to time. However, as a center with enclosed parking and related community functions, it should not be assumed that it was succeeded, if greatly enlarged and more satisfactorily resolved, in Wright's project called Crystal Heights for Washington, D.C., of 1940, or in the grandest and most prophetic of his urban proposals, Point Park, Pittsburgh, of 1947. Monona was imprecise and premature. Another aberration contemporary with Monona was the campus plan of 1938 for Florida Southern College, a project best left to another study elsewhere. The term "aberration" is not used carelessly. There must be inherent and linked qualities of plan, structure, form, proportion, or whatever that connect a work of art to the artist and his oeuvre collectively and in a manner that clearly demonstrates philosophic rigor and development. Aberrations stand obliquely in relative isolation, genetically sterile, even if they may be otherwise interesting—even brilliant—works. It seems that all great artists are allowed such extravagances from time to time.

7 Prejudices Old and New

Art tends not only to discover the truth but to exaggerate and finally to distort it. And, maybe in this distortion lies the essence of art.

Matthew Nowicki

It is important to keep in mind the contemporary context and the prevalent and popular modes of architecture during the 1930s. Not only was there a continuation of traditional historical styles, pure (as in the Nashville replica of the Parthenon in concrete) or hybrids or amalgams, but there were step-back skyscrapers (usually with some historical content) and, as a growing phenomenon, modernism in a Central European idiom. The 1933–34 Century of Progress Exposition in Chicago turned its back—more or less—on historical precedent in favor of various forms of modernism. Some of its buildings were peculiar blends of streamlining, art deco, constructivism, and Central European-isms. Their immediate popular influence was noticeable upon cinema design, but in the long term the exposition's architecture helped legitimize modernism in the United States. While it claimed to announce an American modern style, and in some respects it did (especially in industrial design), the buildings generally were much in debt to the Europeans, including at times an Englishness, and some were suggestive of a revived constructivism. Wright wanted desperately to be involved with

7.1 Perspective of Unity Temple, 1904–06, drawing executed in 1929, perhaps by Takehito Okami. Courtesy and © the Frank Lloyd Wright Foundation.

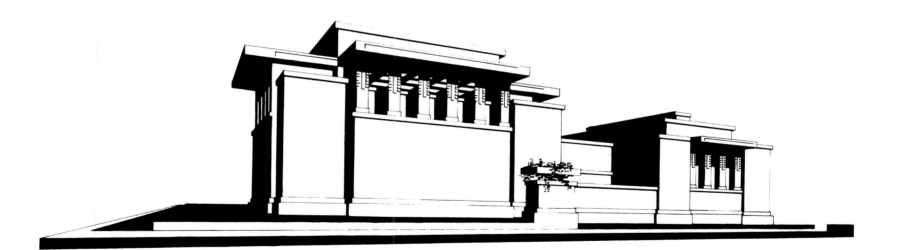

the exposition but failed to gain the organizers' attention let alone agreement: they were Nathaniel Owings, Harvey Wiley Corbett, and Louis Skidmore.

Tied to these varied American architectural products were supporting polemics. The pages of most architectural journals from c.1929 to c.1935 especially not only showed pictures of the architecture in question but offered a discussion of the pros and cons of historicism and modernism. Authors not converted to the "new" architecture were most often represented. In 1932 architect Dwight James Baum summarized what might be termed the profession's view. He was tired of reading about functionalism and the need to meet economic conditions (especially, he suggested, as exposed in the pages of *Shelter*) and wrote that "Packing box architecture with misplaced color may be evidence of a striving for a new architecture but it is quite painful while it is being administered." Baum thought the Chicago Tribune building of 1922(!) to be "modern and new."[1] Architect and academic John F. Harbeson tried to explain modern architecture to readers of *Pencil Points* in a series of articles lasting through most of 1930. His selections were diverse and ranged from pure white boxes to some fanciful extremes (mostly French); nearly all examples illustrated or discussed were European. His very short discussion of the city concentrated on sky-scrapers and included Wright's project for the St. Mark's Towers, Le Corbusier's "Freehold Maison-nettes" and University Quarter, together with Hugh Ferris's charcoal fantasies for a high-rise step-back urban world (all of his sketches lacked people).[2]

For the general or lay public, compilations in book form were essential forums for house and home design, offering ideas to inspire or mimic. With a modest recovery from the Depression in the mid-1930s many of these books were produced. The economic crisis also encouraged a flurry of prefabrication companies that also attempted to satisfy housing needs, and they too were pre-sented in magazines. Invariably the compilations were meant to cater to all tastes. For example, in 1935 and 1936 *The Architectural Forum* edited and Simon and Schuster published *The Book of Small Houses.* It contained all sorts (Cape Cod to Central European), all sizes, all budgets, with a few aberrations such as a revived Southwest adobe (obviously aberrant if not exotic for it was not mainstream New England or Tidewater colonial). Another example was Harcourt Brace's *The House for Modern Living* also of 1935, where results of a competition were published. It too catered to everyone anywhere. So too did later editions of *The Book of Small Houses* in 1936, 1938, and two in 1940. And there were many many more. None of these book compilations or similar but shorter reviews in magazines included Wright. He had accomplished so little through the mid-thirties that there was not much to publish. More to the point, it is doubtful that Wright wanted to be included in such publications. His desire not to be joined with other architects in exhibitions surely would have persisted in principle to other types of association, including magazine and book surveys.

Since Wright had little architectural work during the 1920s and early 1930s, it was his early architecture up to c. 1924 and especially his writing in the 1930s that received the greatest attention in America; and there was much in his writing that was attractive to the English, Europeans, and Soviets. Europe in the 1930s responded enthusiastically to his theories and architectural achievements as manifest, much as it did in 1912–13. A major exhibition of drawings, models, and photographs traveled around European centers beginning in 1931.[3] During the period 1930–36 Wright's architecture and/or his writings were published in France, Belgium, Holland, Germany, Italy, Poland, Hungary, Australia, Japan, England, and probably Latin America, but not east of Poland.[4] No other individual architect from America received so much attention, not the New Englander Henry Hobson Richardson in the 1880s,[5] nor the principals of the New York firm of McKim, Mead and White around the turn of the century. In fact no twentieth-century architects of any nationality, except perhaps Le Corbusier, received so much attention outside their own country during the course of their career.

Wright was popular; Olgivanna and Frank had done their job well.

While some of Wright's writings were meant to disarm in order to gain attention, in the early 1930s his distaste for the so-called modern movement was undisguised. In 1930 Wright shared the galleries of New York's Museum of Modern Art (MoMA), then only one year old, with a Bauhaus exhibition. Wright's exhibition "arranged by himself" came under pointed criticism as "fragmentary and rather confused." Dimitris Tselos acknowledged that a systematic and "complete presentation" of the architecture would have given the viewer an "opportunity to temper the growing uncritical adulation of the architect and the proper perspective to define more accurately his achievements and his intellectual and architectural milieu." Also the exhibit as "arranged" was unsatisfactory. One label "speciously explains," it was said, that the roof plane of any of Wright's early buildings "tipped edgewise will give you the elevation characteristic of the so-called 'International Style'."[6] This strangely imprecise comment of Wright's was given slightly more clarity and some emphasis when, in 1929, perspectives of Wright's buildings of around 1904 were redrawn. It was the idea of Henry Klumb who recalled the event in a letter to historian Donald Hoffman:

Assembled and sitting with F.Ll.W around a fire in the studio one winter day in 1929, . . . I suggested that we might try to reduce his delicate renderings of his best-known buildings to a two-dimensional black-on-white graphic presentation "Modern Architects" were addicted to. His answer: "Do it." [Takehito] **Okami and I went to work and produced several, including in addition to the Robbie House (drawn by myself) the Winslow House, Yahara Boat Club, Bock Atelier, Unity Temple and the Larkin Building. All were drawn in ink on roll-up window shades.** Klumb thought the "stark graphic black-on-white" presentations "emphasized the depth of his [Wright's] poetry and the power of the third dimension."[7] Thereafter the drawings were often used in publications, sometimes in a manner incorrectly implying that they were executed in, for instance 1903, when in fact they were done in 1929.

The 1930 exhibition was followed by the 1931–32 show and in 1932 by another in which Wright also participated. When first approached about the latter he refused because he disapproved of the emphasis to be given to the European style, but he relented and agreed to participate. This show was organized by Lewis Mumford, Henry-Russell Hitchcock, Jr., MoMA curator Johnson, and Alfred Barr who was the primary motivator for the exhibition. The main source, perhaps even the inspiration for the show was a number of publications of 1925–30 in Europe about the new internationalism. Included were many Americans associated with the style, Raymond M. Hood, George Howe and William E. Lascaze, Richard Neutra (expatriate Austrian), and Irving and Munroe Bowman, as well as the now usual Europeans (Le Corbusier, Oud, Walter Gropius, Mies van der Rohe), together with Wright.[8] There was a catalogue entitled *Modern Architects* (MoMA and Norton, 1932) and a companion book of strangely contrived aesthetic principles written by Hitchcock and Johnson entitled *The International Style.*[9]

By his inclusion with the cubic white box crowd Wright believed there was an implication that he was in some way associated or identified with—even approved of—the style and therefore, as he reasoned, with the corollary, Communism's international ambitions. The exhibition was opened in February, and after seeing the catalogue Wright quickly responded in print in April: "I find myself standing now against . . . the so-called international style."[10] Actually, Wright's first attack against promoters of the cubic white box occurred in 1928 in a review published in *World Unity* of Frederick Etchells's translation of *Towards a New Architecture* by Le Corbusier. Of course Wright had no praise for Le Corbusier. Wright's dislike of the Parisian architect may have resulted from Le Corbusier's pretended ignorance of Wright and a refusal to participate in H. T. Wijdeveld's 1925 anthology on Wright, *The Life-Work of the American Architect Frank Lloyd Wright.* Apparently Wijdeveld could find no one to prepare new written material for the anthology, perhaps because of the short notice; so he reprinted previously published articles by H. P. Berlage, J. J. P. Oud, Lewis Mumford, Erich Mendelsohn, Louis H. Sullivan (at Wright's request), and Robert Mallet-Stevens, who might have been Wijdeveld's French choice after Le Corbusier. Wijdeveld may have transmitted to Wright Le Corbusier's refusal in 1925. Anyway Wright's general comments in the review of Etchell's translation were much like those made in response to the MoMA exhibition, which continues:

Do you think that . . . any aesthetic formula forced upon this work of ours in our country can do more than stultify this reasonable hope for a life of the soul?

A creative architecture for America can only mean an architecture for the individual.

The community interest in the United States is not communism or communistic as the internationalists' formula for a "style" presents itself. Its language aside, communistic the proposition is. Communistic in communism's most objectionable phase: the sterility of the individual its end if not its aim and . . . in the name of "discipline"!

But this communistic formula proposes to get rid of this constructive interior discipline's anxieties (and joys) by the surrender that ends all in all and for all, by way of a preconceived style for life—conceived by the few to be imposed upon all alike.

But for a free democracy to accept a communistic tenet of this breed disguised as aesthetic formula for architecture is a confession of failure I do not believe we, as a people, are ready to make.

We are sickened by capitalistic centralization but not so sick, I believe, that we need confess impotence by embracing a communistic exterior discipline in architecture to kill finally what spontaneous life we have left in the circumstances.[11]

He believed that the European architectural "formula" was foreign, "imposed," not American, stale and rigid, that it clearly foreshadowed a second or modern manneristic eclecticism, yet another kind of cultural colonialism. Of the selections available to his country as displayed at the exhibition, why should the American who was creating an American architecture not be the obvious choice for America? The fact that in the 1930s the popular choice became the Central European International Style deeply hurt Wright. With egotistic insight he believed America tended not only to ignore but to dismiss him.

His fear of the effects of internationalism's formula, as expressed above, induced another response when associated publications, including articles, were released by the New York museum. He wrote another of his acrimonious letters, on this occasion to curator Johnson, expressing a feeling of being "out of character" and "out of sympathy with the whole endeavor. I belie my whole cause by coming with you." He said the only reason to agree to participate was in an effort to help Johnson. However, Wright found Johnson's "promotion and propaganda" too "shameless and selfish." He was not certain if Oud or Mies "would approve," adding that Le Corbusier would agree for he was the "soul of your [Johnson's] propaganda." As to the planned national tour of the exhibition Wright was emphatic and final. He insisted that "every trace of my name in connection" with Johnson's promotions be "removed when the show at the Museum of Modern Art closes,"[12] an extraordinary request. Later and to a friend Wright referred not unkindly to Johnson as "Little Philip J. . . . Not an architect—look for him in the international wastebasket."[13] And again, at a public occasion at Yale University Wright greeted Johnson with, "Why, Philip, I thought you were dead!" And later in that evening in 1955 he said, "Why, Philip, little Phil, all grown up, building buildings and leaving them out in the rain."[14] Perhaps these comments were encouraged by the fact that Johnson had become a registered architect and enamored with the post-1938 architecture of Mies van der Rohe.

The fact that the European style was popularly accepted by architect and client alike, and Wright's designs were not, has been discussed quite often since 1930. Ignoring for the moment ethnic and regional differences within the United States, the usual arguments are much like those put by architect and educator Stanley Tigerman in 1986. In the years between the World Wars, Tigerman ventured, which of "architecture's methods" could society accept? "Surely not that of FLW . . . he was too patently individualistic, what with his embarrassing taste in clothes, his unfortunate matrimonial record, and worst of all, an architecture that simply could not be copied. Idiosyncratic at its most normative, FLW's work contained too many elements of unpredictability; it was not something one either could count on or worse, would want to represent stability." If America were to select a style "by which to be remembered, it could not be the work of one arrogant architect alone—certainly not a self-announced eccentric genius such as FLW." This was a good summary of some, perhaps most architects' views and was indicative of perhaps a majority of other people's attitudes. And Tigerman affirmed that even if Wright "could be copied (unlikely), it would be too demeaning for others to commit themselves to such an idiosyncratic original."[15] Are creative artists only selectors and copyists, as Tigerman seems to believe? Wright believed they should not be, but that too many of his fellow Americans were: they "beg or borrow or steal what we have and assume the virtue we have not."[16] Historian Reyner Banham was correct when he put the view that in their book (which excluded Wright), Hitchcock and Johnson did not present a "driving vision," they did not provide "ideological and theoretical support." They "set aside the Utopianism, the zeal for social reform, the Messianic claims that drove the style in Europe, and without which most of us [now] would have difficulty in understanding what the movement was about."[17]

In 1932 Wright carried on fighting. He took an initiative to respond to a circular issued by the New York–based Beaux-Arts Institute of Design, closely linked to the Fontainebleau School of Fine Arts and the American extension of the educational system developed by the Ecole des Beaux-Arts in Paris. He wrote to the Institute's students that they were "unreliably informed as to what modern architecture is. You are told that it is not going to become a style based upon Gropius, Wright, or Corbusier." Wright continued: "But architecture is 'modern' and has a future only because these modern architects, from whom, I am sorry to say, the circular in question derives only language, are what they are and because they have done what they have done in the way they have done it. It is because of their work that the Beaux Arts is now ready to modify its programmes to 'push' all of you back." It was not his choice that he was aligned with the Europeans and he wished to disassociate himself from that nexus. "I am a friendly enemy," he said and then set out to explain that his work was singular, wholly American, and that Taliesin had "already established a living tradition and has good reason to know that youth everywhere is hungry for reality and is everywhere rocking an old boat no longer seaworthy."[18] The note was an attempt to set the record straight and to promote the Taliesin Fellowship to an anticipated eager young audience.

A professional associate and correspondent of only a few years, Ely Jacques Kahn, was then director of the Department of Architecture of the Beaux-Arts Institute. He was at first "warm under the collar" with Wright's "diatribe" but soon cooled off, perhaps realizing that Wright could at times be too quick with unnecessarily sharp and often personal criticism. Kahn suggested that any student would find advantage and value in "personal contact" with Wright. Privately Kahn generously offered advice in the form of praise. "You would be surprised," he said, "if you really knew how much you are liked by the various men whom you are at times inclined to jump on and, in spite of our shortcomings, we are all interested in seeing the vigor of a new endeavor [the Fellowship] . . . if it can show the way.[19] A lasting friendship developed thereafter, if somewhat more giving on one side.

It should be noted that in the 1930s those that set the socially irresponsible (or ignorant) design problems as determined by the Beaux-Arts Institute and its affiliated design schools were under siege from the Central European reformers. (An example of one such problem: an artist's studio on an island in the Nile River.) A serious threat to the Beaux-Arts system of education, however, did not occur until after World War II, in some schools not until well into the 1950s.

Politics, art theory, artists' will, architectural style, and nationalism continued to mix vibrantly—if confusingly—in Wright's view of the modern movement and of Le Corbusier as its protagonist and mentor. So too did individualism, for Wright saw this as the only means to the creative end: the point he argued throughout his life. The mix was understandable. In 1934, in preparation for an article, architect and author Percival Goodman asked Wright: "In a planned society would there not be a restriction of individual taste?" Wright responded yes, "and since individual taste is utterly insufficient to develop an architecture this would mean not so much loss so far as a creative architecture was concerned. But a formula would necessarily be substituted for individual taste and be enforced. Would any formula be nearer the desired source, creation? I think not. Russia is an example of the consequences *to date* [my emphasis]. Only as true sources of inspiration are open to artists and they are free to work upon the knowledge of principle they must possess can any people create a living architecture for itself. By way of taste would then mean not much more than personal idiosyncracy." Goodman then addressed Wright: "Mass design of buildings exist (the tremendous habitable areas of our skyscrapers equal to many square city blocks of old type structures and mass designs of towns in Russia). Will not a few architects be sufficient to design the type-houses? Would architecture become a problem of engineering only, with the elimination of the individual as artist?" Wright responded that "mass design" is "no design. No such thing can live," he asserted. "So to eliminate artist individuality as [an] inspiring element in favour of the test tube and the mechanical laboratory would be to reduce art to an affair of the brain; music to mathematics, architecture to engineering, poetry to rhyme, philosophy to intellectual celebration, religion to ritual. . . ."

The last question put by Goodman was more specific: "if you believe that architecture is an individual expression—, what objection do you have to the works called 'International style,' especially those of Le Corbusier?" In response, "I still believe," Wright said, "that this mass product would only be seen as 'creative' were the effect of a style subordinate and subsequent to the individual perceptions that gave each building composing the whole its own great individuality: . . . Style should be the architect's aim, not a style." Wright believed that "into this category of individual works might fall Le Corbusier et al, until an attempt would be made to make Le Corbusier a style or the style. Then the growth of architecture would stop and such life as it had would depart from it. There was the case with the 'Style Internationale.' It soon became a formula any tyro could cliche and it soon became abhorrent to the feelings of the free man everywhere."[20] It is tempting to alter only one word in the last sentence: "It soon became a 'formalism' any tyro could cliche." These views may have been rather repugnant to Soviet architects during the period from 1925 to 1932. In the 1930s, however, they would have intrigued Soviet regularizers, as will be discussed in the chapters to follow.

On another occasion he was asked if he was in favor of capitalism. He declared, of course! "I believe in a capitalist system. I only wish I could see it tried some time."[21] For emphasis he said, "Money—the System that is destroying us" in America. In other words, only the American version, the one he had to work with and around and through, was wrong: the one that had caused the economic depression in 1929 with such sudden disastrous consequences. To casual observers, therefore, he seemed to be against capitalism per se. To pro-Left observers like Stephan Alexander writing in the June 1935 issue of *New Masses,* Wright's position was all too clear. Alexander reviewed the verbalized ideas of Broadacre City—"Frank Lloyd Wright's Utopia"—then came to what he believed was a logical conclusion: "the significance of Mr. Wright's project is that it points inexorably to the necessity for the removal of capitalism and the creation of a socialist society as the primary condition for the progressive development of architecture." Surely the Soviets were aware of Alexander's observations. Wright's public reply to Alexander was to confess to being somewhat of a romantic and to suggest that his Broadacre City was "a bit Wellsian," but that he had presented only preliminary thoughts about decentralization, "an anathema to Communism" he observed. And yes, he committed the "sin of 'dreaming'" but this was intentional. Alexander was otherwise fundamentally wrong for in Wright's mind Broadacres was anti-capitalistic, anti-communistic, and anti-socialistic "as far as current socialism goes."[22] In Wright's mind socialism was an urban phenomenon, and therein resided another of its problems.

In the 1920s and early 1930s the Soviet Union saw the technical achievements of the skyscraper as monumental, something to be emulated. In the mid-1930s and concurrent with the rise of Stalinism it was not only a negative sign of capitalist achievement but of human degradation: the two always linked. At the Moscow architects' congress in 1937 the Soviet view was of skyscrapers casting long capitalistic shadows over people's homes creating a dark breeding place for slums. Wright's attacks against urban congestion in support of his Broadacre City were well known.[23]

Pronouncements like that offered in his Kahn lectures to Princeton University in 1930 abridge his writings: "Ruralism as distinguished from Urbanism is American, and truly Democratic," he said with Jeffersonian clarity. It was during Wright's formative years that William Jennings Bryan succinctly put the case for practical responsibility in support of America's rural tradition: "Burn down your cities and leave our farms, and your cities will grow again as if by magic, but destroy our farms and grass will grow in the streets of every city in the country."

Two final observations may be made. The first is somewhat less practical, aligned with both the idea of the organic and the affirmation of the modern. There is a compelling thrust to reject historical influences. The past, as Russians are prone to exclaim (and rightly so with respect to their past), is decadent. Less so the English view. The present, therefore, is something positively contemporary and nothing less. Cleanliness is a wiping off of dirty past habits. "Clean" is therefore a common adjective of both the Central European architects and Wright, meaning both clean of line and clean of the past. Sentiment notwithstanding, spring is renewal and therefore cyclical. Hence, Marx could argue that the principles of Greek architecture were due for reevaluation: the principles, not the manners.

The second observation is more critical. It requires a similar oversimplification. Wright's architectural designs were always made in response to given problems: in the problem resided the solution. (There is some similarity between this organic notion and the Central European functionalist idea, but the interpretations are quite different.) Therefore, unlike the European modernists Wright seldom proposed responses to theoretical situations, as noted above, for they would at best be merely theoretical models. There could never be substance in or substantive reasons for their existence. There is no congruity with the Central Europeans on this issue: polemics, manifestos, propositions, abound in the absence of commission but in the vital necessity to persuade. It is true that during the prairie years Wright's buildings were of two types. First the house, the typical low, spreading prairie style; and second the nondomestic building in a proportionally square-volumed style. Of the second type the obvious buildings come to mind: the Oak Park studio, Unity Temple, the Larkin Building, and Midway Gardens.[24] He argued that a building reflects an organic or functional response to given programs. However, all appear rather similar within each of the two types. The same can be said of the buildings of the 1920s. They fall not only into a building type but into a geometrical type. However, beginning with Ocotillo and especially in the 1930s his architecture became a much more vital proposition. Each building was a unique architectural and social entity, each a different response to given social conditions (within the building or without) and, very importantly, to given site conditions.

The site was deemed precious and equal to all other requirements. It was this reality that distinguished his architecture of the 1930s. It also separated him from the Central Europeans and eventually most of his American colleagues. Each anonymous white or glass box or rectangular slab could and did stand anywhere and everywhere, and generally fit any and all internal necessity or social condition. The implications of the Central European polemics were clear for architecture, and since it was an art form that expressed society as well as being totally within society, it too was threatened by the philosophy supporting the common and anonymous box.

Wright believed that a devolved commonality would lead to social disaster; the individual's individualism or ethnic characteristics would be lost through anonymity in collective absorption. His serious worry about internationalism's polemics, therefore, provoked in him a more complete, pragmatically full architecture. Indeed, his stance against "the so-called international style," as he put it, had philosophic premises (Americanism therefore nationalism, ethnicity, transcendentalism, democracy, individuality, etc.) that were almost instinctively grasped. The architectural reality of his position became abundantly clear: while his architecture of the prairie years was revolutionary, his architecture of 1929 to c.1939 was not only revolutionary but *complete* in a way he could not have imagined as a young architect around 1900 or even in the 1920s. The decade of 1929–1939 was his most *creative* period.

8 Broadacre City

Democracy . . . we have started toward a new integration—to an integration along the horizontal line which we call the great highway.

FLW, September 1931

Since it was first proposed much has been written about Wright's Broadacre City by many people who focused on planning or economic or political or social considerations. Perhaps to Wright's delight the result has been a marvelous diversity of opinion. For instance, some authors assessed it as a linear city while others said that it was a non-city or that it was the antithesis of Le Corbusier's Green City and similar centralized and authoritarian ideas. Some authors declared it to be the epitome of decentralized community planning or the ideal place for rural democracy or a release from centralized capitalism. Historian William Curtis synthesized some architectural opinion when he observed that Wright "imagined that architectural form could fashion a new, integrated civilization."[1] At one point urban sociologist Leonard Reissman believed Wright to be a prophet of doom (see Appendix D). Typically, most observers tended to believe that the written words might be more important than the city plan. More so than now realized, Broadacre City was widely discussed during the 1930s and into the early 1960s; it continues without consensus to be so to this day. But it does so in the absence of a proper analysis of the physical form of the proposed city and with little knowledge of immediate practical predecessors, while the "ideological impulses" have been only partially established.[2]

An understanding of the planning methodology used to create the physical form of Wright's proposal will help observers, historians, and designers. If, as well, the organizational units from the smallest in the city to that which was meant to control the regional concept can be identified, then a much clearer understanding will be realized. There will be no attempt to compare Broadacres with other ideas of the 1930s or later, for this has been adequately done by others, in particular George R. Collins, Robert Fishman, John Sergeant, Leonard Reissman, and Lionel March. However, two well-known city/regional concepts will be used comparatively to clarify Wright's intentions. For reasons noted below, this enquiry will concentrate on Wright's initial plan.

Probably in mid-1934 the Broadacres plan was laid out in graphic or pictorial form. That event culminated about five years of serious contemplation and synthesis of substantive issues. The initial impetus for pursuing the subject was provided by an invitation to present the 1930 Kahn Lectures at Princeton University, which published them in 1931 as *Modern Architecture*. (Aspects of his Kahn Lectures, some elliptical reflections, and many assertions were published in 1932 in a limited-edition book he called *The Disappearing City,* a book he confessed he "wrote (badly),"[3] a confession no doubt acceptable to most of its readers.) Offering those lectures to Wright was one way for eastern patrons to support him in his attempt to recover from the harrowing years just concluded. He put his heart and soul into them for he knew they were crucial to success or failure over the next few years. He presented no specific proposals for the physical plan of the American city and its architectural parts, however. Instead, he offered negative expositions of the present physical and social state of cities with only marginal notions about what he considered good about them or their potential for the future. He did not, therefore, present a theoretical proposition, for quite simply he did not present measurable items that might be rationally studied and argued. The present city, he said, was ugly, congested, poorly administered, an economic disaster. But he did not rationally explain how all this might be overcome; there was no obvious solution.

Also in 1932 his article "Today . . . Tomorrow" was published in *American Architect*.[4] This is the briefest summation, barely an outline of his previously presented thoughts about the city. The article was illustrated with an intentionally fuzzy bird's-eye charcoal sketch that showed many roads, possibly meant as major highways, and a few isolated buildings on a rather desolate landscape. The drawing emphasized the importance Wright placed on the car (touring was one of his favorite pastimes) and on the airplane (the illustration was an aerial view). The very brief text indicated some determinants for Broadacres. He suggested that "plane-stations" be located every twenty miles and, rather naively, that highways be used for "take off." He did not mention how the city of Tomorrow might be physically laid out, but one critical detail to reappear in a few later statements was that "farm units and factories that produce"—an interesting qualification—"are within a ten mile radius . . . of each market and within walking distance of home of the workers." That radius fitted the proposal to locate plane stations every twenty miles.

The New York Times Magazine published an article in 1932 about Le Corbusier's architectonic urban place called "Green City" and Ville Radieuse—high-density living in machines for living. Those who knew Wright were aware of his antagonism toward Le Corbusier's ideas about architecture and toward the growing influence in America of the Central European architectural style of the white box. Wright was asked to follow Le Corbusier's contribution with an article Wright entitled "Broadacre City: An Architect's Vision," which appeared on 20 March 1932.[5] Although he did not reveal how his Broadacre City might be planned, he did attack what he believed was the folly of high-rise buildings collected together centrally for work and home living, in particular the ascetic Central European versions. When Wright proposed his own single vertical building systems they were somehow a more correct proposition, he believed. In any event, the two articles by Wright either paraphrased his Kahn lectures or The Disappearing City or they contained short extracts. As Wright's own condensations it can be assumed they contained only essentials.

In 1932, therefore, Broadacre City was no more than a verbalized theoretical proposition based on negative responses to existing conditions with virtually no hints about the composition of his ideal place. Then in November 1934 Tom Maloney in New York City arranged for Wright to display a model of the city in Manhattan and provided $1,000 for expenses. Edgar Kaufmann, Sr., the father of one of Wright's young apprentices, also agreed to help finance the exhibition and a large model.[6] When built it would boldly set out Broadacre City's physical features, functional disposition, and architectural character. Before construction of the model could begin Wright needed to prepare a plan. He quickly set it out on paper (Figure 1) in late 1934. It was sketchy indeed and his notes were almost unintelligible.[7] But the basic outline can be detected: main roads, the position of housing, "little farms," recreational areas, factories, markets, etc. It was a square plan and within that form no exact geometrical formula was applied. Three functional elements dominated. First, roads (with the main artery set in from the square's left boundary); second, green and rural—or semirural and much nonfarm—areas (almost two-thirds of the plan); and third, what he called

**8.1 Original pen and ink sketch of Broad-
acre City by Wright in 1934. Courtesy and
© 1965 the Frank Lloyd Wright Foundation.
Wright's notations on this sketch read:
[*above sketch*] Minimum of one acre to
the family./railroad connected into main
artery/highway/gas stations distributing
center for merchandize of all kinds/gas
stations//[*left of sketch*] gas station/mer-
cantile distribution/Factories/Roadside
market//[*right of sketch*] Residences of
more luxurious class on non tillable land—
more picturesque sites/Natural feature of
the surrounding landscape developed
according to its nature/mercantile gas sta-
tion/expanded into lake for recreations/lit-
tle farms/theatre—Collections. Clubs./
tillable land/2 Factories//[*below sketch*]
fluid traffic taking off main arteries/little
farms/recreations//[*on sketch*] Subsistence
[illegible]/stream/Park/Park and golf
course/market/landing field**

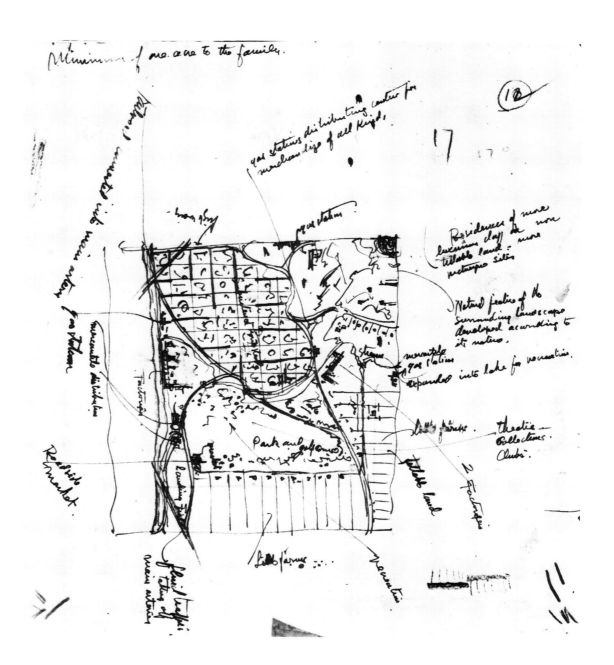

suburban housing. It can be assumed that in 1934 Wright believed these were the most important considerations for the physical structure of an American city.

The next stage in the design process was to refine the plan and devise an effective coherence obvious to an observer. This was achieved by the use of geometric rationale, fundamentally a cruciform as shown in Figure 2. A grid was, of course, the pattern of North American expansion east to west. Wright's plan contained gridded areas, but the principal organizing device was the cruciform, which was defined by major roads. Housing was in the center, the very heart and soul of Wright's concept. At the top of his 1934 sketch, almost as a banner or heading, Wright wrote, "Minimum of one acre to the family." The single family was, in the words of Curtis, to be "the central bond of the community."[8] The other major areas of the cruciform (Figure 3) were occupied by compatible functions. In area A were recreation and county (regional?) administration; in area B were commerce and recreation with little farms—no doubt "Little Farm Units"—on the periphery; in area C orchards and in area D housing and higher education (and a cemetery). In the corners of the cruciform Wright located nonfarm housing ("luxurious" type) in area E, in area F was recreation and administration, and in areas G and H commerce, manufacturing, and industry. The main regional artery or transport route was located on the left edge of the cruciform, and therefore of the city. Beside it and within the cruciform were located related activities (H, C, G). The cruciform was used as spatial geometry; this was explicit in the road pattern and the manner in which it embraced the various quadrants including the four that form the core of the city (area x): housing on one-acre sites.

The final plan as completed in late 1934 was published the following year in *Architectural Record* (Figure 4). It is appropriate to call this final for all subsequent published plans were extraordinarily similar. Future drawings of the Broadacres plan showed a variety of architectural objects, as it were, which over the years mutated for better or worse. But the city plans were all closely related to that published in 1935.[9] The 1934–35 plan departed from the earlier 1934 sketch only in that the regional arterial route was no longer within the square but at its side. While the shape of the single-family housing area was slightly different, it still retained a subtle diagonal across the imaginary site similar to the original sketch. This slight difference was probably a result of defining the single-family detached house as the plan's core and, therefore, philosophic fulcrum. Planning and development of the factories and orchards (agricultural factories?) effectively pushed the main artery further left.

8.2 Geometric rationale of Broadacre City.

8.3 The cruciform plan of Broadacre City.

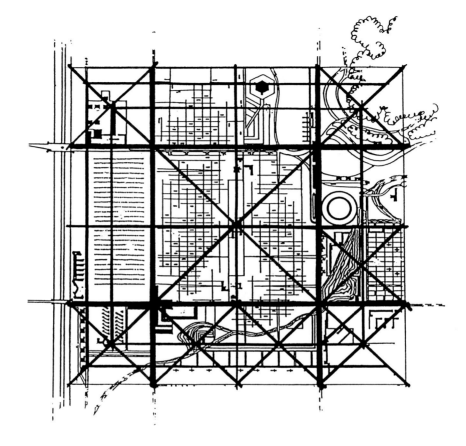

8.4 Plan of Broadacre City as published in 1935 in *Architectural Record,* which supplied this legend: (1) county seat—administration; (2) aerotor—post port and administration; (3) polo; (4) baseball; (5) clubs; (6) lake and stream; (7) crafts and county architect; (8) professionals; (9) stadium; (10) hotel; (11) sanitarium; (12) small industry; (13) small farm units; (14) small apartments; (15) interior park; (16) music garden; (17) merchandising; (18) automobile inn; (19) little factories and dwellings above; (20) factory assembly; (21) aerotor service; (22) aerotor factory; (23) main arterial; (24) vineyards and orchards; (25) homes; (26) schools; (27) temple, columbarium, and cemetery; (28) neighborhood guest houses; (30) scientific and agricultural research; (31) arboretum; (32) zoo; (33) aquarium; (34) luxurious dwelling (House on the Mesa); (35) Taliesin (equivalent); (36) luxurious homes; (37) water supply; (38) forest cabins; (39) country club; (40) apartment houses; (41) small school for small children; (42) automobile objective.

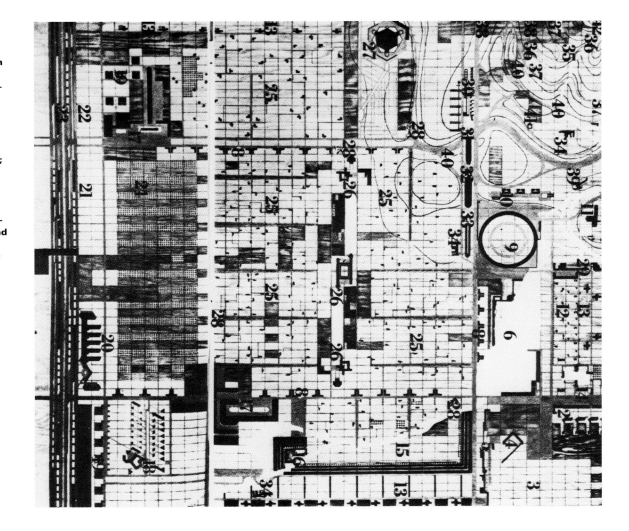

The model was built by Wright's students during the winter, working steadily at an inn in Chandler, Arizona, from January through March 1935. Through Tom Maloney's good offices, upon completion it was displayed at Rockefeller Center, New York, in April–May 1935 at the National Alliance of Arts and Industry's exposition of industrial arts. It is not known if the other exhibits also traveled with the Broadacre City model to Madison, Wisconsin, Pittsburgh, and the Corcoran Gallery in Washington, D.C. Of course Wright's comments and the plan and model were published to coincide with the event.[10] Oddly, the 1934–35 publications did not show the entire plan or model. Therefore the plan illustrated here falls short of the real boundaries. For clarify and simplification a rather more diagrammatic plan is illustrated here as Figure 5.[11]

His model of a possible Broadacre City was accompanied by models of possible buildings and large display panels. His major verbal theses were reduced to a series of negations lettered on one panel. The first three were theoretical economic propositions that he often presented in his writings beginning with the Kahn lectures.

No private ownership of public needs

No landlord or tenant

No "housing." No subsistence homesteads

No traffic problems

No railroads. No streetcars

No grade crossings

No poles. No wires in site

No headlights. No light fixtures

No glaring cement roads or walks

No tall buildings except in isolated parks

No slum. No scum

No major or minor axis[12]

The remaining negations related to the physical plan or some features.

Conceptually and schematically the plan has an affinity with Ebenezer Howard's well-publicized ideas for a Garden City. Howard's "Ward and Centre" diagram (Figure 6), provides a clue to the affection. If that diagram is altered from a pie-shaped—or possibly concentric—diagram to one more rectilinear, then its relationship to Broadacres becomes rather more obvious. To accomplish this we need to look at it from the outside toward the center. If the center is ignored as a point of radius, that is, the diagram is straightened out, it would read not from the center out but from

8.5 Simplified plan of Broadacre City.

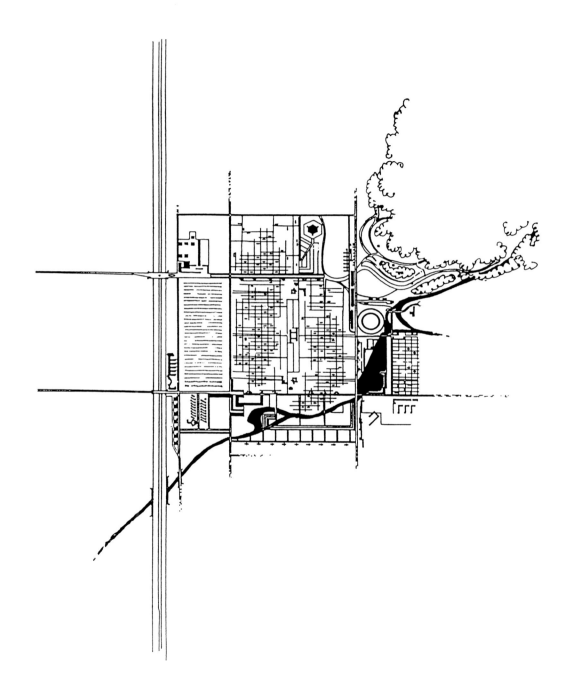

8.6 Howard's diagram no. 3, taken from
E. Howard, *Garden Cities of To-morrow*
(London, 1945). It was also used in Howard's original edition, *To-morrow: A
Peaceful Path to Real Reform* (London,
1898).

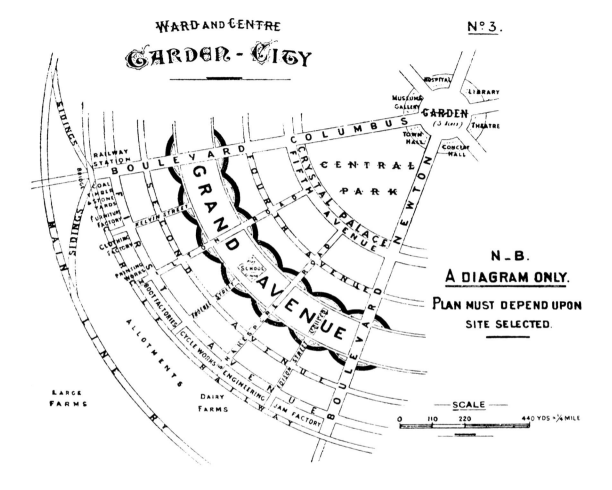

8.7 Howard's diagram no. 3 revised and compared to plans for Miliutin's linear city and Wright's 1934 Broadacre City.

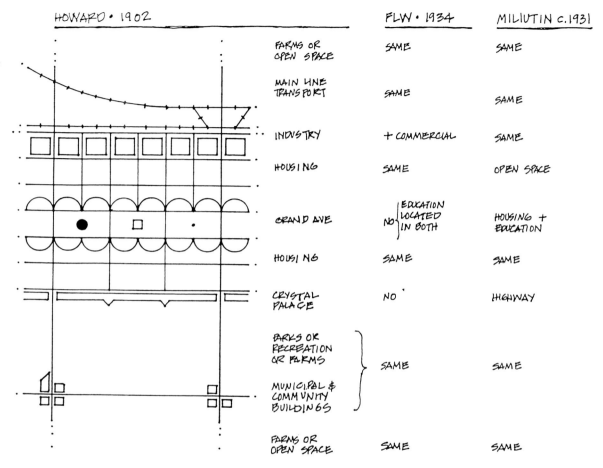

HOWARD · 1902   FLW · 1934   MILIUTIN C. 1931

HOWARD · 1902	FLW · 1934	MILIUTIN C. 1931
FARMS OR OPEN SPACE	SAME	SAME
MAIN LINE TRANSPORT	SAME	SAME
INDUSTRY	+ COMMERCIAL	SAME
HOUSING	SAME	OPEN SPACE
GRAND AVE	NO { EDUCATION LOCATED IN BOTH	HOUSING + EDUCATION
HOUSING	SAME	SAME
CRYSTAL PALACE	NO	HIGHWAY
PARKS OR RECREATION OR FARMS	SAME	SAME
MUNICIPAL & COMMUNITY BUILDINGS		
FARMS OR OPEN SPACE	SAME	SAME

left to right, or in Figure 7 from top to bottom. The resultant diagram presents a very basic formula. It has a slight similarity to Soria y Mata's linear city plan of 1882 as well as plans of linear cities offered in the 1930s. The key to comparison is the rail and vehicle transport spine and those functions that of necessity should be in proximity: industry and manufacturing. Land use zones more distant from transport should need its services less. If we consider that the 1934 sketch was drawn with the bottom as illustrated (Figure 4), and that all plans published by Wright have shown this orientation, then we can assume that Wright's plan reads, as it were, from left to right: that it reads as Western man reads written words and composes pictures. The argument that there is a schematic relationship between Howard's plan and Wright's seems not only plausible but very reasonable. The two schemes have their land use and functional disposition arranged similarly.

We can also compare the schematic diagram of Howard's and Wright's idea with that of Soviet theorist N.A. Miliutin for a socialist linear city in the early 1930s and see a close parallel with Howard's revolutionary diagrams. Perhaps it was the simple logic of Howard's idea that made it attractive and credible: credible, it should be noted, for two conceptual extremes of planning new cities, one Howard's ring of separate cities isolated from one another in semiwilderness, the other Soria's single city linearly additive *ad infinitum.* Miliutin's plan was the first of many very similar authoritarian schemes to follow during the 1930s, in fact through the 1950s. One major difference in the three schemes was Howard's "Crystal Palace" which was not found in the other two designs. In Miliutin's layout an internal road, as differentiated from a regional arterial, occupied a position similar to Howard's Crystal Palace. Otherwise the progression from open space to main regional arterial transport system, to industry, and on to the municipal and community functions was explicit. Using Stalingrad as an example, Miliutin's "Socialist City" was diagrammed and explained to Western audiences in the May 1932 issue of *The Architectural Review.* The issue was devoted to Russian—or more correctly USSR—architecture and city planning. Views of new cities with typical blocks of apartment housing regimentally aligned on the landscape were displayed in dramatically clear photographs: cities such as Autostroy, Dnieperstroi, and Harkov, and plans for Magnitogorsk and Nizhni-Novgorod. To the degree that magazines might inform, Wright was aware of what was occurring in the Soviet Union up to 1932 in architecture and city planning.

In 1934 Wright and apprentice Edgar Tafel did an academic exercise together that included an essay by Tafel about architecture in the USSR including the Palace of Soviets competition for Moscow.[13] The information used in the rather trivial exercise had to be based on information each had gleaned from magazines of 1928–34 that contained articles about Soviet architecture and new cities. The rudimentary schematic similarity of Wright's plan to Miliutin's—and Howard's—was not a matter of coincidence.

The Broadacres concept was one of self-sustaining communities defined and surrounded by rural farm or natural spaces and places, all linked by transport systems combined on the same path. This idea was translated into architectural terms by isolating the city, then isolating the recreational or community or administrative buildings one from another, and then surrounding them in a relatively natural landscape. At an even smaller scale the single-family house was similarly surrounded by its own private green acre.

This family acre was the smallest grid; and forty such acres formed a square. If we study just a small portion of the city plan, an area right of center (Figure 8), we can see the acre grid, various forest plantations (indicated by textured acre rectangles), roads, and buildings. If we super-impose the appropriate part of Wright's geometric rationale (Figure 2) over only that area of the plan shown in Figure 8, more detail is revealed that explains how the plan was further organized. It should be obvious, therefore, that the basic planning module was not the rectangular acre (or the "unit" in Wright's parlance) as implied by Wright and explicated by others, but the forty acres that formed a square. That is, the minor grid of acre units could be anything everywhere and without logical coherence while the major grid, therefore the functional and organizational grid, was the forty-acre square. This is made plain by four samples.

At location 1 (a sports stadium) the square module was used rather untypically but emphatically. Just to the right of location 1 it was used more typically. Or, at location 2 two modules defined the recreation area (including its lake) and municipal buildings, and to the right of that location two modules were used to control another functional area. Or, three modules were used at various times in the plan as instanced by location 3 where another functional land use was archi-tecturally defined by a road and buildings on the periphery. Just below, three modules enclosed a set of "little farms." Four modules were used for the suburban housing indicated by location 4. Four adjacent sets of four modules were grouped to form the sixteen-module core of the city plan; that was the suburban housing at the center of the cruciform, the focus of which was a school. In some instances the diagonal or the center of the grid module was actually acknowledged in the plan (see, e.g., buildings in quadrant G and H, Figures 2 and 3). These samples confirm the design module used by Wright.

If just three basic elements he identified on the 1934 sketch are emphasized together with the ten-mile radius, the plan takes on a significance that can be developed into what was

8.8 Portion of the 1935 Broadacre City plan with geometric rationale superimposed.

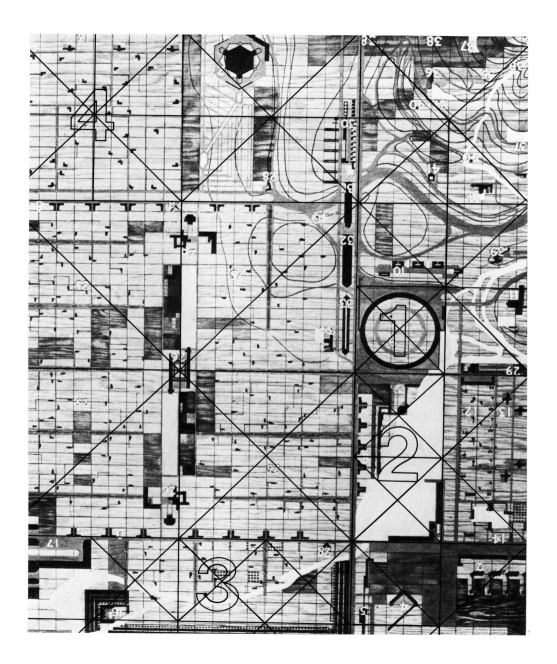

Wright's idea for a regional plan. These elements are housing, either suburban or "finer" houses in hilly sylvan settings; the transitional green areas meant to be more or less natural, whether landscaped environments or small farms or just undisturbed natural areas with buildings relatively isolated within the landscape); and the ribbon regional transportation route and adjacent industry and/or commerce.

Wright's principal city, his county seat or administration center, was effectively and aesthetically a large village because the first two of these elements dominate the plan. Beyond the village were neat areas of either rural farming in all its varieties or wilderness. Therefore the plan must have been for a limited size: in fact the county seat was designed for a maximum of 1,400 families according to Wright, or about 5,000 people.[14] Development beside the regional transport route (which included storage facilities underneath) was not delimited by Wright but it can be assumed that it would have variable functional limits in relation to the village.

From the above disclosures it seems clear that his Broadacres plan was not meant to be a linear city (as often suggested) nor was it meant to be repeated—opposite-hand or otherwise—by an immediately adjacent town across the regional arterial route (also often suggested).[15] Wright implied that regionalism was one of the more important aspects of his scheme. Such a belief is nearly explicit in the words heading a display panel for the 1935 exhibition: Broadacres was A NEW PATTERN OF LIVING FOR AMERICA.[16] The regional pattern—or plan—for Wright's Broadacres concept is a series of villages approximately twenty miles apart (or on a twenty-mile grid) similar to that in Figure 9. In that figure the county seat (that is, the plan referred to as Broadacre City in 1934 and all later editions) is in the center while other perhaps smaller villages are located at various crossroads or fitted between and on principal regional routes, perhaps freeways.

This suggestion for the regional plan follows almost exactly Wright's own interpretation. He described in 1943 how the horizontal line was "the great architectural highway" and the flat plane was to become "the regional field." "The cover-graph of this book, I have called it 'Freedom,' uses the great highway and the regional field of decentralization, uses it as a significant pattern."[17] The top one-third of the "cover-graph" (Figure 10) is an abstracted elevational study of Taliesin near Spring Green (with stylized tree and house) while the bottom two-thirds of the right-hand page shows the regional *pattern* to which he referred. The nodes would be the towns. Interestingly, his statement in the 1943 autobiography is only slightly altered from the same page in the 1932 edition. However, the line referring to his "cover-graph" was inserted and a sentence or two were slightly altered or relocated in the 1943 edition. Arguments in 1932 were for a new interpretation of American

8.9 Map of how the regional grid would have been applied.

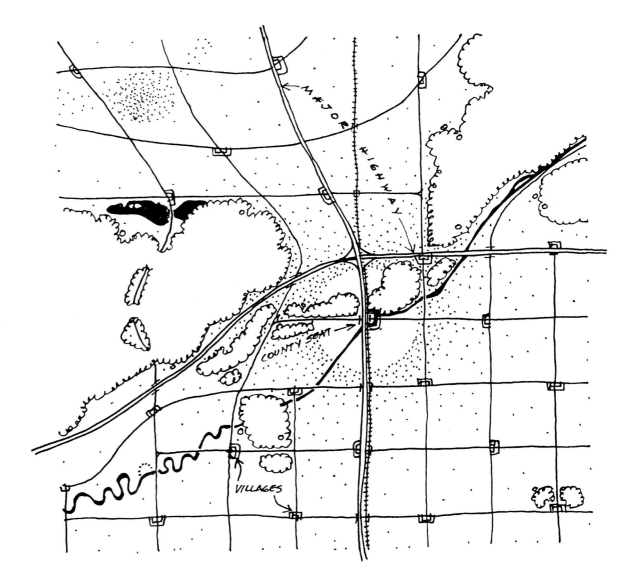

8.10 Graphics for Book 4, "Freedom," in Wright's 1943 autobiography; the original drawing was probably by Wesley Peters. Reproduction courtesy and © 1943 the Frank Lloyd Wright Foundation.

society, one more open for individual expression in architecture symbolized by the horizontal "earth line," the "broad expanded plane" as "freedom for man." It was within this section that in 1943 he chose to explain the regional pattern for Broadacre Cities.

The illustrations used in this analysis should be explained. Original drawings of Broadacre City of 1934–35 are not extant except for the small pen and ink sketch of 1934 (Figure 1). Figures 4 and 8 are obviously important to the geometrical study and are here reproduced from an illustration that appeared in *Architectural Record* in 1935. Unfortunately, when published the plan was spread across the gutter, distorting one portion, but seventy percent remained proportionally correct. (Figures 2, 5, 8, and 9 are reconstructions by myself.) A remodeled model is extant and a smaller, less distinct illustration of the plan was reproduced in the *American Architect,* also in 1935. The same geometry, cruciform, and zoning were used in published plans of 1935, 1945, and the complexly presented colored plan of 1958. However, when the physical plan for Broadacre City was presented in *When Democracy Builds* of 1945 it was considerably simplified from previous publications, perhaps for easier reading or perhaps to emphasize that it was not a specific plan for a specific place. It must be remembered that Broadacre City was the concept; the plan and model were *suggestions* for the realization of the concept and only for one of the larger villages, the administrative center.

The philosophic roots of Broadacre City are within fundamentals outlined in the many works of the great landscape architect Frederick Law Olmsted. The presence or absence of someone in Wright's autobiography means little. A short list of great names appended to the 1943 edition, whose words he "occasionally" remembered, was to satisfy arrogance as much as his publisher's desire for an index. Olmsted was not mentioned; but Wright was familiar with the words and works of the grand master. Wright designed homes to be located in Olmsted's quintessential suburb of Riverside, Illinois (itself a relatively self-contained community), and there were Olmsted landscape and planning works elsewhere in Illinois, including Chicago.

Olmsted's biography and professional accomplishments have been presented by the late historian Albert Fein, long-time student of the landscape architect and city planner. In his introduction to Olmsted's book concerned with a greater New York City, Fein not only condensed an imaginative perception of the late nineteenth century but also effectively paraphrased Wright's own attitude to cities, the historical imperative of rurality in American life, and the vitality and preciousness of the landscape. Like Wright, Olmsted was born and raised in a small town and was therefore familiar with rural scenes and practices. There the two men's biographies depart. The comparison suggested

8.11 Photograph of a detail of the model of Broadacre City as revised 1940, showing the stadium, a motel in background, civic center to upper left, and sanitarium to right. The short tall buildings are models of St. Mark's tower of 1929. From *When Democracy Builds*. Courtesy and © the Frank Lloyd Wright Foundation.

here is to Wright's writings and lifestyle of the 1930s and less to that period of his life around the turn of the century when Olmsted was still a giant among the multitude of design professionals (Olmsted died in 1903).

Fein entitled his introductory remarks "A Changing World":

A democracy born in the countryside—proclaimed by Americans as superior to the aristocracies of Europe—was having its system of government tested in the rapidly emerging cities of the nineteenth century. "Our country has entered upon a stage of progress," . . . Olmsted wrote about 1877, "in which its welfare is to depend on the convenience, safety, order and economy of life in its great cities. It . . . cannot gain in virtue, wisdom, comfort, except as they also advance." The city, he predicted, would shape the modes of thought and basic values of all future Americans. American civilization, in fact, would depend mainly upon the influence of its cities—and unless they were enlightening and uplifting they would not be truly democratic.

Olmsted's knowledge of history and the statistics of social trends [knowledge Wright never expressed] as well as his extensive travels throughout western Europe, led him to conclude by the end of the Civil War that the outstanding feature of Western civilization was the "strong tendency of people to flock together in great towns." He was certain that this process of urbanization was permanently altering the social structure of all Western nations. The growth of London, for example, had been so rapid that from the early part of the century until his own time its population had increased tenfold. Glasgow's rate of growth was six times that of Scotland; the population of Paris increased to account for half the growth of France; Berlin was growing twice as rapidly as all of Prussia; and even rural Russia, he noted, was witnessing a flight by the peasantry from the country into the large towns.

The physical environment shaped by the rapid growth in commerce, manufacturing, and industry by 1865 appeared likely to inhibit social progress. In addition to opportunities for employment city-dwellers required satisfactory homes and educational and recreational facilities in a physical environment conducive to social harmony. Olmsted was determined that cities such as New York use their economic power to become humanizing centers of cultural and intellectual activity. The city, he wrote, must come to epitomize social democracy's "higher" standards of wealth, represented by learning, science and art.[18]

Olmsted's response to his prophetic observations were proven in succeeding decades. While the half century before the Civil War was a period of basically rural commercialism only slightly touched by the industrial revolution, more so than Europe but of course not than Britain, the war itself resolved that industrialism was to prevail over an agricultural gentry. Urban historian Blake McKelvey has defined three great ages of urbanization, perhaps of American civilization: commercial expansion to 1860, then industrialism for the next fifty years, finally and presently "Metropolitanism" from 1910. The general trend toward urbanization in North America and Europe is a well-known phenomenon. As McKelvey summarizes, in less than three and a half centuries the urbanization of the United States had "reached a stage of development surpassing that of all other continental areas." In South and East Asia urban residents "comprised a small portion of their total populations. All the major continents have older cities . . . but only one principal nation, Great Britain, is more completely urbanized" than the States.[19] Olmsted, apparently unlike Wright, was pragmatic and sensitive to history and the future evolution of American urbanism; and the general thrust of his views was persuasive.

Such prophecies as Olmsted's, however, can have greater meaning when connected to action. And Olmsted acted vigorously to personally mold the physical character of much of America's urban future. Fein emphasizes Olmsted's synthetic and artistic contributions.

He consequently devoted himself to the landscape development of such social institutions as parks, colleges, and museums. To ensure that these facilities would be used and supported by a substantial element of the population, he planned them as integral parts of communities; the commercial and social activities of the city were to be physically separated. And these institutions would constitute the harmonizing elements of an organic, democratic metropolis.

[Olmsted] pioneered the professional development of landscape architecture and city planning in the United States. His interest in these fields grew out of his appreciation of the urban experience as well as out of his concern with the social problems challenging American democracy in the nineteenth century. He considered the displacement of rural America by the commercial and industrial city to be the most fundamental change confronting the nation during his lifetime. . . . For Olmsted, the ideal urban environment was to be a *synthesis of landscape and cityspace* [my emphasis]. . . .

There was, he felt, no technical reason why the suburb should not combine the best features of city and country. The cultural advantages of urban life, he realized, would be lost even to "people living in houses a quarter of a mile apart." But the city need not be synonymous with "an unhealthy density of population." In fact, "the advantages of 'civilization' were perhaps best realized in suburban neighborhoods where each family abode stands fifty or a hundred feet or more apart from all others, and at some distance from the public road." Good

roads and walks, adequate sewerage, a pure water supply, gas to light the dark streets, and low-cost, rapid, and comfortable transportation to urban centers could, he believed, "give any farming land in a healthy and attractive situation the value of town lots." He had seen such suburban communities in his travels in England, and by the mid-1860s was actively engaged in constructing them.[20]

Similarities with Wright's perceptions are remarkable, including the view that residential suburbs were a valuable "feature" of the city. Wright never abandoned the suburb and for the very reasons Fein observes in Olmsted. Had he lived another thirty years Olmsted might have praised Broadacre City for its condensation of much that he himself supported.

Practical links to Olmsted's pragmatic historical perceptions can be seen in a series of projects by Wright for Walter V. Davidson during 1931 and 1932. Of the people involved with the creation and administration of the Larkin Company, Elbert Hubbard, John Larkin, William Heath, Darwin Martin, and George Barton had been Chicago residents who went to Buffalo and, except for Hubbard, all became Wright's clients before 1910. Another of the Larkin group was Davidson, who hired Wright some twenty-five years later. He commissioned Wright to look into the idea of prefabricated farm buildings that, by implication, could be delivered and assembled on a building site by the purchaser. Wright's plans included a three bedroom house separated from the farm building by an air lock or party walls. The house contained a "workspace" (kitchen) off a dining area that was part of the living room space. The farm included runs for turkeys, sheep, and pigs, enclosures for cows and chickens, a large greenhouse, an orchard and a summer garden, a feed silo, a machine shed, and a packing-shipping area. This typical house was called a "Little Farms Unit" and was dated February 1932. It seems necessary to repeat that this was Wright's first statement in plan of what became the so-called Usonian house in 1936. A slightly larger version was called "The Integrated Farm Unit on Three Acres" (possibly also 1932) and this plan was refined with only slight modifications and entitled "The Unified Farm."[21] These Little Farm Units were to be typical Davidson prefabricated sheet steel farm buildings. When the model of Broadacre City was exhibited in 1935, a large model of what was then entitled the Unified Farm unit was also displayed (see Figure 20.4).[22]

Intimate to the concept for Broadacre City, therefore, was the incorporation of "little farms" and they were noted on his plan. (The date of the Unified Farm design is probably 1934, in anticipation of the exhibition.) Then in 1937 the Little Farms plan was used as a "Farm Unit" for the Herbert F. Johnson house Wingspread—in 1938 Wright called the Wingspread mansion "The Johnson Cottage." Apparently the Johnsons wanted a working farm, so a manager's house and farm

8.12 Plan of scheme one of a typical "Lit-tle-Farms" house, "Davidson Markets," proposed for Walter V. Davidson in 1932. Courtesy and © 1990 the Frank Lloyd Wright Foundation. The drawing included the following key:

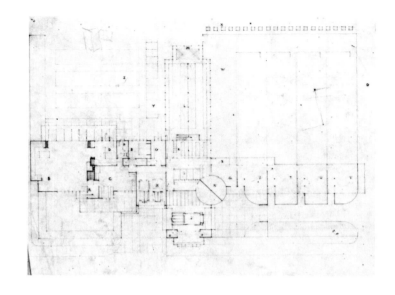

A ENTRANCE

B LIVING ROOM

C KITCHEN

D BEDROOM

E BEDROOM

F BATH

G WORKSHOP

H GARAGE

I COW BARN

J SHIPPING STA.

K CHICKEN HOUSE

L GREENHOUSE

M POOL

N SILO—FEED BIN

O OFFICE

P TOOLS

Q YARD

R MANURE PIT

S COW YARD

T PIG PEN—YARD

U SHEEP

V TURKEYS

W CHICKEN RUN

X BEES

Y HOT BEDS
  COLD FRAMES

Z GARDEN

8.13 "Birds eye view" of scheme one of a typical "Little-Farms" house proposed for Walter V. Davidson in 1932. Courtesy and © the Frank Lloyd Wright Foundation.

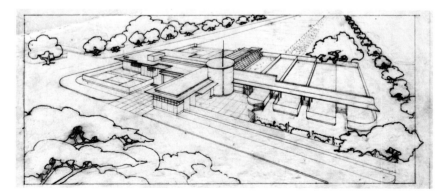

buildings were designed, but the project was not realized. The farm house plan was the same as that of February 1932 (if otherwise appearing on the exterior somewhat like an English cottage), but the farm buildings were quite different. Farm buildings were, of course, a reasonable commission for Wright to undertake. He was from a farming family on his mother's side and a farmer himself—or at least a farm manager, of sorts.

As part of the package for Davidson, Wright prepared a plan for a small town that he entitled "Little-Farms Tract."[23] His drawing listed functions that qualify it as a city (municipal building, gasworks, sewage plant, etc.). It is a plan of no particular inspiration. Vehicle traffic routes are not identified let alone carefully integrated; there is no logical disposition of city functions; and other than a grid of farm sites (and that is only a guess) there is no rationale organizing the plan except that it was proportionally two squares long with the center or core one square. It was all very abstract as if a preliminary study, and it must be assumed that it was a typical design for a flat site to be located anywhere. It was to be a company town and not a cooperative or something like a kibbutz, although Wright's explanatory language suggests that he favored a form of cooperative administration.

Davidson provided further inspiration by way of another paid commission to study roadside markets to be located beside the highways of America's ever-expanding system. Wright explained the market as follows (Figure 15): "Great spacious roadside pleasure places these markets, rising wide and handsome like some flexible form of pavilion—designed as places of cooperative exchange, not only of commodities but of cultural facilities. 'Business' takes on a different character: integration of mercantile presentation and distribution of all produce possible and natural to the living city. These markets might resemble our county fairs, in general, and occur conveniently upon great arteries of mobility."[24] Drawings showed a large central display space covered by a glass and copper pyramid (an architectural theme to reemerge in Wright's work of the 1950s) with shops on the periphery. A car service station was next to one of the parking areas.[25] It was much like a supermarket of farm produce, including flowers, together with a restaurant ("milk bar") with outdoor dining and convenience shops. The idea of a modest form of decentralization via the Wayside Markets was obviously a forerunner of the modern shopping center post-1950 on the periphery of cities: all made possible by inexpensive cars.

Henry Ford had captured the imagination of the world with his notions of industrialization, marketing, management, and the dynamics of American pragmatism. Ford was willing to offer opinions on any and all subjects, he had political aspirations (the presidency and no less), and his

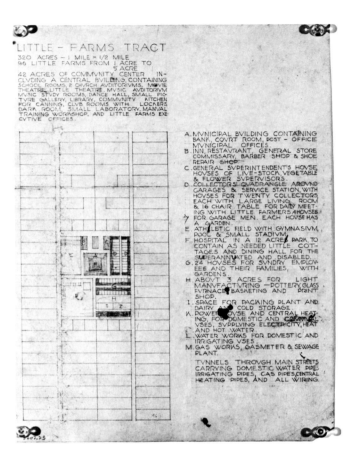

8.14 Plan of "Little-Farms Tract" for Walter V. Davidson in 1932. Courtesy and © 1990 the Frank Lloyd Wright Foundation. Note the English rather than American spelling in the caption.

8.15 Plan of final scheme proposed for Wayside Markets of 1932. Cars from the highway (at bottom) were to enter on the right and exit on the left side of the building or otherwise park on three sides. A service station was to be located in the upper left; its "Y" configuration was similar to Wright's rather naive project for a "Village Service Station" in 1928. Courtesy and © 1990 the Frank Lloyd Wright Foundation.

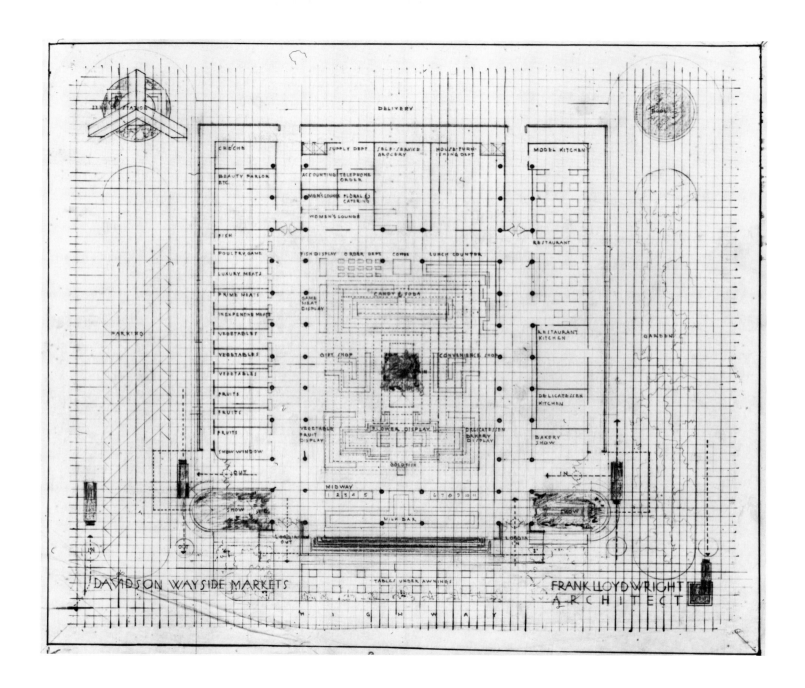

DAVIDSON WAYSIDE MARKETS

FRANK LLOYD WRIGHT
ARCHITECT

words were always preceded by successful and productive action. He knew full well the impact of the car and of transportation generally on the geography of commerce. He and Wright agreed: with the car, airplane, and radio, there was no reason for people to stay at home; communication and travel were becoming widely available and therefore more economical. If there is one measure of freedom it is the ability of anyone to travel anywhere at any time for any reason. The Model T, for instance, emancipated the North American farmer. Through individual enterprise Ford provided one means of cheap, fast mobility, and in the 1920s he epitomized American capitalism, pragmatism, verve, and social mobility. His was a philosophy Wright could understand, and he knew about Ford's enterprises as did most Americans.

Ford commissioned Wright in 1909 to design an appropriate mansion on the Rouge River between Dearborn and Detroit. But before he began Wright fled to Europe with his mistress Mamah Cheney. At almost the same moment Childe Harold Wills also commissioned Wright. Wills was Ford's right-hand man, present from the earliest days in the development of the company's first car. With Wright's departure the Wills commission was taken over by the architect Wright designated to assume his commissions, Hermann von Holst, with Marion Mahony in charge. She designed a house for Wills but it remained a project. The Ford commission was, as historian Allen Brooks has surmised, "a once-in-a-lifetime opportunity." Wright "could have prepared designs in Europe, and remained in contact with Ford by mail until his return" in late 1910. "Yet he did not. Moreover, no attempt was apparently made after his return to pick up where he had left off, which is indeed curious."[26] The same might be said of all the other major commissions including Wills's.

Wright knew Ford and knew of the industrialist's activities. Outside Wright's profession there were family connections. His uncle Jenkins Lloyd Jones, with whom Wright was rather close, was intimately involved with Ford and many others in a pacifistic crusade during 1915–16.[27] When Wright was similarly involved in 1939–40 in arguing against American participation in World War II he called upon his fellow Americans to honor the "true American . . . a staunch man, Henry Ford."[28] But in any event Ford's activities were usually good press, especially in the 1920s when he was idolized by farmers and other sections of society as a paragon of independence and capitalistic virtue. It was early in the decade that he committed his mind and industrial prowess to putting into practice the concept of decentralization beyond merely scattering his "productive centers." Ford in 1918: "I am a farmer. . . . I want to see every acre of the earth's surface covered with little farms, with happy, contented people living on them." In 1919: "Plainly, . . . the ultimate solution will be the abolition of the City, its abandonment as a blunder. . . . We shall solve the City problem by leaving the City."[29]

As always, Ford would put theory into practice and weigh the results. No committees. No endless verbiage. Try it. "I am going to . . . establish plants for manufacturing parts of Ford cars and Fordson tractors, in places where they will be within easy reach of farming districts, and provide employment for farmers and their families in winter. And these plants are going to be operated by water power."[30]

Historians Allan Nevins and Frank E. Hill comment: "Ford was launching a . . . development, designed to alter the basic character of American life, and if anyone could work such a transformation, he had the practical knowledge, experiences, and resources to effect it." The concept was now plain: village industries. "Ford pointed out that rural factories would tend to distribute purchasing power more evenly. His village industry workers would buy tractors for their farms and cars for transportation. Thus they purchased more Ford products, and more products in general, expanding the manufacturer's market while making a better life for themselves."[31] Ford in 1920: "It is far from impossible that with automatic machinery and widespread power the manufacture of some articles may be carried on at home. The world has proceeded from hand work in the home to hand work in the shop, to power work in the shop, and now we may be around to power work in the home."[32]

Perhaps because of higher purposes and more complex deals Ford's village industries were never fully developed. Only a thousand or so families were affected and in the end it was not a financial success.[33]

One diversion was directly related to the village concept yet on a vastly different scale. It was also aimed at breaking the British and South American world monopoly on nitrate fertilizers. Ford proposed to take over by lease facilities and river systems beside the Muscle Shoals of the Tennessee River valley. Among other accommodations proposed was a nitrate plant, farm irrigation, power from dams, and a seventy-five-mile city, as it was at times referred to. Actually it was to consist of activity nodes or small towns located along a highway: not unlike Broadacre City. The layout of the proposed town at Muscle Shoals was to have been very much like a greenbelt town. But in spite of major support, Congress and its allies stopped Ford. As is well known, after a visit to the site in 1931, upon his ascendancy to the presidency Roosevelt announced a program for the multipurpose development of the Tennessee valley. It was of course much like Ford's proposal, only larger and financed by tax dollars. When built, the TVA's town of Norris was greenbelt in concept and layout.[34]

Wright was clear about Ford's contributions to his own thoughts in relation to the problems of and resolutions to city living, or more correctly, the city-country nexus. In 1930 he said that Ford is a man "of common sense."

He has successful ideas. His proposition for Muscle Shoals was one of the best things that I have heard of as a solution of the excess machine increment from this great tool, the machine which this man has now in its hand. What to do with the man at the machine? Ford's proposal was for decentralization of industry. If he could get Muscle Shoals he was going to have lots of little factories. He was going to split up the big factory. He was going to put the men back on the ground. He was going to give every man a few acres of ground for his own.

In the summer the men would work on the ground. In the winter they would go to work with their machines in the factory, the machines in the factory giving such facility that they need only work at the machines for 5 or 6 months each year.[35]

It was that quality of common sense that was so attractive to ordinary people. And Wright's simple analysis of a worker's activities at Muscle Shoals was correct. However, Ford had first proposed in 1919 and soon put into practice that scheme with his village industries. Wright again drew upon Ford's thesis in his lectures at Princeton University in 1930. He took the notion of urbanity to a problematic extreme for the machine analogy.

Only when the city becomes purely and simply utilitarian, will it have the order that is beauty, and the simplicity which the Machine, in competent hand, may very well render as human benefit. That event may well be left to the Machine.

This, _the only possible ideal machine_ seen as a _city,_ will be invaded at ten o'clock, abandoned at four, for three days of the week. The other four days of the week will be devoted to the more or less joyful matter of living elsewhere under conditions natural to man. . . . The country absorbs the life of the city as the city shrinks to the utilitarian purpose that now alone justifies its existence.

Even that concentration for utilitarian purposes we have just admitted may be first to go, as the result of impending decentralization of industry. It will soon become unnecessary to concentrate in masses for any purpose whatsoever. The individual unit, in more sympathetic grouping on the ground, will grow stronger in the hard earned freedom gained at first by that

element of the city not prostitute to the Machine. Henry Ford stated this idea in his plan for the development of Muscle Shoals. . . .

Even the small town is too large. It will gradually merge into the general non-urban development.[36]

As to the desirability and efficacy of the machine, both Wright and Ford were in agreement. Ford however was moved to clear and unambiguous generalizations that seemed to elude Wright. For instance, for Ford the machine directly resulted in freedom for all and especially the oppressed. "Engineering spells freedom. Men were held to a single spot before the engineer came. By steam and motor car and airplane he has liberated man. He has lengthened man's day with light, increased the limits of man's life through food and sanitation, emancipated man's mind, and given him a sense of possible mastery over elements and environment—in short, the engineer found society immobile and left it mobile."[37] Only political freedoms have blocked man's path to that mobility.

When Wright introduced Broadacre City in the magazine *American Architect* he entitled the article "Today . . . Tomorrow." Ford had released his book *Today and Tomorrow* about the integration of industry and agriculture in 1926. It reads as a practical primer for Wright's ideas on economics, pacifism, modern villages, the work ethic, Americanism, and much more.

By 1930, when Wright was putting together his thoughts about the city, Ford was no longer the extraordinarily popular force he had been in the 1920s. A grassroots push—almost a demand—for Ford to be the Republican nominee for President of the United States was thwarted by not only the opposition but Ford himself. During the years he was touted for the presidency, and for a long five years in the early 1920s, he was associated with rather outspoken anti-Semitic comments and other personal attacks. Most Jews who worked with Ford remained loyal as did Albert and Moritz Kahn, who believed, as perhaps had others, that Ford's anti-Semitic notions were "rooted in ignorance."[38] Nonetheless by the time Ford came to make apologies and blame others in 1927, the damage had been done, the momentum lost.

In spite of Ford's difficulties Wright believed that the only way out of the Depression was much as Ford had experienced: individual opportunity gained by individual industry. In his thoughts about small towns, therefore, and perhaps as the primary focus of his thinking, Wright wanted to provide the best possible place for an individual to seize opportunity and exercise industry in intimate contact with nature. It was a place familiar to himself as well as Olmsted, Ford, and many others.

Acting on a proposal of Clarence Stein and with the initiative of Charles Whitaker, the Regional Planning Association of America was formed in 1923. Its purpose was "to discuss regional

**8.16 Preliminary perspective study from
the highway of final scheme proposed
for Wayside markets of 1932. Courtesy
and © 1958 the Frank Lloyd Wright
Foundation.**

development, geotechnics and New Communities," in the words of Stein, the first president.[39] And they were quite vocal, producing many articles and using the pages of popular as well as professional magazines such as the *AIA Journal,* whose editor was Whitaker. In the main these articles were written by Benton MacKaye, Lewis Mumford, Stein, Henry Wright, and later Catherine Bauer. They promoted the regional concept and defined its parts relative to geography, conservation, transportation, industry, housing, farming, etc. The RPAA formally instituted the notion of regionalism and by written propaganda and political lobbying made it a reality in the conscience of planners anticipating the deployment of human activities. Practical results were, of course, irrigation systems and electricity power grids and their new communities such as the Tennessee Valley Authority. A theoretical result was the linear transport, industrial, and conservation systems for New York state of 1926. It has been noted that Wright based his Broadacre City on population and industrial decentralization and on modes of regional transport. These were two fundamentals promoted by the RPAA, if less so in the Regional Plan for New York and Its Environs (1929 and 1931), which was confined to the rather large area envisioned as metropolitan New York City.[40]

The Davidson Little-Farms and markets commissions, although never built, provided an incentive to plan in some detail aspects of Wright's more general and only verbalized thoughts about the American city of the *immediate* future. During this critical period of the realization of Broadacre City the evolution of design connections are clear. The urban market farms (Little Farm Units), the smallest element, were necessarily a part of the Wayside Markets scheme, which were extensions of the Little-Farms community. Derived as they were from Ford's villages and other less pragmatic sources, these various farm-related projects were intimately part of the practical inspiration for the plan of Broadacre City. Indeed, the Davidson commissions *induced the means* by which Broadacres might be realized in plan. Since there was not much else to do at Taliesin, all that remained was to find the money that would enable Wright to develop and refine the scheme.

These then were the *practical* influences on Wright, not the only ones but arguably the most significant. Wright and his historians have listed or described some of the philosophical and literary sources that helped form his corresponding intellectual attitudes. On the basis of the evidence just outlined it can be affirmed with some authority that Broadacres was a concept meant to reinforce and reinterpret the American tradition of rurality and to encourage a return to a democratically formed village life with all its implications, if in modern geometric form. Villages were to be scattered about the vast North American landscape, integrated "along the horizontal line which we call the great highway," disposed by compatible determinants such as work, travel, industry, population density, and other internal or regional needs. As such their physical character and philosophy, as also described and elaborated by many other observers, can be more fully understood. Moreover, the Broadacre villages were to be self-sufficient, part of an invigorated twentieth-century arts and crafts of the machine, a revived Garden City, in opposition to Granite and Concrete Gardens.[41] In the 1880s, Oak Park, Illinois—Wright's first place of independent work, marriage, and fatherhood—was such a place. The proposed villages, therefore, were intimately conservative, yet their vision was liberal and pragmatic while being only loosely utopian.

Many of Wright's buildings designed after 1935 were supposedly part of the Broadacres scheme, that is, they were designed not only with regard to a client but to Broadacre City and were even located on the big plan as it was revised over the years. These can be identified in the model (exhibited again in 1940 and 1951, each time updated with new designs) or in perspectives of the 1950s. Probably the most interesting application was his second significant commission in the 1930s, the Johnson Wax buildings at Racine. Historian Jonathan Lipman has pointed out that the Johnson company was in many ways an ideal Broadacres company. The business was decentralized with plants throughout the U.S. and five other countries; its headquarters was located in a relatively small midwestern city; the company was oriented to products, not solely to marketing; and it conducted its own research. It also had a "no-layoff" policy, shared profits with employees, and had a forty-hour week since 1919.

Even before obtaining the commission, during his first interview in early July 1936 with company officials—not with Johnson as yet—Wright had Broadacres in mind. "The pitch that he gave them was masterful and a shocker," recalled the company's contract art director E. Willis Jones. "In brief, it was not to build on the site adjacent to the ugly old factory, but to raze everything and get out of town four or five miles west, run a railroad spur, plan a Johnson Village around a new factory and office building, homes for employees, their own shopping center . . . the works." A short time later Wright and Johnson met and sparks flew, as Johnson recalled.

He insulted me about everything, and I insulted him, but he did a better job. I showed him pictures of the old office, and he said it was awful. I came back from Spring Green and said, "If that guy can talk like that he must have something." Everything at Spring Green was run down. He had a Lincoln-Zephyr, and I had one—that was the only thing we agreed on. On all other matters we were at each other's throats.[42]

Yet there was mutual respect hidden somewhere for around 23 July 1936 Wright got the commission.

He was in such financial straits that when the letter offering the job arrived at Taliesin he shouted to all, "We got it! We got it!"[43] He continued to persist with the idea of decentralizing the company and creating a Johnson/Broadacre village until Olgivanna's advice won: give in "or you will lose the job."[44] He gave in and the company got not what they expected.

9 Bitter Root

With a firm knowledge of Broadacre City's organization and regional distribution, some observations can be made not only as they might relate to events in Moscow and London but historically within Wright's oeuvre. Before engaging in that discussion, it is important to describe Wright's first commission to plan a city. It occurred during the early months of 1909 when he executed designs for sites in the Bitter Root valley of Montana. Since this design has only recently been properly researched and evaluated and is not generally known, it is necessary to present that information in some detail.[1]

He prepared two plans for the Bitter Root Valley Irrigation Company. The first was for a town (Figure 1) and was his first exercise in city planning; the second was for a village, a term used by Wright on his drawing. The Town of Bitter Root was a design for a complete administrative center for a proposed agricultural community, and like Broadacres it employed precise geometrical and classical proportional systems. The town plan used a square as the basic geometrical organizing device (see Figure 2), which also defined a grid of streets that enclosed square blocks of buildings. Those blocks, the grid and related buildings staggered imprecisely to fit the slope and contour of the land, particularly to the west and north. The street grid recalled the traditional plans for thousands of new towns in the North American central and western prairies and mountains (including Hamilton and Missoula, Montana), but Wright infused it with a personal vitality. The buidlings contained interior courts that were intended as service areas and to act as light wells. The block's peripheral buildings housed normal functions found in a small city; Wright began to identify some—restaurant, boutique—but then erased their titles. There was no indication of multiple housing units such as apartments. In the blocks next to and facing the central green space were located community services—telegraph, post office, fire department, utilities, as well as a real estate office and bank— all identified architecturally by their central position in the block and special plan treatment in the drawing.

On the periphery of the grid were other city functions; most related to cultural activities. North is to the left of the drawing, therefore in the southwest was a hospital, in the west a theater, with a fountain or sculpture axially and directly opposite to the east. In the northeast was a small

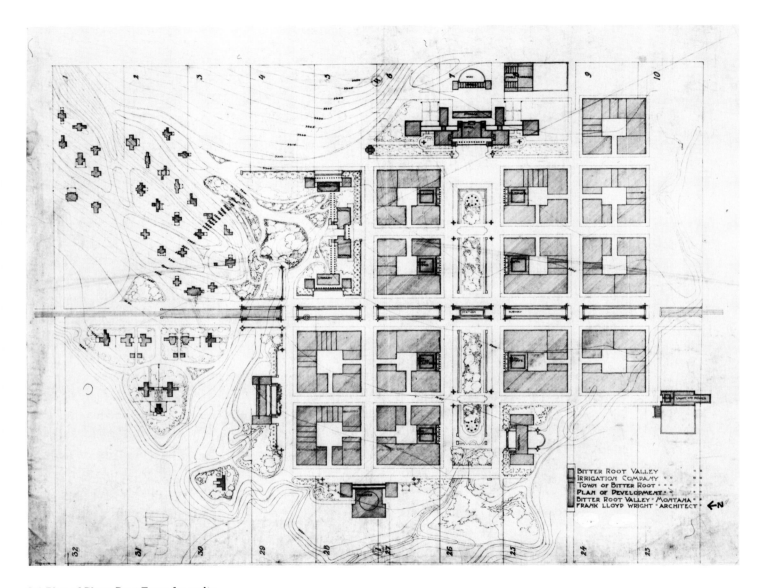

9.1 Plan of Bitter Root Town for a site north of Stevensville, Montana, a project of 1909. Courtesy and © 1981 the Frank Lloyd Wright Foundation.

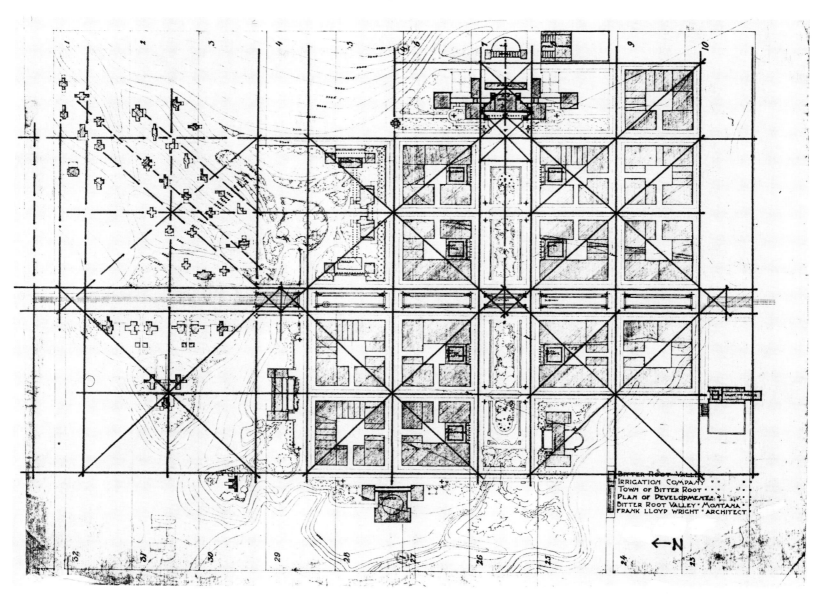

9.2 Geometry superimposed over Bitter Root town plan.

cultural center composed of a museum/school/library complex, and in the northwest the city administration building, which was axially and directly opposite the power tower to the south. Dominating the east was a spacious hotel or inn. The hospital, theater, and administrative center sat on the top of shallow benches overlooking western river bottom lands. All of these buildings on the periphery were formally axial to either street or city block. The inn was obviously the most important complex in the city because of its imposing position on higher ground and its formal relationship to the green. To the northeast was suburbia with a church next to the Eastside Highway, the major north-south road. Also note the very strict axial layout of the houses west of the lazy suburban roads. Exactly why such a formal arrangement was applied to this particular group is unknown.

The Eastside Highway bisected the drawing—and the town plan—and also marked the survey division line. This north-south road was two things: a grand avenue and a two-level transport system: cars above and trains below. But the subway (Wright's term) was only covered where roads and walkways crossed over and it was therefore a depressed rail line. At each intersection pedestrians were to access the rail platforms by stair. At the center of the green space and opposite the hotel was the rail station, while at the northern end there was a vehicular bridge over a shallow gully.

The obvious question: why should Wright devise such a grand transport scheme in the mountain wilderness? During the early months of 1909 there were a variety of proposals for rail lines to run down the eastern side of the valley, and there was talk of connecting eastern Idaho with the Bitter Root valley, of additional spurs to service rural industry, and of a Northern Pacific loop. As well it was suggested that an electric line be extended south from Missoula, perhaps to Hamilton or even beyond to Anaconda. The Bitter Root Valley Irrigation Company was behind both railway schemes. It was the electrified line that Wright proposed should bisect his town, but it was never built. It is clear that the line was not Wright's idea but a response to proposals of the developers, his clients. The introduction of the electrified line, however, gave Wright a chance to test his own thoughts about the separation of rail, vehicle, and pedestrian traffic. The car was not yet crazily popular and traffic engineering not yet born, but carriage, car, and urban traffic had to be considered. In his 1908 design of the Robie house in Chicago he predicted the influence of the car on domestic architecture by placing a garage *within* the house proper. In 1909 he estimated more clearly than most of his contemporaries the practical impact of car and rail on cities by his design for Bitter Root. Perhaps he was influenced by the dirty and unsatisfactory ad hoc arrangements in the large cities of North America and Europe, with their overhead rail systems or enclosed sooty underground lines and stations. He was less likely to have been influenced by the ideas of theorists such as Eugène Hénard, who proposed vertical separation in an ideal scheme of c. 1906 for Paris (which included a helicopter roof landing pad!).

It should be kept in mind that city planning as a professional endeavor was born during the decades from 1895 to 1914. During those years great efforts were directed at resolving the many problems that resulted from sudden urbanization in the nineteenth century—housing, health, corrupt politics, transport, and much more. That energy was focused on the idea of planning future urban places including additions to existing cities. Previously engineers and other technicians had used piecemeal means to serve stopgap ends. Hénard's ideas, as theoretically profound as they were, nonetheless exemplified those efforts. Other professions such as architecture and more especially landscape design began to take serious interest in the increasingly outspoken demands for rational comprehensive planning. Olmsted had many commissions for town additions and suburbs. And there was Wright's friend, the prolific architectural practitioner Daniel Burnham who published his monumental plan for Chicago in 1909. Wright was challenged by Burnham's vision but was in no way influenced by his colleague's baroque Europhilic plan. The perceived need for Chicago to obtain a plan, however, is a measure of how quickly the notion of city planning was rationalized. In 1909 Wright was one of few architects to receive a commission to design an actual town, and Bitter Root remained his only attempt (if only partially realized) until the rather imprecise Little-Farms Tract.

Wright's town design is unique in several of its features: solid blocks tight to the walkways on all four sides; a grid divisible into major sections and minor quadrants; disposition of cultural functions to the edge of the grid as part of a sylvan area; offices of community services facing a green center; separation of car (actually vehicle is a better term), pedestrian, and rail systems; strengthening traditional suburban living by placing it in a wooded garden setting; and the integration of formal landscape and townscape. Olmsted would have been pleased. All applications were tied to a logical geometric system that, it must be observed, did not dictate to Wright but was his design tool. There was neither precedent nor paradigm for Wright's plan for Bitter Root, Montana.

Wright's town plan encroached on platted orchards to the south, a fact that obviously was not relayed to him. In any event, independent of Wright the Bitter Root Valley Irrigation Company devised its own new plan; the city blocks and roads extended west rather than south. Why Wright's town plan was disregarded remains a mystery. One suspects his idea was considered too grandiose, that a smaller town center (if not the town itself) was desired by the client. Having made that decision the company then asked Wright to plan a village center, hotel, and residential areas (Figure

9.3 Plan of Bitter Root Village for a site north of Stevensville, Montana, a project to replace the proposed town of Bitter Root on the same site. Courtesy and © 1981 the Frank Lloyd Wright Foundation.

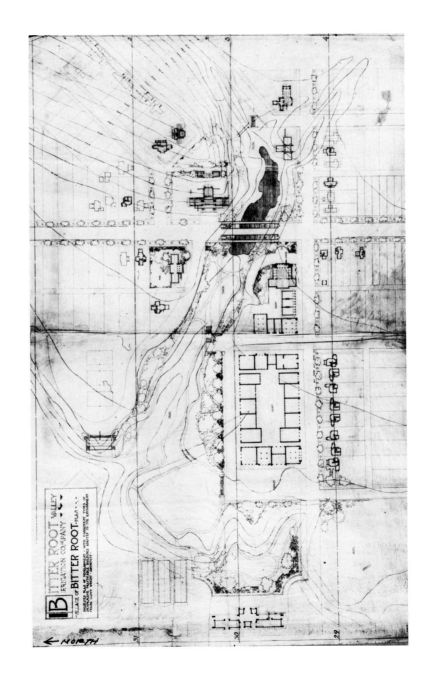

3) to the prosaic new plan. The new street plan was not Wright's; he was only asked to locate the internal functions and provide plans for the village's architecture. East of the bridge (the village is illustrated with north to the left) and south of the pond was a small school next to a church. Near to and east of the bridge was an inn; across the street a library. Land directly in front of the inn and in a shallow coulee was dedicated as a park. South of the park and in a line progressing west were an opera house, a commercial complex, then a large collection of shops and community services around a large court at the west end of which was a market. Furthest west was a railroad station. The subway and electrified line of the town plan were gone and rail transport was relocated west, yet still running north and south. North of the station were, presumably, apple storage sheds. Suburban housing was again in the northeast (now with straight streets) and in the south on narrow lots. There was no village center or square or space as such: just an intersection of two roads. Perhaps the park with its pond was to act as the social or symbolic locus. But in the wilderness of the Rocky Mountains just east of the continental divide a haphazard parkland would have meant very little. On the other hand a formal landscaped park such as Wright proposed for the town would have meant a great deal just by contrast if nothing else.

The grand proposition for a town of Bitter Root was not realized. Even with concentrated advertising and other promotions throughout the midwestern and northeastern states the scheme fell dramatically short of expectations. Many orchard trees were planted, a few roads built, some fire hydrants and a modest water supply were put in place, a golf course was partially constructed and operated for a few years, and an inn was completed in October 1909. It was the only building of many projected by Wright to reach construction stage; it burned to the ground in 1924.

The center of Bitter Root town was to be a great garden that lay before the inn. Bitter Root village and Broadacre City had no identifiable center or urban focus. Just as the idea for Broadacre City was about regional decentralization, within the city there was to be further decentralization. On the periphery of the cruciform certain similar functions were gathered together—for instance government, games and recreation, light industry and markets—but widely separated. This principle was first established at Bitter Root town where certain cultural and town functions were placed on the very edge and widely separated. The Bitter Root town plan and Broadacre City were organized by a compelling geometry and proportional system. Functional location was assigned by Wright's perception of the dynamics and importance of transport—individual, commercial, and mass. Vehicle circulation determined the geometry that defined the zoning of functions. This was also true of Wright's design in 1913 (not 1915 or 1916) of a quarter-section of land for an imaginary suburb

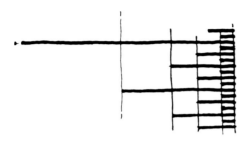

9.4 Progression of lot sizes.

south of Chicago, in response to a competition set by the City Club. It used exactly the same geometry as Broadacre City for the same reasons.[2] A main transport system (a trolley to and from Chicago's Loop) was part of the program, so Wright did not invent it. Its location on the edge was similar to that in Broadacres. The large geometrical center of the quarter-section suburb was detached housing, just as it was at Broadacre City. The commercial center was a strip development along the Chicago trolley line and therefore typical of the period.

In the town plan and in Broadacres, transport was part of a regional system that became functionally multipurpose, at least as it was to pass by or through each city. There is one other intriguing similarity. The plan for Bitter Root village contained a progression from small urban lots to large rural acreage, represented diagramatically in Figure 4. The progression was repeated at Broadacres. Much as he might have wished to be known otherwise, Wright did borrow ideas, architectural or otherwise, from others. At the philosophical level he was extraordinarily eclectic. Other authors have shown that his ideas of economics, ruralism, politics (if that is the proper term in Wright's case), and his holistic organic life were borrowed from others and applied in what might be called a Wrightian manner.

Bitter Root, Little-Farms Tract, and Broadacre City were Wright's only designs for urban form, despite his persistently expressed views about urban America that were carried in the press of his day. Two earlier complex projects were not designs for cities. First there was University Heights (erroneously called Como Orchards even by Wright), a summer colony of only seasonal housing also built in Montana in 1909–10. And second the quarter-section competition of 1913, which was limited to suburban housing, shopping, and cultural amenities; there was no industry or commerce. Broadacres was relatively peculiar in his oeuvre because it was not designed for a client but arose out of his personal musing as a theoretical proposal. That is not quite correct because he did not prepare the plan and resulting model until he had worked the Davidson commissions and then secured the financial support of Maloney and Kaufmann. The fact remains that with few exceptions throughout his career Wright prepared designs almost always in response to a client's needs.

The town of Bitter Root was to have been a more urban place than Broadacres. Bitter Root was to have been physically congested and contain a relatively high population density; it would have had its own suburb, business center, government center, and so forth. Many of those functions were to have been dispersed and physically separated by—but within—the landscape of Broadacres, a fact that enhances its status as village. This demonstrates how Wright's vision of and for urban life had rather dramatically altered after his residence in Tokyo and his personal experiences during the 1920s. One must not lose sight of Broadacres's true purpose, which, for this essay, had been so carefully expressed by Ralph Borsodi, as quoted in chapter 5. Broadacre City could not have been conceived by Wright prior to 1928. But then, like the Fellowship, if all had gone well professionally and otherwise there would have been no time—and no need—to design a theoretical city and build a hypothetical model.

10 And Le Corbusier?

Many ideas for new cities were bandied about during the first third of the century and there had been some practical results: Letchworth Garden City and Radburn, New Jersey, are popular examples. Probably the best-known architectural polemicist of the period was Le Corbusier. Anticipating the context of Wright's excursions to Moscow and London, it is interesting to compare briefly a few aspects of Le Corbusier's and Wright's ideas.

Effectively there were no individual houses in Le Corbusier's schemes for everyone was meant to live in a high-rise or massed housing:

A Man = A Cell

From Cells = A City,

he said as early as 1929.[1] Typical of most European architects since Antonio Sant'Elia in 1913, at least those who were fond of speculating about new urban forms, the city tended to be conceived as a building, as a piece of architecture, as a megastructure rather than a problem that could be solved by rational application knitted to holistic theories.[2] Wright and Le Corbusier proposed to use the highway more effectively—or at least more emphatically—than it was in contemporary experience, but Le Corbusier's elevated roadways crisscrossed his city distributing traffic immediately within. He envisaged a perimeter forest and green "protected zone" around his city. Wright's city was to be within a natural forested garden. Le Corbusier would disperse industry while Wright integrated it within Broadacres and within walking distance of home. The two architects shared some ideas about agriculture but farms were more highly valued in Broadacres. Le Corbusier geographically isolated small villages for "Radiant Farms." Fundamentally he wanted to recreate the metropolis in another form, concretized by inflexibility. Wright wanted to abandon the metropolis completely in favor of a series of unique small towns.

Both men foresaw farms run on a cooperative basis: community power centers, pools of labor, tractors, and other equipment, cooperative storage and distribution—the kibbutz and the Soviet *kolkhoz* are similar. Both architects also believed the state should distribute land and own

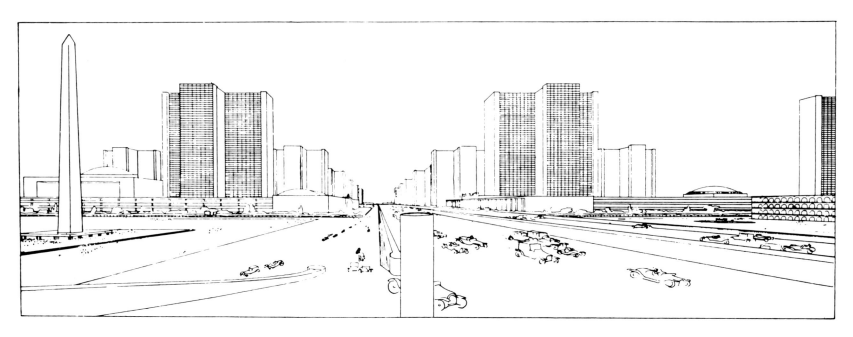

**10.1 Perspective of "Une ville contempo-
raine," a project by Le Corbusier of 1922.
Published often in the 1930s and in the
first edition of Le Corbusier and Pierre
Jeanneret, *Oeuvre complète, 1910–1929*
(Paris, 1929).**

public utilities. Both found much wanting in modern cities. But Le Corbusier was a typical European urban dweller; Wright was of the open lands of western America. Le Corbusier would virtually destroy and then rebuild; Wright would ignore the existing city, expecting grass to grow on its streets, in favor of new towns. Le Corbusier proposed to collect towers centrally for the urban elite, while Wright dispersed single towers isolated in green areas on the periphery of Broadacre City for government, commerce, and business. Only later did he include high-rise housing. While Wright was certain of the value of the gifted artist-architect, Le Corbusier had a faith in "the superior wisdom of the city designer."[3] He unashamedly promoted the need for an autocratic government to see his designs to fruition, and in a very real sense planning power became more important to him than ideology. To fully appreciate this view, consider that central to his Paris Voisin Plan (exhibited in 1925) was the obliterating of the city's traditional fabric; little was to be saved but Notre Dame and the Louvre. As well, during the 1920s Le Corbusier was a member of the proto-fascist Redressement Français, he wrote favorably of Mussolini, and after the German occupation in 1941 he tried "to persuade the Nazi-sponsored Vichy government of France to implement his plan for Algiers."[4]

Even in the 1950s when Wright proposed a single mile-high skyscraper it was aimed to a large extent at satisfying urbanists. Its construction would then enable the freeing of America's land for the more desirable alternative, Broadacre Cities. The Mile High Illinois "would absorb, justify, and legitimize the gregarious instinct of humanity," said Wright, and as far as he was concerned the necessity for people to band together in his building "would mop up what now remains of urbanism and leave us free to do Broadacre City."[5]

However, as historian George Collins rightly observes, "the world was not electrified by Wright's agrarianism in the 1930s the way it had been by Le Corbusier's Futurism [sic] in the 1920s."[6] And there were other dissimilarities and parallels. Is it too obvious to say how extraordinarily different the concept of home and place as expressed in their architectural resolutions? If the words deceived, the drawings were patent: uniformity and conformity versus individuality and pluralism.

On first examination it may appear that the Broadacre City proposal was not influential on the course of city planning and design at midcentury. But further consideration reveals otherwise. As previously noted, Broadacres was widely published and discussed from 1932 onward. The combination of the two concepts, regional planning and Broadacre City (including new towns), had a profound effect on establishing the need for and then offering methods of decentralization in the postwar period. On the other side, one result of Le Corbusier's theories during the same period was "urban renewal"—the demolishing of old buildings and therefore the existing social fabric, to be replaced with high-rise towers.

Wright gambled when he built the model. He must have been aware that by formalizing his idea in architectural and three-dimensional terms he would weaken the concept by specifying all variety of idiomatic detail. Or he might diminish the value of his own architecture by placing it, if abstractly, in an unfamiliar and rather alien context. Broadacre City was, after all, a fluid, undetermined, flexible, existential idea, one that in architectural terms was meant to respond to site and need. His verbalizations from 1930 to 1934 had attracted some attention, but was it enough to induce understanding? Would a diagram have sufficed? And would it have served his intentions adequately? More to the point, he desperately needed money and the commission to build the model was fortuitous; he also *wanted* the publicity that would inevitably come from it. Exhibition of the model, with resulting articles and so forth, was an opportunity not to be missed.

There were two other problems. First, Broadacre City was not a theory, at least not a completely resolved theory. It did not contain a body of ideas or a set of terms that could be measured or could be rationally argued one way or another. His writings were too vague or imprecise to be called a treatise. This imprecision discouraged careful reading and analysis while encouraging equally vague and often emotional responses. Second, he was not proposing a utopia as many observers have suggested. Lyman Tower Sargent's introduction to the subject included one specification: a utopia must describe "fairly completely an imaginary society"; Wright did not. Therefore the architect's pragmatic dream was not included in Sargent's compendium of twentieth-century utopias, and rightly so.[7] Historian John Sergeant was correct when he described Broadacre City as "a scenario for change."

Wright's son John wondered if Broadacre City might have been inspired in part by his father's favorite authors, especially the poets. John listed the New Englanders and transcendentalists only: Henry David Thoreau, Walt Whitman, Emerson, and Henry Van Dyke: all "Papa's friends." Whitman was special, and particularly one poem entitled "Song of the Broad Axe" from which John quoted the following passages.

The place where a great city stands is not the place of stretch'd wharves, docks,
  manufactures, deposits of produce merely, . . .
Nor the place of the tallest and costliest buildings . . .
Nor the place of the most numerous population.
Where the city stands that is belov'd . . .

. . . no monuments exist to heroes but in the common words and deeds . . .

Where the slave ceases, and the master of the slave[s] ceases . . .

Where the citizen is always the head and ideal, and [the] President, Mayor, Governor . . . are

   agents for pay,

Where children are taught to be laws to themselves, and to depend on themselves . . .

Where speculations on the soul are encouraged . . .

Where the city of the cleanliness of the sexes stands,

Where the city of the healthiest fathers stand,

Where the city of the best-bodied mothers stands,

There the great city stands.[8]

The stream of events that composed Wright's career was intimately linked to a vision. With the preparation and presentation of his Kahn lectures, with the completion of his autobiography, and—even if intimately indebted to Wijdeveld—with the formation of his fellowship, he was more strongly convinced of the propriety of his organic theory, which he perceived as holistic and spherical: "I now realize that organic architecture is life and life is organic architecture or both are in vain."[9] With purpose defined, by December 1933 he could announce with certainty his intention and means:

Well Taliesin believes the day has come . . . for a rejection of the too many minor traditions in favor of great elemental Tradition that is decentralization; sees a going forward in new spirit to the ground as the basis for a good life that sets the human soul free above artificial anxieties and all vicarious powers, able and willing to work again as the first condition of true gentility. Taliesin sees work itself where there is something growing and living in it as not only the salt and savor of existence but as the opportunity for bringing "heaven" decently back to Earth where it really belongs. Taliesin sees art as no less than ever the expression of a way of life in this machine age if its civilization is to live.[10]

11 Lectures and Exhibitions: Willcox

The discussion so far has shown that in the 1930s lectures, talks, chats, speeches—whatever they were called but most certainly not formal papers—were important financially and as polemical vehicles, more so than any other period of Wright's life. This is also true of exhibitions. In most instances lectures and exhibitions came about as a result of exercising a friendship. Most relationships were related to his architectural practice and to the Fellowship once it was under way, or to his movements in that part of society in which he found succor or intellectual support for his often singular interpretations of art, politics, economics, or philosophy. Strangely, he had few close friends within the architectural profession, or to be precise, his friendships with professional colleagues were usually of relatively short duration; but a few stood the test of personality strains and jealousies over time: Cecil Corwin (perhaps his dearest friend, he was to say), Raymond Hood, Jens Jensen, and Andrew Rebori come to mind.

Two examples, presented in some detail, will help explain the complexity and concentric nature of these relationships, together with the reasons and means for the lectures and exhibitions. They are examples only, but typical of this period of Wright's life. The first occurred in the early 1930s. It involved a social and semiprofessional event little known to Wright aficionados or people in the Pacific Northwest. It exemplified Wright's transition from the troubled twenties to the viable thirties. The event had its beginning in the heyday of his private practice in Chicago and Oak Park, Illinois, at the turn of the century. The second example extended through the thirties and culminated almost at the same instant he left for Moscow. In both cases Wright formulated responses to challenges inherent in personal trials of the moment, in a decade of rather dramatic economic and political change as well as artistic consolidation.

When he received a letter in October 1930 from Walter R. B. Willcox, head of the Department of Architecture at the University of Oregon, expressing interest in an exhibition of his work, Wright was most receptive. Relations with Willcox went back thirty years to the Oak Park days. In the 1880s and 1890s Willcox had worked in Chicago for an electrical firm and through the building industry he came to know Louis Sullivan. His admiration for the elder architect lasted throughout Willcox's life. In fact, on learning of Sullivan's death in 1924 he proposed and designed a memorial to his mentor. It was in Chicago that Willcox decided to become an architect; he was in his mid-twenties. An encouraging letter from Sullivan helped him begin in the Boston office of the professionally impeccable New Englander R. Clipston Sturgis. Willcox also took an occasional class at the Massachusetts Institute of Technology but he did not favor Boston's educational citadel of propriety, so when he began formal studies he elected the University of Pennsylvania. "Poverty and overwork contributed to an attack of yellow jaundice" that ended his student days.[1]

Returning to his hometown, Burlington, Vermont, he started from scratch and soon built up a good architectural practice. During this time he traveled now and then to see his brother-in-law, Lew Porter, whom Willcox described rather inaccurately as one client with whom Wright "started" his architectural career. On these occasions Willcox sometimes stopped to see a close friend from Burlington and fellow architect Charles E. White, Jr., who was then working in Wright's studio at Oak Park. That was during the years 1903 to 1905, after which White left the studio to set up his own practice. (He designed mainly houses in the beginning, not so much in Wright's prairie style but more English in character.) These visits to the Oak Park studio familiarized Willcox with an exciting period in Wright's architectural career.

Despite his developing Burlington practice, disturbed by the demand of New England society for historical eclecticism, architectural and otherwise, he again uprooted himself in search of, to paraphrase, a place untamed by social fetishes and pedantry. He settled in Seattle, Washington, in 1907 and established a partnership with William J. Sayward. Together they developed a creditable practice. The indefatigable Willcox contributed much to the profession, a fact recognized by his election as Fellow in the American Institute of Architects as early as 1910.

At age fifty-three, in 1922 Willcox accepted the headship of the Department of Architecture at the University of Oregon. There he created probably the first non–beaux-arts course of architecture in America and over the next twenty-five years he nurtured the course to some renown. But he did not see the rise of somewhat similar and often parallel systems that grew out of reactions to the beaux-arts in America after World War II, for Willcox died in 1947. As well as devising a new, open educational system he also argued strongly against the aesthetic imperialism of the Beaux-Arts Institute of Design in New York and the Francophile beaux-arts architectural style, or styles. Impressed with Sullivan's Transportation building erected for the Chicago World's Columbian Exposition in 1893, he had followed Sullivan's career and then Wright's "own efforts with great and continued interest." His visits to Wright's studio in 1904–05 were only one indication of his admiration for Wright and for the architects and craftsmen attracted to the studio. It was Willcox who informed Sullivan that Wright was a promising young architect, and it was Willcox who informed Wright of the opening with Adler & Sullivan where Wright began working in 1888.

In 1929 the University of Oregon began a search for a director of the Department of Sculpture, which was administratively in the same school as the architecture department. Willcox recommended Richard Bock, who had executed sculptural works for Sullivan and many of Chicago's Prairie School architects including Wright. Notable were pieces for Wright's Larkin Administration Building in Buffalo of 1903–06 and Midway Gardens in Chicago of 1913–14. Willcox contacted White in Chicago to support his recommendation and by 1930 Bock was established on the Eugene campus.[2] The Chicago connection with Willcox was tenuous but vital.

11.1 Walter R. B. Willcox in about 1936, courtesy Mr. Wallace Hayden and the University of Oregon Library.

It is not surprising, therefore, that in October 1930 Willcox wrote to Wright expressing a hope of obtaining an exhibition of Wright's works that was then on display at the Art Institute of Chicago. Willcox reintroduced himself, refreshing Wright's memory of those earlier days in the studio when they talked about projects "in progress" or Wright's recent trip to Japan and the prints he brought back. Willcox believed the exhibition "would be a great interest" to his students, greater, he thought, "than that felt in the eastern schools." Willcox explained: "My assurance is founded upon the fact that Sullivan and yourself have had my inspiration in revamping the course here from the pattern of all other architectural schools in this country I know of. . . . All competitive projects have been discontinued, each student having his individual problems, developed from actual topographies. The importance of the human being, his needs and circumstances, rather than scholastic [architectural] patterns, is emphasized." He added a tempting morsel for iconoclastic Wright to savor: "Style" is "never mentioned in the drafting room, and of course no copying of anybody is done, however much the students are influenced by their experience of buildings. Practicality of plan, reasonable use of materials, composition in design are sought without conscious resort to formal precedent."[3] These brief comments reflected his own training to some degree and exposed an egalitarianism that pervaded much of Willcox's thinking. In a parallel manner his architecture often carried vernacular theses. Indeed, tasty stuff for a like-minded architect.

Wright replied immediately, allowing Willcox to be "no doubt right about The Show going West." While it had been mounted at the Architectural League in New York City and at Princeton University, Yale and Cornell universities could or would not raise money for The Show; the exhibition therefore had few further prospects in the East. In his reply to Willcox, Wright specified the exhibition's needs: the installation required his personal attention; "there are over 600 photographs and about 1000 Drawings, sets of plans and four models. I might decide to send it to San Francisco and Los Angeles instead of East,—in which case it might go to you first and then down the coast. It would take $350.—to get it to you, set it up and knock it down again, together with such local help as we may need,—have you got it?"[4]

After a few weeks the two men reached general agreement. At one point in their correspondence Wright did not hide his financial dilemma: "I hate to have any money consideration attached to the show," lamented Wright. "Were I not financially floored there would be none. As it is I am unable to undertake to properly set the thing up and transport it . . . without knowing where the money is coming from." Wright suggested that a "lecture by myself usually goes, and should go with the exhibit and I should like to give these on the Coast after February 10th."[5] This was often the case. The exhibition at the Art Institute of Chicago, for example, was accompanied by two talks called the Scammon Lectures. These had been published by the Institute in a little-known pamphlet called *Two Lectures on Architecture*.

Moreover, Willcox agreed to arrange the coastal tour for The Show. The Portland Chapter of the AIA did not want the exhibition in their town but sent some money to help install it at Eugene. The architecture department at the University of California at Berkeley said no. So did the University of Southern California, whose dean of architecture, A. C. Weatherhead, in rejecting the show stated that he failed to agree "with all of Mr. Wright's philosophy."[6]

In fact Frank's first son Lloyd Wright, an architect then living in Los Angeles, on behalf of his father attempted to make most arrangements in California, but without much success. For instance, Lloyd was refused by the Los Angeles County Museum which was unable to schedule such a show, and by the Art Department, University of California, Berkeley, which could not find the money. A similar reason was offered by the California Palace of the Legion of Honor.

An underlying problem facing Lloyd was competition: an exhibition was being prepared for the Western Association of Art Museum Directors by Pauline Schindler, wife of one of Wright's former employees during the period 1917–1921, Rudolph Schindler. When first planned in 1930 as "Contemporary Creative Architects" it included Richard Neutra, Jacques Peters, Schindler, and Wright. Except for Wright they were part of Schindler's Los Angeles professional circle, all of whom were protagonists for some kind of European modernism (also, oddly, some American art deco) in California even though Schindler and Neutra had worked for Wright. Schindler and Neutra were Austrian immigrants; Schindler had arrived in Chicago in the teens and Neutra in the early 1920s. Wright's work had been included by Pauline Schindler, but when he was informed of the plans for the exhibition Wright had responded that it was a principle of his never to display his products "except in an exhibit on my own work." Therefore, he said, "kindly omit me from the proposed exhibition."[7] Without Wright the exhibition was prepared for various venues on the West Coast during 1931 under the title "Contemporary Creative Architecture of California."

If this was his principle it was one quickly bent, for about this time he was enticed by the prestigious New York Museum of Modern Art to join their exhibition of "Modern Architects." Those selected were all practitioners of the European architectural style of the chaste cubic white box, except Wright of course. Even so, Henry-Russell Hitchcock, one of the MoMA organizers, confessed that Wright reluctantly participated—without his "enthusiastic approval" were Hitchcock's words.[8] Anyway, Pauline Schindler's show was under way in 1931 as was MoMA's, which eventually was mounted at Bullock's in Los Angeles in 1932. Preparations for Wright's show for Willcox nonetheless went ahead smartly if not under full steam. Up north Harlan Thomas, head of the Department of Architecture at the University of Washington, said yes and negotiations between Willcox and Thomas began at once.

Over the years Wright's various lectures were sometimes published and often covered in the local press. All were thematically related. As he hoped, they did in fact have the effect of reuniting the architect with his profession, lay bodies, and the general public. His determination to acquire public attention—as well as needed cash—is revealed in a January 1931 letter to Willcox urging the academic on with his arrangements. In part he said that he was scheduled to give two lectures, "University and Art Museum," in Minneapolis on February 10. Then he was to be a "Speaker" at the AIA banquet at the University of Michigan on February 21. "I have five lectures to give in New York City the week beginning the 23rd of February—'Twentieth Century Club, School of Social Research, Women's University Club, "Audac"'—etc. . . . Seattle is a likely City—so my son Lloyd writes, and he is getting in touch with someone he knows there." He mentioned that Europe was "bidding for the show" including Amsterdam and Berlin.

His commitment to Willcox was acknowledged in a letter to his cousin Richard Lloyd Jones just before the Northwest tour. He confirmed "The Show" (his capitalization) for Eugene and Seattle and mentioned that New York "went over swell. Six addresses in five days—all the best possible auspices—and plenty of great publicity."[9] Addresses in Minneapolis, Ann Arbor, and New York (especially to the New School of Social Research) were essentially paraphrases of his Princeton lectures and aspects of his thesis of a disappearing city.

In fact publicity took precedence over money. As the West Coast tour approached he offered his show and lectures at less than cost: "Why not charge admission to the lecture—giving away tickets to students—swell the funds maybe? and turning over to me what-ever was above your own expenses?—or something like that."[10] (Tickets in Eugene were fifty cents.) The records show that the fees agreed upon were not forthcoming and Wright was out of pocket: as a matter of pride Wilcox personally made up the difference.

After much toing and froing The Show was on. Wright's itinerary was to travel on the "Olympian" across the northern states to Seattle, then by the "Cascade" down to Eugene, and then back to Seattle. Because of a train accident he missed a Portland connection and so continued to Eugene by car. His Show preceeded him and opened on 6 March 1931 in the University of Oregon's Art Museum. He had been informed that Bock was the school's sculptor and they must have renewed shared memories. Wright gave the lecture at the university's Music Auditorium on the seventh. The Show was not a modest affair: displayed were all types of drawings plus photographs and models that together numbered over 500 items. Considering the quality of his artifacts and their number it was most assuredly a major exhibition.

Wright also attended an evening Club Night, as they were called. These were informal gatherings at Willcox's home for the purpose of "discussion and cordial debate on any issues of current relevance or controversy."[11] Students, faculty, and out-of-town guests participated including architects such as Serge Chermayeff and the German emigré architect Erich Mendelsohn. Topics were not preannounced and none was excluded. This informal, rather familial, social and educational practice became one of the hallmarks of Wright's own relations with apprentices of the Taliesin Fellowship.

While in Eugene Wright received an invitation to visit Salem on his return journey north. The offer was initiated by J. M. Clifford of the Oregon Board of Control's State Purchasing Department, who was acting with the "informal consent" of his board.[12] Clifford's purpose was quite clear: he had made arrangments for Wright to visit Oregon's capital city so he might become involved in plans for a new capitol building. Wright was to visit possible sites in the afternoon and then over dinner to meet "influential persons" about the project. Clifford confided that he hoped "to bring about . . . a demand for your services as architect of the proposed development." Clifford, who was also president of the Salem Arts League, arranged for Wright to give a public address under League auspices and invited Portland architects to attend. Clifford's plans were an attempt "to crystallize sentiment" in Wright's favor,[13] and Clifford optimistically suggested to Willcox that the Salem stopover might result in a job for Wright in the future.

Apparently it all went much as planned. In Salem he met the new governor, Julius Meier, the secretary of state, "several Portland architects," three newspaper editors, and, as promised, some "prominent citizens."[14] Indeed, a capitol design board was established and Willcox was asked to be a member but declined, yet continued to promote Wright. With the opportunity at hand, Wright asked Clifford to propose to the powers that be that he be retained with $10,000 to prepare preliminary sketches and a model, a proposal not accepted.

It was at the Salem dinner that George Putnam, publisher of the local newspaper the *Capital Journal,* asked Wright to design a new printing plant and office building. Putnam (no relation to the New York publishing family) was born in New Orleans, attended the University of Nebraska, worked for a number of newspapers on the West Coast as well as the Scripps-McRae press service (now United Press), and founded the *Spokane Press.* He had purchased and merged most of the Medford, Oregon, newspapers before selling out and buying the *Capital Journal* in 1919, for which he had since acted as publisher and editor. His relationship with the newspaper ended in 1961—a forty-two-year association—when he died in a fire that burned his home. At the Salem dinner in 1931 a rather "lit" Putnam sat next to Wright and seemingly the publisher "took to me," to quote Wright. "Suddenly," Wright said Putnam said, "I've found my architect." Putnam offered a commission and retainer of $1,000.[15]

After the rather exhilarating prospects suggested at Salem, Wright proceeded north to Seattle. The Show ran in the Puget Sound city from 11 March through the weekend of 15 March in the Henry Gallery on the University of Washington campus, to modest publicity. (It is rather sad that at both venues The Show had such short exposure.) The lecture—by the "Einstein of Architecture"—was presented on the twelfth in the university's Meany Hall and was sponsored by the Department of Architecture, the AIA, and the Seattle Art Institute. On Friday the thirteenth, among other adventures, he visited the new *Seattle Times* building which he described as a "splendid" example of modern architecture "at the same time a manufacturing plant of highest efficiency."[16] One of the more satisfying social functions of the tour must have been a family dinner with a former employee of the Oak Park days, Andrew Willatsen, who had been practicing in Seattle for nearly twenty years. Willatsen also arranged for Wright to attend an AIA luncheon. On Sunday, Wright and Olgivanna boarded a train for the return journey to Wisconsin. The exhibition was quickly bundled into cases that were shipped back to Spring Green on the nineteenth. In a letter to Willcox of 24 April, Wright acknowledged that "The show is back here again."

Considering everything the architect was pleased. His thanks to Willcox included an exquisite original Sullivan pencil drawing executed in 1922 of a design for terra cotta.

However, politics intruded upon the future course of events. The trouble went back to the strangely wrought Oregon gubernatorial election of 1930. The Republican candidate, George W. Joseph, died early in the campaign and the party declared the conservative old-guard Phil Metschan its candidate. His selection did not please liberal Republicans who then enticed Julius Meier to run as an independent. The opposition candidate, Edward F. Bailey, was nominated by a narrow ("razor-thin") margin in a faction-ridden Democratic primary. The party would not unite behind his candidature and Bailey felt he was making useless efforts, "running against a dead man."[17] As a result of the Democrats' ambivalence and Meier's advocacy of relatively popular resolutions to issues related to public utilities and ways of combatting the Depression, Meier was elected governor by what has been estimated as the largest majority ever given a gubernatorial candidate—double the vote of both his opponents combined. Fiscal responsibility in a variety of forms, as it turned out, was one key to Meier's eventual success as governor after he took office in January 1931. Clifford and many of his colleagues were among early causalties of severe budget cutting and liberally dispersed patronage. During late 1931 most of the Oregon Board of Control was fired and some of the State Purchasing Department.

In a long three-page typewritten letter to Wright explaining some of the problems and his own bitter disappointment, the Oregon bureaucrat added his hope that the architect would obtain the state capitol building commission. Clifford earnestly and sincerely believed that a Wright-designed capitol "would be a 'Mecca' for art lovers from all parts of the world," and that could be only good for Oregon.[18] In response Wright asked the beleaguered Clifford to continue promoting him and to ask Willcox to do the same, adding with characteristic ambiguity but unusual humility, "I am a poor politician for lay[ing] wires for work."[19] Now well outside the circles of power, Clifford advised Wright to work through publisher Putnam or reliable politicians. Clifford's personal crusade to obtain Oregon's most important architectural commission for America's greatest architect came to zero.

And Wright's disappointments continued to accumulate. He worked on George Putnam's Salem printing and office building through the remaining months of 1931 and into 1932, program details of which, together with the retainer, arrived soon after his return to Spring Green (as did some financial support for the tour). Encouraged by affairs in the Northwest, in June he went so far as to propose to his son Lloyd that he work as administrator and supervisor for whatever commissions might arise and that they share fifty-fifty the profits. Immensely satisfied, in March 1932 Wright sent the plans and other drawings to Putnam. The response was unemotional and rather brief. Putnam liked "the general scheme," though he was not sure of certain unspecified aspects, and he saw "little chance of . . . going ahead with construction at the present time." In view of events in Oregon his reasons were as might have been expected—"conditions have changed materially since you were here"; there was a shortage of cash, sales were down, the Depression.[20] And so another of Wright's ideas became a dream unfulfilled.

Wright's design was brilliant. Glass exterior walls hung from a mushroom structure; the illuminated building was meant to glow at night and reveal its inner workings of giant presses rolling and folding newsprint at dramatic speed. Around and above the press floor was to be a mezzanine for administration. The press floor was to have been separated from the "stems" of the

11.2 Ground-floor and site plan of the
Capital Journal **building, Salem, Oregon, a**
project of 1931–32. Courtesy and © 1979
the Frank Lloyd Wright Foundation.

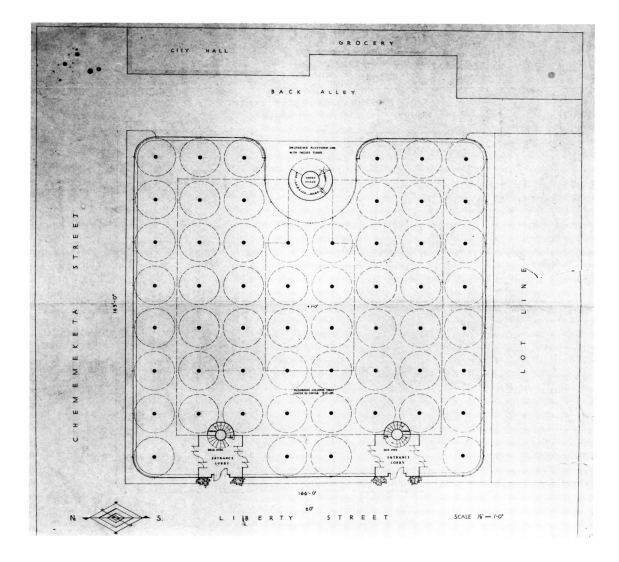

**11.3 Section of the *Capital Journal* build-
ing, Salem, Oregon, a project of 1931–32.
Courtesy and © 1979 the Frank Lloyd
Wright Foundation.**

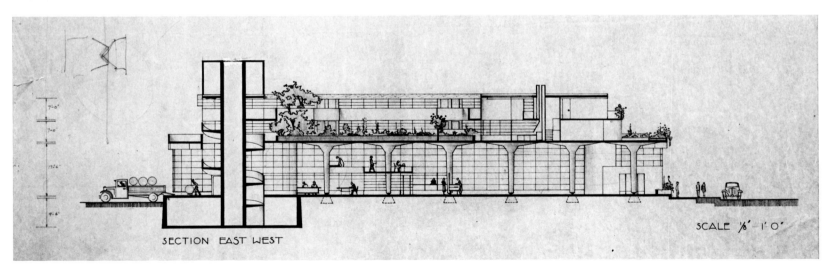

SECTION EAST WEST

SCALE ⅛'-1'0'

11.4 Perspective of the *Capital Journal* building, Salem, Oregon, a project of 1931–32. Note that the interior mushroom columns are outlined, indicating an intended transparency. Courtesy and © 1985 the Frank Lloyd Wright Foundation.

mushrooms so that the inevitable vibration of the presses would not transfer to the upper floor, roof, or exterior walls. The top two floors were to contain one owner's and twelve bachelor apartments placed around a roof garden. It was an architectual concept that extended the notions of the Central European structural aesthetic of glass and prism beyond what other architects had articulated at the time; yet it was purely Wrightian. As well, the plan was academically secure in its plain symmetry.

It is true that Wright used the mushroom structure and some of the broader details of the *Capital Journal* building in the Johnson Wax Administration Building (1937–39) at Racine, Wisconsin, especially in and around the administration hall, the great "Workroom." It takes little imagination to picture the presses aligned within the interior, roaring noisily. But the Johnson building could only partially have mitigated the architect's disappointment.

There can be no doubt that in Wright's mind the Racine building was based on the Salem building. Architectually it is obvious, and on one drawing entitled "Glass Building for the Capital Journal" Wright later wrote, "Original of the Johnson Bldg." But note: the primary reason for the mushroom structure was to keep vibration away from roof and upper-floor structures. Such a requirement did not exist in the Johnson building. On the contrary, the great high-ceilinged administration workroom is for quiet, solitary office work, not for giant vibrating presses or other huge and noisy machines. Also note that the exterior walls for the Salem building were to have been transparent glass. On the Johnson building they are solid brick; all exterior life is excluded to office personnel. He used the same plans (ground floor, mezzanine, and second floor of rented offices rather than apartments), section, elevation, materials, and the mushroom structure for the unrealized Freund y Cia. department store in San Salvador, El Salvador, in 1954; that is the first scheme, not the later corruptions. Here the great space and mezzanine were to be devoted to static display and sales.[21] The "dendriform" columns were enlarged and employed in a design for a relatively large defense plant in 1942, to have been located in Pittsfield, Massachusetts. The primary consideration for industrial and manufacturing buildings is open unobstructed space well lighted from above. With a forest of columns twenty-five feet on center as proposed by Wright there would have been great difficulties in locating machines, assembly lines and other processes and equipment. And it is doubtful if the use of the ball joint at the base of the column would have served any real purpose. Perhaps these are reasons why the project did not get beyond preliminary sketches. The mushroom columns were then employed in 1955 within another proposed office and factory building, the Lenkurt Electric Company, San Mateo, California, and again there is little sense in their use. As with

11.5 Interior photograph c. 1939 of the
Johnson Wax building, Racine, Wisconsin,
1936–39, courtesy of S. C. Johnson and
Son, Inc.

most good ideas derived from a specific need, when transferred to another clearly unequal situation they often became weakened.

This was not the first nor last instance in which Wright carelessly reemployed a concept, an idea, or a detail. Further, it needs to be said that the Johnson Wax Research Tower of 1946–49, located next to the administration building, was perhaps too obviously inspired by—maybe "copied" from is a better word—Buckminster Fuller's 4-D tower housing as published from time to time beginning in 1932. Fuller was a close professional colleague around 1932–33 and Wright was quite familiar with his theoretical and conceptual presentations.

Other than Putnam's preliminary drawings Wright was unable to secure work as a result of his tour. Prior to his visit he had, of course, produced works for the Pacific northwestern states and southwestern Canada. First was the University Heights summer community, a complex of buildings outside Darby, Montana, designed and partially constructed during 1909–10. Then a few months after University Heights was commissioned he was asked to design the town and village of Bitter Root, near Stevensville, Montana. The village was begun in 1909 and an inn to his design was constructed in 1909–10.[22] In 1911 at Banff National Park a pavilion was completed in association with Canadian architect Francis C. Sullivan. There was the little-known Schindler and Wright design for a large riverside soldier's memorial park and recreation area in the city of Wenatchee, Washington, of 1919; but like Putnam's building, it remained a dream.[23] Beginning in the 1940s a few houses were designed and built in the Pacific Northwest, commissions that resulted from the massive publicity he received in the late 1930s and from the success of the second edition of his autobiography which appeared in 1943.

There was one rather nice result of the trip, presumably an outgrowth of the Salem visit. In July 1931 the young Portland architect Pietro Belluschi sought Wright's advice about a proposed museum for the Portland Art Association. Belluschi's plain design was meeting resistance, and more generally he found it impossible for young architects "to be spiritually alive in the right sense. In this country we are inevitably kicked between fashion and dead tradition." And further: "You [Wright] have sounded an intellectual awaking throughout the world, but our great public needs to have the trumpets blown into their ears." How Wright must have loved those remarks. Belluschi enclosed drawings with his letter. Wright found the exterior "sensible" and the floor plan "simple and sensible." Of the prolific A. E. Doyle, the architect with whom Belluschi was then working, Wright wondered: "can't Doyle stand up for Architecture?"[24]

Wright's contacts at this time with artists or posh society, so to speak, were nearly nonexistent; he did not seek them and they did not seek him. Typically, the Pacific Northwest Academy of Arts was not involved with Wright's presence in Seattle; just five days after Wright's lecture the Academy held their "Architect's Night," where only local professionals participated as speakers, as well as Harlan Thomas. The event was announced while Wright was in Seattle. In general, Wright did not aspire to be part of such society-driven enclaves, in fact he avoided them with success, though individuals within those enclaves were another matter (as in the case of J. M. Clifford).

Wright's published recollections of the visit to the Northwest were brief and uncharacteristically appreciative. "From the excellent state university at Eugene, Oregon, came a hand-lettered appeal for an exhibition of my work signed by all the architectural students and their shepherd, Walter Wilcox [sic]. Walter Wilcox is one of the best shepherds. That it came at all touched me at this time. And though so far away I managed with their help to get there with the exhibition. Then I went to Seattle. A success."[25] (Obviously the students' appeal *followed* Willcox's initial inquiry to Wright.) The choice of the word "shepherd" was a careful acknowledgment of Willcox's close association with his students as exemplified by the stimulating educational evenings held in his home. But typical of Wright's postmortems of similar affairs, he said nothing else. His private recollections were more interesting if not wholly relevant. To his friend and former client Aline Barnsdall (who had sent her daughter to Taliesin to be a Fellow) he included the following comments in a long, chatty letter of May 1934. The only region, he said,

is the all year round climate of the far Northwest—the most beautiful part of our country and destined because of its beauty and wholeness to be the future center of culture for our country. I mean Oregon and Washington with their beautiful seas, snow capped mountains, forest, fruits and flowers. If the good "God" had cast my role there how lucky I should now consider myself. As for . . . the great midwest. . . . It bores me."[26]

Wright abandoned the city, in his case Chicago, in 1910 to return to his family's Wisconsin farm. He left the Midwest for Japan and the American West Coast in 1916, and after his troubles in the 1920s he often traveled west. In 1936, after a bout of pneumonia, he was advised to find a dry, warm climate and immediately decided on central Arizona. Thereafter he divided summers and winters between rural Wisconsin and the desert: he did not reside in an American city after 1910. There is no doubt that his boredom was induced by sad memories and lost causes associated with those old and too familiar places.

Documents indicate that essentially the same exhibition material had the following itinerary. It had been organized for venues in the northeastern U.S. and began at Princeton University in mid-1930, where Wright gave six lectures. In September and October it was at the Art Institute of Chicago, where he presented two lectures. It then went to the Architectural League in New York City, and there he gave lectures during February 1931 on succeeding dates to the 20th Century Club, Brooklyn, the Women's University Club, AUDAC and the Art Center, and the School of Social Research.[27] Appearances at the University of Oregon and the University of Washington followed. Wright had said that Cornell, Harvard, MIT, and Yale had rejected it; perhaps others did likewise. By this time he had enticed Wijdeveld to organize—and prepare mounts, print catalogs, and all else for—a European tour.

The Show began in Amsterdam (where the U.S. Ambassador attempted but was out of ignorance unable to open it, then to Berlin where architect Erich Mendelsohn opened it, and then Frankfurt, Stuttgart, Brussels, Antwerp, and Paris. Wright hoped it would visit Munich, Hamburg, Zurich, Prague, and even Tokyo, but it did not make these venues. It ran in Rotterdam before Wijdeveld finally returned it to Spring Green in January 1932. The Show was then mounted in Milwaukee.[28] (The 1932 Museum of Modern Art exhibition in New York City in which he participated was a separate affair.) Wright was unashamedly hustling Wright by any and all means. He did not accompany the exhibition overseas because he could not afford to. And anyway, he was paid $1,000 plus all expenses to act as a juror of final designs for the Columbus Memorial Lighthouse competition held at Rio de Janeiro, Brazil. He and Olgivanna traveled during September 1931 courtesy of the Pan American Union. The money must have seemed heaven-sent; the job perhaps less so: "The first Jury has already ruined the competition by picking out ten imitations of N.Y. skyscrapers, or man-eaters of wolken krabber [sic] for a light-house."[29]

The presentation of Wright's exhibition in 1931 was the result of a long if not continuous interest by young European architects in Wright's theories and practices. After the remarkable reaction to his Wasmuth publications of 1909, 1910, and 1911, there was a second, less generative period of interest in the 1920s. It began in Holland as early as 1913, was revived there in 1918 and continued thereafter. With few exceptions all articles used illustrations from the 1910 and 1911 German books, from Wijdeveld's *Life-Work of Frank Lloyd Wright* published by Wendingen in 1925, or from Wright's articles "In the Cause of Architecture" for *Architectural Record* during 1927–28, for which he was highly paid: $500 for each.[30] The *Record* essays were digested in Europe and other foreign centers.

While not all are yet recorded, the count so far of known publications on Wright in Europe is revealing: two in 1921 and again in 1922; none in 1923; two in 1924 when the 1910 portfolio was republished by Wasmuth and the Parisian journal *L'Architecture vivante* joined the widening circle; four in 1925; sixteen in 1926; eight in 1927; none in 1928; three in 1929; and only a couple each year thereafter except during the 1931 exhibition.[31] The statistics reveal the sudden interest in Wright, the impact of the Wendingen articles and book, and then the virtual collapse of that interest no doubt attributable to the establishment of the modern movement. The final European presentation of Wright of real significance was the great display in two parts in the July 1930 issues of *L'Architecture vivante.*

So in one sense The Show in 1931–32 was somewhat anticlimatic because it displayed only a few new works, mainly unrealized projects, and generally they were not appreciated. The Show did, however, provoke considerable discussion in Europe about the evolution of modernism and a fresh examination of Wright's role therein, and about the direction that twentieth-century architecture had taken during the 1920s. In response to these various views, Wright charged that his ideas had been thoroughly corrupted as exemplified by Oud's and Le Corbusier's products. Thereafter argument in the 1930s tended to polarize around Wright and Le Corbusier, without satisfaction for Wright. As far as he was concerned, discussion in magazines and newspapers only confirmed two things.

First, that regardless of the results that followed, he was the source of modern twentieth-century architecture, and second, that the U.S. ignored him whereas the Europeans praised. This last concern was patently incorrect, but such protestations always provoked one of his basic needs: attention. Moreover, through his replies he was effectively asking his European colleagues to reject their own architectural style, which he believed had so obviously eliminated individual will in favor of collective rationalism. Wright was asking them to develop something that would *allow* a better expression of both their nationality and individuality with less obvious recourse to political or aesthetically formal bias. The fact that they could not alter history, resist the dynamic vortex of fashion, or, more importantly, revise their convictions when faced with idiosyncratic impressions—Wright's, or the Amsterdam School's or expressionism's—did not faze Wright. And anyway, much as the Europeans felt a genuine debt to him they did not agree with his analyses (if they understood his writing) or with most of his architecture since 1922.

Wright and Willcox sporadically and affectionately corresponded over the next fifteen years, and the academic was invited to Taliesin in 1934 and 1935. When together they probably talked not only about architecture but of shared beliefs in a single tax and a democraticized socialism (Willcox also supported the Industrial Workers of the World), but there is no evidence of such matters in their correspondence. Nor is there any evidence that those beliefs prompted Willcox's invitation. Rather, the issues were practical and straightforward: education and architecture—Wright's.

A postscript to this episode reveals Wright's continuing search for money as a result of too few architectural commissions. It also indicates that all the hassles in personally arranging lectures and shows was too complicated and tedious for him. He registered with the Leigh Bureau of Lectures and Entertainments, New York. W. Colston Leigh's stable of lecturers included Louis Untermeyer, Joseph Wood Krutch, Fannie Hurst, Dashiell Hammett, Thomas Craven, and Mortimer Adler: nice company. Through Leigh and barely a year after The Show, Wright again offered lectures—$300 each or less if several could be arranged in the same area. No one in the Northwest could raise the money, though the University of Washington tried. People in California did, however, so a 1932 tour was put together. Wright and Olgivanna were again off to the West Coast.

12 Lectures and Exhibitions: Brownell

White, Wright, Willcox, and Bock represent one kind of continuity through architecture, its profession, and secondarily education. The other representative example of a productive social relationship is not concerned with pedagogy or friendly professional continuity. It is of a relatively new personal friendship developed with a local academic who, through a meeting of minds, prompted Wright to define more precisely his attitudes toward architecture, America, and its democracy.

If there was any doubt that Wright was flirting with theories of socialism, if not its practice, then his words in support of Broadacre City and his association with Baker Brownell should have dispelled that doubt. Brownell and Wright produced a book about *Architecture and Modern Life,* which was copyright in 1937 but dated 1938 on the title page. They coauthored some chapters (two) and independently wrote others (Brownell three, Wright two). Before embarking on their book the two had been friends for a number of years and shared ideas about human society. These prompted Brownell to invite Wright to give lectures during the 1932–33 academic year in an undergraduate course conducted by the professor in the School of Journalism at Northwestern University.[1] Such an arrangement continued for a few years and an honorarium was always paid. Often guest lecturers in "science, society, art and philosophy" spoke to Brownell's students about their special subject. The course was also meant to explore "relations," as Brownell put it, between these apparently diverse disciplines.

11.6 Wright's opinion of Los Angeles in
particular but most American cities in
general, called a "Wisconsin Valentine,"
drawn by Shoppe, as published in 1937.

The general theme was one that had intrigued Wright for most of his career. In fact it was first expressed in a talk he called "Architecture and the Machine" given in 1894. That was followed in 1901 by the more famous and often reprinted essay "The Art and Craft of the Machine."[2] After those expositions he had spoken from time to time about adaptations of science and technology to art and specifically architecture. From 1933 to 1937 the academic and the architect visited one another a few times. In 1934, much as Willcox had been, Brownell was recipient of one of Wright's letters seeking support for the Fellowship.[3] When invited again to lecture in 1935, Wright spoke on modern architecture, no doubt concentrating on his own efforts.[4] In 1937 his lecture was on the future of architecture;[5] that would have been before his departure for Moscow, and it was his last talk for Brownell.

During 1935 Brownell was trying to organize a book that was to have been based on the theme of the course on "contemporary thought." He wanted to bring together two disciplines under one book cover and explore their "relations." Initially he worked with a couple of other academics; one of them was Paul Douglas of Chicago University whom Brownell described as a "prominent young radical economist."[6] But it seems that those collaborators would not take time off from other more personal projects to work with Brownell. In December 1935 he conceived a "departure," as he described it, and wrote to Wright in a belief that the architect might wish to participate in a "delightful and significant book" to be written "on architecture and music, frozen and fluid form."[7] He suggested Wright collaborate with Dean Carl Beecher whom Wright may have met a few months earlier; apparently Beecher specialized on Tahitian music. This collaboration came to naught, but having got Wright's interest in a book related to Brownell's pedagogy and philosophy, they eventually agreed in October 1936 to work together on a book about the art of architecture, coincidentally incorporating Broadacres and political philosophy.[8]

During the winter of 1936–37 Wright persisted even though he was seriously ill with pneumonia, the illness that pushed him to build his winter home in Arizona. In February 1937 two of the book's six sections had been completed,[9] and by midyear 1937 the text was complete in spite of Wright's threat to pull out of the deal because of Brownell's unilateral revisions of Wright's text.[10] This resolved, proofs became available in August.[11] The possibility of *Harper's Magazine* serializing parts of the book did not materialize, even though Harper's was to publish the book.[12] Brownell had to rather vigorously push Wright along. Not only was Wright slow but Brownell was rather anxious because the book was most important to the academic's career. He saw it as a "stepping stone" whereby he hoped "to leave the university" and begin the work he "should be doing."[13] After World

War II he did leave academe (but only on a leave of absence) to put his philosophy into practice. His experiences and those of his colleagues were sympathetically and adequately described as was Brownell's linear fluid society (to borrow his phraseology) in two books by Richard Waverly Poston, *Small Town Renaissance* (1950) and *Democracy Is Yours* (1953), as well as within Brownell's own *The Human Community* of 1950. Just the books' titles indicate Brownell's philosophy and its compatibility with Wright's thinking.

A poet, author, journalist, educator, Brownell has described himself as liberal but quick to qualify his liberalism as not falling into "that snare" called Communism. He acknowledged that the "social evils that have given rise to Communism must be faced."[14] It seems clear that Wright and Brownell were promoting their own—yet not entirely separate—themes within the one book; themes of a social philosopher with strong ideas about participatory democracy that approached classical socialism (but fell short), and an architect with strong ideas about individualism that did not fall short in words or practice. *Architecture and Modern Life* was a book about art, architecture, politics, and urbanism. Wright's contributions about architecture and Broadacre City were similar in content to his earlier writings but with greater concision.

Brownell's thoughts about architecture were partly outlined a few years later when he said that Architecture "lays down patterns of movement for those who live in buildings. It directs their left turnings and their right turnings, their comings and goings, their pauses and speeds in a great dance. . . . It writes thus a rhythmic score," Brownell made an incorrect assumption if illuminating charge when he elaborated: "This kinesthetic function of architecture is almost unrecognized by architects and others, although its significance in building as an art is, in my opinion, great. In a recent book written in collaboration with Frank Lloyd Wright I twice introduced the idea, but so far as I can see neither Mr. Wright nor any critic who read the book—good men all—had any notion what I was driving at, or even saw that I was driving. . . . Architecture is treated too much as a picture."[15] Obviously Brownell was not aware of contemporary architectural theories. The main purpose of their book, however, lay on another intellectual plain.

In a scathing review, Meyer Schapiro outlined the book in three sentences. According to Wright and Brownell "a primitive state of democratic individualism in the Eden of the small towns and the farms was perverted by the cities," Schapiro said. "A privileged class arose which did not know how to administer its wealth in the common interest . . . ," and the "deurbanizing of life, the fusion of city and country on a high productive level" is the ideal. This ideal was, Schapiro said, one "shared by socialists and anarchists."[16] (The belief that the fusion was shared with socialists and anarchists might seem strange until Schapiro unnecessarily points to his own interpretation of a true socialism.)

For Brownell and Wright, Broadacre City was the exemplar of an ideal that would indeed fuse city and country; a place for urban refugees. Those urban products, socialism and communism, were seen synonymously. The terms even share exactly the same page numbers within the index. "Highly organized society, in a word, is a disintegrating influence on persons," they said. "It moves towards impersonal ends. It gains in power and fluidity at the person's expense." And further, in "fascist Italy, in [Nazi] Germany, in communist Russia this of course has happened."[17] The authors contended that

socialist theory, which in general is based on an urban conception of life, proposes that the present evils of the city, the slums, the injustice, the predatory savagery of man towards man, can be removed by the evolution of the industrial urban system—the dialectical evolution, indeed—towards more mature forms of organization. This evolution will take place, they think, through the mechanism of class conflict. This is again the competition motif, applied now to classes, that is characteristic of the modern city and of the capitalistic system that produced it.[18]

After arguments against "extreme concentration and governmental ownership" they concluded that the "socialist assumption that centralization in all fields is itself the natural and best pattern of economic and social life is by no means justified."[19]

Brownell and Wright were against socialism as then defined or as exemplified in the Soviet interpretation that was so popular in the late 1920s and throughout the 1930s. The two authors were attempting to redefine socialism—if by another name—and place it in the hands of the people rather than the selfish elite of a political party. The idea of developing an elite from labor unions united with the aristocracy as promoted by the aristocracy in Britain was also ignored. Brownell and Wright were not interested in Fabian socialism or its notion of "gradualism."[20] Yet abrupt or violent change was abhorrent to both men: the elemental freedoms in the American system of capitalism based on constitutional guarantees were too precious. Rather, they wished to induce change by example and allow the results to be inclusive of those guarantees. Brownell's experiments after the 1945 armistice confirms this. He and Wright wished to disarm the inherent centralizing nature of the single-party system (one party on a long-term basis as in the USSR, or short-term as with the English and Australian parliamentary systems). They wanted to decentralize, to regionalize government and spread its influence through what might be termed a participatory democratized socialism where grass-roots politics persuaded a less dominant hierarchy. In this way they believed that the evils of modern industrialized urbanism might be less pervasive and hopefully dissipate. Villages would abound; Broadacre Villages. Land, Work, and Home would again unite.

It was clear: while Wright's writings were elliptical if punchy, with his concurrence Brownell clarified Wright's position. Wright's interest in socialism was dialectic, passive, and, as suggested, flirtatious. And it was hardly a desirable mode for him to practice; others surely, but not him. Wright's professional and personal lifestyle were in opposition and asymmetrical to his urban and political theories. Indeed, he tended to apply those ideas that had some sensible application to his architectural practice and supported his anarchistic individualism. Yet what could have been more highly and centrally organized, less a place for the expression or practice of individualism than membership in the Taliesin Fellowship? Contradictions.

As noted above, production of the book had reached galley stage in August 1937. By then Wright had been home at Taliesin for four weeks, resting after his arduous journey through Europe and east to Moscow.

It was during that rest at Spring Green that Mies van der Rohe visited Wright. It occurred shortly after Mies had arrived in the U.S. and was contemplating an academic position from a few offers, including one from the Armour Institute in Chicago. Wright had previously and rather rudely rejected requests by Gropius and one by Le Corbusier to talk or to visit Taliesin. But Wright liked Mies's work. As William Wesley Peters has said, and therefore Wright had said, Mies was the only European who had not only the good sense to follow Wright's lead but the independence to create something original in the process.[21] Mies arrived on a Friday morning, meaning to spend but a few hours; he stayed over for a long weekend. Of the buildings and landscape that were Taliesin, Mies exclaimed "Freiheit! Es ist ein Reich!" Freedom! This is a kingdom![22] East had met West; the old culture had met the new; patient reserve had met a babbling magician; student and mentor touched. The two architects found a friendship and understanding that, while it did not mature, lasted for nearly a decade; not a bad run when one considers the egos involved.

M o s c o w

In June 1937 Frank Lloyd Wright attended the First All-Union Congress of Soviet Architects held in Moscow.[1] Curiously, the episode has not been discussed by observers or historians beyond borrowing Wright's own published impressions, such as they were. Even the most recent biographies fail to treat the subject.[2] It was an extraordinary meeting, not only in the opinion of the man from the midwest prairies but in that of his hosts. As well, he gave a talk to a consortium of colleagues gathered in Moscow for what was a dramatically serious occasion. That paper has only recently been presented in English.[3] Four fundamental questions need to be asked about this event: why was Wright invited, why did he accept, what occurred at the conference in respect of his presence, and what effect did the sojourn have on him?

Wright's activities preliminary to his Moscow visit have been explained in some detail. Yet it would be well to look at pertinent events in Russia leading to the Congress: events that occurred in the 1920s immediately after the Bolshevik seizure of power, and events initiated by Stalin in the 1930s. Only with an outline of those events can the questions be properly answered.

13 The 1920s

The miserable withdrawal from World War I, the internal war of 1918–21 to revolutionize Russian social and political life, the debilitating famine in 1921, and the conquest of neighbors by the Red Army immediately preceded a period of amazing optimism, at least in comparison to the past. And the past had been rejected through great effort and pain during those four years. There seemed to be a release of previously constrained impulses, buoyed by great anticipation and a belief that the only path must be upward. One result was a period that can fairly be described as one of the most vigorous, most exciting moments in the course of architectural history; ideas flowed uninhibited to direct enormous creative energies. The upheaval was far more dramatic architecturally than that which took place in Paris in the late 1000s, in Florence in the late 1400s, or in Central Europe concomitantly in the mid-1920s.

A paraphrase of constructivist Aleksei Gan, a member of the First Working Group of Constructivists that was formed in 1921, sets the political and therefore the practical realities of architecture as one of the arts in the new Soviet Union. Old concepts of art must die with old cultures and the "enemy are those unable to grasp the 'fact,' which [the] . . . Marxist rationale makes logically inevitable, that there cannot be a peaceful evolutionary transition in Russia's concept of art

13.1 "Lenin Tribune" (according to one source, but the sign says PROJECT) produced in El Lissitzky's Moscow atelier in 1920, as published in Mendelsohn (1929).

if there has been a violent Revolution in her politics."[1] Tradition was not to be allowed a natural death; rather, it was executed.

Theoretically therefore, all hierarchies associated with religion or politics or social distinction had to be destroyed. It was a cultural purge that had a sensational impact on all the arts; architecture was no exception. There were to be new styles, new forms, new materials, new ornaments or none, new plans (especially for housing), even new cities for new functions, especially in the late 1920s and 1930s. There were to be new symbols for a new nation, symbols that would help identify and covet the new Soviet idealization of Marxist materialism. "Historical evidence never worried the functionalist who, in the face of contradictory evidence, decided to ignore it," said Russian emigrant Berthold Lubetkin, "and proceeded to liquidate history, proclaiming it irrelevant, and relegating to the scrap-heap such embarrassing concepts as the national characteristics of art, in the name of world wide internationalism and technical progress."[2]

In the milieu of demands for wholly contemporary arts free of the shackles of historicism, the role of the futurists prior to World War I cannot be overemphasized. "Fighting their way towards a new liberty against apathy, nostalgia, and sentimentality," Joshua Taylor outlined, for the public they became a "symbol of all that was new, terrifying, and seemingly ridiculous in contemporary art."[3] Filippo Marinetti and his performing troupe of polemicists visited many European urban centers during 1913–14, including a few in Russia. Marinetti lectured and performed to "enthusiastic audiences" in Petrograd and Moscow during January and February 1914.[4] The futurists, who were more committed to architecture than the cubists, were not accepted by all, including Kandinsky, but even those who were not captivated were nonetheless indebted to futurist propaganda and their style of two-dimensional design.[5] In the process of arguing rejection of the very persuasive, if often defaming Italians, the views of the prewar Russian theorists were to become more precisely defined.

The growth or evolution through suprematism to constructivism has been nicely outlined by historians Camilla Gray, Anatole Kopp, and K. Paul Zygas.[6] The influence of De Stijl is the only missing link in the outlines. Constructivist theory was quickly transferred to reality in the first serious architectural proposal for the 1922 Palace of Labor, designed by Alexandr, Viktor, and Leonid Vesnin. Zygas believed the genesis of the Vesnins' design "owed little to programmatic considerations, to the 'machine aesthetic,' or to the Vensins' ideological preferences." Rather they "drew from existing typologies to create an unprecedented architectural configuration which, in turn, affected the entire complexion of Constructionist [sic] architecture."[7] Like a number of projects and completed works to follow, it was published in early 1926 in *L'Architecture vivante* and in Walter Gropius's *International*

**13.2 Sketch for a mass festival setting
called "Struggle and Victory of the Soviets," a 1920 project for the third Communist International for Moscow by Alexandr
Vesnin and Lubov Popova. This sceme has
an obvious affinity with "Instant City," a
project in 1969 by Archigram.**

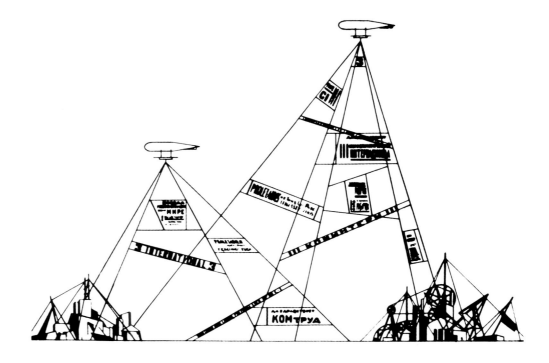

13.3 Palace of Labor, Moscow, a project of 1922–23 by Alexandr, Leonid, and Viktor Vesnin, as published in *L'Architecture vivante*. The industrial appearance of the building was induced in part by exposing industrially made steel components and concrete, wires, and ships' air scoops, and by a general rectilinearity of each facade that intentionally recalled American manufacturing buildings pre-1920 (see also Figures 17.1 and 17.2). The plan of the oblong theater, or meeting hall, was influential on Walter Gropius's "Total" theater project of 1927, a factor not often realized.

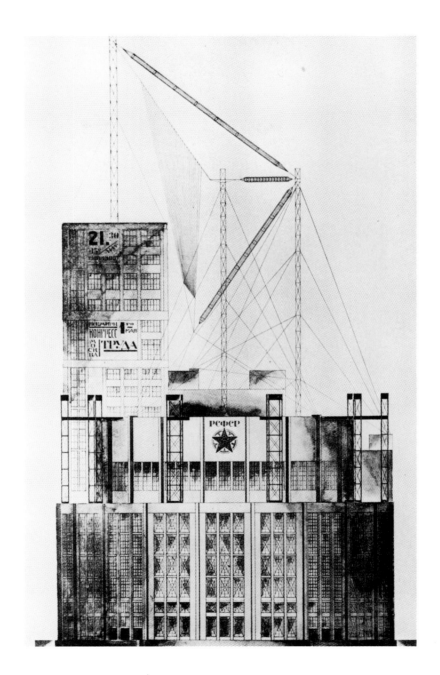

13.4 Elevation, second-level plan, and section through stairs of the USSR Pavilion, Paris, in 1925 by Konstantin Melnikov, as published in *L'Architecture vivante*, a journal with which Wright was familiar and that in 1930 devoted two issues to his work.

Architektur (Munich) released in early 1926. *L'Architecture vivante* was read by Russian architects who also contributed to Morance's Paris magazine.

While a prophetic statement for constructivism in Russia, the Vesnin project was not the first to reach Western presses. Konstantin S. Melnikov's USSR Pavilion for the 1925 European decorative arts exhibition in Paris preceded the Vesnins' work in the western presses in a much more dramatic manner. The official exhibition publication referred to Melnikov's building as a mixture "analogous" to Le Corbusier, André Lurçat, Gropius "at Dessau," and other Central Europeans; and a photograph displayed those influences.[8] However, the elevation of the street promenade revealed a distinctly obvious Russian constructivist piece only hinting of the suggested analogy to Le Corbusier et al.[9] This was the first constructivist building to be constructed outside the Soviet Union. Progressive Soviet art and the ideas of constructivism were known to those who made the effort. For instance, in 1922 William Lethaby issued what might be called a British constructivist document and earlier, in 1919, Walter Gropius became chairman of a group *Arbeitsrat für Kunst* (Working Soviet for Art).

Freedom from traditional social and economic structures also allowed a release from artistic historicism and enabled wholly fresh studies of the fundamentals of architecture. It was the constructivist movement that grasped the ideological, theoretical, practical, and idealistic lead and enunciated its position in 1920–21. Its adherents began practical training for young architects; particularly notable was the Higher State Artistic Technical Studios (Vkhutemas) in Moscow. Products emanating from their art and architecture departments were revolutionary, yet practically and aesthetically brilliant. The Moscow school was a place for "the production of qualified Constructivists"— of "artist-constructors."[10] The young intellectuals, architectural theorists, and teachers were partly, and only partly, influenced by the Dutch De Stijl or more particularly van Doesburg, by Le Corbusier, and by aspects of the architectural aesthetic being developed in Central Europe. The Europeans were not persuaded by North American skyscrapers, although the technology that allowed their achievement (including grain silos) was eulogized. They were persuaded as were the constructivists by the architecture of American factories and warehouses.

While constructivism contained a revolutionary dynamism for which buildings were "turbid dreams of romantic engineering," as historian Bruno Zevi had said, objective symbolism was a countering force of the mid-twenties. Also free and unrestrained by tradition, its proponents sought the "objective" and the "absolute and universal" significance of architectural forms. The symbolists even conducted laboratory experiments on reactions of spectators, the proletariat per-

13.5 Photograph of the USSR Pavilion,
Paris, in 1925 by Konstantin Melnikov,
architect, as published in *L'Architecture
vivante*.

haps but more than likely other intellectuals: scale, mass, rhythm, modulation, or whatever were itemized to form a vocabulary, a list to draw upon for proper design; canons. Cube = integrity. Sphere = tranquility and equilibrium. Etc.[11] It was a kind of codified Russian expressionism, incomprehensible to the uninitiated, devoid of an obvious social responsibility.

There emerged three main groups who argued that they were the true theoretical voice of a true Marxist architecture, each openly opposed to the others. In the end the Pan-Russian Organization of Proletarian Architects (Wopra) won the ideological war through compromise. They were formed in 1929, perhaps on the instigation of the party, and immediately attacked the work of Konstantin Melnikov, for instance, who was of the older (1923) group, and Moisei Ginzburg who had been a voice for the constructivists. As an extension of the Party they also argued against the influence of the Central Europeans. Soviet architects had visited Le Corbusier in Paris and he won a limited competition in 1928 for the Tsentrosoiuz Building in Moscow. When built it was supervised by N. D. Kolli and partially completed by 1935. Yet Le Corbusier's winning design and his entry for a later competition, the Palace of the Soviets, appear contrived to satisfy the constructivist camp in Moscow.

A recounting of Russia's dynamic architectural projects of the 1920s is not necessary, for they have been analyzed and presented in many books and journals. English-language publications of the recent past, which began around 1970 in the London magazine *Architectural Design* with some articles written by Soviet historians,[12] were—and are—staid, dull, unnecessarily detailed, descriptive; especially those translations from the Russian. They tend to be apologetic and lack the historical, realistic, and objective insight of Berthold Lubetkin, for instance, and the verve and attractiveness of Bruno Zevi in his much earlier book *Toward an Organic Architecture* of 1949. Predecessor to all recent studies, however, and the most succinct view of relevance to this study of events around 1930–32 is that of Lubetkin.

The simple, classical concept of internationalism underwent a considerable change towards the end of the twenties, when hopes of immediate world revolution receded and the most autarchic stage of "building of socialism in one country" was initiated. Simultaneously, the exuberant romantic conception of techique gave way to a sober realisation that technique, in Russia, meant a hard uphill struggle to transform a peasant economy into a modern industrial organism. . . .

Their failure to understand the significance of these changes, and to adjust themselves, led the profession . . . to the brink of complete impotence. . . .

The disparity between the vision of a super-charged technique and the reality of a

primitive and backward building industry, in which, more and more, idealised technology had to give way to ordinary ingenuity on a lower level, led other [architects] to a hollow and insincere aestheticism, indistinguishable from that of the formalists they had set out to replace, inasmuch as they were forced to reproduce the adulterated forms of an advanced technique in the absence of its real media. . . .

[Events] did not wait for the various groupings of architects to settle their internal difficulties: and, with the continually expanding building programme brought by the [first] Five Year Plan, the search for architectural competence became more and more pressing, for these were the years which saw the planning and the foundation of such gigantic industrial towns as Kuznetsk, Magnitorgorsk, Zaporojie, and many hundreds of smaller centres.[13]

It must be noted that some of those cities were built by American contractors. Moreover hundreds of factories were designed by and construction was supervised by the American architects Albert and Moritz Kahn. Their significant contribution at the request of the Soviet government has been wiped from official histories. All nonofficial and western histories also fail to mention the Kahns.

In any event the Lubetkin recollections echoed concerned sentiments current in Moscow in the early thirties. As he suggested, all of the uniquely creative productions directed toward defining a new architecture for a new society were to end—suddenly.

14 Prelude to the 1937 Congress

The June 1937 All-Union Congress of Soviet Architects was intimately caught in a swirling tide of disarming and often horrific events: events that defined political and personal power; events that turned the joy of creating a new culture one hundred and eighty degrees and into autocratic orthodoxy; events explicitly determined by Joseph Stalin's political machine.

Warnings to those who would not follow the dogma of Communist Party policy had slowly turned to action. For instance, in 1932 internal passports were introduced, thereby reviving one of Peter the Great's most despised means of controlling the peasantry, and there was the controversial Party-made famine of 1932–33. In 1933 a series of concentration camps were established in the north and east of Russia where peasants and technical labor from throughout the USSR were impounded. The peasant had his title changed to "worker"; he no longer belonged to a landowner but to a soviet cadre. And there were other repressive acts.

The murder of Sergei Kirov in December 1934 was the public act enabling Stalin to control, and where necessary purge, a rising and expanding opposition to his leadership; Stalin had no rival. The switch from liberally applied social—and artistic—experiments in the 1920s to constriction and constraint in the 1930s has been summarized as follows: "the Communist Party . . . shrank the individual into an instrument for the achievement of material progress and the construction of socialism." In consequence, said historian Marshall Shatz, the "liberalization of many areas of Soviet life in the twenties gave way to strict social discipline and cultural conformity." The political and bureaucratic mechanism was the Five-Year Plan. With its advent "the emphasis was now on productivity, work, and self-sacrifice for the collective good as defined by the Party, on harnessing individual energies for the benefit of the state rather than releasing them for the fulfilment of the individual" and society.[1]

Obviously Trotsky's deportation in 1927 (he was murdered in 1940 in Mexico) did not effectively eliminate Stalin's opposition. Kirov's murder highlighted the policy of terrorism that continued for at least the next four years. Old Bolsheviks of the left and right opposition as well as members of the Red Army were executed or exiled or committed suicide. To give the spectacle a sense of justification a series of show trials were staged. Fake and unsubstantial charges were trumped up and often staged for public consumption. They were given great publicity.[2] In all, millions of people were arrested, deported, jailed, or simply disappeared: poets, artists, musicians, architects, and engineers were included, as were Stalin's own cadre.[3] The GULAG (Main Administration of Correction Labor Camps) was dramatically increased and by 1941 it administered 11,000,000 prisoners, mainly political, guarded by half a million secret police.

Historian Isaac Deutscher defined two fundamental interlocking questions raised by the purges, especially since they occurred nearly parallel in time—and in kind—with Nazism in Germany. "If so many outstanding politicians, administrators, and military men," said Deutscher, "had in fact formed a monster fifth column, it was asked, then what was the morale of a nation in which this could happen? If the charges were faked, then was not the regime that indulged in such practices rotten from top to bottom? . . . this is how it presented itself to outsiders."[4] Russian diplomat Andrei Y. Vyshinsky's admission that Marxist doctrine was merely an outward cloak legitimizing the machinery of despotism was plain. Stalin's Marxism and Hitler's Nazism were based on socialism, could be equated, could be synonymous, did occur simultaneously. In art in 1934 the Soviets censured the avant-garde, in 1936 the Nazis declared expressionism and modernism "degenerate."[5]

In spite of the Soviet's announced aim of crushing capitalism, there was a time in the 1920s when the Russian mind welcomed progressive influences of European and American thought in the arts. Some architects from Europe, the northern Mediterranean, the British Isles, the Americas, and Australia[6] were excited about the prospects of Soviet architecture and city and regional planning.

In order that they might participate, these idealists traveled to the USSR in comparatively large numbers. Then, with the terror at least partially revealed, they pressed their embassies to get them out. They left the USSR not because they had fulfilled a task and satisfied their desires: they fled. Hannes Meyer, who had directed the Bauhaus from 1928 to 1930, traveled to Moscow to take up a position as a professor at the Higher Institute for Architecture and Building, and then became a member of architect Karo Alabian's Organization of Proletarian Architects. Alabian was one of the Party's more devoted managers and Meyer was outspoken against the constructivists. But around 1936 Meyer pleaded for and received permission to return to Switzerland. At about this time, or 1935–36, the first arrests of architects began.[7]

Therefore the 1930s reversed the trend of the 1920s: Russia isolated itself from western nations. Terror as a political tool swept aside the noble words of Soviet idealism. A partial halt to the process of self-destruction finally arrived in 1938, perhaps only because of the threat of an external war.

While Wright may not have been privy to details such as arrests of architects, he seemed unconcerned and, it must be observed, at times unmoved by the revelations about Stalinism. Wright was certainly aware of them for he mentioned the atrocities in his autobiography.[8] As well, when he arrived in Moscow in that June of 1937 the American ambassador, Joseph Davies, most probably counseled the American architect and definitely informed him that Marshall M. N. Tukhachevsky had just been executed. Naively, as if it just occurred to her, Mrs. Wright remarked that the execution "may have aggravated political unrest."[9] The Soviet architects' union, however, was concerned and moved by the politically inspired events orchestrated by Stalin.

It is now generally understood that neither Stalin nor the Party selected one particular architectural style. However, the Union of Soviet Architects together with Party bureaucracy most assuredly determined what was and was not acceptable. No individual or artistic or professional clique would be permitted to make such determinations, unilaterally or otherwise. It was the Union that carried Party policy to the architectural profession. The Union was a sieve through which the Party allowed Union members to believe they were initiating and effecting professional and artistic ideas by a process that was not democratic but may have appeared to be so to outside observers. It was a process whereby loyalties were to be displayed at a convention attended by a select few dominated by a Party clique. And always the cunning Georgian was watching and listening. In a written overture Stalin's words greeted delegates to the June Congress.[10] Comrade Schteinberg from the Ukrainian S.S.R. was one of many speakers at the Congress who plainly acknowledged "the great architect Comrade Stalin."[11]

The 1937 Congress was the culmination of a long, awkward process of attempts by the state to control the arts. In 1932, the Seventeenth Conference of the Communist Party proclaimed "that within five years socialism must be achieved within every sphere of Soviet life."[12] It was unclear how the architectural profession would achieve such a broadly based prescription. As we have seen, throughout the 1920s a remarkable and idiomatic architecture flourished on paper if seldom constructed.[13] But around 1930, groups, associations, and individuals, vying for ideological and/or personal supremacy, factionalized the profession. Attempts were made to pacify certain groups or individuals or to amalgamate other informal groups or semiofficial associations in an effort to defuse, so to speak, the rather bitter polemics. Amalgamation was slow and in response the Party, wrote Soviet historian S. O. Khan-Magomedov, "was compelled to intervene." Under a decree of April 1932 entitled "Reconstruction of Literary and Artistic Organizations," all such professional groups were dissolved.

In July 1932, therefore, the Union of Soviet Architects was formed "with members of the earlier societies elected to its committee."[14] But the realities of events in 1932 are not quite as simple or innocent as Khan-Magomedov outlines. The April decree was the first step to enforcing Party control over all aspects of literary and artistic life in order to direct all aspects of artistic production. The second step was to force all architects into one Union of Soviet Architects. The third step was the establishment of Arplan (Arkhitekturno-Planirovochnoi Komissii or Architecture-Planning Commission) under the direction of super-bureaucrat L. M. Kaganovich, which occurred almost simultaneously with formation of the Union. "A controlling organ," noted architectural historian Milka Bliznakov, "Arplan, was established to review and approach each design before acceptance for construction." "Its function was to review and approve each design before acceptance for construction, not only from a functional but mainly," it should be emphasized, "from an aesthetic viewpoint."[15]

This review by the Party fit specific arguments that had been put by Lenin, including the following. "Every artist, everyone that considers himself an artist, has a right to create freely according to his ideals, independent of anything," and here Lenin was referring specifically to the marketplace. But he quickly added that in fear of possible chaos, "we"—the Party—"must guide this process according to a plan and form its results."[16]

A contradiction of monumental proportions.

This exposé together with other revealing comments were innocently presented in the

London magazine *The Studio* in 1935. Articles for that issue about all aspects of Soviet art were written by a group of official Soviet authors. David Arkin's article on architecture—he was then Secretary of the Union of Soviet Architects—succinctly outlined the official interpretation and defended the Party prescriptions.

Naturally, after the heady years of c. 1921 to 1932 this enforced bureaucratic control was bitterly resented. Yet nothing could be done about it. Similar proposals were desperately resisted in 1932 by writers, the more immediately obvious propagandists, but without success. For architects, factional divisions remained for many years in spite of Union efforts. Resolution of many ideological questions was not achieved, especially those of artistic will and definition of an appropriate socialist architecture. Therefore, the Party called the Union to exercise authority over its members. Architecture was the last art form to come under restrictions of the new Soviet policy. The turning point, in fact, had already been passed. Unity by political control was achieved by 1937 and the Congress was a formality for ratification of the new professional orthodoxy and a new architectural formalism.

Yet one problem persisted—and persists: Soviet architects and the Party bosses did not know how a new—or old—architecture could in fact be explicitly socialist. As far as the 1937 Congress was concerned such a refashioning of the past or a rejection of constructivism was too vague. And so the Congress was, "by its own standards, premature," wrote Frederick Starr; the "leaders of the Union of Soviet Architects had no choice but to celebrate the triumph of a program that did not exist. Unsure of what they could affirm, they concentrated their attention instead on what they could safely deny. . . . Formalism best fit this need, the more so since it had already been linked with Trotskyism. Accordingly, the Congress turned into a kind of orgy of denunciation of formalism."[17] It may have been artistically premature but politically for the Stalinists it was overdue.

The Party revisionists believed the Soviet architecture of around 1932 was wrong, therefore Le Corbusier was wrong, therefore constructivism and so-called formalist ideas and modern architecture were wrong. Modernism was wrong for the following reasons: it had no roots in Russia or elsewhere in the Soviet Union, it was too formal and based on preconceptions some of which led to "fetishism," it was not Marxian, it was individual and therefore not collectivist and consequently counterrevolutionary, it was not sufficiently expressive as witness the clichés produced around 1928–32 in the USSR, and it was contrary to "the methods of socialist realism."[18] Only the proletariat could determine artistic taste but invariably, of course, the Party prescribed and the proletariat accepted without choice. Indeed, *Izvestia* exhorted local soviets "to draw the masses . . . into a discussion of the shortcomings in architecture" in preparation for the Congress.[19] From a destructive, negative test of what was wrong, could what was right be found? Perhaps from the remnants? Not the best way to begin anew. Yet Wright's own polemics attempted to verbally destroy in the hope that rebuilding would be to his ideas.

The word "formalism" is a rather fuzzy, imprecise term that relies on context. In the 1920s formalists were historicists; around 1930 formalists were the Central European architects. In 1932 Anatoli Lunacharskii, Commissar for Education, urged a return to the antiquities and cited Marx's well-known admiration of Greek civilization. Therefore, as historian Arthur Voyce succinctly put it, ancient Greece and Rome were invoked "as an inspiration for a new Proletarian Renaissance— Athens and Rome reappraised, revitalized and refashioned, so as to fit the purposes and ideas of the young Soviet Republic."[20] It was a process of selective retrieval, one often used by fundamentalists. Exactly the same rationale was used by Hitler in the 1930s. Russian expatriate architect Berthold Lubetkin, who had left Russia for Paris and then London in the late 1920s, described formalism of the mid-1930s as substituting "the sense-experience" for "rational judgement"; or to put it another way, romanticism for rationalism. The Commissariat of Light Industry building in Moscow, Tsentrosoiuz, designed by Le Corbusier, was greatly admired when first proposed in 1928 but ignored on its opening in 1934–35 and ridiculed as formalist in 1937.[21] Clearly, formalism is what you wish it to be.

This definition, such as it is, was affirmed by what happened in the 1930s. "In the attempt to define beauty," wrote historian Bliznakov, Soviet "architects and theoreticians turned to the past. Analysis of the architectural achievements from ancient Egypt to the Rococo led to the conclusion that a synthesis of all the arts . . . would inevitably lead to a perfect and beautiful building . . . the search for synthesis in the 1930s was concentrated exclusively on the past." Bliznakov described the devolution from traditional hierarchy to bureaucratic power and dependency: "In their writings on the principles of synthesizing the arts of the past, theoreticians naturally made extensive use of illustrations. This handy research led architects to a literal transposition of illustrated elements rather than to the search for new forms based on principles of abstraction. Image led to image. Gradually this eclectic imitative art came to be accepted as the official style under the name of Socialist Realism." Beauty therefore "was not a goal in itself but only a means of propagandizing for socialist ideology,"[22] another tool for building Marxist materialism.

A more practical definition was contained in a series of official prescriptions issued the day before the Congress opened. In *Pravda* on 15 June 1937 the Communist Party explained the purpose and defined the role of the Congress.[23] The directives were diverse and can be paraphrased like this. The Congress was important since in its long history architecture had never been so closely associated with the masses as in the Soviet Union. American architecture, by contrast, served the bourgeois and not the people. (In all the denunciations of American society, Wright was never mentioned, not even in the most subtle manner.) Soviet life actually creates artists while lifestyles in bourgeois countries only degrade architecture. In a socialist country the architecture is a participant in creating a new society. Working people need to admire beautiful buildings that are also functional. The contrast between beautiful areas and slums is an undeniable fact of capitalist cities. Thanks to the love and attention of Stalin and Lenin, Soviet architecture and many other artistic fields are showing results of which one must be proud. (And then the ordinances became more precise, almost as warnings.) Stalin's rule in construction is a concern for the people, and while some architects realize this they are not cooperating. It is the duty of architects to free architecture from formalism, trickery, or routine. Divorced from life, many architects do not pay attention to the needs of the people and therefore they must be criticized at open meetings. Planning must be performed in an unselfish way. A failure to understand politics and to follow Party lines explains many failures in architecture and building. The task at hand was then announced: the opening of the architects' Congress must bring about the complete destruction of formalism and falseness. The Congress will create a Soviet architectural style whose sole responsibility will be the needs of the people of our time. "We are now in Stalin's third five year plan and we must rise to the great task before us," said *Pravda.* "Greetings to the first Soviet Congress of architects." Political reality was gravely emphasized by Molotov, who stressed the Party's will to arbitrate rules governing architects.[24]

The constrictions introduced by Stalin's Party exerted a basically conservative, reactionary strain that would not allow experimentation, would not countenance explorations into realms unknown or potentially dialectic: dialogue was forbidden. Liberal investigation of what might be (or what existed, as far as the constructivists were concerned) was also forbidden. A selection of a series of known, traditional, therefore accepted quantities was not only more theoretically viable but bureaucratically easy. Indeed, quantifiable convenience must have been seriously persuasive although usually couched in other terminologies. It was, therefore, difficult to define such a style. And yet the word "style" cannot be used with confidence for such a futile and perverse eclecticism. In fact, Soviet architect Karo Alabian in his statement as president of the Union lamely and imprecisely defined Soviet Realism as an amalgam of "ideology" and "truthfulness" that meets the demands of technology, culture, and practicality. It was an acceptable definition, however, even if contradictory in the face of eclectic historicism.

The All-Union Congress was crucial for four interlocking reasons. The first and most important was the outwardly visible and verbal acknowledgment of allegiance by the profession's individuals to Stalin's rule. The emphasis of Congress events and eulogies on Stalin, a kind of groveling, is part of the dynamics of the cult of personality that initially grew out of a Russian ecstasy for Lenin and was successfully if forcibly transferred by Stalin to himself. In view of the chilling climate and the acts of terror orchestrated by Stalin between 1932 and June 1937, this simple statement had special meaning. Second, the Congress was designed to demonstrate that, as artistic and professional spheres within the Soviet republics, architecture and city planning were in tune with and executing the ideals of Soviet socialism as determined by the Party, therefore the Union. Third, the Congress was also crucial for the careers of individual Soviet architects and, fourth, it shaped architectural design and stylistic acceptance. The actual wording used to announce the Congress was, however, innocuous. During a meeting on 19–21 April 1937, the Union of Soviet Architects determined that the All-Union Congress would meet in June with the following agenda: (1) task of Soviet architecture, (2) the general plan and reconstruction of Moscow and other planned cities, (3) the architecture of the home, (4) architectural schooling and training of building craftsmen, (5) statutes of the Union, and (6) elections.[25]

The stage was set. Into this physical and ideological turmoil guests were invited to attend and participate. Their involvement was both passive and active: to listen, to visit, to see, to talk, and to give papers. People were much like show pieces brought in from various places in the USSR, from Europe, the Mediterranean, and America. In June 1937 the constructivists took the brunt of criticism, denunciations, and demands for confessions of waywardness, even "wreckerism." So too did individualists such as Moisei Ginzburg, Viktor and Alexandr Vesnin, and Konstantin Melnikov. Yet America's most eminent and well-known architect and an outspoken individualist and experimentalist was also invited as a foreign guest of the Union and Party. He would serve the Congress well if he were to accept their invitation.

15 Wright, Architecture, and the Soviets prior to 1937

There may have been several reasons for the Soviets to invite Wright as well as other foreign architects. The struggle, to use their term, of world Communism would be given a new life in spite of the notorious difficulties of the mid-1930s. In any case, the next meeting of the Comintern and the Party was due in less than two years. It was necessary to provide evidence that socialism and Stalinism were active in all spheres of artistic life as decreed in 1932. The internal problems of the USSR would seem less onerous if emphasis could be shifted to positive world developments. As well, people from countries girding Hitler's Germany were invited. It was one manner of signaling unity among various national Communist parties in Europe. But more than this, the Congress organizers would wish to be seen not only as accountable to the Party and its government but also acceptable to the Soviet Union's various republics and, hopefully, the rest of the world. If foreigners, that is non-USSR citizens, participated the Union of Soviet Architects would appear to be fulfilling its proper roles. Many, in fact most of the foreign guest architects were Party members in their own countries or something like fellow travelers. But why specifically Wright who was not a fellow traveler and who was the only internationally eminent foreign architectural figure present in Moscow?

One problem in responding to the question is that we do not know if he was the only eminent foreign architect invited. Others may have refused invitations, even architects with known Communist sympathies such as Le Corbusier in Paris, Oscar Neimeyer in Rio de Janeiro, and William Lescaze in Philadelphia.[1] But in the mid-1930s Le Corbusier was seen as an initiator of the new formalism. As the Congress progressed he was judged passé, his followers as enemies. Similarly, because of his obvious explorations of constructivism and Central European idioms, Lescaze was tainted. Neimeyer and Le Corbusier had been collaborators on at least one project in Brazil, the Ministry of Education building in Rio, begun in 1936.[2] Neimeyer therefore was also unacceptable. But what of other leading architects in England or the Americas? Of the emigrés, perhaps we shall never know whether or not the Europeans were invited. Of the Russian emigrés we can be more certain; they could not be invited for they were tainted by commission of a sin—their rejection of Communism.

The Soviet Union was not ignorant of ideas and practices in architecture in Europe and other areas of the Western world. Theoretical treatises and architecture as manifest were well published and eagerly read. Until 1917 Russian architects came from the ranks of the aristocracy. After 1919 they came not entirely from the remnants of the aristocracy but in any event were literate and necessarily knowledgeable in a Western language. In fact before the 1920s many members of the aristocracy could not speak or read Russian, preferring French. Even in the 1930s parts of Russian architectural journals *Academy Architecture* (Moscow) and *Architecture of the USSR* (Moscow) were in both French and Russian. A reading knowledge of European languages was a necessity for architects before 1917. Moisei Ginzburg mentioned that while a student in prewar Milan he studied one of the famous German Wasmuth editions of Wright's architecture.[3]

However, in the early 1930s a concerted effort was made to present the architecture of the Western world to the body of Soviet architects. A few examples reveal the general trend. In 1932 David Arkin edited a book on *The Architecture of the Contemporary West* published in Moscow. Arkin was then Director of Theory and History at the Moscow Academy of Architecture and he claimed to have translated all of the key texts. He included in his illustrated survey architects Bruno Taut, Gropius, Le Corbusier, Richard Neutra (then in the U.S.), Ludwig Hilberseimer, Ernst May, J. J. P. Oud, and André Lurçat. In issue number six of the 1933 *Architecture of the USSR* there were edited texts by, among others, Joseph Frank, Robert Mallet-Stevens, Raymond Fischer, Hans Schmidt, Hannes Mayer, and Lurçat. This was balanced by an article by N. Brounov on "The Evolution of an Architectural Theme," the role of the Roman Pantheon, which was offset by an article by Arkin about Adolph Loos. Then in 1934 Lurçat himself wrote an article on "Today's French Architecture." It was the result of a paper he gave in Moscow on 31 January 1934 to Soviet architects who were meeting to discuss the "Architectural Decade" and included a pictorial survey of "The latest work of Le Corbusier" that showed the Paris Swiss Pavilion of 1933 and the City of Refuge "l'Armée du Salut" in Paris of the same year. It can be seen that in spite of official Party wishes, those who supported the Central European aesthetic were persistent.

Other indications of a continuing Wrightian influence were not usually published. For instance Wright had played with kindergarten wooden blocks as a child under the tutelage of his mother. He believed that they were instrumental in shaping his desire to become an architect and his attitude toward and implementation of elemental geometric shapes, a fact publicized in 1900. Constructivist artist Aleksandr Rodchenko devised some wood block "spatial constructions" that were very similar to the kindergarten blocks of Friedrich Froebel, whose works were widely read in Central Europe from 1880 onward.[4] But publications were the most useful inspiration. From 1924 to 1927 the pages of *L'Architecture vivante* constantly displayed buildings by architects obviously indebted to Wright's style, the more obvious being Antonin Raymond (with works from Japan). Oud, Erich Mendelsohn, M. de Klerk (at times), R. van 't Hoff, Mies van der Rohe, van Leusden, and Bijvoet and Duiker (especially their trade school near The Hague). Wright's work was published in the magazine (1924, 1927, and 1930) and concurrently there were the famous *Wendingen* publications in the mid-1920s of his work and of those influenced by him. Oud, Mendelsohn, Gropius, and Mies were included in the foreign section of the First Exhibition of Modern Architecture held in Moscow in 1927. During the early months of 1927 Richard Neutra had published in Stuttgart (by the prestigious Julius Hoffman) his book *Wie Baut Amerika?* which was eagerly seized upon in central Europe, especially as it addressed American technology and prefabrication. Among other subjects Neutra

15.1 Perspective of the Rowing Society De Hoop on the Amstel, built 1922, by M. De Klerk, architect. Associations without resorting to mimicry to Wright's prairie style are in the off-center massing of the upper floors linked to a general asymmetry, a strong horizontality; and an openness in plan with service spaces located similar to a Wright domestic house plan, that is, off-center of the open spaces. The building is not typical of de Klerk's work. As published in 1921 in *L'Architecture vivante*. Demolished by the Nazis in 1943.

talked about and illustrated Wright's Los Angeles concrete block houses of the early 1920s. Commissar Lunacharsky of the USSR Ministry of Education promised the book "would be read by Soviet artists and architects." (*Architect's Journal* in London thought it basic, only a textbook for students.) As early as 1912, Russian architect Pantaleimon Golosov had built his own version of Wright's prairie-style Warren Hickox house of 1900.[5] But there is no record of books or articles about Wright in the Russian language, at least not until 1933.

In response to an initiative of *Pravda* in 1932, probably by the newspaper's New York office, Wright replied to some short, very general questions about how the "economic crisis" affected American architecture. He avoided economics in preference for disparaging remarks about "bad" decoration. Then he exclaimed that "Capital will only spend money to make money." This should have pleased *Pravda.* Asked his view of the USSR, he described Soviet endeavors as "heroic" but failed to note which endeavors. He used his word "organic" in the context of a new society. It was left to his readers' imagination, perhaps, to discover exactly what this word meant and then how to apply it unless, of course, *Pravda*'s audience (its staff more than likely) had read Wright's most recent writings. If so, his brief polemic would have made just a little more sense. He added that he believed a nation should be ruled by its "own bravest" and "own best," appending a peculiar and provocative qualification, "whether from within or from without."[6]

A year later *Pravda* again approached Wright, this time asking how American intellectuals were coping with the Depression. He responded by stating that there was little "visible change," that the "Capitalistic system is a gambling game" anyway (he tended to equate capitalists with intellectuals), that America's education breeds inertia and was for middle-class minds (he had just opened his Taliesin Fellowship), that no radical changes were noticeable but only "tinkering and adjusting" by Roosevelt's New Deal, and he called for a "repeal of special privilege." As usual his reply wandered but it contained provocative stuff for the Soviets. A cursory survey fails to discover the publication of either of the very brief responses;[7] perhaps the Party was collecting information that could influence future decisions.

There was another brief contact via the mails. In 1933 he was asked by the professional journal *Architecture of the USSR* to respond to another set of questions. The editor-in-chief David Arkin wanted to learn something of Wright's "Method of Architectural Designing."[8] The Union's journal was running a series and the same questions were asked of other foreign and Soviet architects, including Melnikov.[9] Wright answered relatively tersely to nine questions. First, architectural problems are solved within themselves, by "the nature of the site, the nature of the materials

..., the nature of the system using them, the nature of the life concerned ... the nature of the architect himself." Second, architectural composition "is dead"; architects should proceed from "generals to particulars" in a natural way. Third, drawings and sketches record and clarify ideas and are a means of communication only between the architect, client, and builder. Fourth, the study of classical or contemporary monuments can only serve the architect who learns how they were "serviceable or beautiful in their own day"; their architectural forms can only be "harmful" in respect of today. Fifth, great works of art can be achieved through the creativity of one person who "conceives and another [who] executes." That is the only reasonable collaboration. Collectives and committees at best produce compromise. Sixth, sculpture and painting should be sympathetically embodied in architecture by the composer who orchestrates the concept, namely the architect. Seventh, completing a harmony by appropriate details is the final design work. Eighth, only the architect can supervise construction on the site. And ninth, corrections and additions as work proceeds should be limited.[10] Very little was revealed about Wright's actual design methodology. In most respects he offered opinions that conflicted with the orthodox eclecticism of Socialist Realism. His belief in the supremacy of the individual over collective action would not have been appreciated.

Melnikov's responses to Arkin's request were similar to Wright's yet more intellectually constructed and theoretically positioned, therefore more profound. Since negative reactions to the architecture we now generally construe as constructivist were gathering momentum, Melnikov's comments were remarkably candid. "At the first stage of work on a project there is no *a priori* law governing the creative process to which one is subject. A great deal depends on intuition and on what is commonly called the 'creative impulse,'" Melnikov's biographer Frederick Starr extended and summarized the Russian's response to Arkin. "Architecture is the undetermined product of subjective perceptions, rather than the inevitable end-product of the interaction of objective forces. It is *for* society, but it is not *by* society. And since the 'creative impulse' of individuals is central to its existence, architecture is inescapably an art in the fullest sense of the word." Intuition, therefore, "could be guided by many elements."[11] As might have been expected, Melnikov's words were interpreted as heretical.

When translated and printed in *Architecture of the USSR* in February 1934 as "How I Work," Wright's comments about method were similar to his typescript. Translating Wright's writing into another language is, as can be imagined, difficult at best. Liberties must be taken to correctly place his words within the logic of the new language. For instance, to close the first paragraph where he introduced his responses he wrote in his typescript: "But to answer your questions as may be"; this was translated as "I will attempt to supply answers to your questions," a more reasonable sentence in English or Russian. Wright's answers to Arkin's nine questions were published together with illustrations of drawings not of Wright's latest work but of the Bock Studio and Robie House, of 1906 and 1908. This selection suggests an interest in the man who fathered modern architecture and not in the man of the 1920s and 1930s. They were interested in the youngish radical who offered promise for a machine aesthetic, ideas that had infected the futurists, and for architectural forms independent of the past neatly linked to a methodology that infected the constructivists and Central Europeans. Arkin did not substantially alter or edit Wright's comments, including those about the evils of facadism or the comment that collectivism and "committee meeting" do not "give anything. They can only create compromises." The essence of his architectural theory, if not adequately distilled, was thinly revealed. It would have been recognized by those who had read Wright's writings of 1908, 1911, 1931, and 1932, but not from a reading of Arkin's "Notes on American Architecture" of January 1934 in the same magazine.

It seems that Arkin was responsible for the dissemination of information about Western architecture during the critical years when the State was wrenching control of the arts from artists, that is 1932–35. His January 1934 "notes" about American architecture were a survey that concentrated on the skyscraper and urbanism. Arkin commented on neoclassical and neo-Gothic works and on "romantic" architecture which he believed was exemplified by H. H. Richardson. And Arkin noted the USA's "own early modernism in the personage of Arthur [sic] Sullivan" and "finally, its own natural attempt at a folk appearance, the so-called 'prairie style,' with a large contribution by the innovative and courageous enemy of eclecticism—Frank Lloyd Wright." Later in his piece Arkin said that Wright was a "prominent and eccentric"—perhaps he meant "original"—"spokesman of a contemporary architectural thought" and had made "critical remarks about what is called architectural formalism." Moreover he believed that Wright "boldly undertook new methods and means of architectural creativity" and that the "radical-Utopian" ideas of a "dispersed city," of decentralization along highways, was a "theme developed by Wright" in his Broadacre City. There were a number of illustrations accompanying the article, all about tall buildings or buildings with a plain reduced classicism or of urban situations. The two illustrations of Wright buildings were outside the general theme, however, for again they were buildings of his early years. First, the greater interior hall ("operations room") of the Larkin Building, 1904–06, and the Barton House (identified only as a "country house"), 1903–04, both in Buffalo, New York.[12]

Arkin's articles and editorial comments make it clear that he was not wholly committed to the changes, aesthetic and administrative, that the Soviet Party was demanding. His hesitancy and no doubt that of his editorial colleagues at *Architecture of the USSR* is reflected in their selection of articles and of architects as well as in content. As mentioned earlier, those who supported modernism were persistent; but not after 1937.

The annual enquiries from Moscow continued in 1935 when the Society for Cultural Relations with Foreign Countries asked Wright five questions, each related to promotions for a traditional aesthetic orthodoxy. His replies were in a manner similar to those for *Pravda* in 1933 but more terse. The "situation of Art and Art Workers in Europe and America" was at a "stalemate confusing old and new." And "perspectives" for 1936 were of more confusion. His note about the "methods of Soviet Art" and the "position of Soviet Art Workers" was coupled with a view of the influence of Soviet realism: it needed more "organic character." And his "wishes for Soviet Art in 1936" were for a "Russian art for Russian life."[13] Wright preferred to ignore pet Soviet terms such as "art workers" (in the 1980s a popular term in semisocialist countries such as Britain and Australia) and instead quite correctly referred to artists and architects. These various written requests for Wright's views were constructed in such a way that suggests they probably were sent to many architects, perhaps in the Soviet Union or outside. It is not known if this last response was published, but for purposes of this discussion it is not too important. The desire of the Union hierarchy to maintain contact with the venerable architect is important.

Wright was primarily and preeminently a producer of architecture for the entirety of his career that began in 1886. In the 1930s his architectural productivity was knitted to and extended by ideas for cities; city planning, perhaps. Soviet city planning was rather vaguely known in the West,[14] except that for Moscow, the spiritual focus of Mother Russia. Beginning in 1928 sixty new industrial cities were proposed for the Russian and Ukrainian areas of the USSR.[15] With the introduction of the first Five-Year Plan in 1929 those cities were constructed, many to designs in which Europeans participated like Ernst May who, with Mart Stam, proposed a plan for the new city of Magnitogorsk that replaced Leonidov's proposed linear scheme of 1930.[16]

But Moscow was in disrepair and in need of renovation and enlarging. Many proposals were offered including one for a ring of Garden Cities.[17] In 1931 the Party decided that Moscow would remain where it was and decreed a limit to its growth. Planners set to work and prepared a comprehensive ten-year plan for the city which was approved in 1935. In the process of their deliberations they consulted many people including architects in Germany and France. Le Corbusier suggested Moscow be preserved as an urban museum, so the story goes, and a city of super-high-density towers be built nearby;[18] in other words a reiteration of his 1925 Paris plan. May, who was in residence in Moscow from 1930 until 1933 when he left hurriedly, also proposed a satellite town.[19] It has been reported that Wright was asked his views, although there is no record of such a request.[20] However, at the 1937 Moscow All-Union meeting in May, Professor S. E. Chernyshev summarized the basic elements of a similar Moscow general plan in six parts. Part four said that in the socialist city "there is removed the difference between the rich center and the poor outskirts with their slums. In contrast to the capitalist city, where all the public and cultural buildings are concentrated in the center, in our Soviet cities there follows a planned distribution of these buildings over the entire area with the aim of bringing them nearer to the population for convenience and service."[21] Such a distribution was an essential part of Broadacre City theory as published from 1931 to 1935 and known in Russia.

 After the theoretically challenging city designs proposed c. 1929 to c. 1931, including the linear plan for Stalinsk, later Stalingrad, the Moscow plan was plain and practical.[22] Its general layout was probably based on the Prost plan for Paris of 1934, and that was no doubt indebted in Eugène Hénard's proposal of 1905.[23] While the plans of other socialist cities were not well known outside the Soviet Union, the revitalization of Moscow was well publicized.

 Were there other architectural ideas and products getting out of the USSR of which Wright might have been aware? Not very much but enough to intrigue. Melnikov was the only Soviet architect given his own section at the Machine Age Exposition in New York in 1927. Again in 1933 he was selected by a jury of the Milan Triennale as one of the twelve great contemporary architects. The only American selected was Wright. The others were Sant'Elia (Italy), Pierre Jeanneret and Le Corbusier (Switzerland/France), August Perret and Lurçat (France), Adolph Loos (Austria) and Willem Dudok (Holland), Josef Hofman (Austria), and from Germany Mendelsohn, Mies van der Rohe, and Gropius.[24] Four of these greats, Gropius, Mies, Mendelsohn, and Dudok, have confessed to being greatly influenced by Wright prior to 1925; all showed stylistic knowledge of Wright, and we now know that Le Corbusier imitated the American's early work, an admission he was unwilling to offer personally.[25] The fact remains that Soviet architectural ideas revealed by their many projects, competitions, or completed works were seldom published in English prior to the 1930s. The exception is the publication of theoretical proposals (in the main) in *L'Architecture vivante* from time to time from 1925 to 1927, at the same time that the magazine was publishing Wright's work.

 As to Wright's ability to read foreign languages we are not certain. His mistress Mamah Borthwick had translated some of Ellen Key's writings from Swedish to English as well as some of

Goethe's works.[26] Mamah lived in Germany during 1909–10 and together they lived in Italy. After Mamah's death, Wright was in Japan on and off from 1916 to 1922, usually with his new mistress Miriam Noel. His interest, though, in languages other than English remained peripheral. His main source of information would have been English-language magazines and journals, and of course drawings and photographs regardless of the publication's language.

Soviet architectural ideas were published only parsimoniously in Britain and the United States. Even so, Wright would have been aware of them. For instance, Roderick Seidenberg's article about "Symmetry and Ornament Discarded as Russia Casts Off the Past" appeared in *The American Architect*.[27] Seidenberg had just returned from Russia in 1930 "where he acted as consulting architect on a number of projects." He listed six characteristics of the Soviet-inspired architecture he witnessed: it was "akin to engineering"; strict economy encouraged a solution stark and barren; ornament was discarded in favor of "expression," which was achieved through placement and relation of form alone; symmetry was also discarded, for it was "arbitrary and lifeless"; circular and rectangular masses were mixed; and lastly, he asserted, architecture was only propaganda—it was "communal in nature."

The May 1932 issue of the English periodical *The Architectural Review* was devoted to a splendid survey of Russian architecture with one part written by Berthold Lubetkin. Also included was a report on Soviet city planning ideas, including those of Nikolai A. Miliutin, and a note that the German architect Ernst May was working with a team of twenty-five of his countrymen at the State Institute of City Planning in Moscow. Then in 1935 *The Studio*'s special autumn number was devoted entirely to "Art in the U.S.S.R." with Soviet authors. David Arkin, then secretary of the Society of Soviet Architects in Moscow, wrote about architecture. He warned that constructivism had led to the "fetishism of technique."[28] Some incidental information was also revealed that helps build a picture of the progress of Russian theory and practice. An example was Moisei Ginzburg's prefabricated concrete structure for a one-family house, which appeared in *Decorative Art: The Studio Year Book* in 1933.[29] Not typical was an influential book by Wright's friend Erich Mendelsohn, *Russland, Europa, Amerika* of 1929. Short, gentle, yet optimistic, even prophetic opinions accompanied what was mainly a picture book of universal themes. The opinions, however, should have been more highly valued. Since a Wright building was illustrated, suspicion suggests a copy may have been sent to Wisconsin.

Generally speaking, American professional magazines covered European architectural events from time to time but invariably excluded eastern Europe. In the May 1934 issue of *The*

Architectural Record, however, Sigfried Giedion, European propagandist for the International Style, put together a large picture portfolio of European work and included the USSR. He commented on the "experiments" of 1927–29 and lamented the "reaction in favor of classical styles." However, he believed Soviet city planning ideas were "of international importance."

In 1930, Buckminster Fuller financially took over *T-Square* (formerly *T-Square Club Journal*) of Philadelphia and became its publisher and editor. The magazine became an organ of Structural Study Associates (SSA), a loose confederation of like-minded people that included Simon Breines, who was invited to the Soviet architectural congress in 1937; Henry Churchill, New York City architect and a friend of Wright's; Theodore Larson, then editor of *The Architectural Record;* and Knud Lönberg-Holm, a Swedish emigrant who also wrote about Wright and signed as a Friend of the Fellowship in 1932. In 1932 Fuller renamed the magazine *Shelter* and also asked Wright to write a couple of articles. Fuller published a series of articles about Russian architecture and American architects in Russia in November 1932. American O. K. Fulmer talked of his experiences in "An Architect in Russia"; one "M. M. R." wrote a letter from Moscow that elicited a response from Larson of little consequence; Matthew Ehrlich wrote a note from Sverdlovskii, Siberia; and a confessed former employee of Wright's (name unfortunately withheld but other evidence suggests Michael A. Kostanecki)[30] challenged the magazine to publish an article by S. T. Woznicki, Managing Editor of the Polish magazine *Architekture i Budownictwo.* The article was about the proposed Palace of the Soviets, entitled "U.S.S.R.—On the Problems of Architecture," and when published a copy was sent to Wright.[31] On a few occasions Wright also contributed to Fuller's magazine. Fuller closed *Shelter* after the November 1932 issue, probably for financial reasons.

Certainly none of the Western architectural journals contained information about political events within the Soviet profession or instituted by the Communist Party of the USSR. From his own remarks we know that Wright read these American and British magazines.

In the early 1930s an architectural competition for a Palace of the Soviets was begun and among other intentions it was to signal a new architectural awakening in Russia. When completed it would be the most important building in the USSR, rather like a new Palace of Westminster, London, or a new Capitol building for Washington, D.C., or the more recent competition for a new Parliament House in Canberra, Australia, in the 1980s; or perhaps, as Kenneth Frampton suggests, it was a "deliberate" response to the League of Nations building. In the obvious and intense light of totalitarian Soviet Russia, the design and style (if there was to be one) would be enormously influential. Indeed, during the period 1932 to 1938 it was the most widely publicized architectural piece promoted by the Soviets. Historian Bliznakov mentions that the building was "to symbolize the power and express the ideology of socialism."[32]

The first competition was held as early as 1923, without material result. The competition announced in 1931 for the Palace of the Soviets (note the conservative revivalist symbolism of the title "palace") was conducted in four stages. The first was an internal competition in 1931 to determine the scope of the project. The second, announced in that same year, was an international competition, which in early 1932 drew 272 entries, twenty-four of which were received from foreign architects. In the May 1932 issue of *The Architectural Review* entries were illustrated (all too small) and discussed for an English-speaking audience. Included were designs by Le Corbusier; Gropius and the partnership of Blum, Lubetkin and Sigalin; August Perret; B. M. Iofan (the "most highly commended"); Hans Poelzig; Langbard; Barzini (the "Fascist Italian"); Mendelsohn; and the Americans Hector O. Hamilton and Joseph Urban. Thirteen projects, not necessarily prize winners, were selected for the third stage to be completed by June 1932. Of those only five made it to the fourth stage, due in February 1933. Hamilton of New York won a special prize and traveled to Moscow by invitation but was eventually disappointed; he was not to be invited to participate in stage three. The following brief description by Bliznakov reveals the subordination of architecture to political ends by bureaucratic means.

While there was no exact problem in the first stage . . . the second stage carried functional requirements but no specification regarding style. For each succeeding stage the stylistic requirements became more specific, thus gradually diminishing the possibilities of success for modern designs. . . . In the hope of uniting all Soviet architectural factions behind a project of such exceptional importance and of arriving at a design solution that would combine the best features of modern and classical styles, the jury also invited the Vesnin brothers, Ginzburg and Golosox . . . and Ladovsky . . . to join in the third stage. The leaders of Constructivism, however, were over confident about the inevitable triumph of their principles regarding proletarian architecture. Only the Vesnin brothers were asked to rework their project for the fourth stage and compete against four of the most eclectic projects. The Vesnins arrived at the simple solution of hiding the extensive glass area of their original project by encircling the entire building with rows of [classical] columns. But this compromise was not sufficient to satisfy the jury.[33]

Iofan's project eventually won, so to speak, but construction never began. It was not a style but a grandiose eclectic collection that captured international attention not so much for its quality but for

**15.2 Aerial perspective of the Palace of
Soviets by B. Iofan, architect, a competition (of sorts) of which this was the final
proposal of 1934, widely published, never
constructed.**

its gigantism and tendentiousness. But then architecture has always served propagandists from king to prince to government to business corporation to political party.

An American observer of things about the Soviet Union for whom Wright designed a small apartment house in 1930, Elizabeth Noble, wrote a summary that parroted official party views about the palace. She based much of her article on reports from Moscow and from a catalogue edited by Talbot Faulkner Hamlin for an exhibition held in February–March 1938 at the Architectural League in New York, possibly seen by Wright, called "Architecture and City Construction in the U.S.S.R." Only a few months later the League held an exhibition of Wright's work. While written after events presented here, Noble's comments are valuable to the present discussion. Writing in the 15 March 1938 issue of the American magazine *New Masses,* she said in part that final instructions of the committee for construction "stated that the tendency to design low buildings should be overcome by a 'bold composition of great height,' adding, 'It is desirable that the structure should be given a tower effect, at the same time avoiding cathedral motifs.'" Noble wrote that the resulting design might offend "bourgeois taste," that the proposed structure "would outsoar the Empire State building by 200 feet," that the volume would be greater "than all the buildings of Rockefeller Center together," and that the statue of Lenin on top would be "larger than the Statue of Liberty." She noted that Iofan's design embodied the "fluted modernism" of Hamilton's preliminary plan. She also believed that in spite of Wright's adverse criticism of the design he was otherwise "full of enthusiasm for the broad, democratic 'social upbuilding' now in progress in the U.S.S.R."[34]

In another study in preparation of Wright's architecture of the period 1886–1913, I explain how Wright embraced the past inasmuch as each instance was a model of its time. It was his view that to adore those older models was narcissistic, even potentially self-destructive. Wright was indeed critical as Noble indicated, but the full import of his criticism, directed to all works exemplified by Iofan's palace, or rather his response to the Party's demands, had been succinctly stated many years earlier at Princeton University in 1930: "this modern ideal of an organic architecture" is an architecture no longer "composed or arranged or pieced together as symbolic," it is an architecture intimately and continually destroying "the Old by the New," it is an architecture that was "no longer symbolic sculpture." In his view, therefore, the Soviet's proposed palace was burdened with a grossly displayed symbolism and vulgar monumentality, characteristics abhorrent to the constructivists as much as to Wright.

It is not too difficult to understand and appreciate reaction against constructivist architecture as presented by the built product. It was dull (proponents would say severely chaste), uninteresting, lacked ornament (proponents would say it showed proportionally refined cubic massing); but more importantly, when constructed it was poorly detailed, weathered badly, and often looked downright ugly. At least Wright found it so, and he believed it naive. Clough Williams-Ellis, who toured the Soviet Union in 1932 and was possibly "the last of the English Arts and Crafts Architects,"[35] seems to have got it partially wrong when he said retrospectively, "On my first visit [1932] their architectural gods had been Ernst Mai, le Corbusier and Wright and starkness was all," but got it right when he continued, "but now [1937] I found them gone all Ritz with the classical orders, marble, carving, and gilding proliferating everywhere."[36] Engineering works were another matter, for there was no tradition of artistic excellence for comparison. It should be remembered that there was negative reaction in the West to the modernism produced just after the turn of the century. There was an important and critical difference. Western architects and clients retained the ability to make a choice; tradition and modernism existed and evolved side by side in pluralistic excitement. Such choices were forbidden in the USSR.

As previously noted, articles in English about Soviet architecture were few in number, a persistent trickle. After 1933 the trickle dried up. The dearth of information was emphasized in 1937 by *The Architectural Record,* which noted, perhaps in the view of editor Larson, that American architects "have followed the fragmentary accounts of recent trends in the architecture of the Soviet Union without obtaining a clear picture of what is going on there."[37] If Wright received any information during those years it would have been filtered through propaganda channels, at occasional Soviet-organized exhibitions, or appearing in the pro-Soviet press including magazines such as *New Masses* or *Soviet Russia Today* (after 1951 *New World Review*). As might be expected, not even the Western socialist or Communist press was kept abreast of—let alone fully aware of—actual happenings in Russia during 1934 to 1938. Certainly propagandists gave subjects such as art and architecture a low priority. It was highly unlikely that Wright would have been aware of the struggles within the Soviet architectural profession between the Party reactionaries, the formalists (to use their vernacular), and the revisionists of the 1920s who, by 1937, were no longer the vanguard but virtually the enemy.

16 Why Attend?

It is not clear why Wright accepted the invitation to attend the Moscow Congress. He was to celebrate his seventieth birthday in June 1937 but before that happy day he had been seriously ill. During the week of 28 October 1936 he gave a lecture at Columbia University in New York. However, probably by early December he developed pneumonia. His strength may have been sapped by a fall from a road grader in June 1936 at Hillside near Taliesin. He suffered some bruising, twisted limbs, and crushed ribs. Also, his left leg was put in a cast in September 1936, "phlebitis (pneumonia aftermath) . . . I broke it up in Tokyo building the Imperial Hotel and it seems a weak place." By 17 December the fever broke but even as late as 26 January 1937 he was still "house bound." His recuperation continued through February and finally in March he traveled to San Francisco and Hollywood, a tired but well man.[1] His major commissions, those with Kaufmann, Hanna, and Johnson, had not received the personal attention he desired. So he was both quite busy and still weak from his recent illnesses. One reason for beginning to build a home in Arizona was to obtain desert warmth in winter. Yet he elected to undertake the long, tiring journey to Russia.

While not clear, reasons provocatively assert themselves as to why he should have visited Moscow. Some are interesting individually while collectively they are quite persuasive. Wright was titillated by exotic places; he needed an occasional change of environment for revitalization; he loved to travel and then to write and talk of those places and the people he had met. From 1917 to 1922 he spent most of his life in Japan. He had traveled to Europe, England, South America, the Caribbean, and all about North America by the time the Moscow invitation arrived at Taliesin. By traveling to Russia his wife would return to a place whose culture would stimulate memories of adolescence, and she would have a chance to see "old friends who might still be alive." She was always reluctant to discuss her family, especially those relatives, possibly only her older sister, who remained in the Soviet Union. After World War II her brother and sister-in-law lived at Taliesin at Wright's insistence. There is no record of meetings with family in Moscow or while traveling to and from the city in 1937. Nevertheless the possibility of some form of contact may have been considered, in fact may have been a major determinant for the visit.

They enjoyed things, whatever they might be, that were outside of—or a challenge to—their view of the Establishment. A trip to Russia was such a challenge. They showed foreign films to the young people of their Fellowship and some were Russian. This proved to be disturbing to rural Wisconsinites. Historian Twombly discovered that when Wright was accused in 1936 of showing too many Soviet films, he replied "that Russian movies were no more propagandistic than American westerns, and that as citizens of the world the Fellowship had an obligation to explore the cultures."[2] Wright even wrote reviews of Russian films for the Madison newspaper *The Capital Times.* The ruralites' views were an understandable conservative response, even though Russian films were not excluded from American movie houses in the 1930s. For instance, during the week in 1932 that Wright visited Seattle, *China Express* was showing at a city cinema (admission 25 cents):

A marvelous Superfilm, portraying

the struggle of the Chinese masses.

A stirring, realistic drama

you will never forget.

MADE IN

SOVIET RUSSIA

In a theater just down the street Rex Lease was playing *The Utah Kid.* By 1943 people at Taliesin had viewed nearly eighty Soviet films,[3] all rented since 1935 from the Soviet-controlled Amkino Corporation in New York City.[4] All this indicates one or two levels of interest in the Soviet Union: but there are more substantial reasons.

Foremost, it seems Wright wanted to test his intellectual liberality. His own life had been one of action in and reaction to society, its norms and shibboleths. He left his first wife for a woman who shared his notion of free love as propounded by Ellen Key and other popularizers of the notion. From 1908 onward he acted out a belief in himself as an institution outside, if not above, his profession and the society it served. Not that he was always antagonistic; he simply believed in the necessity for people to act out their roles individually. He refused to acknowledge the rights of states to protect their people by setting competence tests through professional registration. The list of his protestations, if that is the correct word, against collective society in the name of liberality could be extended, and has been by other historians. Perhaps equally persuasive was the presence of Soviet Union military volunteers, as they were called, overtly fighting totalitarianism in Spain where the fascist forces of Mussolini and Hitler were materially engaged. Further, the Bolsheviks fought czarism and then displayed enormous internal fortitude by a vigorous and repressive reshaping of society into a potent, self-sustaining if demogogic whole. Suffice is to say that Wright was a revolutionary spirit. A personal evaluation *in situ* of the Sovietization of a former monarchy was indeed an enticing proposition.

Practically, then, Wright saw the Soviet experiments of the twenties and early thirties as a challenge to "dead cultures," to use his words, therefore to dead architectural style. He shared at least a portion of the *Zeitgeist* theory then so prevalent in Central Europe and Russia. He believed that the Russia of the 1930s should be the Russia of the 1930s just as he argued that America should—must—be similarly motivated. To the Soviets he prophesied that they would "create a worthy architecture which will be in harmony with the Soviet way of life, just as the Kremlin was in harmony with the social environment which gave birth to it."[5] He saw that in the 1920s established academic roles played by architects and art theorists in Europe and European-based cultures—like the U.S.—were subjected to critical evaluation and scrutiny in the Soviet Union, and that was good. He believed that reappraisal, even revision, was necessary but not of those elements traditionally national: "I see no necessity for Russia to die that the Soviet Union may live," he said.[6] With parallel and equally candid vigor, architecture and American nationalism (his interpretation) dominate his writing from 1930 to at least 1950.

The USSR's possible interest in Wright has been noted. His knowledge of some of those interests must have intrigued him. He knew, of course, that Europe had been thrilled with his ideas and his architecture. He believed that they believed, therefore surely the Soviets believed there was something "correct" in his theories and practice as revealed in his architecture. Perhaps, he might have reasoned, the European response also resulted because he said that he believed, that he was forthright. Did opportunity offer a new platform to proselytize? Did they invite him because they needed him; that is his ideas about architecture, but more importantly about his vision for an organic life? When he confirmed his intention to attend the Congress he said his "sympathy with Russia's need in architecture impels me to go."[7]

A study of Wright's written works in the 1930s, including the collaboration with Baker Brownell, indicates that he was not enamored with American capitalism, so what was the practice of Soviet socialism really like? Was the Taliesin Fellowship, his and Olgivanna's notion of a working school, professional office, and farm, similar to a communal *kolkhoz* or, less likely, a local soviet? And what of those highly praised engineering works, dams, and those new cities and housing projects, underground railways, theaters, and convention halls? Wright must have been intrigued by Moscow's ancient architecture, its tradition as capital of the Russias, the changes proposed, and, since many of the constructivist buildings were built in the big city, its modern architecture.[8] How did Roosevelt's large and expensive Tennessee Valley Authority compare with its Soviet predecessors? How did Russian constructivist architecture look in reality, in its environment?

In the 1930s, for someone disappointed or, in Wright's case, despondent over aspects of the American system as highlighted and exaggerated by the Depression, a trip to the USSR was a tempting proposition. For a man needing heaps of aggrandizement, the opportunity was heaven-sent. In any event the trip was free.

Wright's need of publicity, of being newsworthy, cannot be glossed over as a superficial part of his personality; rather, it was a dominant feature. And if one looks at his manuscripts or literary output after his visit to Moscow, one cannot help but be persuaded that he wanted to become a voice knowledgeable about Russia and only secondarily about Soviet architecture. Indeed his and later Olgivanna's views on Communism, praising yet cautionary, were voiced in writings that began in 1937 and carried well into the 1960s.

17 To Moscow and the Congress

Wright may have intentionally promoted himself in such a way as to obtain the invitation to Russia, and the Congress may have provided a reasonable excuse for the invitation. Yet it would be silly to suggest he ingratiated himself or begged the favor. In January 1933 he sent his former student Michael A. Kostanecki a relatively long letter. In one section he wrote that it was "the time to acquaint Russia with the principles and ideals of an organic architecture." Wright wanted to go himself but since he could not he asked Kostanecki, "why do you not run over and have it out with the young architects in charge of the Soviet architectural destiny?" Wright added that he thought his thoughts about the disappearing city would be "good medicine for them—too."[1] Later in the letter he thought a show he was preparing for the Milan Triennale might thereafter travel to Poland and Russia. Perhaps the young Polish architect passed the word along to the right authorities.

Then in March 1934 Wright wrote to Moissaye J. Olgin, American correspondent for Pravda, that he, Wright, was anxious to know if Olgin had received an earlier letter on a "pressing personal matter."[2] All other correspondence is apparently lost, so the exact subject is unknown. It may have been about Mrs. Wright's family, for instance, or about a visit to Russia, or what? In 1934 Wright was also trying to obtain at least three scholarships from the USSR for their people to attend his Fellowship. Later in 1935 one B. A. Verdernikov in Kiev apparently asked to study with Wright. Wright agreed to take him, and wondered if perhaps "the Soviet" might provide Verdernikov with a scholarship since Wright understood "they are sending young men abroad for special training with different masters."[3] Nothing material eventuated from these letters although correspondence continued sporadically for many years with Kostanecki in Krakow. These letters together with all the evidence previously presented here indicate the extent of Wright's involvement with Russia and the Soviet government prior to June 1937.

Exactly how or when Wright was invited is unknown, but it was in late April and he refused. Then sometime in May 1937 he changed his mind. His acceptance by telegram on 22 May to the Soviet Consul in New York was brief but revealing: "Sir: Felt I must refuse the kind invitation of the Soviet being extremely busy besides feeling unable to undertake expensive journey but circumstances have changed so now pleased to attend convention Moscow June 15th. Mrs Wright will accompany me. My sympathy with Russia's need in architecture impels me to go."[4] It was sent from "Taliesin, Spring Green." As has been noted, he had only recently recovered from an illness. More demanding of his energies was the Kaufmann house which was under construction, and the Johnson administration building and Hanna house had just come into the office. He was indeed busy, busier than he had been for nearly two decades. He was in the second year of his second architectural renaissance. The changed circumstances that he referred to in the telegram probably related to organizing supervision of his new work, perhaps to money and to travel costs and arrangements made by Moscow. The date of the telegram must have been very close to the last moment for such a decision.

Wright's trip to Moscow began in early June 1937. Apprentice Edgar Tafel acted as chauffeur and drove Wright, Olgivanna, and their child Iovanna from Taliesin, through dull Racine and on to Chicago.[5] The Wrights traveled by train from Chicago to New York where they boarded the liner *Queen Mary*. At Cherbourg they disembarked and traveled by train to Paris (where they saw Iofan's Soviet Pavilion for the Paris Exhibition[6]) then, following a short stay, on to Berlin.[7] After a brief time in the German capital, then Hitler's seat of power, they were off again by train for the Russian border. On the final leg of their journey they were accompanied by the English architect Clough Williams-Ellis.[8]

In his autobiography of 1943 Wright described the border area around the town of Njegorieloje. "There was a wide blank space at the frontier, trees all cut down, a kind of no-man's land, a barbed-wire entanglement both sides. Towers with sentries were marching up and down the station platforms on the one side, Polish sentries on the other." At the border some difficulties developed with two customs officials, a man and a woman. Wright said of the incident only that their "examination . . . was getting acrimonious and more and more complex." Olgivanna was more explicit. She warned Wright to curb his normal freely spoken opinions (keep his mouth shut) and reminded him that his tongue might land them in prison. Olgivanna spoke a little Russian and after she intervened things proceeded more smoothly. However, when Wright was asked to open a roll of drawings he carried under his arm he became indignant. "I will not open my roll of drawings."[9] He agreed that customs had the right to inspect all material but he was emphatic; "I will not have you pawing through my drawings."

As Olgivanna described it, things again became rancorous indeed. There were threats from both sides; on one side guns were drawn. Wright could see his country defending his honor with "warships on the Black Sea." A telephone call was made by customs to their Moscow office and while this was in progress Olgivanna again warned Wright that his conduct might land them in jail. Moscow must have said something to the effect that all was right and proper concerning the Wrights. They were then put on a train on which they ate "sumptuous meals" *alone,* Wright emphasized, in the dining car. They were advised to lock and chain their compartment at night. Wright raised the logical question: "Is someone afraid of us, or afraid *for* us?"[10] It needs to be remembered, indeed stressed, that, as historian Kathleen Berton said, "The year 1937 is generally accepted as the beginning of the worst period of the purges in which ten million [sic] were reckoned to have lost their lives. It was in this atmosphere that the First Congress of the Union of Architects was held."[11] On their arrival in Moscow on 21 June, six days after the conference began, the Wrights were welcomed by architects Iofan, Kolli, Arkin, and their spouses who presented Olgivanna with bouquets of flowers. Later, the American Ambassador ("Joe Davies . . . a Madison U. boy," said Wright)[12] privately informed the Wrights of the execution of Marshall Tukhachevsky.

Once the Wrights entered Russia everything was paid for by "the Soviet." Such generosity could not suppress the obvious. In a fleeting, almost parenthetical thought in his 1943 autobiography Wright somberly summarized one lasting impression: in Russia, "Too much going into building up the defense which would inevitably have to be used," he said, "and perhaps just because it was built up to such proportions! It was a subject of which no one spoke. I don't know. The world was in a jam. Great changes coming. And there was something in the air then—May [June], 1937—that made everyone afraid of something he couldn't define."[13]

Outside the Congress Wright saw much of the country in and around Moscow. Aleksei Shchusev took him to see the Russian's design of a "Soviet Hotel" and Iofan described his winning design for the Palace of the Soviets.[14] Of course Wright saw many other buildings during his visit and there was a large exhibition of Soviet architecture mounted in the House of Unions lobby.[15] He found the constructivist buildings a little shabby, "indeed, drab, lonesome, technically childish." He visited a *kolkhoz,* a collective farm where, he said, the same flowers and trees and weeds were seen as those at home in Spring Green. In another Russian village that was part of the official tour and notable for prized nineteenth-century eclectic architecture, he saw "the same herds and the same birds and similar architecture" as those at his Wisconsin home.[16] (In his autobiographical reminiscences he recalled the days in Tokyo during 1917–21 while working on the Imperial Hotel when he entertained Russian expatriates and refugees from the Bolshevik wars—princess so-and-so and "Countess C.")[17] But the thousands of sea and land miles traveled in 1937 were not for the purpose of touring, rather for business of sorts. The business of the Congress had been announced in the Soviet architectural press in May as follows: "The first All-Union Congress of soviet architects is

17.1 Perspective of proposed *Izvestia* building, Moscow, 1926, G. Barkhin, architect.

summoned to complete, amongst its other important tasks, that great spade-work which was conducted for some years in organizing the united creative society of soviet architectural cadres—the Union of Soviet Architects."[18]

Guests at the Congress were divided into language groups and provided with two interpreters who alternated in translating proceedings. The English-speaking group consisted of Harald Hals and Edvard Heiberg from Norway, Sven Markelius from Sweden, from England B. Garrett and Williams-Ellis (who sat with Wright), and Simon Breines and Wright from the USA. The French-speaking group included the Spanish government architects Manuel Sanches-Arcas, J. Martin, and J. Vaamonde, and the Frenchmen Francis Jourdain, Lurçat (a "militant communist" Parisian who was then designing a large hospital group in the USSR),[19] and Marcel Lods. Also present were architects from a few other European and Mediterranean countries; Turkey, Belgium, Rumania, and Czechoslovakia were mentioned.[20] Major papers and discussion resumés were made available in French to all guests.

Breines was an interesting fellow, an architect fully committed to European modernism in thought and practice. He worried about what he saw as social and economic inequities ("evils")—the business, finance, and credit systems—but he did not labor on these. On one occasion he expressed concern over perspective renderings of mainly urban buildings, like those by the popular Hugh Ferris, who in 1929 had published his "ode to the skyscraper," as Manfredo Tafuri has put it, *Metropolis of Tomorrow.* Breines believed they were too impressionistic and false. Honesty was also missing in architectural education and professional practice. They were all linked. Implied was a socially irresponsible Beaux-Arts system infecting education and architectural design. Breines found Wright to be honest as a designer, his own "judge," and this was reflected in his plain "line drawings." Breines confessed to a liking for the new Central European architecture: it did not need the "assistance of artistic paper compositions." His attack was not well received by New York's architectural establishment but at least it was given public air at a lecture and on the pages of *American Architect.*[21] In the early 1930s he was actively involved with The Federation of Architects, Engineers, Chemists and Technicians, a union of sorts dedicated to assisting those groups of professionals during the Depression and promoting their cause to Congress in the hope of inducing employment and a variety of monetary reliefs.[22] In 1946 Crown published a book by Breines and John P. Dean, *The Book of Houses,* on how to make selections in postwar America.

Breines was impressed by efforts in the Soviet Union generally and the Congress particularly because constituents from all the USSR participated and because, he said, "the proceedings were carried on in an atmosphere of vigorous, free, and objective discussion and self-criticism." Breines reportedly collaborated with Joseph Vanderkar and they were one of the place-getters in the international competition for a Palace of Soviets. They traveled to Moscow as a result, possibly in 1932–33. However Breines and the Wrights may have got along in Moscow, Wright subsequently makes no mention of Breines. With Ralph Pomerance, Breines maintained a partnership in New York from the 1930s into the 1970s. In 1938–39 they were associates to Soviet architect Karo Alabian and site architects for the USSR pavilion built for the New York World's Fair.[23]

The papers presented at the Congress were routine and repetitive. They praised Stalin; they dealt with achievements in various states and cities in the USSR, with tasks for Soviet architects, with reports on the Palace of Soviets, with city planning, especially for Leningrad and Moscow, and with "reconstruction" for housing, industrialization, and education.[24] The first day set the pace, style, and tone. Karo Alabian, by then "principal scribe and purveyor of the official party line in Soviet architecture" and general secretary of the organizing committee of the architects' Union, offered the keynote address.[25] He "plunged directly into the question of the hour" when he asked, "What is the social function of architecture in the USSR and what form shall it take?"[26] He gave no answers, finding it easier to list those architects who failed "to serve the interests of the people," such as Melnikov the individualist, Nikolsky and the Vesnins the constructivists, "who adhered to the 'modern' or 'functional' style."[27]

Pravda noted in one of its daily postmortems that architectural styles and ideas as well as architects themselves came under scrutiny and were praised or damned. The newspaper continued its resumé. The only true realistic architecture was that which had been formulated by the Party. Were ideas of present-day Europe and America of use? . . . we have to learn from them . . . "we must catch up," said Aleksei Shchusev.[28] Soviet architects must learn to express truth (wisely left undefined). Ancient architecture should be a source of ideas but not copied mechanically. The architecture of the capitalist countries was experiencing a decline because it had exploited the masses. Technology would be a key to success. Architects must be reeducated. Within the ranks of our architects were enemies of the people, and they and their works were "exposed." True Party lines had not been achieved by academic architecture, i.e., the schools were not providing a proper education (Ginzberg, Viktor Vesnin, and Melnikov were professors). Some architects followed the leftist bourgeois art—the Central European modernists—because they did not understand the political ideas of Lenin. One of the more important aspects of Soviet architecture, said N. J. Kolli, was the influx of constructivist architectural ideas in the 1920s. French architect Le Corbusier was one of its promoters and, emphasized Kolli, his style became a basis of Soviet architecture.[29] And on and on it went for a very long week like a Russian novel.

The Congress papers had been more-than-less prescribed by *Pravda*.[30] As well, factory workers, Red Army personnel, writers, painters, sculptors, and artists participated or performed publicly or criticized architects and their buildings. Architects, planners, and bureaucrats from all the Soviet republics and major cities attended, with representatives giving papers. The good and the bad in their realms were exposed. A desire for regional identification was a rare positive contribution, the implication being that ethnic cultures should be allowed to express themselves. Some architects confessed the error of their ways and pledged closer adherence to the Party. Viktor Vesnin pointed out that while it was true that many postwar architectural ideas from the West had been adopted without sufficient criticism and with an incorrect ideological approach, nevertheless it was equally true that in the 1920s constructivism contained much of value.[31] He admitted that he and his brother Aleksandr had erred in not vigorously combatting extremists in their ranks. But, he said, "the way to overcome constructivism is through the application of socialist architecture," and by a scientific method.[32] He was politely suggesting that if one was to redefine socialist architecture, precision was necessary. The exact method was left undefined, perhaps purposely so.

After summarizing the papers, the Party took the architects to task in the pages of *Pravda*. For instance, Viktor Vesnin was old-fashioned. He and Moisei Ginzberg followed individualism and did not disclose their own mistakes in their speeches. Their confessions and new pledges soon followed this.[33] The Congress purged Melnikov from the profession and his teaching position; he was ostracized. Then resolutions were passed including a demand to overcome formalism and, oddly, eclecticism; medals were given; and new pledges of solidarity were offered.[34] In the foreword to his book *Constructivist Architecture in the USSR,* Anatole Kopp was concise: one result of the Congress was to "erase" all reference "to the achievements, projects and theoretical research that had made the Soviet Union one of the poles of progress in architecture and town planning during the 1920s." That censorship was effective for the next forty years.

The Congress closed on 26 June. On that day before the closing ceremony Wright's paper was read.

18 Wright's Paper

There are four versions of Wright's speech in Moscow in 1937: two are Russian, one by *Pravda* and one by the journal *Arkhitektura SSR* (or *Architecture of the USSR*), and two by Wright. Each version served a different purpose. Not one wholly agreed with the others and for good reasons. The first

17.2 *Izvestia* building, Moscow, 1927–28,
G. Barkhin, architect, photograph by Frank
Yerbery in the early 1930s, courtesy of the
Architectural Association, London. The
distance between paper theory and reality
was often dramatic.

**17.3 Red Army Theater, Moscow, 1934–40,
K. Alabian and V. Simbirtsev, architects. A
building often photographed as represent-
ing the Stalinist notion of socialist
realism.**
**Illustrations for chapter 13 and the *Izves-
tia* and Red Army theater buildings are
representative of what Wright would have
seen in European magazines or in Moscow
in 1937.**

version was prepared by the editors of the newspaper *Pravda* as a resumé for public consumption, especially Russian. The other was prepared as a quasi record of proceedings for professional consumption by architects and city planners throughout the Soviet Union. This second version and the *Pravda* resumé are close in content, different in length. Two were prepared for Wright's public, one a 1943 version and another of 1977.

As previously noted, *Pravda* published a running account of the major events at the Congress a day or two after they occurred. The resumé and edited selections by TASS of Wright's speech were short and, as was typical, accompanied by a photographic portrait. The summary lost much of Wright's flavored and elliptical prose, giving only a dry presentation of detail suitable for a nonprofessional audience.

Speech of American Architect
Frank Lloyd Wright

My dear comrades. I come to you from afar having crossed the borders of five countries to get from America to the USSR. I find that thanks to Soviet aviation the USSR and USA are the closest neighbors.

I am happy to be among you as I am already aware of your countrymen's struggle for an architecture worthy of your new Soviet life.

Due to our need for new architecture we in America have followed the wrong path. The path of imitating fallen or dead cultures and our official architecture is a disgrace to a free country. Our highly acclaimed achievements—Skyscrapers! What do they represent? No more and no less than a victory for engineering and the defeat of architecture.

Hidden by their facing of stone which are attached to steel frames, the skyscrapers imitate the stone masonry of feudal towers. They are stunning but they are false, as false as the economy that made the building of them possible in dull urban districts.

The left wing of the so-called modern architecture did not proceed beyond smooth walls, flat roofs and corner windows while the right wing was satisfied in advancing ornamental buildings. Both are signs of the death of modern Western architecture.

Organic architecture knows (and America is slowly and painfully realizing it) that grandomania is not greatness.

It seems to me that the Soviet Union must concentrate their efforts on good planning and construction and refrain from attempts to impart to them unneeded farfetched shapes. I

am sure that your architecture will find a way of expressing your new Soviet life. The USSR will justify the hopes of the world by not creating a false architecture and I hope that the USA will learn this too.

F. L. Wright further dwells on planning of cities.

America is far behind, he says, from correct city planning. Her economic system interferes with this and private ownership makes planning impossible.

Addressing the young architects of the Soviet Union Wright says.

I call upon you to gradually achieve the heights of building that we call architecture. Learn construction and structural principles that have their basis in technology and organic architecture and having mastered these principles create architecture harmonious with your Soviet life.

Country of freedom, such is the Soviet Union. It must leave a treasure for the future.

I take home with me brilliant impressions of your achievements and the greatest hope I have ever nourished for the wonderful future of life on this earth.[1]

These selections were what one might expect. There were references to Soviet achievement in aviation (Wright acknowledged the just-completed flight of the Soviet air force over the north pole from Russia to Seattle which had been proudly announced to the Congress);[2] to problems in the United States; and even a note about freedom in the Soviet Union in spite—or because—of the persistent revelations during the mid-1930s of conflict, purges, and death. But a more careful examination of Wright's speech can be made only when the full text is known.

The *Architecture of the USSR* version was next chronologically with a publication date of July 1937. As a congress of importance to the professional body and to the profession as a functioning, pragmatic serving group, it seems reasonable to assume that a full record was kept. There are other reasons for trusting this version of the speech. One cannot think of a creditable reason for the Soviets to dramatically alter Wright's speech. It was relatively praiseworthy of Russian efforts. As will be discussed, it supported at least part of the political and theoretical—architectural—stance of the Union organizers. Also, it would come under the scrutiny of the journal's overseas subscribers and the Wrights probably would see the publication, though it is unknown if they did.

Of the two versions of the speech published by Wright himself, he altered the 1943 text to form the 1977 account, so one can assume he made changes to the 1937 original to form the 1943 text: an assumption supported by changes to a suspect manuscript held by the Wright archives. It is also supported by the fact that articles written by Wright and published in the 1930s were changed by him for their republication in his 1943 autobiography. There are, for instance, alterations to his article "Architecture and Life in the USSR," which had appeared previously in both *The Architectural Record* and *Soviet Russia Today*. Since those magazines served different audiences Wright's text was edited to suit; again differing versions. In any event he stated in his autobiography that he prepared the Moscow text which was then translated into Russian by *Pravda* correspondents.[3] Such a process could have allowed a tempering of language and structure of his speech. Then that translation was vetted by his wife. The fact that the speech was carefully prepared was unusual in Wright's long career as an off-the-cuff speaker, something he was rather proud of.[4] But why did Olgivanna not provide the initial translation? The reason is clear: the language of her childhood was Montenegrin and of her teen years Serbian, both Slavic languages but not Russian. Her third language was Georgian, Russian her fourth, and French her fifth. English was well down the list by the time she and Wright met in 1924. Anyway, Wright spoke a few introductory and concluding words in English to his Moscow audience, the first and last paragraphs below, which are not part of either Wright version. His text as prepared and translated was read in Russian to the Congress by Nikolai Kolli[5] of the Union of Soviet Architects.[6]

Frank Lloyd Wright (USA)

Before embarking on the essence of my address, I should like to express my sympathetic admiration and to point out that I have seen your country's quite remarkable achievements. Architecture is a very complex matter; it represents a distinctive interpretation of life. Hence one has to approach the solving of architectural issues with very careful forethought and attention.

Dear Comrades, I came to you from afar having crossed on my way here the borders of five countries. I have arrived from the USA, a country that is the great hope of the world, to the USSR which is equally a country of great hope for the world. But since I arrived here it has turned out that, thanks to Soviet aviation, the USSR and USA are very close neighbors indeed, living almost side by side in the center of the northern hemisphere! . . . [ellipsis in source]

I am happy to be among you—already I have had time to acquaint myself with the struggle you lead for the creation of an architecture worthy of your new Soviet life.

I understand you better since, in that struggle for new technique, my country was at one time in the same situation you presently find yourself. We too were faced with a choice— either crawl back into the shell of an old culture, or barely go forward and create our own

18.1 Wright with Soviet architects and politicians in the Palace of Unions in June 1937. The four people either side of Wright are, left to right, N. A. Bulganin (Chairman of "Moscow soviet"), perhaps N. Zholtovsky, Alex. Nikolsky, and G. Kochar. The man partly hidden by Wright may have been N. Kolli.

social order. With this obvious direction before us, however, we made a mistake—we proceeded on the wrong path, that of imitation.

The rapid growth of science, industrial technology, and mechanical means, applied to the exploration of huge natural resources of our country, suddenly presented us with great wealth. These advances considerably surpassed our knowledge of the basic principles of art. Developing an extensive and great building activity, we were guided by architectural samples from the arsenal of dead or decayed cultures. Hence our official professional architecture is a disgrace to a free country. Our official buildings indicate, at best, merely the achievement of our very considerable triumphs in the field of science and industry.

Only now, in ours as well as some other countries, from the standpoint of modern needs, there is beginning to break through a genuine architecture to replace the artificial ornamental style with which we previously adorned our cities. This new growth of a genuine culture emanates from the people and is based on a truly national culture.

The fact that our buildings excel in top-quality workmanship is a poor consolation for us architects. Our highly acclaimed architectural achievement is the skyscraper. But what does it really represent? The skyscraper is no more and no less than a victory for engineering and the defeat of architecture.

This rising, steel framework of a skyscraper is generally hidden behind a thin facing of stone blocks imitating the masonry of feudal towers.

Skyscrapers are stunning, but they are false and artificial, like the economic structure that gave rise to their emergence in dull congested urban areas.

In some of your buildings, constructed to serve the people, I noticed architectural motifs created in the old days by the aristocracy's culture. The adornment of this very hall speaks of that idle lifestyle and of a considerably lower standard than the level of that which we call organic architecture.

It is difficult to overcome the palatial style. The tendency toward grandomania when prevailed upon in one place, sometimes becomes apparent in another—and where it is least expected. Aspirations for such magnificence at times become popular because it becomes apparent that there is difficulty in finding another, more refined expression of life in architecture.

Just at present, with the day of a new freedom dawning for mankind, we are imbued with new ideas, loftier than those ideals that occasionally inspired the old cultures. The old cultures were able to create only the outward signs of well-being, whereas a flourishing new culture springs from the basis of internal growth. Such growth develops slowly, but I am convinced that this is the only right and safe course to genuine growth.

The USSR must now construct buildings on a scientific basis, guided by common sense and making the most efficient use of high-quality building materials. The left wing of the so-called "new" architecture also advocated the principles of creating an organic architecture but, to all intents and purposes, did not proceed beyond plain wall panels, flat roofs, and ornamental corner windows; and the right wing of said "new" architecture turned the buildings into ornament. Both tendencies are generated by decaying old cultures. The correct path to the creation of organic architecture consists of the scientific organization of building activity and animating it with a genuine spirit of humanity.

In the USA, slowly and painfully we are beginning to realize that megalomania does not stand for greatness. That exaggeration is alien to organic architecture.

Architects of the Soviet Union must now concentrate their efforts on good planning and sound construction, refrain from superficial decoration on their buildings and from attempts to impart to them forced and far-fetched shapes, until your young architects find new technical forms and the images expressive of the new ways of Soviet life, in the same manner as the architecture of the Kremlin similarly expressed old Russia. Under these conditions, the USSR will doubtless justify the hopes of the world, and create in it a new genuine architecture. I hope that some day the USA will learn this too.

Do not squander your talents on trivialities; do not be carried away by superficial "taste." Architecture is more and more coming into the spheres of science and philosophy.

America is far behind from correct town planning. Its economic system interferes with this. Private property ownership makes correct planning impossible. Soviet Russia, however, came to the realization of the value of correct planning ideas. Organic architecture will not only express such ideas of a new free life but also ensure, in the USSR, the possibility of living one's life better than anywhere else. Ideas of Soviet Russian organic architecture will spread to those other countries on the continent if they continue their insular way of life in those continental countries.

Young architects of the Soviet Union, I call upon you to continuously improve so you may reach the very heights of architecture. Overcome all difficulties. Study your design meticulously, thoroughly master construction and structural principles that have their basis in

technology and, inspired by your Soviet vision, you will create a worthy architecture that will be in harmony with your Soviet way of life just as the Kremlin was in harmony with the social environment that gave it birth.

The Kremlin, when relieved of its later decorations, represents one of the greatest treasures of all times and nations. Soviet Russia must honor its great architectural monuments, but not imitate them. Genuine architecture retains its significance eternally. But new principles of freedom, embodied in the Soviet Union itself, will generate other great art treasures.

I take away with me from the USSR many impressions of brilliant achievements, and the greatest hope I have ever nourished—the hope for mankind and the future of life on earth.[7]

Writing in his autobiography, Wright thought his speech was splendid. "I have never had so great an ovation in my life," he said. "Again and again I had to go back, the applause continuing until I reappeared to take my seat beside Olgivanna."[8] But the report in *Architecture of the USSR* and *Pravda* said otherwise. Response to Wright's speech was controlled. There was a more or less spontaneous applause after he said that the skyscraper rather than being a triumph for architecture was its defeat. And a rather sustained and vigorous ("stormy") but polite applause at the end. By comparison Manuel Sanches-Arcas, who was a guest from "Heroic Spain," received ten almost intrusive "cheers" and applause and a "standing ovation" on a few occasions.[9] But then he was highlighting the few successes of Soviet-supported troops and the role of architects in and out of uniform in Spain. With much optimism Sanches concluded his paper, "They will not pass!," *no pasarón.* There is, however, a more plausible accounting for the disparity. Elements of Wright's speech contradicted some aspects of Stalinism, at least certain cultural notions. Neither the architectural magazine nor *Pravda* would have wished their readership to know that such heresy received a warm response.

The three themes in Wright's talk were technology, aesthetics, and new societies. His approach to them in 1937 was not too different from that of previous years. It is not technological achievement in itself that is important, he argued, but how it is applied. For architecture it is not enough, for instance, to be able to build skyscrapers. They must be necessary in the grand scheme of things and they must not be sham masonry. It is not correct to achieve technological break-throughs without concomitant changes in theories of art, in aesthetics. To apply technological advances to buildings that look like those of the old "dead cultures" is wrong. New societies must demand new aesthetic responses, especially in architecture and town planning. The thread that runs through and knits the speech is Wright's vision of an organic architecture—the complete theory—

and individual artistic responsibility to interpret the needs of a society.

Some interesting points were made by Wright that now seem rather obvious in their support of the revisionists, especially as laid out by *Pravda* on 15 June and some of the papers outlined above. Skyscrapers in general reflect capitalist ventures with resulting slums. The "left wing" to Wright were the Central Europeans and their impotent internationalism. To the Soviets the "left wing" represented naive followers without a proper ideological knowledge of Lenin. To both sides they were formalists and wrong. It is not clear what or who represented Wright's "right wing," but one suspects those styles similar to or less modern than art deco—ideas and ornament derivative of the past. To the Russians the right approached the old traditionalists. Both Wright and the right advocated technology and science as necessary. Both were discouraged by certain aspects of American society and its architecture. It is difficult to explain what Wright meant by "official" architecture, perhaps governmental or that which is generally accepted by fashion or by the American Institute of Architects. Either way, the parallel with party policy was clear. "Grandomania" was a reference to Iofan's winning design for the Palace of the Soviets—an apt term. Wright did argue against eclecticism but not effectively. And, as previously mentioned, he encouraged a search for an architecture worthy of modern Soviet aspirations. That was one of the terms of reference for the Congress as set out by *Pravda.*

All these and other issues in the speech had been raised and argued by Wright before. He almost certainly was not aware of the ideological and hierarchical battles within the Soviet architectural profession that had preceded the Congress and was therefore ignorant of those lingering potently within the course of the Congress. His reading of articles in the Philadelphia architectural magazine *Shelter,* for instance, where the discussion of the Palace of the Soviets competition was reported, would not have given him proper insight into those problems, only that there was an ongoing discourse. The heat of that debate would have eluded him. But the Soviets were most certainly aware of Wright's views.

His speech, therefore, must be seen in two lights. First, it was only a courtesy that they asked him to speak. Note that his talk was in the evening of the last day. This courtesy can be interpreted as one means of publicly acknowledging the presence of the patriarch of twentieth-century architecture. But then many of the foreign guests gave a speech. Wright's speech was not meant to set the tone of the Congress or to be something similar to a keynote address; it was rather like an after-dinner speech. So they allowed him to sit through six days of proceedings without saying a word. Then, as recorded by *Pravda,* the speech was somewhat confusing if short, rather naive professionally; yet much of it fitted nicely into the Union leaders' schemes. All things considered it was probably somewhat disappointing to Wright's hosts—the architects if not the Union leaders and the Party.

And again some interesting questions arise. Was he invited in the hope that he would reiterate his well-known dislikes of aspects of American politics and economics and its architecture, and thereby add credence to the position of the Union and the Party? Or was he asked to talk about those subjects after his arrival? Or did he respond to some of the issues raised at the Congress, those that fitted his ideas? Or did he prepare his manuscript before arrival in Moscow? Perhaps a comparison of his responses to *Architecture of the USSR* in 1933 with his talk in 1937 may help toward an answer to these questions. His replies in the early 1930s were straightforward and uncompromising. Eclectic compositional planning and its facades were dead. So too formal drawing which, he might have clarified, was merely Beaux-Arts composition. It was important to understand why monuments of the past were created, for the process might lead to the discovery of "the same characteristics" to make great buildings today. But these "would be necessarily very different." And, most importantly, the individual architect conceives, creates, and controls the construction of great architecture, not committees, unions, or collectives. A further comparison of his brief answers to *Pravda* in 1933 is similarly instructive, especially where he wrote that a nation should be ruled "from within or from without" or that American education breeds inertia for middle-class minds. For audiences at the 1937 Congress, many of his previously uttered subjects or themes of personal importance were either ignored, politely suggested, or reduced to banality.

Differences between the July 1937 text and Wright's 1943 version are of such magnitude that analysis or comparison is almost embarrassing.[10] They are also unnecessary. In the 1943 text whole paragraphs were inserted or ignored or ballooned; sentences were rearranged, altered, magnified; words were changed, dropped, added. So too the 1977 version where more changes further adulterated the text. The 1943 version was considerably longer than that of 1937. Two lines may have been left out where the ellipses occur at the end of paragraph two in the *Architecture of the USSR* text; but then other sentences were probably omitted, at least according to the suspect typescript in the Frank Lloyd Wright Archives. Nevertheless, suspicion points to the *Architecture of the USSR* transcription being only slightly abridged. Allowing for Wrightian vernacular and American language and phraseology, even allowing that the 1937 text is probably condensed, the 1943 and 1977 versions remain disturbingly false. There are good reasons why they came to be so and they relate to reactions to his Moscow and London adventures.

London

One of the most useful events of the 1930s to Wright was the January 1938 *Architectural Forum.* On his return from Moscow Wright missed the sailing of the *Normandie* on 7 July 1937 and therefore returned from Europe on the *Bremen,* arriving in New York City the week of 14 July.[1] He began immediately to work on the *Forum* articles.

Probably the result of working on occasional articles about Wright for the *Forum* as a "consultant" to editor Harold Myers, George Nelson had come to know Wright. From 1936 into the 1950s they often visited when Wright was in Manhattan or Nelson would drop in at Taliesin for a few days to unwind; he was always welcome. Nelson wrote a scathing review against the set designs for the 1949 film of Ayn Rand's novel *The Fountainhead,* making certain that his readers were in no doubt that the designs were not Wright's.[2] Anyway, apparently Wright asked Nelson if the *Forum* might be willing to publish the preliminary designs of the Johnson Wax administration building. When put to editor Myers he agreed. In November 1936 he offered—and Wright accepted— $500 for exclusive publication rights of the Johnson Wax building. Wright was slow in getting the drawings to New York so Nelson visited Wright in May 1937.[3] On seeing the drawings for Falling-water, with photographs of its construction and as completed, he asked Wright if it might be included in the *Forum* with the Johnson building, in fact with other projects as well. In a follow-up letter to Wright he implied something like a special issue and offered his opinion that the "collection" would "call attention to the fact that while the so-called International Style has been taking advantage of every possible bit of publicity, the cause of organic architecture" is being "carried on by its first and chief exponent."[4] Naturally Wright thought this a splendid idea and agreed to "a number" about and for Taliesin, but he could not put the material together until his return from Moscow; and this he did.

After hearing of Nelson's plans for the Wright issue Myers was quite "excited" about its prospects and wondered which issue of the 1938 volume would suit: Wright suggested January.[5] After anxious and hurried preparations at both ends the special was released in mid-January 1938.[6] Other than front and back matter and advertisements, the one hundred and six pages of the magazine were designed by Wright.

The astounding revelations in that issue showed that the new Wright was creating new architecture and that it was without formula, informal, diverse. Buildings and projects from the first golden decade were pictured along with those more recent: St. Mark's Towers, the Willey house, the Paul Hanna house, the *Capital Journal* project, Herbert Johnson's mansion, and so on. Also included were drawings for the Johnson Wax building, of course, and photographs of it under construction; beautiful photographs by Hedrich Blessing of Fallingwater; and seventeen pages about and photographic views of Wright's home and the Fellowship facilities.

It was a very important product in the Wright campaign, equal to the autobiography. In fact it was much more valuable to his image as a master architect because it proved his creative abilities were not diminished, still extraordinary, unique. Together with the revolutionary *Architectural Record* article in 1908 and the January 1948 *Architectural Forum,* it forms a triumvirate of architectural journalism in kind and in quality of production unequaled for another American architect. Myers was fully aware of the importance of his January 1938 issue and as early as January 1940 he was pushing Wright for the next "magnum opus."[7] However, those plans were postponed because of the war.

The *Architectural Forum*—and *Record*—were widely read in Britain and that fact leads to the next event to concern these essays: Wright's acceptance of an invitation to the Sir George Watson Chair.

19 Interest and Preparation

The Sulgrave Manor, north-northwest of Banbury in Northampton, England, was purchased in 1914 by a committee that in turn gave it to the British and American people as a memorial of friendship between the two nations. It is now administered by a board whose purpose is to foster U.S.–British relations.[1] The manor was opened to the public in 1921. It is a fine example of a small, somewhat Elizabethan manor house completed c. 1560 by Lawrence Washington, direct ancestor of America's first president, whose family lived in the house until about 1660. The Sir George Watson Chair, established in 1919 and administered by the Sulgrave board, is meant to be a series of lectures (usually six) by a prominent if not eminent person on a subject of their choosing. There are no other responsibilities except perhaps social.

In March 1938 the board invited Wright to occupy the Watson Chair.[2] In recollection Wright noted that he was preceded by, therefore in company with, people like Woodrow Wilson and Theodore Roosevelt.[3] (Postwar recipients of the Chair have included Alan Nevins, Marcus Cuncliff, and Oscar Handlin.) The year Wright gave his Watson Lectures he received £500.[4] After mutual agreement about the lectures he suggested a theater at the University of London would be an appropriate venue since that was the traditional location. On the other hand the Royal Institute of

British Architects (RIBA) thought their new Henry Jarvis Memorial Room at Portland Place, London, was more appropriate, and that was finally agreed to. Because of the demands of the war a limit of four lectures was settled on.[5]

A number of basic questions arise from our knowledge of Wright's invitation: why was he selected, why did he accept, what did he present, and what was the response? He accepted because it was a prestigious and singular honor, one difficult to reject. What he presented and said is a matter of public record for it was published soon after the event in a book entitled *An Organic Architecture.* There remain, therefore, the reasons for the invitation and reaction to his lectures.

The beliefs people held in the 1930s about who or what Wright was or was not varied with their information about the man, mainly as he would release it. It was Harry Seckel who rather neatly summed up Wright's reputation and popular image in 1938. By this year Wright had received honors from around the world and many from within America. Yet "never has a person been more generally misevaluated than Wright. People either despise or idolize him. One must peer through a cloud of adoration and aversion to see the real man and his architecture." (One suspects that Wright would have enjoyed that observation.) Seckel continued:

Personally, he is what the French would call a numero. He is small, white-haired and has a flair for dress. He is immaculate and dapper, and follows a style that is his very own. In the country, or at a building under construction, he will sometimes appear in rough clothes, but even then his apparel suggests the deliberate effect of a costume.

He has a pride in himself that at times is rather childish, but it is of the kind that amuses rather than irritates. When he tells how his Imperial Hotel withstood the Tokyo quake it is somewhat as an angler might describe a very large fish.

He shamelessly parades his rather miscellaneous erudition. Occasionally he enriches his conversation with a Japanese word.

He adores adoration. Disciples are a necessary part of his existence.

In short, he is an architectural Isadora Duncan. How much like Isadora the arresting personality, the enormous ego, the illogical, piquant, clairvoyant mind, the odd mannerisms! How similar the unconventional life, the silly publicity!

Like Isadora he has a sense of showmanship. He makes the usual seem unusual.

Perhaps Seckel's most perceptive remark followed: Wright "reasons as far as reasoning accords with what he, himself, does by instinct."[6] Wright was intuitively an architect; words or rationaliza-

19.1 Wright with some of the Fellows gathered about him in the Spring Green studio in 1937, a photograph by Hedrich Blessing that became the most widely issued and published photograph of Wright and apprentices, from *Architectural Forum*, January 1938.

tions were unnecessary. His reputation stood out and his architecture was outstanding. Such a genius was fair game for almost anyone who wanted to try. Perhaps that is why, except for half a dozen from Ireland, Peter and Mary Matthews from England, William and Geraldine Deknatel from Paris, Michael Kostanecki and Marya Lilien from Poland, and the Swiss Rudolph Mock were the only Europeans in the 1930s and 1940s who dared become Taliesin Fellows.[7] And further, Wright realized no architectural commissions in Britain and only one in Europe, Venice, either before or after 1939.[8] Perhaps it was felt that he was a peculiarly American phenomenon.

Interest in Wright by only a few British architects and theorists began, as Wright and historians have noted, around the turn of the century with Wright's knowledge of the arts and crafts movement and personal contacts with one of its proponents and activists, Charles Robert Ashbee. After about 1912 there was a noticeable lack of interest on both sides of the Atlantic until a revival was started by the English author and historian John Gloag who, in the 1930s, was at the initial height of his long public career.

In the autumn of 1934 Gloag visited the United States. Among others he chatted with "probably the greatest living gossip," as he described Alexander Woollcott.[9] Gloag also visited Wright at the architect's farm and studio in Wisconsin. It was October but especially cold, "a dark night."[10] He was met at the railway station by one of the apprentices (probably Edgar Tafel) and driven by car to the Taliesin farm. "All I knew of Frank Lloyd Wright was derived from photographs of his work," said Gloag, and "from reading that biographical essay entitled 'The Prodigal Father,' in Alexander Woollcott's book, *While Rome Burns,*[11] and from a vast disconnected body of gossip and legend, lit here and there by his own writings; and from all this I gathered that he was a modernist and a humanist with a splendid disregard for the pettifogging restrictions that make such miserable, meek and timid creatures of most of us."[12]

Gloag's meeting with Wright was a pleasant surprise. He was thoroughly impressed with the "old man with the carriage of a youth." And Gloag was persuaded to the point of admiration by Wright's program for apprentices, the Fellowship. Gloag saw them at work, noted their studies—literature, film, painting, drawing, sculpture, music—their architectural models, and most of all their infectious enthusiasm. The crisp autumn evenings encouraged fireplace fires; rooms were strangely elegant, evocatively natural and cozy. The affectations of the Spring Green Manor House probably seemed quite normal to the Englishman. For Gloag it was an impressive, aristocratically tasteful yet very different social and architectural experience.

On his return to England he wrote about his visit and his impressions of Wright and the apprentices. In one instance he concluded that except for a small "discerning" group of architects, writers, critics, and their publishers "he is unknown and unhonoured among the people who make loud public noises in America." This lamentation, not at all accurate and obviously paraphrased from Wright's lips, was followed with a remonstration that in hindsight was less than justified. "He made me feel humble, ignorant and encouraged," said Gloag, "and he made me feel ashamed for the great country that knows so little of his work and understands nothing of his greatness."[13]

Gloag followed this article with a talk to the Design and Industries Association in late January 1935. He again lauded Wright and spoke mainly of Wright's architectural achievements and some of his ideas, if rather sketchily. But he had second thoughts in relation to his earlier article: "I think I should hesitate to call [him] a humanist"; rather Gloag would call him a "functionalist." He continued with a personal summation of the Fellowship: "I suppose [it] is about the only really big research station for machine design that exists today. The Taliesin Fellowship is not an 'art colony.' It is not an 'escapist' school. It is a social research station, unrecognized and unsupported by the country which will benefit by its work."[14] Based on only a two-day visit that is a somewhat erroneous impression, one probably encouraged by conversations with a persuasive Wright; "machine design" and "research station" are Wrightian phrases.

In mid-1933 war was in the balance and there was an economic Depression. In art and architecture there was a wobbly stability in "modernism." When English architect Clough Williams-Ellis looked back at the first third of the century he was singularly ashamed for both architect and patron and their collective results. He poured out mournful phrases about national disgraces of kind and attitude. In his view it was all sham, tasteless and tawdry and too full of social formalities. He welcomed the escape afforded by the new architecture, suggesting something like the words of Hubert Hastings, "Scholarship is no longer the bottle-neck of Design."[15] But there remained the "sick land," as Williams-Ellis described Britain, which fostered those disgraces. What of the future? Who knows, he said, "there may be a *deus ex machina* lurking around the next corner, the turning of which still so bafflingly eludes us, and it may be that some great political upheaval, some national or international cataclysm will suddenly render abortive the dilatory and rather planless patching that is all we have thus far put our fumbling hands to. Meanwhile," continued Williams-Ellis, "with what hope we may, those few of us who feel concern must needs continue to preach repentance and individually try to mitigate the mess wherever we can and however forlornly."[16] And so he concluded his mournful cry. He was not alone, for his grumbling read much as an architect might write for or interpret a page of Victor Gollancz's Left Book Club newsletter. He was a pessimist.

More optimistically John Gloag's searches found a king in an architect's utopia. His unrestrained enthusiasm for the Fellowship and enjoyment of Wright the man and his ideas may be a reaction to the gloom then hanging over Europe exemplified by Williams-Ellis's grief. Frank and Olgivanna's wholly positive outlook for the future they envisioned and, by the time of Gloag's visit, were in the process of building, was quite antithetical to the negative morale and the threatening events in Europe.

Gloag too had felt remorseful dissatisfaction with, even fear of those events, as revealed in some 1933 prognostications for the next third of the twentieth century—he saw war, revolution, a moral breakdown, the threat of a black (negro) Crusade, and so forth. "Anyone who thinks about the future," said Gloag, surely must come to the conclusion that "civilization has learned so much more about the technique of suicide."[17] The contrast was extreme between those words of 1933 and those uttered in the aftermath of his visit to Wright's farm at Spring Green. He was thrilled with the optimism displayed by the young apprentices; the survival of the art of architecture was assured with prospects of regeneration and potential newness; it was a humane approach, not mechanistic. As Wright said in his Princeton University talks of 1930:

Now, a chair *is* a machine to sit in.

A home *is* a machine to live in. . . .

And, as I've admitted before somewhere, a heart

***is* a suction-pump. Does that idea thrill you?**

Wright projected an attitude contradicting the gloomy analyses of the materialistic political left, the antiart technical propositions and extreme functionalist notions pervading so much European writing about architecture. Antihumanist expressions such as those of Hannes Meyer (Gropius believed Meyer's philosophy culminated in the assertion "life is oxygen plus sugar plus starch plus protein," to which Mies added, "Try stirring all that together: it stinks") were dismissed, as were negative words such as those of the Viennese architect Adolf Loos who said a "work of art is the artist's own business; a house is not," or his dictum that "architecture is not one of the arts."[18] Gloag saw Wright proving otherwise, that a house was the concern of both the artist-architect *and* his client and that architecture was supremely an art, the supreme art; an art that transcended mere visual perception or social engineering. Gloag was ecstatic.

Gloag's reports are important in another aspect. He had personally visited Wright and reported his discoveries, he had not presented hearsay evidence or vicarious impressions. He was an English author of some reputation involved in and committed to the design industry; his views carried weight.

Indirect information or even propaganda about Wright had been published in the English professional press prior to Gloag's visit to Taliesin. The most important was an analysis of architectural events during the first third of the century, something closely approximating a history, by Englishman Philip Morton Shand, a Francophile theorist for *The Architectural Review.* Then in 1936 Nikolaus Pevsner published his art historical piece on *Pioneers of the Modern Movement,* which owed a debt (unacknowledged) to Shand's earlier synthetic work. Shand and all others owed much to an even earlier study, the charismatic presentation by American art evangelist Sheldon Cheney in his *The New World Architecture,* published in London in 1930. His balanced approach to both European and North American architects mixed with an infectious prose was superior to a host of similar texts to follow. Henry-Russell Hitchcock and Philip Johnson narrowly academicized Cheney's enthusiasm in their study of *The International Style* in 1932. Even Oud, a founding innovator with De Stijl, was caught in the analytical tide sweeping the western world when in 1933 he briefly summarized "The European Movement Towards a New Architecture."[19]

But to return to Shand's historical series, entitled "Scenario for a Human Drama" and in seven parts, published between July 1934 and March 1935. The first article was in fact not by Shand but a summary by F. R. S. Yorke of his soon-to-be-popular survey in book form entitled *The Modern House.* The book concentrated on the Central Europeans' aesthetic and their followers and included a section about prefabrication. It was given considerable press coverage on its release and went through a number of editions. Shand wrote an introduction to Yorke's summary describing it as "memorable" and saying that it took up "the story at the point we have now reached," or 1934. (Actually, it told only one story. Cheney's book and Australian expatriate Raymond McGrath's book *Twentieth Century Houses,* also of 1934, were far more comprehensive and valuable.) It was going to be Shand's job in the series, he said, to explain "how we got there," that is, how the one strain evolved in Central Europe up to 1934. Shand looked to certain individuals for continuity: Walter Gropius, Robert van 't Hoff (and his Dutch colleagues), Peter Behrens, Erich Mendelsohn, Otto Wagner, Henri Van de Velde, Adolph Loos, Josef Hofmann, Charles Rennie Mackintosh (the "Glasgow Interlude"), concluding his reverse chronology with William Morris, John Ruskin, and John Soane.

In each case the role of cause and effect, the lineage of idea and architectonic form was discussed. Of concern to this essay was his placing of Wright as a principal hub around which much of modernism revolved.

American Anglophile historian Henry-Russell Hitchcock had been imprecise, merely suggesting Wright's influence in 1928 when he wrote a short introduction to a French pamphlet on Wright published by Cahiers d'Art.[20] But any implicit recognition of a European connection with Wright was encouraged by the French publisher. Shand was more explicit. And he knew the architect well when he said that there were "two Frank Lloyd Wright's—the visionary architectural prophet and the dynamic architectural practitioner—and more often than not they are at variance with one another, execution belying profession. And in much the same way there are two architects in Lloyd Wright, the local, regional and the international, universal." It was Shand's opinion that, unfortunately, "Europe blunderingly confused them; which is presumably what Oud meant when he said that Wright's influence on the Continent had been a by no means happy one."[21] This unhappiness needs clarification.

In 1926–27 a unique event took place in Stuttgart, Germany. A new housing settlement was proposed and Mies van der Rohe became the coordinating director. The well-endowed Deutscher Werkbund and the city of Stuttgart sponsored the project. It was a permanent exhibition of sorts in the form of model housing that included not only the buildings but also furniture, furnishings, and finishes. Mies, who was first vice-president of the Werkbund in 1926, gathered together the leading protagonists of Central European modernism from Germany and Holland, and from Paris Le Corbusier and Pierre Jeanneret. It was Mies's belief and that of the Werkbund that "the new dwelling" was much more "than a purely technical or economic problem and accordingly only to be resolved by creative abilities, not by means of computation or organization."[22] By 1926 the Werkbund was no longer interested in fostering ideas of the arts and crafts but in concentrating on architecture and technology as they might influence habitation: a decidedly materialistic emphasis. As well, it was hoped that various factions arguing their particular interpretation of modern architecture would, by this exhibition, present a united front. How this might have been accomplished when factions such as the expressionists and the Amsterdam School were excluded is not clear. It also gave modern architecture a credibility and, if not a popularity, at least a recognition that it suffered previously. (In fact the Congrès Internationaux d'Architecture Moderne, or CIAM, was formed in 1928 by twenty-four founding architects.) After it opened in July 1927 the settlement, or

19.2 Left to right, Henry-Russell Hitchcock, Robert Kahn, a Mr. Soby, and Le Corbusier (on his first visit to the U.S.), 1935, courtesy the Architectural History Foundation.

the Weissenhof Exhibition, became well known throughout Central and Eastern Europe and England if slightly known in North America.

In spite of Wright's relative professional obscurity during the previous fifteen or so years his influence was still measurable at Stuttgart. Of those architects who were invited by Mies to design and build some form of domestic housing, Mark Stam, Oud, and Gropius had previously and openly acknowledged Wright's influence, as had Mies. Mendelsohn, Hugo Haring, and Heinrich Tessenow were invited in 1925 but did not participate or were eventually excluded, and their debt to Wright was also admitted and substantial. Wright's presence was with the architects. It was also within the theoretical notions of some buildings.

The problem given to the architects (and to Mies as overall planner) was the provision of cheap housing (not realized!) for the changing character of family life—mechanical aids, cars, freer lifestyles, etc. One contemporary observer and Weissenhof publicist, the German architect and disaffected ex-Bauhaus student and member of De Stijl Werner Graeff, noted that, "it has hitherto been impossible to create decisive new forms for domestic architecture, since the process of transformation is still in full swing. Indeed the customary dwelling which has served us for centuries seems unbearably ill-suited to the new generation—almost as if they were given frock coats to wear."[23] The open plan, plainly demonstrated by Wright at the turn of the century in his many prairie houses and seized upon by European architects, was at least part of the answer for three architects. As Graeff explained for the exhibitioners, people must be shown

the new technical postulates of domestic architecture, they must be acquainted with the most practical domestic equipment and machines; they must be made aware of the fact that the most talented architects throughout the world are striving after something new, even if their schemes prove merely fanciful. And so long as one gives practical examples of the different types of dwelling, it is preferable to fix things as little as possible, to show on the contrary that everything has yet to be given its final shape, which will be developed out of the way it is used. This is the *reason* [Graeff emphasized] for the variable ground plans in the skeleton buildings of Mies van der Rohe, Le Corbusier, and Mark Stam. In this way we can help to discover people's preferences in their domestic arrangements.[24]

Wrightian forms and materials aside, the open-plan principle was applied before Stuttgart by the De Stijl group in Holland under the influence of Wright. A particularly dynamic example was Gerrit Rietveld's Shröder House in Utrecht of 1924 where internal walls could be moved to redefine an open internal space. This was a house that altered to meet the needs of family changes on a weekend or over the years. The dynamics of space and form produced for *De Stijl* magazine gave way at Stuttgart to similar clean, crisp, white cubic shapes; a fact that indicates the united front was one of conformity. Indeed, it would not be unreasonable to characterize the exhibition's architecture as having been seduced by its own formalism.

An outline and resumé of the seduction has been written by art historian John Willett, who said that "nothing did more to characterize the emphatically urban civilization of the later 1920s than the rapid development of this new architecture." Willett noted that in the six years prior to 1925 "men like Gropius and Mies van der Rohe had built little; Swiss architecture still seemed conservative; Adolf Loos had left Vienna; so that about the only truly modern works in the whole of central Europe were certain buildings of Erich Mendelsohn's . . . and the first of Otto Haesler's Celle estates." Weimar Germany became the new movement's

effective centre and was for many years the one country where it made a real impact. . . . For all the deliberate unpretentiousness and impersonality of its aesthetic, this architecture embraced some outstanding individuals who could handle it with elegance and perfectionism. . . . But what gave it its particular dominance was not so much the occasional building of genius . . . as the more humdrum activities of countless lesser architects and, above all, its harnessing to a major social aim . . . modern housing.[25]

The art of architecture had been subsumed by sociology. Flats and housing estates were built in the white box idiom in Vienna, Celle, Breslau, Cologne, Dresden, Frankfurt, and other European centers, but mainly in German-speaking countries from about 1924 to 1929. Almost all were pretty dull, uninspired cubic boxes attached to one another in endless rows much as the housing for new cities in the Soviet Union from 1929 to 1935.

It was in response to this aesthetically deprived monotony as well as the unsuitable traditional form that the Werkbund promoted the exhibition at Stuttgart, only to produce equally monotonous buildings. A cursory study of published surveys produced during the 1920s such as Morance's *L'Architecture vivante* or later his *Encyclopédie de l'architecture* shows the diversity of architectural design, in particular the theoretical projects, which evolved in less than a decade. The charge of monotony at Weissenhof, therefore, is modest criticism to that which might be leveled, especially in view of the housing studies and projects done between 1900 and 1925 in England, Holland, and Germany.

Two books by Ludwig Hilberseimer, more or less a propagandist for the Werkbund and Gropius and an architect who proposed some of the most ascetic and inhuman urban landscapes imaginable, not only revealed architectural diversity but several other interesting aspects relevant to this essay. Hilberseimer's *Internationale neue Baukunst,* published in Stuttgart in 1928, was the second volume of three published on behalf of the German Werkbund about modern architecture and housing. (The first volume was Richard Neutra's *Wie baut Amerika?,* in which he wrote about not only his and Schindler's American work but Wright's concrete block houses of the early 1920s in southern California.) Hilberseimer naturally included the Weissenhof buildings. The book was about the new "International" building art, echoing the name Gropius used in 1925 to categorize much of the Central European aesthetics. Gropius and Hilberseimer thus supplied Johnson's and Hitchcock's title, if not their arguments, and it should be obvious that the Americans' *The International Style* (1932) merely ratified the observations of the European practitioners and theorists, presenting those views and works to a North American audience. Hilberseimer's book was composed only of illustrations with no text (or only half a page), and Wright was given the honor of the first four plates. (Strangely, Charles McArthur was also represented with an awkward house design reminiscent of American Southwest colonial architecture. His inclusion at a moment when Wright was working on the Arizona Biltmore suggests Wright was aware that Hilberseimer was putting a book together, or a shorter version by the same title as an article in *Moderne Bauformen,* and may have recommended to Hilberseimer—or someone—that they include McArthur.) The only other Americans included in the otherwise all-European display were immigrants Neutra and Schindler.

Hilberseimer's other book *Groszstadt Architektur* of 1927, also published in Stuttgart, acknowledged the theme of the "international character" of modern architecture for big cities which was carried more emphatically into the 1928 book. The work of the Werkbund was acknowledged but Hilberseimer presented a much broader survey of nationalities (most of Europe plus the USSR) and building types (high rise, house, factory, etc.) with ample text that included some historical emphasis, at least of the immediate past. He spoke, therefore, of Louis Sullivan, Peter Behrens, and early Wright, for instance, and selected pictorial samples of their work as well as contemporary designs by Raymond Hood and Hugh Ferris, for example. This historical interest was also made plain in the text and a bibliography of only thirteen books, two of which were the 1910 and 1911 Wasmuth monographs on Wright. Some of Hilberseimer's illustrations of Wright's architecture, however, were taken from the 1925 *Wendingen* volume compiled by Wijdeveld.

At this stage of Wright's career, because he was included in these and similar publications as well as magazines, he was intimately linked to internationalism and the Central European aesthetic. Wright was not disturbed by this association until (and this is speculative) he saw the publications that so dramatically displayed the severe European and Soviet stuccoed aesthetic. Those publications—and Hilberseimer's are only two examples—began to be produced in great abundance in Europe in the late 1920s. During his early years in the offices of Joseph Silsbee and Adler and Sullivan we do not know what his political position may have been other than that his mother was committed to promoting Hull House and the kind of practical socialism it espoused through its many endeavors. Wright was more or less involved with that same group of people for many years. After about 1893 and until 1929 he was not politically active, or at least did not overtly push any factional view. After 1929 he was very outspoken but always used architecture as a catalyst for his political ideas.

He invariably responded to the actions of those architects who were themselves energetically promoting those things espoused by the political left that could reasonably engage the architect: housing of all sorts but always for the masses, nice factories for workers, centralized urban places, or whatever. Based on evidence presented in French, Dutch, and German publications of the late 1920s—and later similar Italian evidence—Wright believed they were always tied to the same basic architectural style. In 1930 that style was being promoted by a few professionals, or para-design people, as right and proper for America. In the 1930s they increased their promotions dramatically.

The link between the Central European aesthetic and Soviet Communism—and later Italian Fascism—was clear to Wright. That aesthetic symbolized the suppression of individual freedom in the name of the collective will. Such a symbol needed to be vigorously refuted and an American alternative offered. Wright had to disengage himself from the European social/political/aesthetic nexus. He did not like the boxes anyway, stuccoed or otherwise. More important, he believed that the black-trimmed white boxes of the Central Europeans and Soviets were too red. Historians have recently revealed that "after 1923 the Bauhaus was subject to influence from VKhUTEMAS,"[26] an acronym for the Higher State Artistic Technical Studios, Moscow, and that the extreme left was a factor in Dutch and French housing, city planning, and architectural ideas after 1919. Mussolini as well embraced the international style, showing that the aesthetic could be associated with totalitarianism of other stripes. Further observations and relevant information are presented in the chapter about Wright's trip to Moscow. Suffice it to say that by c. 1929 Wright was aware of many of the political and architectural placebos offered in Europe, if not in detail then in summary and especially with their visual symbols.

Wright was also present at Stuttgart in what might be termed a subliminal manner that revealed itself to those who would remember. Graeff remembered in 1927 when writing for the Werkbund's journal *Die Form*: Wright "had the necessary qualities twenty years ago. He knew the way to a new kind of living." (Note that Graeff connected quality to domestic need, not to building materials or abstract form.) This was the kind of comment that would encourage other observers and historians to declare—or perhaps assume is a better word—that Wright was no longer a viable influence. However, Graeff correctly and prophetically continued: Wright's compatriots in America "have so far been unwilling to follow him, and he will have to be patient for another ten years."[27] Mies would have agreed; and Graeff was correct almost to the year!

Quite clearly Wright had not been forgotten in Europe. If further evidence of his presence is needed then statistical data extracted from Sweeney's bibliography is most revealing. It is incomplete as a bibliography (for instance the Neutra volume and two Hilberseimer books are not listed) but the entries can at least be taken as indicative of trends. During the eleven years between 1916 and 1926 only fifteen articles were published by or about Wright in the U.S. Of those, ten were about the survival of his Imperial Hotel during Tokyo's 1923 earthquake. Two minor pamphlets were also published. During the three years of 1927 through 1929 there were twenty-nine published articles by or about Wright of which thirteen were in the *Architectural Record,* most as part of a series commissioned by the magazine. Again there were two minor pamphlets. In 1930, the number of publications increased dramatically. The shortage, until 1927, of published information about Wright clearly indicates the degree to which he was consumed by his Japanese experiences and the domestic strife that followed. This conclusion is also supported by statistics for European publications. During the critical stabilizing years of the Central European architecture, now called the International Style, four books about Wright were published in Europe: *Ausgefürte Bauten* in 1924, the Wijdeveld compilation in 1925, de Fries's monograph in 1926, and the Cahiers d'Art pamphlet in 1928. All were important publications for their visual and verbal presentation. From 1916 through 1924, seven European articles were published about Wright. During the three years of 1925 through 1927 there was an increase to twenty-one: ten were German, one Czech, one French, and nine Dutch. Beginning in 1930, there were many more articles published in an increasing number of countries. For unknown reasons it appears that Wright wished to establish closer ties with his European contemporaries rather than his American colleagues.

As well, a number of European architects began to work for Wright, not as fellows, of course, but as employees. The highly regarded Werner Moser of Switzerland, for instance, sent his son Karl to Taliesin around 1926–27. Shortly thereafter Karl Jensen arrived from Denmark to stay for a few years and briefly act as Wright's secretary. Earlier, in 1924 the Viennese architect Richard Neutra began his short but obviously absorptive moment under Wright. Heinrich Klumb traveled from his home in Germany to work with Wright and help construct Ocotillo. (Moser returned to Europe; Neutra went to California to be with Rudofph Schindler; Klumb to Puerto Rico.) Perhaps Wright sensed that the European architectural theorists were on the threshold of something new, perhaps based on his own works, and therefore wished closer ties.

The American aberration out of Chicago was a prophetic force in the scheme of things architectural. He most certainly haunted the minds of European architectural theorists in the 1920s, but his was not otherwise an overt presence.

Considering the fact that he was a relatively inactive professional from c. 1915 through the 1920s, why was Wright's architecture so attractive to the Europeans (less so to Americans) during the 1920s and 1930s? Was it only an intellectual and theoretical stimulant? Architect and historian Gilbert Herbert, has stated concisely what many have observed:

The architecture of revolution was deliberately narrow, dogmatic, manifestoes in concrete, steel and glass. Wright's architecture was instinctively admired, but it was for all that an ideological embarrassment; for the borderline between Wright and the past was too blurred, not sufficiently clearcut, to serve a revolutionary purpose. Indeed, perhaps the appealing romanticism of Wright's work, the seduction of his architecture, the very temptation of it, helped to drive Europe, seeking the provocative forms of a revolutionary architecture, to the opposite pole of abstract rationalism. Wright stood diametrically opposed to the purist forms of the International Style, at the other polar extremity of the modern movement.[28]

His was an idiomatic architecture, easily identifiable, very personal. Oud's frustration is more understandable; so too that of the perplexed English.

For a contrast, we can look at the city planning ideas of the leading European practitioner and theorist, Le Corbusier. As part of the aesthetic and social revolution of the political left, ideas for the city needed to be easily comprehended, that is, emphatically doctrinal and related to a clear organization with obvious regularity. His ideal city, "une ville contemporaine" for Paris of 1925, 1930, or 1937, possessed those qualities and was also very architectonic, an architect's solution. Too obviously it "enshrined hierarchy and command, looked to Authority to accomplish its plan."[29]

Quite deliberately Wright's Broadacre City was declared open, diverse, and internally and externally expandable, not rigidly regular, not linearly additive or compacted vertically. As historian Robert Fishman has observed, diametrically opposite to Le Corbusier's ideal city, Wright's followers "would need sufficient intelligence to comprehend Broadacre City, the initiative to act on it, and most important of all, the vision to see it as the necessary alternative to the centralized society. . . . In his own prophetic mission, Wright assumed that his fellow citizens would share not only his values but also his imagination."[30] As previously noted, Wright's abused listeners and readers refused to believe it was potentially all true, not altruistic.

Some general points seem plain. Change in the 1920s as touted in Europe needed obvious but nonpersonalized organization for both architecture and the city; to be successful the structure of change needed to be clear, concise, and unambiguous. By the early 1930s it became so. Wright's dialogue, on the other hand, was not precisely quantifiable. In the 1930s his dialectical pronouncements were too ambiguous. They became irritatingly confusing to fellow Americans if more clearly anarchic to a few Europeans and the English. Yet Wright was extraordinarily attractive to those few and a kind of intellectual curiosity to many, more often a result of his pen which was always ready to flow freely and unhindered by protocol or politeness.

After some neglect a number of his writings began to appear in the English press beginning in about 1932. Many were extracts from works published in America. Of more importance to events around 1938 were a number of items published in England beginning in 1933. As examples, in that year his House on a Mesa project was illustrated in the London magazine *Decorative Art* where he shared a page with an illustration of one of Joseph Urban's houses. (A nice happenstance, for Urban helped form Wright Inc. which had bailed out the financially troubled Wright.) The year before, the constitution of the Fellowship was published in the London edition of *The Studio*. The magazine's editors incorrectly referred to "a Utopian community of craftsmen suggestive of a medieval guild."[31] There was a review (of sorts) of a book by his former employer Louis Sullivan, *Kindergarten Chats* (published by Scarab Fraternity Press in 1934). When the review typescript was sent to *The Architectural Review* in January 1935 the cover letter implied that the manuscript was not commissioned. In any event Eugene Masselink, Wright's secretary, wrote to editor Hastings in part:

The next time John Gloag comes across you must come with him or come alone. The Fellowship group is starting soon on a caravan to the Arizona desert. One great new truck—ten cars—red

flags flying—we will stay about three months in new country. We look forward to a departure from Taliesin that will be as classic as that of Ulysses and the Children of Israel.[32]

Of more importance was his article subtitled "Recollections. United States: 1893–1920," commissioned shortly after Gloag's return to London and published in 1936. In it he reminisced rather inexactly and talked of his architectural theories, of his importance, about education and the future. The article followed familiar themes, much as those of 1930–32. It ran as a series in four consecutive issues of the London *Architects' Journal* from 16 July to 6 August 1936. Then in 1937 *The Architectural Review* in an impressive non-page-filling two-page spread published a short article on "What the cause of architecture needs most."[33] Parts of it were typical of Wright's unintelligible prose, but at one point he confessed to an "inconsiderate illness." He acknowledged that other things aside, his "characteristic modesty which has endeared me to you all" caused him to "sometimes wish veterans might be inviolable." He then sermonized: "as I write—convalescent—it seems to me that what the Cause of Architecture needs most . . . is love": the man was the message, not his words.

Of course the American professional press was now very alert to Wright's new and fabled life. The justly famous January 1938 issue of *The Architectural Forum*—designed and laid out by Wright—was the most impressive array of information by and about Wright to that date (see Appendix C). It can be compared with the *Architectural Record* in 1908, the series of articles in the Dutch magazine *Wendingen* during 1924–25 (together with the 1925 Wendingen book), and the July 1930 *L'Architecture vivante:* two European, two American magazines. The January 1938 issue would have arrived in London in late January. All of this coverage in the 1930s, together with Gloag's intervention, pricked the interest of the Sulgrave Manor Board.

There were, moreover, other secondhand bits of information, some even thirdhand: reprints of Wright's lectures at the Art Institute of Chicago, his lectures at Princeton, and the minibattle for Wright to become involved in the 1934 Chicago Century of Progress Exposition. Chicago was after all his town; his exclusion hurt deeply, and perhaps he remembered the apparently shabby treatment of Louis Sullivan (at least in Sullivan's view) at the 1893 Chicago fair and that fair's gloriously regressive architecture.[34] Wright and his friends, including supporters of his Fellowship such as Lewis Mumford and Alexander Woollcott, tried by public meetings, letters, and articles to encourage or shame officials—or anyone else—into including Wright; but to no avail. One of Wright's first criticisms of the fair was published not locally but in distant London in *The Architect's Journal* of July 1933.[35]

American expatriate Howard Robertson reviewed a small pamphlet that resulted from Wright's two lectures at the Art Institute of Chicago in 1930. One of Robertson's opening remarks demonstrated that in 1931 Wright was still held in high esteem by his fellow professionals. In Europe "there has been, and still is," said Robertson, "a disposition to regard him almost as the Father of Modern Architecture."[36] This observation was followed by a note about the many publications about Wright appearing in France, Holland, and Germany. Also, though the exhibition of Wright's architecture touring Europe in 1931–32 failed to make an English venue, *The Studio* still reported on the exhibition and about the "stormy petrel of American architecture."[37]

In 1937 Henry-Russell Hitchcock wrote an article for the London magazine *Architectural Review* on "The Architectural Future in America." It was mainly about Rockefeller Center and other high-rise complexes; more or less a review of tall buildings built during the 1930s. Wright was again mentioned for his contributions in the past and not those of the 1920s or 1930s. At one point Hitchcock said he supported a "sense of form wholly of the twentieth century and wholly American, as was Wright's in the days when he was an active architect before the War."[38] Eugene Masselink responded with a letter pointing out that there was most assuredly a directing genius in America and that Hitchcock's statement was "not only blatantly ignorant but, in the circumstances, libellous."[39] John E. Lautner, Jr., also of the Fellowship, wrote a letter supporting Masselink. Hitchcock, responding, said that he considered Wright "America's greatest architect and the only American architect who has had a fructifying influence upon the outside world," but it seemed to Hitchcock that Wright's "creative force was more consistent and effective" between 1900 and 1914. (He also noted that the point of view of Wright's followers at Taliesin "somewhat resembles that of the immediate Wagner circle towards that master in his later years.")[40] This opinion was offered in spite of Mumford's previously published persuasive arguments. Hitchcock's view was somewhat typical, though, for it must be conceded that most knowledgeable theorists and historians saw Wright as somewhat of a father figure. But then the Johnson Wax building at Racine and the Kaufmann house on Bear Run were yet to be published.

As Wright accumulated awards from nations and institutions, he began to receive many more commissions and of a wide variety although houses remained his mainstay. The period just before World War II was one of great activity, full with achievement and all varied. He had traveled to Brazil, Italy, Germany, Poland, Russia, and around the United States. Soon he would go to England. He gave speeches, informal talks, chided American city fathers about their horrible towns, saw clients, gave interviews, and designed and built buildings that deservedly attracted world-wide

19.3 Cover of the January 1938 *Architectural Forum*, probably designed by Wright but drawing executed by someone else. The dark square was in vivid red. The *Forum* was ring-bound for most of the 1930s.

attention. Just before the Sulgrave Manor offer was made *The Architectural Forum* of January 1938 was released with its excellent illustrations of Wright's architecture.

Suffice it to say that the English profession was well aware of Wright, his architecture, some of his influence, and some of his ideas. There was less interest, though, in his architecture as manifest and more in his historical position, the character of his inventiveness, and his theoretical notions. The continental Europeans (except the French) tended to look at his architecture and to publish his drawings and photographs, while the English tended to study his writings. Robertson observed that there was "little here which cannot be read with advantage, and probably also argued and contested, by the English architect."[41] There was of course some practical influence by Wright on the English architect. Some of the houses by Thomas Tait and John Burnet in the late twenties showed that influence even if tempered by a knowledge of the work of the Dutch architect Willem Dudok,[42] as did certain works by F. E. Towndrow of the same period. As suggested by the indirect route of Wright's influence through Holland, the English looked to the continental Europeans for their inspiration, even their eclecticism, rather than to former colonies. So Wright was a kind of New World theorist and artistic curiosity, already a museum piece.

Was Wright interested in the English? Other than the arts and crafts movement, William Morris, architects C. F. A. Voysey and Edwin Luytens, and designer C. R. Ashbee—no. Yet there is something Anglophile in his very early architecture because of that interest. The roofline and its shape, sets of windows tucked up under the eave, plain wall surfaces, windows collected in bands, a cozy inglenook with a fireplace, bold plainly geometrical forms especially reminiscent of Edwin Luytens; all have had a place in determining the shape and character of the classical prairie houses. But without further investigation this observation must be considered of less value to the present discussion than the negative fact that there was no reciprocal interest after Ashbee at the turn of the century, only momentarily in 1925, and briefly after Gloag's visit in 1935. It is not that Wright dismissed English architects as much as he displayed no curiosity about their architecture. Their literature, yes. But not their literature on architecture. After all, he might have said, after Luytens, Voysey, and Ashbee's school what was left? Conversely, his interest in Germany was full—music, architecture, architects, and literature including architectural writings.

Historically his British associations were a result of his mother's Welsh family. He did not seem to be aware—or at least he never displayed an active interest in the fact—that his father was of English stock. (It has been traced back to the 1600s when the family first arrived in New England.)[43] As late as 1956 Olgivanna wrote about a trip to the British Isles, in particular Bangor.

She wrote enthusiastically about discovering the old Welsh soil. She and Frank had searched for his ancestors' names and finally found "one tombstone with the name Wriaeth."[44] But the name Wright was of course his father's, therefore northern English, while Jones was his mother's Welsh family name. Further, neither he nor any of his biographers have shown any interest in the fact that in America the English strain became fundamentalist Baptists and the Welsh strain became liberal Unitarians, or that one strain was not only Bible-oriented but musically talented, the other pragmatically wedded to the soil and education, secular and theological. Anyway, in the 1930s the British were not aware of his English ancestry.

While one can understand the influences prompting the English to take an interest in Wright, one other consideration seems relevant and important. Some people in England believed they were filling a void left by America's confusion over Wright. That is, if America would not give Wright justly deserved recognition then England should. One English editor thought that though Wright would never achieve the acclaim he deserved, "the fact remains—and the sooner Americans accept it the better—he is by far the greatest architect the United States has yet possessed."[45] Gloag was insistent that the English present a proper and fitting acknowledgment. With no evident display of prior interest in Wright it appeared that the Soviets had recognized his worth by a simple invitation to their Moscow architectural congress in 1937. Did that incident act as a catalyst for England to take some similar action? One event followed the other closely. How important were the British who had been infected by the liberal promises of Soviet Communism?

The vigorous reshaping of Russian society into an apparently potent, potentially self-sustaining entity was quite attractive to Westerners and in particular the English in spite of crudely applied governmental controls and parallel cruel repressions to save the Bolshevik takeover. After his visit in 1920 H. G. Wells believed the Leninist system and its measures were necessary to stave off collapse. Wells visited in 1914 and again in 1920 when he was sponsored by Maxim Gorky. Bertrand Russell visited in 1920 to return skeptical and by 1930 was more or less anti-Soviet. Wells and most others who wrote about the USSR from 1920 to around 1932 tended, however, to be apologists for the Bolshevik exercises to form Communism. While those who visited in the 1930s were aware of the purges they could be overcredulous. Others like G. B. Shaw said little, a silence strange for such an outspoken socialist. Around 1930 Julian Huxley objectively analyzed events but retained mixed feelings. In 1932 Malcolm Muggeridge hastily denounced the Soviets, but his was a minority opinion. These passages from West to East are adequately portrayed in many biographies, histories, or sometimes more directly in the pages of the English-language *Moscow News.* As well, legitimate international conferences (quite different from the Soviet all-union meetings) were held in Moscow or Leningrad. For instance, concurrent with the architects' meeting in 1937 was the 17th International Geological Congress. The *News* seldom mentioned individual visitors unless there was an obvious propaganda advantage. During the purges fewer Westerners traveled to the USSR except stalwarts such as Sir and Lady Simon (as they wished to be known, probably John Allsebrook Simon and his wife, he a government minister and statesman and advocate of appeasement with Hitler) or Victor Gollancz. In 1937 British publisher Gollancz spent many weeks in Russia on holiday. His views and impressions were recorded in the 10 March issue of the *News.* Also during June 1937 seventy physicians from the United States visited Moscow.

A good summation of British interest has been provided by historian Charles Harrison who has studied the period 1900–39 in depth and with objectivity. Generally speaking, those who had been "capable of assimilation in the popular imagination into some vague picture of leftist activity," said Harrison, "can be seen as symptomatic of a polarization in English—and indeed European—politics during the early thirties, and of a general, if vague, identification of modern design and architecture with Socialism, if not with Bolshevism." Harrison then pointed to some political events: "The Labor Party had been destroyed as an effective independent force in Parliament when it fell in September 1931 [and] England was ruled by a National Government for the rest of the 1930s." During a period "which saw massive unemployment, the formation of the British Union of Fascists (1932) and the establishment of Hitler as Chancellor of Germany (1933), 'leftism' came to be loosely associated with a wide range of attitudes or activities more easily and accurately characterized in terms of what they appeared to oppose than of what they proposed."[46]

The situation was ripe, especially in 1937. For instance, the growth of the Victor Gollancz Left Book Club from zero in 1935 to 57,000 in 1939 was phenomenal. Perhaps the success of the Popular Front in France was another influential factor but necessarily coupled with the Soviet Union's lone stand against German socialists—in their new guise as Nazis—and in a like manner against the fascists in Spain.[47] On the other hand, most people including the left in England, Europe, and the USA for a variety of inexplicable reasons dismissed or ignored evidence of the human tragedies in the USSR from c. 1930 to 1938, Wright included. But as might be expected of a conservative profession, architects with leftish leanings in England were not numerically persuasive; noisy but a minority—at least in the 1930s. The English were aware of Wright's visit to the Soviet Union, and the well-known and garrulous Williams-Ellis had attended the Congress. Wright had returned from Moscow in mid-July 1937. The Watson Chair was offered only a few months later in March 1938.

While a look at what happened in London will not clarify exactly why he was invited, it will be revealing.

20 To London

As we [the *RIBA Journal*] go to press we hear . . . that Mr Frank Lloyd Wright has cabled to say that through unavoidable circumstances he has been compelled to postpone his visit to England, during which he was to give a series of four lectures at the RIBA on 8, 10, 15 and 17 November [1938]. The Sulgrave Manor Board will announce the revised dates for the lectures as soon as they have been able to arrange them with [Mr Wright].[1]

Supervision of the Johnson Wax Building was the reason given for the postponement.[2] Wright's sudden decision on 16 October was not happily received in London; much preparation had been completed and his first lecture was scheduled for only three weeks hence, on 8 November. It took until March 1939 to set a new course.

Wright first planned a visit to London in July 1901, then again in 1909 during his sojourn in Europe with his mistress Mamah Borthwick. She and Wright finally traveled to London and also visited Charles Ashbee in September 1910. As far as we know his next visit was not until the eventful months of April and May of 1939. Frank, Olgivanna, and daughter Iovanna, who was then thirteen years old, left Spring Green on 19 April, traveling across the Atlantic on the *S.S. Europa* to arrive at Portsmouth on 30 April.[3] In the evening on the 1st of May they had dinner on invitation of John Gloag at the Architectural Club in the Savoy Hotel.[4] The next day there was a 4:30 tea party at the RIBA and at 5:30 the inaugural lecture was given. This was followed by a dinner with the Council of the Architectural Association (AA). From 12:30 to 3:30 on 4 May they had lunch with students and staff at the AA where Wright also looked in on the design studios, giving an impromptu talk that wandered about many architectural fields; "random thoughts" was his term.[5] There was another dinner, this time with the Goldsmiths' Company. That evening at 8:30 he gave his second lecture.

After a day visit to the Building Research station at Watford, Wright had dinner at the English-Speaking Union where he took part in a debate on the proposition that "The Architectural Beauties of London are in Greater Danger from the Builder than the Bomber." Other debaters were architects A. E. Richardson, W. Craven-Ellis (also an M.P.), Edward J. Carter, E. Maxwell Fry, D. J. S. Adams, and A. E. Oliver. On the sixth he met Carter, who had gathered a few friends including Serge Chermayeff. The seventh was a free day. The President and Council of the RIBA entertained Wright at dinner on 8 May and on 9 May he gave his third lecture at 8:30. In the evening of 10 May Wright took part in a BBC television program. (High-resolution electronic TV began in England as early as

**20.1 Wright with a group of students out-
side the Architectural Association, Bed-
ford Square, London, in 1939, as
published in the Association's *Journal*.**

November 1936. By 1939 there were 100,000 receivers in England. Transmission was suspended in 1939 simply because the signals could lead Nazi aircraft.) Gloag arranged for Voysey and Wright to meet for the first time. The fourth and final lecture was given again at 8:30, on 11 May, and the following evening he was "entertained" by the members of Modern Architecture Research (MARS) Group, the British arm of the Congrès Internationaux d'Architecture Moderne (CIAM).[6] It was a group dedicated to architectural and social research in support of the Central European architectural theorists. Among founding members of MARS apparently were E. Maxwell Fry, Yorke, Hastings, and Gloag, with Lubetkin soon joining. The group had been formed primarily for research that, within the terms of the task the members had set themselves, included "not only technical investigations into purely architectural matters such as planning and structure, but," as historian Anthony Jackson notes, "rather deep probings into the whole structure of society."

For a man of nearly seventy-two years all this activity formed a fairly tough itinerary. Wright remembered that when Iovanna was not invited to some of the functions John Gloag's daughter took her "about."[7] However, the doyen of architecture thoroughly enjoyed himself. As he recalled: "The British lectures . . . I regard as a great experience: one of the most gratifying of my life." He noted that most of those attending were young and the size of audiences "increased until they were turning many away." During the second lecture, the chairman, the Earl of Crawford and Balcarres (whoever that might have been) leaned toward Wright to ask, "What is this, Mr. Wright? The board has never seen anything like this before." Wright responded, "Your lordship, I can't imagine!" Olgivanna attended each lecture and tells us that many people asked her "if it was true that [Wright's] speaking was entirely spontaneous—not because it didn't seem so, but because it *did* seem so spontaneous. She assured them it was so." Wright also remembered that "one ponderous Duchess" who sat next to a friend "raised her lorgnette and asked, Who *is* this charlatan from Texas who comes way over here to talk *us* down!'"[8] The Sulgrave Manor represented the inherited aristocracy he found so repugnant, and it seems Wright enjoyed attempting—and that is probably a correct term—to put them down; not in London, only in his autobiography.

The London lectures had a mixed reception. Lay people responded much as the ponderous duchess. The press outside the profession practically ignored Wright's presence in England; understandably so. There were many more pressing and demanding issues than the artistic ramblings of a man from midwest America; he wasn't even from New England. One of the few mentions of Wright in London outside the professional architectural press, a single five-inch column, was headlined "Architecture of London. Builders and Bombers." It was of course about the debate in

20.2 Wright between engagements in London in 1939, as published in the RIBA *Journal*.

20.3 Wright, Iovanna Wright, and Mrs. Wright in their London hotel in 1939, as published in the *Architects' Journal*.

which Wright participated; the penultimate paragraph stated: "Mr. F.L. Wright, an American architect, who is delivering the 1939 Sir George Watson Lectures at the RIBA, advocated, 'a new sense of spaciousness, speed, and wing-spread.'"[9] A more complete if not well-balanced view was presented by *The Spectator.* It introduced Wright not only as "America's greatest architect but also as one of the representative men of his time. Yet his name will be unknown to all except a tiny minority."[10] The reporter used one of Wright's statements about the future of cities to remind the British government that some action was needed to resolve the problems of centralization and slums. The lead article said that the "essence of Mr. Lloyd Wright's ideas lies in the thought that man has now an untrammelled command of space which destroys the necessity for the vast cities of today," that there was a need for smaller urban units, implying Broadacre City. It was noted that Wright believed architecture should not just "please the eye" but be "right minded," have a moral purpose. *The Observer* not only reported on two of the lectures but interviewed Wright. It picked up Wright's well-rehearsed theme that cities were a "menace to life" and described Wright's Taliesin Fellowship as an "experiment in arcadia"; it was a favorable interview.[11] There was nothing else in the public press.

Coverage by the architectural press, however, was extensive. There was a series of articles to better acquaint British architects with Wright. In one instance Nikolaus Pevsner wrote on Wright's "Peaceful Penetration of Europe," and in another, E. Maxwell Fry wrote about Wright in *The Listener* not only for the professionals but also the lay audience.[12] Geoffrey Jellicoe, who had replaced the reactionary H. S. Goodhart-Rendel as head of the AA, published his rejoinder to Wright after the afternoon impromptu talk: Wright "feels England is in rather a bad way at the moment; but I think you will agree with me, I can tell him *right now* [he emphasized] we are not."[13]

The International Union of Architects and the London Building Centre sponsored a display of photographs and drawings that opened on 3 May.[14] Almost all the material had been brought across the North Atlantic by Wright. By then the Johnson Wax Building was nearly finished and the Kaufmann House was complete and they took honors for presentation. They were also the subject of a number of separate articles that were amply illustrated.[15]

At the 1 May dinner of the Architecture Club Wright showed an amateur color film by one of his Fellows that was about Taliesin and the Fellowship. John Gloag gave a short appreciation and John Summerson summed up what Wright meant to England. It was in 1930–31, he said, that "we began to strain our eyes across the North Sea. Sweden, with its arts and crafts, was the first revelation; then came the expressionism of North Germany, the Sachlichkeit of Dessau, and, far

20.4 Photograph of a portion of the model of the Broadacre City site with highway on left; behind, an exhibition panel with the plan. To the rear is a model of a section of the main highway bridge and a model of the 1929 St. Mark's Tower project. All were displayed at the 1935–36 exhibition in New York City. Also in the background is a model of a theater project for Woodstock, New York. The photograph was taken in the old assembly room of what was the Hillside Home School, and it was exhibited in London 1939. From the January 1938 *Architectural Forum*.

more congenial to English sensibilities, the new architecture of Holland. We visited Amsterdam; we enthused about Hilversum" (effectively that meant Dudok). "But did we realise—I don't think many of us did—that the real source of this revelation of a new architectural humanism was not Holland at all, but far-away Wisconsin."[16] It is a good guess that Summerson had read Shand's articles and so had Fry and Pevsner. *The Architects' Journal* picked up Wright's charge that the Central Europeans were "another eclecticism, a stylism—a fifty-eighth variety." In fact the *Journal* believed that Wright came along just at the right moment. "The romantic factor needed re-emphasizing. (Or, if that word is still too dangerous, the *intuitive* element.)" The magazine believed Wright was administering "a strong and necessary dose of salts. Perhaps he yet can save English progressives from a new stylistic constipation."[17] Writing in *The Builder,* "Murus" was elatedly confused by Wright—"I repeat, he is right, but his opposition is the whole of England," and he is an egoist, he is an idealist. If "Murus" were to throw a party the most desirable guests would be Gordon Craig, Ouspensky, Augustus John, and Wright, while his co-hostess would be Isadora Duncan—all "profound and free."[18]

As these names suggest, perhaps the substance of Wright's lectures did not seem as important as the presenter himself, the man who conducted such an extraordinary life. His architecture and his architectural philosophy were less important than his philosophy of life and his unflagging persistence in seeing it fulfilled. The circle in which "Murus"—and Harry Seckel—placed him was one with interesting, often close relationships that touched or paralleled the careers of Olgivanna and Frank. Most of the figures were connected with the arts.

Edward Gordon Craig, son of actress Ellen Terry and architect Edward Godwin, was a British expatriate of sorts who lived in Florence nearly all his life. He was famous as a theater critic, historian, and notable set designer. Craig supported Russian and Soviet theater during some of its most creative years. He designed Ibsen's *Rosersholn* for Isadora Duncan, which she promptly discarded after the first performance. Duncan was an American dancer who rejected conventional ballet dress for flowing draperies and bare feet. She danced in Russia in 1905 and influenced Diaghilev as well as Fokine and Benois. She led an open, very public unconventional life. She bore Craig's child in 1905 and introduced Craig to Constantine Stanislavski, which developed into a significant theatrical relationship. Her attitude to free love was well known through publicity of her own not-so-private activities as well as personal tragedies. Two of her children (one by Paris Singer) died when her automobile rolled into the River Seine. Duncan died in 1927 when her flowing scarf caught in the rear wheel of the sports car she was driving, snapping her neck.

Another member of the set mentioned by "Murus" was Augustus Edwin John, a British portrait painter who spent some of his early life living with Gypsies. He was part of the London Bohemian scene, outwardly unconventional, and casually knew the New Zealand expatriate Katherine Mansfield. Still another member was Ouspensky, or Petr Demianovich Ouspenskii, the Russian journalist and author and follower of Gurdjieff, in whose Institute for the Harmonious Development of Man he had met Olgivanna. Ouspensky lectured far afield and it was in London that he attracted Mansfield, who eventually attended Gurdjieff's institute.

During the period c. 1910 to c. 1935 the society-based circle of followers and occultists was extensive. So too was the similar and often interlocking circle of so-called individualists and existentialists (Jean-Paul Sartre's and Simone de Beauvoir's entourage for instance) of about the same period. As well, Wright was linked to the famous or infamous Round Table that gathered in the 1920s and 1930s at the Algonquin Hotel in New York City. It was a fairly tight forum of writers and critics that included Alexander Woollcott (who in 1930 wrote a chatty insignificant piece about Wright and who always seemed enamoured with the aura of the architect, openly praising him, which Wright reciprocated even in his 1943 autobiography: "I have seen Aleck bubble with wit in his lair by the river and scintillate in his seat with the mutual admiration society at the Algonquin"[19]), Dorothy Parker and Robert Benchley (who lent their names to the Fellowship venture as a "friend" in 1932), Ring Lardner (a visitor to Wright's house), George S. Kaufman, Edna Ferber, and Marc Connelly (who signed Wright's petition to President Roosevelt asking the government to finance further study of the Broadacre City concept).

When Wright Inc. was created in 1928 one of those to invest was Charles MacArthur, Oak Park schoolboy, Chicago then Manhattan newspaper journalist, and also a member of the Round Table. That Algonquin association precipitated his decision to become a full-time playwright. In 1932 MacArthur signed as a Friend of the Fellowship; by then he had successes on Broadway and in the film industry. Independently and in collaboration, usually with Ben Hecht, his films became many including *The Front Page* (1931 and 1974, based on a play of 1928 written with Hecht), *The Scoundrel* (1935, again with Hecht), *Gone with the Wind* (1939, among the many uncredited), *Gunga Din* (1939), and in the same year *Wuthering Heights*.[20]

Wright was seen as one of America's leading contributors, so to speak, to those fluctuating, popular and, it should be noted, publicity-seeking associations. It was a role he enjoyed, and the British could not have missed those vocal players (Gloag had read Woollcott on Wright) and their excellent literature, poetry, plays, films, or shenanigans.

Perhaps the English response to their guest is best summed up by an editor of the RIBA's *Journal* who offered praise, then advice ("the atmosphere was . . . inimical to coherent and constructive discussion"), and then sought clarification. After Wright's visit he said,

the London architectural world, a bit dazed perhaps, is looking around to see how many of its old beliefs, or new ones [the Central Europeans] too, remain intact after the big bang. By the force of his personality, and the force of his provocative ideas, Mr Lloyd Wright succeeded in making us stop and listen and think out quite a lot of things anew. It is too early to gauge how deep are the sympathies that have been made to exist between London modernism and Taliesin. The whole argument has, as it were, been left in the air. The atmosphere of the meetings somehow was inimical to coherent and constructive discussion; probably there never can be really good discussion at meetings so large and so charged with feeling! Nevertheless, there were many there left with their doubts unresolved who, if circumstances had allowed, would easily enough have been satisfied.

Mr Wright's critics and Mr Wright seemed so easily to get at cross purposes, Mr Wright presenting a formula, a general pattern of development, a Marxian way, extending rationality in human problems to include spheres of life in which radical changes are all the time taking place; the critics all the time looking for an exactitude of solution which this extended reasoning could not allow. All along mystics have been asking such questions as, "Please, Mr. Wright, where do I put the soil pipes in organic architecture?" and have had in reply answers which, to the people who put such questions, are certainly inadequate, and ever frivolous, or seem dully of the "render unto Caesar" class of answer. But there is a lot more that can and will be said than ever has been said in the last few weeks, and certainly more than can be said in a paragraph here.[21]

Wright's talks were published in book form as *An Organic Architecture* (publication was part of the conditions of the Watson Chair) and in the foreword Edward J. Carter hedged much as the RIBA editor had done by asking each reader to "interpret for himself." He also gave an interesting impression of the four events. There is "one feature of the lectures which no literary publication alone can convey, and that is the part which his audience played in making these meetings perhaps the most remarkable events of recent architectural affairs in England," said Carter. "No architectural speaker in London has ever in living memory gathered such audiences. The atmosphere was charged with a strange expectancy . . . to meet in person a seer." A serious though teasing editorial in the 11 May *Architects' Journal* approached a discussion of the lectures as follows:

By the time this *Journal* appears the third of the four Sulgrave Manor sermons—for sermons they are . . . will have been delivered. . . . The white-haired prophet was in form, disciples and disbelievers spellbound by his natural dignity, his obvious sincerity, his easy manner—or rather, his lack of anything so superficial as a manner. He has an irresistibly persuasive voice, mellow, smooth-flowing.

Frank Lloyd Wright is nothing if not American. . . . We are apt to forget, because of the tie of language, that Americans are "foreigners." Americans have an idiom not only in the expression of their speech but in the expression of their being. They have no taboos, for instance, about communicating what might be termed a nature-experience: they don't mind, most of them, admitting to a romantic reflex if they feel that way. We do. When Frank Lloyd Wright tells us he was born in the prairie, "out in the long grasses," we shift uneasily in our seats. When he talks of a building growing "out of the earth into the light" we get slightly clammy. But he gets away with it.[22]

It seems fairly clear that Wright's words were almost of secondary importance. The talks were experienced more as a happening; Wright the legend was the show. The spoken words had been often said before in a variety of places. But the films of Taliesin and the photographs of the Johnson building under construction and the completed Kaufmann house were new, remarkably interesting— a celebration. Were some of those gathered willing to be converted? Well, Carter believed that one fundamental consideration "was the modern English architect's hunger for criteria."

The audiences, or at least the larger parts of them which were not composed of complacent "traditionalists," were out not just to hear an architect expound his faith, but to catch from his faith every gleam of light that could serve to clarify or direct their own beliefs and practice. And in this Mr Frank Lloyd Wright can have disappointed few. His critics and questioners were not from the rearguard forces of classicism, as might have been expected, but were people who, being inside the modern movement themselves, were able sympathetically and critically to relate . . . Wright's ideas to their own.[23]

But Carter (who, beginning in the early 1930s, was close to Lubetkin,[24] befriended Walter Gropius in England,[25] and later became director of the AA) tempered it all with characteristic English calm and the hope of an internationalist when he advised that "English modernism is too tough for sudden conversions." *The Architects' Journal* was also skeptical; "To most of us, this labouring the 'of the earth' idea is a weakness. Today, when so many building materials are synthetic, the natural

[sic] effect of most buildings must be to *contrast* with their terrain," it emphasized, "not to grow out of it."[26]

Englishman, publisher, wanderer, writer, and Gurdjieff "student" Stanley Nott remembered the event. Olgivanna had invited him to the lectures and sat at his side. Nott recalled that the "lecture room was packed" with mostly "young men." He found Wright's talks "extraordinarily stimulating, full of ideas"; films were shown of "students working at Taliesin," and so forth. At the end of at least the first lecture "the applause, as they say, nearly lifted the roof."[27] Architect Lionel Brett also remembered the event well. The RIBA, he said after the war, "seldom finds itself the scene of a revivalist meeting, yet Frank Lloyd Wright's appearance there in the hectic summer of 1939 turned out to be nothing less. . . . No one enjoyed the atmosphere of lese-majeste more than Wright himself. 'Architecture', proclaimed the leonine figure with its mane of white hair, eyeing the youthful and rather grubby audience, 'architecture; my lords, ladies and gentlemen, is poetry'. . . . We were carried away."[28]

21 Reaction

The book containing the four Watson lectures was released in early 1940 by Lund Humphries. Before its release, however, there was a reevaluation, or rather those who were not so enamored of the living legend began to assert themselves. Since extensive extracts of the lectures had been published in *The Builder* a few days after each was delivered it was possible for those who had attended the lectures to test their first impressions and for those who had not attended to evaluate what they may have heard from others.[1]

Sculptor Naum Gabo remembered studying Wright's architecture after leaving Russia and attending a polytechnic in Munich. After Wright departed England Gabo had discussions at the Architectural Association that were of confusion and disappointment, to use his own words. The sculptor attacked Wright's concept of a new city and evaluation of the old and implied that Wright was hiding from life at Taliesin. Gabo also stated that "there are lots of young architects today who build quite good houses, and I can say that anybody of the MARS group, if he were given the means to build *as he liked,* would do a house *just as well* as Wright is doing it now, if not better"[2] (emphasis added). How very naive. He then reversed his view, stating that cities are indeed evil places but that smaller urban communities are the answer.

Measuring responses to Wright is usually rather easy; as Harry Seckel suggested, people either loved him or hated him. In the case of his London lectures there was ambivalence. Apparently some leveled criticism that did not surface in the public or architectural press; only the ramifications were revealed. The nature of the reproof can best be understood by a series of letters and by Wright's attempt in response to clarify what he thought he had said.

The letters disclose four important points. First, John Gloag was the inspiration for and organizer of Wright's visit. Second, people were confused; some felt bamboozled. Third, his architecture as proposed or as built was a far more eloquent synthesis of his ideas than his quirky words and phrases. The fourth needs little amplification—Wright's "spontaneous" style of lecturing was not all that he might have hoped for. To understand more completely the reaction to Wright's London visit it seems important to quote most of the content of the letters, which also rather nicely reveal attitudes and personalities. The correspondents were Gloag and Patrick Abercrombie with the *RIBA Journal* as intermediary where they were given public air.

Dear sir,—I had sailed for the United States [on 6 May] before Mr. Frank Lloyd Wright had concluded his visit, so I was unable to follow all the reactions here to his lectures; but among a few ill-informed and vocal exponents of what used to be called "the modern movement" (which ceased to move a long time ago in the matter of imagination) I detect a tendency to belittle Mr. Wright's influence, and to suggest that he is merely romantic.

It is inevitable that people from whom the gift of imagination has been withheld, and who hide the nakedness of their inspiration in reach-me-downs, copied from Corbusier fashion plates, should misunderstand the rich humanism of Mr. Wright's work and teaching.

It would perhaps have been better if he had confined his reply to the statement that he had outgrown "functionalist" childishness about 1900. That is the real answer to his uncomprehending critics.

Yours faithfully,

John Gloag (Hon. A.)[3]

Exactly what provoked Gloag is not clear, but in his letter he was concerned about two things. One was that the modern movement was aesthetically sterile. The other was more serious: that Wright was not merely idealistic but rather had practical ideas that would enrich everyone's life. Gloag's letter was published in November of 1939. Response was less than a month in coming, and it would appear that Abercrombie was speaking not only his own thoughts—and prejudices—but was spokesman for the opposition, so to speak, although not necessarily those supporting the Central European architectural theorists.

Sir,—I had begun a humble contribution to the Frank Lloyd Wright affair when the word Marxian was applied to the pattern of his philosophy by a writer in the Journal: but I desisted—it seemed

a little discourteous to our visitor. But now that Mr. Wright has written and Mr. Gloag has spoken, something may be said. Mr. Gloag is really to blame. For years he had punctuated nearly all of his delightful writings and talks on architecture with the three magic monosyllables; he had built up a wonderful legend, and then, when the Prophet was to be displayed, Mr. Gloag skipped off to America without acting as producer, with that inimitable flair for publicity for others which he possesses. Never has a Prophet been worse treated by his disciple; perhaps he thought the figure so impressive (and indeed it was) or the English architectural public so stupid that no preparation of utterance was needed. For I can tell Mr. Gloag that "Romantic" was one of the milder descriptions used. This gives some measure of the disservice which Mr. Gloag's doubtless unavoidable absence in America did to his Prophet.

Perhaps Mr. Gloag had suggested the titles of the four discourses, which promised a closely argued philosophy. He should have carefully supervised their contents as well. For there was a first-rate audience, receptive and highly favourably disposed. But Mr. Wright, the descendant of preachers, forgot that he was not at home! The extempore preacher relies upon his own congregation, which glows as each disjointed phrase falls from the beloved lips: excellent phrases, true fragments of doctrine (often, of course, contradictory); but how worthless for the stranger who has come to listen. . . . And we were nearly all strangers. . . .

When the first Lecture dried up abruptly after half an hour's talk, punctuated by the declaration of independence . . . enlivened with some well-worn jokes at Renaissance architecture . . . and enhanced by the display of an impressive personality, I said to myself: "Ah, the Rheingold, the preludian opening of the Tetralogy! The Leitmotifs will be woven into a coherent pattern, the whole will be presented, not indeed as a formula (or reach-me-down) but as a vast cosmology; and for a conclusion, instead of the Twilight of the Gods, the 'Dawn of a new Era.'"

The second Lecture quickly dispelled any such illusions. The prophet-preacher had clearly made no preparation for his sermons. He gave us first some pretty, flimsy but . . . unsatisfying moving pictures made by one of his "Boys" . . . then a further instalment of the Rhein-maiden's song, whose haunting strains again intoxicated the few Complete Wrighterians present (no development, no emergent Siegfried); and, lastly, to eke out the time he called for questions. This part was the least satisfactory: the questioners were mostly young and serious and they very thoroughly searched his material. Mr. Wright, who has a distinct gift for wisecracks, set himself to score off them and to raise a laugh at their expense, which he easily did. But he didn't face up to a single point and the questioners showed great restraint and politeness under equally great provocation. Mr. Gloag cannot have heard these questions or he would not have thought (if these are the reactions to the Lectures he refers to) that there was any attempt to belittle or misunderstand Mr. Wright. It was a genuine desire for elucidation of the Lecture which was displayed.

There were, perhaps, two special features that caused puzzlement in the audience. Firstly, the paradox that an architect doesn't need to learn anything: schools are useless . . . but remember you must be equipped with all the latest scientific knowledge of materials and their possibilities; secondly, the difficulty of applying Mr. Wright's theory of scattering the population over the face of the land . . . with the needs of industry and a densely populated country. . . . I did not dare to ask a question as to how the architecture of Democracy came into the picture, for he appeared to work for a clientele of millionaires. But perhaps in the Marxian future we shall all be able to afford Hollyhock Houses or Ranunculus Villas or, at any rate, Forget-me-not Flats.

At this point Abercrombie spoke of Wright's architecture.

But, seriously, the best antidote to these Lectures was a visit to the small but beautiful exhibition of the drawings of his buildings. It was there seen that Mr. Wright is a first-rate architect working in a rich and (in spite of Mr. Gloag) romantic medium, well tuned to a highly emphatic natural surrounding. . . . In one example the trees, the rocks, the rushing stream were all taken into consideration, even to the extent of preserving a surface of living rock for a hearthstone. In others he exploits to the full the contrast of textures and the juxtaposition of a geometrical form in an irregular surrounding.

No, sir, I repeat that Mr. Gloag is to blame for the misunderstandings that quite naturally occurred. He should either have kept Mr. Wright, a mythical figure, in his remote Arizona, or he should have carefully staged and produced him. Let us hope that in the books which we have been promised Mr. Wright will be able to demonstrate that he is a coherent thinker as well as a logical architect.

I am, sir,

Your obedient servant,

Patrick Abercrombie[4]

"A mythical figure": nice.

If one reads the lectures as reprinted a few days after each was offered, and the questions and the book, it seems that in spite of his wanderings in paragraph five Abercrombie was closer to the truth about the lectures than not. His disgust with the American's flippant, casual, almost insulting presentation was directly put. The Watson Chair was, after all, an honor carrying certain expectations. Abercrombie was also having it both ways: Wright was a charlatan but his architecture was great, and Gloag was irresponsible but thank you for inviting the American. To some extent Abercrombie echoed Carter's more measured response put in the foreword to Wright's book of lectures. Gloag's reply to the professor's long letter suggested that his reading of the lectures may not have been too dissimilar to Abercrombie's. Gloag did not take up the challenges presented by Abercrombie. Rather, he maintained that the talks were stimulating and well attended.

Sir,—I don't want to prolong a correspondence about Mr. Frank Lloyd Wright's visit to England, but I feel that Professor Abercrombie's letter in your issue of 11 December demands a reply from me. In making this reply I find myself in some difficulty, for my respect for Professor Abercrombie's judgement equals my admiration for . . . Wright and his work.

So far as my movements are concerned . . . I didn't skip off to America until the programme of Mr. Wright's visit was well under way. . . .

I was not wholly unconcerned with some other items in the programme of his visit, and I had many talks with him, although it was not possible for me actually to attend any of the lectures, for I sailed to the U.S. during the week they began. But if the lectures were as queerly obscure as Professor Abercrombie implies, I can't help wondering why they were so well attended. I have heard from reliable sources that they were packed. Apparently they exercised a strange fascination for Professor Abercrombie, because he seems to have sat through all of them; but I doubt whether anybody would have taken the trouble to attend a second, let alone a third or fourth, lecture if they had been as dull and complex as he suggests.

Yours faithfully,[5]

Word about the rumblings and "misunderstandings that quite naturally occurred" reached Wright in Spring Green soon after his return. Wright's concern that he may have been— was—misunderstood was evidenced in a short statement received in London in early October. Abercrombie was probably referring to the publication of Wright's statement rather than his lectures when Abercrombie said he could air his views "now that Mr. Wright has written." Wright extracted some comments about stylism of the fifty-eighth variety from his lectures (one more than Heinz 57 Varieties?) and entitled his rejoinder "To the Fifty-Eighth." It was published by both *RIBA Journal* and *The Architectural Review*.[6] Did he clarify his position, or positions?

In his first line he confessed the obvious, that he was not a lecturer, "no speaker really," he said. In truth he did not enjoy giving lectures or talks. He did so and very often in the 1930s just to bring in money. But they were rather tedious affairs for him, and often for his audiences. In his foreword to the publication of the lectures, dated 20 May 1939, he admitted that the talks were spontaneous and not lectures: "Had I been commissioned to give them by the Royal Institute of British Architects instead of the Sulgrave Manor Board they might have been, properly, so limited." Why that might have altered his attitude or encouraged him to be more thorough in preparation was not made clear. Later in the foreword he offered a perceptive note that should have guided him more often. "I find it safer to try to build it rather than to 'say it' because in construction sophistry falls down whereas tactful language has the disconcerting knack of outliving itself."[7] He was saying, of course, that architecture was his forte and that it came easily to him. Words were another medium, and so therefore speech.

Next in his letter "to the fifty-eighth" he mentioned published responses (few in number, as we have seen) to his talks. He noted that he had succeeded in getting himself "misunderstood and well disliked." He challenged the notion that his Taliesin was the refuge of an "escapist." In support of his contention he suggested to his contemporary architects that he was the seed of their theory and thus that "their own European creed, every form they use at least if not their every way they use it, came either directly or indirectly from my own 'escape'." And further: "Can they believe that we at Taliesin advocate a 'back-to-the-land' movement? Do they really imagine that I build self-indulgences for capitalistic parasites in the name of esoteric philosophy and work for the rich, that my buildings are expensive, etc., etc. . . .? I would like to compare the cost of them with the cost of theirs." (If such a comparison were made, the architects who made the accusation would have been somewhat embarrassed.) He then picked up the arguments of the political left. "Is the idea that good architecture must be, first of all, good building and the architect a master-builder first and an aesthetician afterward—heresy? Is the idea that good community life is the life of the individual raised to the nth power rather than the life of the individual reduced to the lowest common denominator—idealistic hallucination? Cake?"

In this connection I ask MARS . . . again . . . which came first—hen or egg? Well, if the egg is the *Idea* then the egg came first—and, just so—society. First the great individual (the Idea or Egg) then Society (the Hen). After that what have you? . . .

All great cities are slums now—communism or no communism. They like them. Why?

Perhaps they (the Communists) like them, he suggested, because they do not see them as cities but only as laboratories for theoretical study. "Are they so in love with intellectualisations they can't see any true surface, or see any surface true, because of obliterating reflections? Then what hope to escape some universal pattern for the individual human soul named after some European?"

When he talked about his architecture and their reaction to it he became more lucid, or at least less emotional. He suggested that his architecture was obvious. So too his talent: "concerning this constantly repeated reference to my contribution to Architecture as a kind of romanticism . . . they drag in the term 'Romanticism' to conceal their own impotence whereas it really only explains it." He offered that it should be evident in the "revelations of principle eternally fresh and new in every building I build." (Wright enjoyed promoting Wright.) He was saddened to learn that people misunderstood him; that people thought "because we are not newspaper addicts" that life at Taliesin was monastic; that imitations of his work had become what was called the International Style, a style he believed "could never be Democratic because it is *the use of man by the machine,*" he emphasized. "Are 'they' striving to perfect that?"

"To the Fifty-Eighth" vaguely and partially summarized his talks to the London audience and partially answered his critics, though it was illusively pedantic, rather abusive, and lacked precision. Wright was slightly more intelligible in a lecture at Hull House, Chicago (an old venue for Wright) soon after his return to the Midwest, or in about July 1939. The subject occupied only a small portion of what was obviously another off-the-cuff talk, idiomatically Wrightian and difficult to reduce a resumé. He repeated the beginning of his first lecture in London: "England had had a Declaration of Independence from us, July 4, 1776, concerning taxes and now England was going to have another, May 7, 1939, concerning the spirit. (A minority report I confessed), and I politely invited cultural England to get off our cultural chest." He declared that Americans "had been harrassed long enough by English 'old Colonial' and that I didn't think it was ever worth much even to them because it was the dwindling end of a decadant French culture when they got it and it was all certainly worth less than nothing to us when we were confronted with the building of a new nation." Surprisingly he believed the English not only understood him but shared his opinion, for his next and last line on the subject was: "Well strange to say, they readily agreed with me."[8] His sword of gentle confrontation was, of course, double-edged: the art of architecture (new) and the politics of colonialism (old). While in Russia both Wright and the Soviets also presented a double edge: architecture and nationalism (or republicanism) but also new versus new, that is, new art versus new power.

It can be seen that the motivations of the British to invite Wright were more involved than those of the Russians, yet they seem more easily described. Wright's reasons for going to London were less complex.

Was there a Russian or Communist connection to his invitation to London? From the evidence, no. Influence yes, but not directly. The invitation was a reaction by certain sections of the architectural profession who held concerns somewhat similar to Wright's. Those who were involved with promoting Wright were moderates, interested in Wright's theories about architecture and the city and his concern about the impact of Central European architectural styles on the English scene. They were also intrigued by his positive, uplifting attitude. Berthold Lubetkin—as individual in England in his demands for a socialist architecture as Wright was for a freely individualist architecture—and other architects with socialist ideas were not included in promoting Wright's presence in London.[9] MARS and Lubetkin's followers were probably too divided on ideological issues. The English architectural left was anything but a coherent or cohesive lot. And in any event Wright and his architecture would have been more of a curiosity than an intellectual threat to their ideas, diverse as they were. In opposition Wright confused issues to such a degree that he was indeed a more usable foe than reliable friend.

Wright did not believe that radicalism was necessarily the province of the political left. On the contrary, he viewed his own position, as outlined in some arguments above, as closer to that of a revolutionary. Certainly he came to that conclusion about his architecture at the turn of the century in reference to his prairie houses and those monumental theses, Unity Temple and the Larkin Building. "I used to wish they would dub me 'radical', and let me go home today," he said in his 1943 autobiography. It was a comment not found in the earlier 1932 edition. So his problem with radicalism was induced by events in the 1930s, by the misunderstanding he thought others had of his continuing influence through design, theory, and education. He thought "radical" a good honest word. "It means of the root"; radical to the academic usually meant "red" because, he said, "the hypocrite instinctively hates the radical in the United States." He concluded the statement with a tinge of elderly concern: "But if so, was I no longer radical, or were they overtaking me?"[10] He argued with Hitchcock and others that he was not overtaken as much as they thought. In England he declared that they had not overtaken him but were regressively eclectic, their "European creed," every form of architectural design "they use at least if not the very way they use it, came either directly or indirectly from my own 'escape'." He was the source, the root of European radicalism in architecture.

Later in his 1943 autobiography he restated his case, again in a passage not found in the 1932 edition. His various polemical arguments put around 1940 were induced in part by his financial difficulties and to some degree resulted from the problems he saw with American capitalism, Roosevelt's centralized government, and taxes. In the late 1930s he tried to gain tax exemption on the grounds that Taliesin was an educational institution, but without success. At Taliesin "We have . . . been compelled to work for the construction of an indigenous Architecture as revolutionaries in a far too uncommon War. . . . Yet, never really having any money. No . . . throughout these forty-five years an out-and-out culture-bootlegger, forced by the nature of our national tumbled house to work and live under the banner of a bandit: that is only to say, the banner of the Radical!"[11] He wanted to be radically different but not tainted by the word's common meaning, that of a left-winger. Being a bandit of taxes was somehow also acceptable.

Set aside the fact that Wright patently did not give the care and attention to the Watson lectures that he lavished on the Kahn Lectures for Princeton University in 1930. From Wright's affairs in London and immediately afterward, two impressions arise. One is more a question: had the man and his ideas not kept the promise of conceptual stamina and intellectual vigor that sustained him through 1932? It would appear this was the case. Wright in his late sixties and seventies was more flippant than in younger years. His remarks in the 1920s and early 1930s (often uttered to attract attention) had devolved in the late 1930s to caustic, even mean comments, especially when spoken in his own America. Where there was once a rather provocative mix of genius strained by vanity, that vanity attracted its usual ally, arrogance, and together they assumed command. He seemed unable to control his "wisecracks" and derogation. Did he honestly and consciously believe that he would influence a nation or its intellectuals or even gather a following about him larger than a handful with such a course of action?

The following is a by-product of his London adventure, and another example of incidents to come to the public's attention off and on throughout his life but especially in the thirties. *Time* magazine reported that

In Williamsburg, Va., Architect Frank Lloyd Wright told a dumbfounded audience that the only value of the town's restoration by the Rockefellers was to "show us how little we need this type of architecture now." Said he: "What has been done for you, or to you, here in Williams-burg, has advanced our cause of modern, organic architecture greatly, but not in the way it was intended. It shows how narrow, how shallow life was in Colonial days. I have long ceased

to take off my hat to our forefathers, seeing what a mess they left us." Up in arms, as one man, rose Colonial-conscious Virginia.[12]

The themes are recognizable. Sadly, the genius of architecture was not the genius of diplomacy when facing what he believed was an ignorant, intolerant if not hostile mobocracy. His objective was obscured by abuse, even vitriol. After the chilling years of the 1920s overbalanced by successes that followed 1935, and his frustration with his audiences of all social kinds and levels, such displays of his own intolerance and animosity may be understandable: not acceptable, but understandable. It also was a conscious program as revealed in Chapter 25.

The other impression is that again his visit as an important guest in a foreign city was moderately successful, if socially very pleasant, while his professional engagement was not a success and not a failure. As a public relations exercise he thought it was great. On his return he wrote Dr. Ludd Spivey at Florida Southern College that "London and Paris 'signed on the dotted line.' We had a grand reception everywhere. Gene [Masselink] is sending you copies of a telegram and letter from the Earl of Spencer just to show you how it all turned out."[13]

The book *An Organic Architecture* is a better retrospective of how it all turned out. In fact the book, which is very close to a verbatim record of his talks (not "formal lectures") and answers to questions from listeners, is a good outline of many of his ideas as of 1939, and they did not much alter—except about the USSR—after 1939. And for a close insight into the personal manners of his verbalizing the book is indeed most interesting.

While in London a representative of Parisian interests (of the Ecole des Beaux-Arts, the "president of the International Society of Architects," and the mayor) dined the Wrights and invited him to give lectures in the French capital. He declined to lecture: dinner yes, "in my honor, yes," lectures no. "I will lecture in no language but my own, distrusting interpreters almost as much as stenographers" (was this an oblique reference to Moscow?). And so Wright visited Paris. He was thoroughly impressed with the architecture he was guided to by his hosts. "I saw many extraordinary modern buildings there as I had also seen them in the Balkan cities. I don't think we have many as genuinely advanced as those. I was surprised because I was familiar only with reactionary Beaux-Arts attitudes in the schools of my country, I saw I would have to reverse my feeling about the Paris Beaux-Arts. Said I, 'I have never thought much of the Beaux-Arts training in our country.' Said the president and the director-general, 'We don't think much of it in your country, either.' They probably didn't realize the brick they were handing me."[14]

Actually Wright had briefly visited Paris on his way to Moscow in 1937. He saw the Paris exhibition and in a press release published in August 1937 revealed his liking for the Norwegian, Danish, Finnish, Polish, and Russian pavilions, which, he thought, incorporated "to some extent his teachings of the past twenty years."[15] Shortly after Wright's visit in 1939 and with probably no connection, Jean Prevost published a book he called *Usonie.* It was a series of essays about American civilization, at least so he said. One chapter was about Wright, the next about Walt Disney. "Usonia" was a word contrived by Wright, not by Prevost, a word to symbolize a revitalized USA/America.

The trip to France gave Olgivanna a chance to visit Gurdjieff at his Paris apartment. Stanley Nott was also visiting the mage and his recollections of Wright are quite revealing. They tell us much about the great architect that is often only implied or assumed as a result of scattered evidence. Nott expected Wright to ask interesting questions of Gurdjieff and then Nott would listen and watch the ensuing discussion. But Wright's behavior was like a "brilliant under-graduate" who "understood nothing" of Gurdjieff's ideas. It was a difficult evening. During a toasting Wright said to Gurdjieff he found his "idiots" (students? or Gurdjieff's "group of women" who were then in attendance?) "very interesting." He then told the occultist he should be a cook, that he could earn good money cooking.

Later in the evening Gurdjieff produced a chapter from his book manuscript later published as *Meetings with Remarkable Men,* which he was then laboring. He asked someone to read from it, so Wright began because he did not wish to "hurt the old man's feelings." After reading for a while he told Gurdjieff he found it "very interesting," but it was "a pity" it was so poorly written. "If I had the time you could dictate to me and I would put it into good English for you." Wright resumed reading but soon feined tiredness for himself and Iovanna. Better stop, he said, for his daughter's sake. Gurdjieff agreed, saying that she was still young and "only begin," but Wright was an "old man" whose life was finished. Wright got "red in the face" and angrily stated that his life was *not* finished, that there was plenty he could "do yet!," or words to that effect. With family he left in "high dudgeon." Nott observed of the evening's events that he found it "gratifying to discover that 'great' men" have weaknesses, that they possessed "vanity and self-love" like everyone else, and remarked that when Gurdjieff "provoked Wright's prickly vanity, something malicious in me had a feeling of mild satisfaction."[16]

Wright's fondest recollection of the visit to England was of luncheon at the country home of Charles Ashbee, then also in his mid-seventies, "my one friend in England" said the American wistfully. On a visit to Oak Park Ashbee and his wife had witnessed and were attentive to both

Wright and his first wife during the difficult months before Wright fled to Europe with Mrs. Cheney. And then in 1932 Wright had asked Ashbee to add his name to the list of Friends of the Fellowship. The only other Britisher invited to be a Friend was DeCronin Hastings who was then deeply involved with the RIBA and headed the Architectural Association. As part of the public relations designed to coincide with Wright's visit, Nikolaus Pevsner reported Ashbee's claim that "amongst his other titles to fame" was that "of having discovered Frank Lloyd Wright for Europe."[17] Wright also enjoyed other private engagements particularly with Luytens and Voysey: "loved them both," he said. He met Voysey for the first time when introduced at a private London club. Gloag and Wright remained friends and Gloag sent his children to Taliesin during the bombing and war.[18]

The mission to London had taken its toll. The sojourn and its business were almost too much. He was nearly exhausted; "frankly, I am getting tired," he said, "I've been so rushed to and fro giving four hard lectures" and other talks. He confessed that tiredness made him "bored and want to escape." So the last two lectures and his hassles with the slightly antagonistic MARS people were difficult exercises for the seventy-two-year-old architect.

On the evening of 11 May 1939 the Wright family, Frank, Olgivanna, and Iovanna, took the night train to Paris. They remained there as guests for three days, resting, dining, talking, and regenerating. Then they traveled to Dalmatia for another day or two of relief and sight-seeing. Wright made his comments about his tiredness and desire to escape London in a letter to Ashbee.[19] It was written from the Garland Hotel, London, on 11 May just before departing for Paris. Ashbee and Wright first met in Chicago during the winter of 1900. The spring of 1939 was their last meeting for Ashbee died in 1942.

Soon after returning to Spring Green Wright received a visitor from Europe who was on a mission. Sigfried Giedion had been appointed Norton Professor at Harvard University for the 1938–39 academic year. The subject of his lectures he described for Wright as a study of the "formation of architecture since the Renaissance, with stress on modern architecture and urbanism."[20] They met in July 1939 and there can be no doubt that Giedion probed Wright's thoughts and furthered his knowledge by visiting the architect's many works in the northern midwestern states, not only then but later. Giedion's thoughtful, perhaps revolutionary lectures were published in 1941 as *Space, Time and Architecture.* The book presented the first synthetic and historical study of Wright's architecture, providing cogent analysis and stimulating analogies. The influence of Wright's words during interview and discussion is apparent throughout the relevant text of Giedion's book. But this does not detract from Giedion's independent evaluation. Wright "belongs among the great preachers of his century," Giedion said and then specified which century was Wright's. Wright

has by nature the will and the courage to protest, to revolt, and to persevere. He carries on in architecture that tradition of sturdy individualism of which in the middle of the last century Walt Whitman and Henry Thoreau were the literary spokesmen. He regards this tradition as part of himself. As prophet, preacher, and agrarian individualist, he preaches hatred of the city and return to the soil and to the productive, self-sufficient community.[21]

And further, Wright's "real influence, his great and educative influence . . . is that of his methods and ideas, as they are reflected in his work." Giedion then noted that Wright's conception of space "was developed and changed in the hands of [Europe's] leading figures." Since Giedion was an intimate of most of those leading figures, that was a note of some importance as was the following: "This may explain why Wright is somewhat repelled by what has been done in Europe since his appearance."[22]

After an active but tiring trip to Britain and Europe those must have been stimulating days talking with the Central Europeans' chief propagandist.

Gold

The Sulgrave Manor Board had asked Wright to speak on the "science" of architecture and on his interpretation of "America to England in architecture" as occupant of the Watson Chair of American History, Literature and Institutions.[1] When completed, in at least one polite English opinion the lectures had "greatly contributed to the advancement of good will between [the] two countries," this "irrespective of any question of politics."[2] In Wright's opinion it was a good show. In early June he returned to the midwestern prairies somewhat chuffed, as his British hosts would have phrased it.

Surrounded by the warmth and relative security of his home at Taliesin West in winter of 1939–40 the septuagenarian architect began to write about his London experiences of the previous spring. He wrote of those "intelligent" audiences and their "fine character." In retrospect he enjoyed what he called their "purposeful heckling." He remembered more seriously that the hereditary lords and ladies were "rather a bore, don't you know." His association with those London audiences and the RIBA was to culminate the following winter in an episode that reflected the highest level of British cultural diplomacy. He and his work were again weighed in London. If not as broadly as Wright might have wished, nonetheless after their personal experience of 1939 the imperialists were to study more closely America's feisty living heritage. The episode that engaged Wright's professional British colleagues was the determination of the 1941 Royal Gold Medal of the RIBA. The affair remained outside Wright's knowledge and was not of his making: he merely accepted their offer. One immediate result of his award was an optimistic request from an English newspaper asking him to comment on how to approach postwar rebuilding. This aspect of the episode was of his making: a response that dramatically and pompously denounced the war and British society, economics, and their war effort, and supported a vocal and influential stream of intellectual argument in America against participation in the war, an isolationist view.

22 Royal Gold

In October 1940 it was time for the RIBA to begin the process of selecting a gold medalist for 1941. In March they had given the 1940 medal to English architect Charles F. Annesley Voysey. Now, because of the war, the Institute noted that there were difficulties. Just getting people together was one. More importantly it was feared that some British architects might agree to a suspension of the award for the duration of the war. The president of the RIBA was informed that there had been only two breaks in continuity in the medal's long history. The first was when Queen Victoria died in

January 1901 and the schedule was put "out of gear." The other break was in 1924 when Englishman W. R. Lethaby rather dramatically "upset things" by refusing it. The gold award was given right through World War I, so why not through the new war? The president was also informed that there was no rule to say that the award should go to a Britisher for two years running and to a foreigner in the third year. A more or less regular practice to that effect had been established but there was no constitutional requirement as such. In fact the practice had been broken eight times between 1869 and 1912.

William Henry Ansell was the new president. He had just been invested and thought it necessary to be counseled on procedures as well as problems induced by the war, and possible courses of action. When accounting for the "existing conditions abroad," the number of countries that might have been seriously considered in 1940 was severely limited and by January 1941 even more so. From a political and practical point of view people of German, Polish, Norwegian, Danish, Dutch, Belgian, French, or Italian nationality were excluded. Those of Soviet, Swedish, or Swiss nationality were not easily considered. "Some unimportant countries," to use their phrase, were dismissed but not named. There remained four possible choices, a Spanish or Portuguese nominee or an easy option of someone from the United States or the British Dominions. Ansell's counselor offered the view that the easiest thing to do was to give the award to a British architect but cautioned that it might be difficult to find the right man.[1]

On 2 October 1940 members of the RIBA Council were solicited for nominations to be received by 12 October. Conditions of the award as approved by the King were:

The Medallist must be a distinguished Architect or man of Science or Letters, who had designed or executed a building of high merit or produced a work tending to promote or facilitate the knowledge of Architecture or the various branches of science connected therewith, or whose life work has promoted or facilitated the knowledge of Architecture or the various branches of science connected therewith.[2]

Strangely, only the RIBA Council could nominate and then determine the medalist. The Council was large, indeed the better word is enormous.[3] The membership was obviously considerably greater, yet it was officially excluded even from offering suggestions. The medal was to be decided secretly by a comparatively small elite, a practice that appears to have been consistent over the years. Before 1940 therefore, those variously formed elites had chosen fifty-six British recipients. To give an indication of the influence of the Beaux-Arts during the late nineteenth and early twentieth centuries, fourteen Frenchmen had been honored. Four each were from Austria, Germany, and Holland; two each from Sweden and Italy; one from Canada and three from the United States.

In 1940 nine nominations were received; seven were British. They were Stanley Davenport Adshead (in his seventies, he had been professor of town planning at Liverpool University for twenty years); the late Earl of Crawford and Belcarres (apparently he died March 1940; his name, his familial identity eludes us but he had held the chair at one of Wright's Watson lectures); Banister Flight Fletcher (author of the classic *History of Architecture on the Comparative Method*); E. Vincent Harris; Charles Herbert Reilly (head of the architecture school at Liverpool University during its remarkable development from 1904 to 1933); Albert Edward Richardson (a professor of architecture at the University of London before becoming Director of the Royal Academy School of Architecture in the 1930s); and Thomas Smith Tait, partner of John Burnet. Four were identified as academics; others may have been but were not so designated. Two others nominated were foreigners: Otto Rudolf Salvisberg (architect and teacher from Switzerland who worked for thirty years in Germany prior to 1930), and Frank Lloyd Wright. These were, in pragmatic terms, safe and reasonable nominations. Adshead was a well-known neo-Georgian;[4] three of the nine were best known as teachers, and one as an historian and eclectic. Only Tait could have been considered a modernist of some—but no extra—competence.

Wright had been nominated by Herbert Kenchington, Norval R. Paxton, and Howard Robertson. Members of the Royal Gold Medal Committee were president Ansell (Chairman), Charles Henry Holden (Gold Medallist in 1936 and a sponsor of Le Corbusier for the Gold Medal in 1953), Howard Robertson, L. Sylvester Sullivan (Honorary Treasurer), Michael Theodore Waterhouse (Honorary Secretary who later became president in 1948–49), and Ian MacAlister, secretary of the RIBA (as differentiated from Honorary Secretary). Of those committee members Holden nominated twice and in so doing diminished the value of his nominations and later his vote. Fletcher was the sole nominee of Ansell. And, of course, there was Robertson's nomination.[5]

Robertson was active in the RIBA, in professional affairs and in debates about architectural theory. He was also a man of considerable influence. An American expatriate and cousin of Morton Shand, he was appointed to the Architectural Association School of Architecture in 1919 and became principal and then director before he resigned in 1935. His little book *The Principles of Architectural Composition,* first published in 1924, went through many impressions (my copy is the eighth, of 1955). It was a preeminent teaching guide for British traditional notions of composition. (In it Robertson included a plan of Wright's Imperial Hotel, Tokyo, suggesting that it expressed its concrete structure.) One of the first serious presentations in Britain of French modernism was by Robertson and his colleague F. R. Yerbery, whose *Examples of Modern French Architecture* was published in 1928. Together in 1929 they began a series "A Pictorial Review of Modern Architecture in Europe" for the American professional journal *Architecture,* using Yerbery's photographs. Later Robertson helped to encourage the introduction of modernism as touted by the Central Europeans. His association with their Congrès Internationaux d'Architecture Moderne (CIAM) and its English wing Modern Architectural Research (MARS) was not a happy affair, but his influence in England remained notable and steady until the mid-1940s. He not only showed an interest in Wright in the 1920s but reviewed Wright's publications in the 1930s and 1940s. In September 1940 he authored an article on American architecture for a special issue of the London magazine *The Studio* about America, one of a number of such efforts of that time. Robertson gave Wright plenty of notice as the architect with "the most individual influence in America." In a general survey concerning "domestic architecture and the second great war" for the annual *Decorative Arts 1940* he again included Wright, erroneously placing him between tradition and the "complete breakaway" of the Central Europeans. As well, Robertson and John Gloag were good friends, as witness the dedication to Gloag of Robertson's book *Architecture Arising* of 1944. In an otherwise relatively conservative committee it would be safe to say that Ansell, MacAlister, and Robertson would have been the persuasive members; persuasive toward an architect who practiced modernism of a type not too radical.

During Wright's visit in 1939 to give the Watson lectures, the English public and its press were not interested in his presence in London or his esoteric talks. There were more pressing matters in Poland, Germany, and Italy, matters that attracted nearly all public and political attention. Troop movements, Ribbentrop in Italy or Poland, conciliation moves, Lord Halifax in Russia, Japanese bombing of Chungking—all this and much more took place during May 1939, just before Wright's visit. And in the same month the King and Queen went off to Canada for a royal tour coast to coast and then, via the New York World's Fair, to Washington, D.C.[6] One reason for visiting Washington was to enlist United States moral support for the British position. Then on 1 September 1939 Hitler's armies attacked Poland, and on 3 September England and France declared they were at war with Germany. By mid-1940 the British were desperate for U.S. physical support—troops, weapons, transport—for full military participation against Germany and Italy. But the American people and the politicians on Capitol Hill were deeply divided between participation in and independence from European problems. Because of isolationist and antiwar sentiment President Franklin

D. Roosevelt was reluctant to act positively and openly and physically support England. In this situation British cultural as well as political figures appealed to their American counterparts' sense of kinship. As president of the RIBA, Ansell sent a long letter "to the Architectural Profession in the U.S." supposedly written while in an air raid shelter. It was published in the November 1940 *Architectural Forum.* It spoke of the British profession's attempt to participate in defense and then in war and then optimistically to look to future reconstruction with the eventual peace to come. About forty percent of the text was about the war and its idiotic ways, of unexploded bombs in innocent villages, the need to protect freedom, and about a link between British and American people and the two professional groups. As with all messages from Britain, and the above is only an example, there was an implied urgency on the need for unity of the two countries against what was surely a common foe and of material activity through engagement.

In view of the desperate situation that faced Britain, it is reasonable to ask whether those that determined the royal gold medalist were reacting to events of the day, more precisely to diplomatic needs. Did the committee receive certain suggestions *sotto voce* from elevated places and people? There is no firm evidence either way, yet the medal committee must have been aware of the potential publicity that would come from recognizing Wright, a man of immense stature in his profession and one so prominent—and newsworthy—in America. Announcements of the medal always received wide publicity in architectural and building circles in both the USA and Britain. Was the committee alert to the international role they were playing when in mid-1944 they decided that the Royal Gold Medal for 1945 would be given to the Soviet architect Viktor Vesnin?[7] Was it meant to perform a similar role in 1940?

Previous American medalists were given awards during periods when American support, political or military, was of no particular concern to Britain. The socially aggressive Richard Morris Hunt received his citation in 1893, Charles Follen McKim (of McKim, Mead and White in New York City) in 1903, and the last before Wright was the aesthete Thomas Hastings in 1922: all *New* Englanders. Yet in Wright's case the question of diplomatic need, so to speak, is reasonable, while an unequivocal answer difficult. Moreover, those who granted the distinction may or may not have been conscious of any diplomatic pressures, covertly coercive or otherwise.

Wright had been invited to give the 1939 Watson lectures in part to fill a void. "It is almost impossible to name any one man as the leader of modern architecture in England to-day, but it is perhaps Maxwell Fry," said architect F. R. S. Yorke, "who should be given first place by his colleagues. He has been responsible for a number of houses in which rational planning and delicacy of treatment are combined with a precise selection of materials to produce a fine finish."[8] Yorke was not sure; "perhaps" Fry, and only for some nice houses. Housing, single-family or multiple-family units, was the social issue around which many, if not most, theoretical arguments in Europe were focused during the 1930s: housing for the "masses," for the workers. Its structures were relatively inexpensive on the one hand (single-family) and on the other they were a politically viable proposition (multiple units). But proficiency in their design only is not a sufficient premise to assume leadership in a profession as dynamic and diverse as architecture. Wright was the master house designer (to some) and the leading architect in America (to most) and of world renown.

The obvious aesthetic quality, however it is defined, of Wright's buildings was extremely important to observers, particularly those not enchanted with architecture as promoted by the Central Europeans. Their architecture was seen by most people as cold, didactic, unresponsive to human needs, and plain awful. Wright's architecture was indeed romantic, natural, warm, and full of human dialogue. Although the Central Europeans and constructivists had attempted to reject the notion of beauty in favor of an aesthetic tied to socialist ideology, they had in fact invoked the functionalist idea that beauty was an absolute found in necessity and that it was an end in itself. People, the political proletariat, were denied participation in understanding the new aesthetic, or more particularly in developing it. Wright always charged his audiences with failing to understand that function was only a means to better comprehend how beauty might naturally evolve and be clearly understood. And he was unafraid to search for and speak about beauty.

In England there was utter confusion. Many dilettantes flirted (some dangerously as it turned out) with notions of the political left. Others were trying desperately to find some coherence in a modified modernism, i.e., aesthetic dilutions like art deco or similar fashions. Others looked for someone to sort out the true modern architecture from the false evangelists and pretenders; someone to find an architecture that was new yet familiarly English. In short, someone to fill that leadership void. When historian John Summerson tried to identify contemporaries who were leading British architects of the 1930s, his choice was exactly the same as others' such as Trevor Dannatt or P. Morton Shand. Their choices included Wells Coates, Fry, the firm of New Zealand colonial expatriates Amyas Connell and Basil Ward, the immigrant Berthold Lubetkin, and the European emigrés Chermayeff, Gropius, Marcel Breuer, and Mendelsohn. Of these last five only Lubetkin stayed in England. He arrived on British shores in 1931 and had established a modest and respectable international reputation by 1935. But he was single-minded in his commitments (which included MARS for a short time) and outspokenly antiestablishment especially toward the RIBA.[9] Summerson's view and probably that of most observers went like this: Lubetkin's architecture was "oversophisticated for [its] time and even had the war not intervened, it is doubtful if . . . [Lubetkin's] creations would have helped to form an English 'school.'"[10] Oversophisticated is an odd observation and the emphasis should have been on the word "helped." In short, there was no English hero and no indigenous cult. Perhaps someone who had found an American architecture might have ideas about where or how to find a new, truly English and modern architecture. Or was the fountainhead elsewhere overseas?

Architect Lionel Esher recalled the grand tours, so to speak, of the 1930s rather well. Architects traveled to Stockholm and Hilversum; a few visited America and occasionally held audience with Wright. But the vital center was Paris.[11] And Paris was the place for avant-garde artists and Le Corbusier. He was best known in England for writings about his own work and his association with Soviet Russia; his dominance virtually depressed international recognition of other French architects. However, in June 1940 Paris belonged not to art but to Hitler. There was confusion among English architects. People were trying desperately to find some satisfaction in a modified modernism, i.e., aesthetic dilutions like art deco or similar fashions. With the Beaux-Arts the route has been clear—eclecticism and its rules of proportion, planning, and ornament. There was added in the 1930s, however, a series of European continental ideas seemingly without order or responsibility to acceptable aesthetic tastes and architectonic properties.

The RIBAs award was not about architectural styles or movements but about people and ultimately one person's contribution to architecture. In 1940 it was also and primarily about nationalism. Howard Robertson alluded to some of the difficulties when in 1940 he wrote about "domestic architecture and the second great war." He believed that in recent years architecture had been "influenced by party policies" and "sociological" developments. Russia had "experimented wildly in a new architecture" and then suddenly reverted to a traditional style, which then became a simplified "modernised classic work not unlike that of Fascist Germany," forbidding all other styles and particularly modernism. Robertson was not optimistic. With "officialdom" ruling the "human roost to-day" he could see collective houses with people sleeping in a collective bed listening to a dripping of collective water in a collective bathroom.[12] Indeed, with bureaucracies in a war mode and in control throughout the western world who could exemplify optimism and a reasonable hope for threatened democracies?

There was a need for Britain to find and then sustain an inner strength and cohesion. At the same time it was necessary to secure and hold allies who would help repel a probable invasion.

The allies at that critical moment in late 1940 were in disarray. The French had again lost face, America was not yet engaged, the Soviet Union was always suspect, and so on. Frenchmen who might have been considered by the RIBA had spent many months, even years, working on projects in the Soviet Union—François Jourdain, Le Corbusier, and Lurçat for instance. Their loyalties were ambiguous, perhaps divided. Those of the political left who openly supported the USSR's international Communism probably were viewed as nonnational, perhaps dangerous. Those even vaguely associated with the Axis nations surely were outside consideration. Salvisberg's many years in Germany tainted his prospects and anyway, what could Switzerland offer Britain in 1940? Some had become almost without national identity—emigrés such as Mendelsohn, Gropius, and Mies. The selection of the architect to receive the RIBA gold medal at this critical juncture in English history had to be one who could in some way serve immediate national needs and who, considering persuasions within the committee, was a modernist.

In horrific national crises perhaps architecture becomes irrelevant. In any event, in such moments motivations become confused or hypersensitized, actions imprecise, intentions either vague or exaggerated. Suffice it to say that the paternal figure of Wright was of interest to the English for a variety of reasons, but he seems to have wholly satisfied none beyond veneration and perhaps curiosity. For most, Wright was still one of the masters; petulant, eccentric, but a master architect. A leader? No; at least not in the manner or degree desired by some in the English profession in the late 1930s, as evidenced by the reaction to his Watson lectures. Yet this lack was not crucial to the nomination; nor was the curiously displayed affection by the British for the American from the Midwest prairies critical, though it was not ignored.

The meeting of the RIBA's Royal Gold Medal Committee to determine the medalist was held on 17 October 1940. After what was described as a "thorough" discussion of only slightly over an hour a resolution was passed. By a vote of four to one Wright received their nomination.[13] Apparently it was that easy. All lobbying had been done before and outside the committee room. The result was submitted verbally by Robertson to the RIBA Council on 29 October 1940 and they approved the recommendation. The Keeper of His Majesty's Privy Purse was informed that the RIBA Council resolved that "subject to His Majesty's Gracious Sanction" Wright receive the medal for two stated reasons: "for the Promotion of Architecture" and in "recognition of his work as an architect."[14]

It is now reasonable to propose that after his return to Taliesin near Spring Green, Wisconsin, in 1939, Wright played another and unsuspected part in Anglo-American diplomacy. Was the medal deserved? Of course. When all is considered, however, it appears fortuitous that he gave those 1939 Watson lectures just one year before nominations were called and that they were published and released in February 1940.

If the award was not manipulated then it was a fortunate windfall for England, in a small yet not an inconspicuous way. The British public was informed in January 1941 that Wright had received the medal. Most importantly, it was emphatically and widely publicized in the United States in all press media. Further, a propaganda campaign began at the same time that presented America and Americans to the English. For example, America was "introduced" to readers of *The Listener* by among others the American journalist Edward R. Murrow and his English counterpart Alistair Cooke, in a series that ran for many months;[15] Charles H. Reilly wrote on "Modern Movements in Architecture" for the same government-controlled magazine and included Wright;[16] and there was Robertson's article—one of a number—in *The Studio.* More overt propaganda continued throughout the year in all communication fields: attempts to hold American friendship and win their material commitment. Suspicion coupled with circumstantial evidence suggests that Wright's award neatly fitted into the British campaign.

Wright said he was "listening to the New Year's Eve broadcast" at his Arizona hibernacle and heard that the medal had been "bestowed" upon him. He was astonished, he said, but that could hardly be true. Why he would dissemble on such a small matter is a mystery.[17] He had received a letter much earlier, dated 4 November 1940, informing him that the RIBA had decided "to rec-ommend to His Majesty the King that the Royal Gold Medal for Architecture for 1941" should be given to Wright. The decision was confidential until he accepted and the King approved. They obviously did not want another Lethaby affair. The letter called to Wright's attention the long roll-call of medalists since the award was first established in 1849 by Queen Victoria. It gave particular notice to the thirty-one "non-British architects" and the Americans "Ric." Hunt, "Chas." McKim, and Hastings. It continued in a relaxed manner to say that

One of the most interesting names of all is not in the list for a particular reason. Fifty or sixty years ago the medal was offered to John Ruskin. He refused it, not because he was not greatly impressed by the compliment, but because he had just received the news that the Italian government had destroyed a beautiful old building in Northern Italy. He said that at such a time all architects and people interested in architecture ought to be sitting in sackcloth and ashes and mourning their failure to prevent an act of vandalism rather than awarding Gold Medals to one another![18]

Wright replied by cable on 16 December to simply "Macalister" that he accepted, adding, "A culture like that can never lose."[19] To make it all more acceptable to everyone Wright was proposed by Council as an Honorary Corresponding Member of the RIBA in November 1940.[20] Wright did not complete and return his application until after he was officially notified that he was recipient of the medal.[21]

Possession of the royal gold eluded Wright. On 31 December he was informed that the King approved of the award.[22] On the same day a public announcement prepared by the RIBA was broadcast especially by the BBC. The statement included the Institute's view that the honor was the highest "that any architect can obtain" in the world.[23] The Institute then informed the American Embassy of the award.[24] Then on 17 January 1941 the RIBA caught up with Wright on a small matter: "You may be wondering when the actual Royal *Gold Medal* is going to reach you." The explanation offered was that the striking of medals awarded by the King had been "postponed until the end of the war." (Actually, Wright received a letter from Windsor Castle at the end of December 1940 stating that he was the gold medalist for 1941 but that the Medal was to be presented after the war.)[25] This freeze was to help maintain the "Gold Reserve," a precedent that had been set, it was noted, during World War I.[26] For the time being both Charles Voysey and Wright received certificates prepared by the office of the Secretary of the Privy Purse.[27]

So Wright had to wait and Voysey would never see his gold, for he died in February 1941.

Three British architects nominated or otherwise considered at the same time as Wright were eventually given gold medals: the elderly Charles H. Reilly in 1943, Edward Maufe in 1944 (the practice of a foreign recipient every third year was again abandoned on that occasion), and the aged Albert Edward Richardson in 1947. Viktor Vesnin was picked for 1945 and the durable Patrick Abercrombie for 1946.

Finally, in response to a query the Privy Purse office informed the RIBA in 1946 that restrictions on gold were raised and the Royal Mint was preparing "The King's Medals."[28] The RIBA then made plans to make presentations to those medalists of 1940 through 1947. A grand party, an "unprecedented event," took place on 15 April 1947.[29] Five medalists attended the ceremony; Voysey's son accepted his father's medal. Wright preferred not to attend and his medal was sent to him. Viktor Vesnin did not attend but acknowledged the award with a telegram to the RIBA. It included the message: "In this act I envisage not only such high appreciation in recognition of my modest efforts in the field of architecture but also a symbol of the further promotion of creative cooperation between architects in Great Britain and the Soviet Union."[30] In June 1945 Vesnin wrote a more formal letter of acceptance saying,

It affords me particular pleasure to find my name included in the glorious roll of Medallists now, at a time when the people of my country and Great Britain are waging a heroic struggle shoulder to shoulder against a common enemy. In this struggle difficult and honorable responsibilities have been laid upon the shoulders of architects. We have to give new houses to millions of people who have been deprived of heart and home by barbaric Hitlerism.

Vesnin's capitulation to the Communist Party's dogma and the tortuous eclecticism it favored must have continued to trouble him, for he stated that he was still hoping to "create new forms of contemporary architecture which will satisfy the great demands of the age."[31] There is no record of a similar courteous letter of acceptance from Wright, only his quick cablegram. Soviet architect David Arkin (who personally assisted Wright on his 1937 trip to Moscow) was also an Honorary Corresponding Member of the RIBA. He too wrote on the general enthusiasm of all Soviet architects about Vesnin's award.[32] The medal was presented to Vesnin in 1946 in Moscow by the Press Attaché of the British Embassy.[33] Wright's medal was delivered to Taliesin in July 1947.[34]

Wright's son, John, recalled his father's "open joy" at receiving the Royal Gold Medal and believed that Wright "treasured it above all [awards]."[35]

It is of interest to note that Wright and Olgivanna next traveled to England in 1950. Again he was a guest. There was brief report to the membership of the RIBA in its *Journal.* The Wrights' visit to Britain appeared to "have been a great success."

Age has not enfeebled his acute mind nor dulled the edge of his provocative wit. Both were vigorously exercised at the three gatherings of architects at which he was entertained, namely, the annual prize giving of the A.A. School of Architecture (the original purpose of his visit to the country), the luncheon held by the Executive Committee of the R.I.B.A. Council and the dinner held by the Architecture Club.[36]

It was a social occasion.

But the story of Wright's gold award does not end with the RIBA's medalists' party in April 1947. There was some interesting correspondence between Wright and an English newspaper that effectively illumines his professional relationship with Great Britain immediately before the U.S. entered the war.

23 A Touching Affair

Writing about experiences during the spring of 1939 for his autobiography, Wright commented that "there is something indomitable in British pluck and splendid in British character," and he wondered what England "might have been like . . . were it not for the 'white man's burden'—her Empire. Surely such qualities as hers are good for far more than war and conquest and the conduct of subjugated peoples." He concluded that if England was free "on her own—developing slowly the characteristics and strengths of Englishmen from within, the nation might have been small, but the world would have had one mighty, genuine democracy by now. . . . Empire has ruined England." He recalled his long personal and unsuccessful struggle to save America from the unfair economic and undemocratic forces he saw within. He dwelled on his vision of a "genuine democracy" free from past hegemonies. He then added two lines: "A disease took root and spread by way of her [Britain's] success. Dismal reflection: it has now spread to us."[1]

We can understand the tag to his telegram accepting the gold medal: "a culture like that [not Britain but England] can never lose." He used a similar phrase in Moscow when arguing that the varied Russian traditions should not be lost in the rush to Sovietize. Wright wished to differentiate the British Empire (as one evil political function) from England as a discrete culture and tradition. This is further evidenced in personal notes, such as a letter to author John Gloag in 1938 where Wright looked forward to seeing Gloag "on the spot that was England"; perhaps "was" should have been emphasized.[2] Public exclamations were also forthcoming.

It was the war that dominated Wright's thoughts in those years as it did most everyone's. Events took their course by the thrust of their own destructive velocity. With its own power and impetus there was not much he or anyone could do about the war. Protest, yes. Encourage conscientious objection, yes. Fight for the isolation of America from those European troubles, yes. Perhaps now was the time also to finish the revisions to his autobiography, to bring it up to date, more or less. It might show by example a path that avoided the idea of war, its centralized government, and its profiteering. The new autobiography could illuminate not only a personal struggle but his success through steadfastness, through striving for ideals held high. Perhaps his words might stimulate an understanding of his philosophy and provide an apocalyptic inspiration. Or perhaps his architecture of the past might inspire others. Perhaps the publications *On Architecture* and *In the Nature of Materials* also might provide ideas for reconstruction after the war. But first the war . . .

Of course Wright was not involved with policy at the national level or with international diplomacy. He chose to try to persuade, to protest, or to critically attack from outside. During 1940 a great deal of propaganda was generated for and against America's becoming involved in the European war. Proponents for participation laid particular emphasis on the obvious need to defend Britain. In Wright's attempts to dissuade people he used Britain as an arguable example against participation in the war. His main thesis was that democracy had failed to counter by example. The best defense, he suggested, was to "put better ideas" than those offered by Hitler's "total state and total war"; and one example not to follow was Britain's. It was one typical antiwar position.

In a letter published November 1940 in *The Christian Century,* a Chicago religious and missionary magazine, he observed that America's "most creative minds" were ignored by the "by-party act" to save Britain. To "save Britain" he maintained America would be on the road to self-destruction. "Wake up, America!" he exhorted.

Such standards as we have been aiding Britain to maintain or have been ourselves aided by Britain to maintain are played out! They are senile, a demonstrated bottleneck without issue except war. To beat our enemy *his way* [Wright emphasized] we have not got a good foundation. We won't get one with extravagant preparation for war no matter how far we go. English culture will not die but British imperialism never was anything but a foolish challenge to the world and more than ever an empty one.

Democratic ways and means are gone wrong or rotten just when the world needs us most as the great forces of life again surge forward in the ceaseless tide of change. Fearful as we are, we the exploited must face great organic change and we must face it on our own merits. We cannot face it on Britain's! If we go on in that old way of life, we are lost anyway.

Perhaps his presentation is somewhat confused but it can be understood as an open display of disgust with the kind of system—colonialism and its economics—that America should not support, especially by shedding America's "young blood." Those who were properly educated, he argued, should make decisions concerning weighty philosophic matters, not the politicians, not the journalists (the propagandists), and not even the voters *unless* they were properly informed by the country's "most creative minds." He continued with his views that closely approximated Jaeger's text on *Paideia:*

The only safeguard democracy has is a free, morally enlightened, fearless minority. But democracy deprived of either the vote or the voice of that minority will stay in infancy, a pushed or helpless drifting mediocrity. Democracy's very life depends upon entire freedom to choose from among its free minority the bravest and best thought. If party pacts are made to end or continue the way of life before they go before the voters, what has democracy? Any influence

whatever designed to keep the people ignorant of the real issue by falsifying or by stultifying the enlightened minority is soon fatal to democracy. Must manipulated mediocrity overwhelm the real issue in a democracy? If so, let's say mobocracy, not democracy. To mobocracy dictatorship is inevitable. We have it in conscription.[3]

(In 1949 Wright published a book *Genius and the Mobocracy,* ostensibly about Louis Sullivan and containing illustrations of the elder master's drawings. In it, among other familiar themes, he discussed discursively the topic of a "fairly decorated mobocracy," which was a substitute "for a thought-built democracy.") Wright had now and then expressed his view that the U.S. should stay out of the war and that the British establishment and its empire were not worth saving. If the British or Europeans wished to know his position they had only to look or ask.

The Christian Century letter exemplifies Wright's attempt to insert his ideas into the war debate. As might be expected he attracted some not irrelevant attention, and some flack.[4] More extrovert utterances followed. And interestingly, they seem to gain momentum after receipt of the Royal Gold Medal. In fact the medal prompted one response that centered on London and one of its morning newspapers was the intermediary.

The haphazard growth of London had been of concern for decades if not centuries. In the late 1930s there was a surge of renewed interest in how to rectify the city's many problems, caused mainly by industrialization's inherent impetus toward centralized population and industrial power. That interest was due in part to the evolution of the idea of regionalism promoted in the late nineteenth century and into the 1930s, and to a kindred planning notion, the popular green belt that grew out of the garden city movement. In the 1930s that interest brought into being a series of studies of industrial cities in Britain. The hope was that a total national plan might result. In 1938 a law prohibiting the expansion of London was passed that effectively halted building at certain boundaries and established a surrounding relatively undeveloped green belt. Then the bombings of 1940–41 destroyed large parts of the city.

By 1942 planning was optimistically again under way to an extent that encouraged the presentation of ideas for a new physical plan for greater London. In that year, for instance, MARS revived their 1937 proposal for a theoretically viable linear physical plan of green areas alternating with developed built-up areas divided by a narrow core of central facilities. It was obviously derivative of the many linear-city notions proposed in the USSR in the early thirties. But a traditional physical plan (foreshadowed by a proposal for Paris as early as 1928 and Moscow in 1937) by Patrick Abercrombie and J. H. Forshaw in 1943 was officially accepted in 1944. As soon as practicable, i.e., in 1946, a total plan for the English industrial centers was enacted: in a few words, decentralization by the creation of new towns. It negated the intense urbanization favored by MARS. Although we have no evidence, at least such a general concept (if not the particulars and the architectonic results) must have found favor with Wright whose decentralization proposal called Broadacre City was well known. While not involved in the planning for—or debates about—London, he was at least asked to participate: only once.

Three weeks after his Royal Gold Medal was announced, with optimistic zeal the London newspaper *News-Chronicle* asked Wright on 21 January 1941 to write 1,500 words on his suggestions for the planning and rebuilding of London after the war. The actual title requested was "How I would re-build London."[5] He telegrammed a manuscript on 25 January.[6] The time spent on the piece suggests it was hastily drawn; all extant copies strengthen the suggestion.

But again, there are a number of extant versions. One version was, as expected, published on the morning of 17 February 1941. The next version was published in Wright's sporadically released newsletter *A Taliesin Square-Paper,* probably in March 1941. Another version was published in his 1943 autobiography and yet another in the 1977 edition of the autobiography.[7] This last is, of course, the least reliable for reasons outlined in the references at the end of this book. The 1943 text is similar to that published in London, only condensed. The *Square-Paper* version was quite different from the other three in some parts, for reasons that will be discussed in the next chapter.

Wright's article in the *News-Chronicle* was presented in an interesting manner. It was entitled "How I Would Do It"; the introductory remarks noted that he invented "a new era: B.B.—before the bombs," cited his "Welsh extraction" (again he disregarded his father's family), and mentioned his Imperial Hotel and its survival. Above the article was a reproduction of a drawing by British architect Hubert Bennett, five columns wide and entitled "London Rebuilt," supposedly as the city would appear if planned to Wright's specifications. In fact the drawing shows an urban scene, obviously London but more like Le Corbusier's dream of a congested city of towers proposed in the 1920s. Preparation of the drawing may have delayed publication until February. (A cable to Wright on 27 January acknowledged receipt in London of his article and it was published two weeks thereafter.[8] Wright's reaction to the drawing is not a matter of record.

Wright rewrote his favored old themes and inserted some that were for the occasion. The bombing of London was sad but must be seen as fortuitous, for planning could start anew. There was some detail. "London should be a motor-car aeroplane London" with wide spaces and tall buildings on the periphery. Railways should be elevated and truck routes set low. Traffic problems

solved in his Broadacre City plan should be emulated. Land for all, each to have his own ground. There must be a "good modern plan for a Democratic people." He saw no reason for "difference in quality of thought between the house of a man with more and the house of a man with less: only difference in extent" (more and less of what and which extent?). Were his organic city planning ideas executed the British Empire "might disappear." This was followed by a confusing sentence, "Were Germany to win this war it would be to lose it on any basis of a plane and gun future." He then asked Britain not to grieve if the Empire were lost for it was not essential, "the Empire of Imagination is more enduring."

Wright, as usual, vaguely and elliptically presented many ideas through a series of assertions never refined. The result was always a perplexing diminution. But he was persistent. The political and economic Empire may die, he argued, but England will live: "Traditions must die in order that great Traditions may live." Linked to these notions was a question to be answered: was England humanitarian or only English? If humanitarian, it should decentralize London. Then boldly he stated that "Great buildings always begin at the beginning." Strangely this meant that there were "necessary items" to begin with:

1. No very rich nor very poor to build for—no gold [bullion?].

2. No idle land except for common landscape—no real estate exploiters.

3. No holding against society the ideas by way of which society lives—no patents.

In short, no speculation in money, land, or ideas; not one of them must be . . . a speculative commodity but *must be used* [Wright emphasized] as the actual necessities of human life, like air and water. This is the true basis for what we could honestly call democracy.[9] These three "items" he had listed before. In fact much of the article for the *News-Chronicle* paralleled an address Wright had given to the Chicago Real Estate Board on 2 June 1938.[10] It should be noted, however, that in six decades of writing he never once specified how his varied political/economic declarations were to be achieved. Fortunately other writers have since shown the derivations of some of his ideas but also avoided the subject of implementation.[11] Both they and Wright, notably in his 1943 autobiography, offered Henry George, Thorstein Veblen, and Silvio Gesell as sources for at least those ideas related to contemporary economics and parapolitical needs. To his mind, adoption of the three items would cause a "liberation of human individuality." The intellectual logistics of such a transfer were avoided, not only on this occasion but on all others. Perhaps he reasoned that dogma was not only a virtue but an aspect of logic.

All money, land, and ideas were to be magically and freely available to all, and with his unclear notion of the new undefined state, he asserted that there would be no unemployment, therefore war impossible. To his London audience he shouted over the cablelines:

Skeptic? Well, laugh and be bombed![12]

Was he actually naive? Had he lost all pragmatic reason? Were his personal ideas and ideals above the obvious realities of death and destruction by an accelerating war? Was he wholly and imperiously arrogant? On the other hand, what better time to institute an "honest democracy" than during postwar reconstruction? What better time for a social reformation to throw off the shackles of squireism, to be finally and irrevocably free of the iniquitous and divisive class system inherent in the British form of aristocracy? Entwined within the article and knitted to his planning ideas was the need to drop the "grandomania" that physically enshrined the aristocracy and to drop economic as well as cultural enslavement. Perhaps he was prophetic. After 1945 and in awkward twitches the Empire died; but unhappily the aristocracy persists.

However . . . that extraordinary outburst was not published in London: it was edited out. It was published in *The Architectural Forum* in August 1941 in what was supposedly a short resumé of the *News-Chronicle* article. It was not published in either the 1943 or 1977 autobiographies but it was retained in the 1941 *Square-Paper* version.[13] Wright added in the *Square-Paper* that a cable had been received by him from the London newspaper offering news that the article had been well received.

Reaction to the article was measured, or as New York correspondent for the *News-Chronicle* Robert Waithman said, it "inspired a certain amount of waspish criticism."[14] The socialist bits pleased Clough Williams-Ellis. As well, he found Wright "a Prophet with a philosophy of life, as sentimentally romantic and unrealistic as the poetic eloquence wherewith he delights to decorate his thesis." As to the London plan, "this sort of thing just will not do."[15] Another reader found the message "stirring" and "heartening."[16] Elizabeth Denby thought Wright's intention was to make Londoners laugh. "Jokes can, however, be in bad taste, if not risky: there may be some who will take these empty phrases seriously, who will think that London's slums were in fact 'blasted out of the way in a few days,' . . . who would not notice the confused mind." She doubted if Wright knew where London was, and in any event his "empty phrases" were based on "complete ignorance," and so forth.[17] Soon after publication of Wright's article, W. H. Ansell as president of the RIBA gave a talk to the Royal Arts Society and asked for a "vastly improved old London" rather than a new city, with "shining gold and ivory, reliefs and panels."[18] Well, Wright might have said, at least Ansell's paper offered old tasteless spice to the affair.

Wright received twenty guineas or about US$100 for the cablegram. "In the circumstances," he said, "a touching affair—that check."[19] What that meant is anyone's guess.

24 AIA Gold

Patterned after the RIBA, the American Institute of Architects (AIA) began awarding its own Gold Medal in 1907. The first award should have been an announcement of national and professional pride, but instead the medal went to an Englishman, Aston Webb, R.A., RIBA, etc. Other foreign architects were honored in succeeding years, without much misgiving but no doubt with factional and personality problems. So it was when the controversial Wright became again controversial during deliberations for the American medal. His receipt of the AIA Gold Medal in 1949 is well outside the decade under study here. However, some knowledge of how it came about, if only in outline, allows an interesting comparison to the British honor and exposes causes initiated in the late 1930s. The equanimity of the British architects in determining Wright as their medalist for 1941 was not evident with the American professionals. Richard Guy Wilson, historian of the AIA medal has noted that in spite of the fact that Wright had never become a member of the Institute and had often publicly criticized the average professional and most twentieth-century American architecture, thereby implicating many of its architects, his "omission from the AIA Gold Medal list became embarrassing," to use the AIA's words.

Just two years after Wright received the RIBA tribute, in 1943 architect Ralph Walker proposed him for the AIA Gold Medal of 1944. Also nominated were Louis Sullivan (posthumously) and the West Coast architect Bernard Maybeck. Various local and state Institute chapters and members submitted letters of endorsement. As the minutes circumspectly recorded, "letters opposing this award were also submitted." Both Wright's and Maybeck's nominations were subsequently ruled incomplete; supposedly they lacked portions of a biographical statement and a "history of attainments." Perhaps in response to other problems with his nomination, in 1945 Wright replied to a query of the AIA as to why he was not a member. His response was as might be expected: he was interested in Architecture, not the Profession; he was a freelancer and an anathema to the old guard; no man can cooperate and still maintain independence "of his Spirit"; the Profession is for personal gain not for Principle; and so forth. In the past and when asked, however, he had never refused "the boys" anything "on decent terms."[1]

Wright was again proposed in 1946 together with Eliel Saarinen and Charles D. Maginnis by a Gold Medal committee on which Walker served. Saarinen won the 1947 medal to be followed the next year by Maginnis. At the June 1948 annual meeting where Maginnis received his award, a member's petition was presented asking the Institute's board of directors to give the next Gold Medal to Wright: attached were 140 signatures of members, friends, and students. Such a petition publicly presented was a rather special occurrence.

The board was sympathetic to the petitioners but not all directors were convinced. Further, William A. Delano was also nominated for the 1949 medal. At the December board of directors meeting, Joseph D. Leland, chairman of the Gold Medal committee, "summarized the extensive correspondence received with regard to Mr. Wright" and announced that most were in favor, "few opposed." As president of the Institute Douglas William Orr spoke strongly in favor of Wright's nomination, mentioning that the AIA's image might suffer if it denied the award to one of the very few American architects who had received international public acclaim and recognition. Was that the all of the arguments? (It is most interesting to note that a similar discussion took place when Wright was nominated for the AIA's Centennial Gold Medal; see Appendix G.) A few board members were opposed and, as Wilson recorded, they "discussed Mr. Wright's morals (personal) and his unethical conduct, such as stealing jobs, bidding for work, and undercutting other architects in his quest for desirable commissions." It is not known if these serious allegations were substantiated, for if not they most certainly should have been withdrawn and so recorded. They seemed to grow out of hearsay that began early in his career and proceeded through the 1930s.

Anyway, the Delano nomination was dispensed with and there remained a single holdout who was strongly opposed, Brandon V. Gamber, personal architect of Henry Ford. Understanding the mood of the board, Gamber "announced that he would absent himself from the room, and in his absence The Board could take a vote!" The board then voted unanimously (sic) to give Wright the medal. A very tricky question now arose. In view of his antipathy to the Institute, would he accept? The Board wanted to be able to privately rescind the award if he refused. A hurried telephone call was made and Wright accepted.[2] These machinations from 1944 to the boardroom affair in 1948 were conducted—performed—by mature-aged professionals. As with the RIBA, an elite board determined the medal in secrecy, not the members.

When the medal was finally presented at the next annual meeting Wright made another of his off-the-cuff ("extemporaneous") talks. It included an opening remark to the effect that it was about time he received the medal, and words such as "I really feel touched by this token of esteem from the home boys."[3] But Wright had heard about the allegations, so to his colleagues he said that beginning in the Oak Park days and since, his services remained at ten percent. As far as stealing jobs was concerned he maintained he had never competed for services, had never hawked himself "on the curb." He spent nearly one quarter of his rather short speech defending that position; one quarter was about the sad state of architectural design (Houston was the bad example), and one third about the cold war and the House Un-American Activities Committee's action of the day. From his temporary pulpit before professional colleagues he offered them salvation in honor: honor of self and of nation. It could only be achieved through truth and creed, through philosophical constancy and through the daily living of it all. With great pride—and *not* in reference to architecture—he announced, "I have built it. I have built it! That is the source of my arrogance." That was why, he said to them, I can "look you in the face and insult you."[4] He did not need to add that they knew this was true.

And so finally Wright was officially recognized by his professional brethren not so much in acclamation of his architectural genius and good deeds for architecture (and therefore for America) but out of embarrassment: everyone in the world had honored him except the "home boys." How sad. But of course none of this was revealed when President Orr read the award's citation to those gathered at the annual meeting in Houston, Texas. The first three lines read:

Prometheus brought fire from Olympus and endured the wrath of Zeus for his daring: but his torch lit other fires and men lived more fully by their warmth.
To see the beacon fires he has kindled is the greatest reward for one who has stolen fire from the gods.
Frank Lloyd Wright has moved men's minds.
A belated but fitting tribute.

In relation to the British medal a couple of further observations can now be offered. If Wright was true to his beliefs and very serious concerns about the British and their involvement in the war, then how could he reasonably accept their medal? Rather should he have overtly protested in some significant manner? His emphasis on a strangely argued theory about English culture opposed to or oppressed by British imperialism was more or less correct but appeared polemical at best, self-deceit at worst. As esoteric as it may have been, Ruskin's example offered him a respectable yet potentially dramatic model for protest. For instance, England's aggressive defense against the imperialism of Hitler witnessed the destruction of thousands of beautiful old buildings.

In their name and in the cause of peaceful construction, he could have refused the medal. Or more to his point he could have rejected it on grounds that it was offered by a nation who used war in the attempt to solve problems.

Was his passion tempered by practicality? Answers cannot be accurately gauged for lack of evidence but two possibilities converge to suggest probabilities. First, his ego—so brittle as often revealed in his writings—would not allow rejection of such a high kudos. The RIBA medal was after all the most important international recognition that can be given an architect. Second, by accepting gold his words and beliefs (regardless of the subject) might gain more authority in public arenas. It is not difficult for the knowledgeable observer to believe Wright capable of conceiving such a calculated plan. After accepting the medal his activities with a political bent, together with his verbal strutting, increased. He seemed to gain confidence in his already imperial vision, in his intellect and self-announced influence. If the British were using Wright as one element in an attempt to win America and also trying to gain Wright's support of the war, then they failed as evidenced by the *News-Chronicle* article and thereafter. Wright's thank-you to the RIBA was to more openly attack Britain, its war effort, and its attempts to engage the United States against Hitler.

The Closing

With Wright's life and concomitant architectural works in the 1930s now better known, a short piece he wrote in 1929 can be more easily understood as his own rather sketchy outline for action—and reaction—in the forthcoming decade. He was asked to answer several questions put to him by Oliver M. Sayler, an observer and historian of Soviet theater arts. It is valuable to know Sayler's attitudes to the arts generally and how he conceived and produced, so to speak, his book entitled *Revolt in the Arts* of 1930. Intended to be a survey of the creation, distribution, and appreciation of art in America, to be simply a "coordinated symposium on the subject by typical workers in the several arts, the book suddenly enlisted the author's own interpretive interest when he detected unmistakable trends and feasible goals emerging from the general chaos." He then wanted an analysis of the "multiple forces at work in the several arts, to determine the relative importance of esthetic, economic and moral factors, and their reciprocal interplay, to inquire causes and to formulate implications." Sayler conceived the arts "as handmaids to science"—it should be noted—"in the effort to explain life, replacing religion and metaphysics for those who have lost faith in these aids to cosmic understanding and supplementing their service for those who still retain faith in them." In a Machine Age "intimate art may exist alongside mass-production art, deriving support from the latter in return for serving as its laboratory, testing ground and inspiration."[1]

With notable exceptions (reflected in the phrases "handmaids to science" and "replacing religion" and in the Marxist emphasis) Sayler's attempt to homogenize the arts had only the slightest affinity with Wright's and Baker Brownell's ideas. The bringing together of well-known artists in a symposium was similar to Brownell's university course, to the initial intention of the book he coauthored with Wright, and to his later essays of 1939 published as *Art Is Action.* Wright could see the polemical value of participating in Sayler's 1929 effort, and it was also nice to be among "distinguished contributors" at a time when his newly reformed career was about to begin. His contribution for Sayler was short.

Architecture—"In Between"

The first declaration—that I know anything about—of the value of the machine as an artist's tool was made twenty-seven years ago at Hull House, Chicago. I read a paper there called "Art and Craft of the Machine," since translated into many languages, making the assertion.

Today, Holland, Austria, Germany, Switzerland and recently France have contributed work that not only subscribes to that ideal, but is more "protestant" than my own. There is distinctly now a modern architecture,—in world-wide preparation. America has less in quantity to show.

Among the forces, factors and circumstances which stand in the way of complete and general recognition of architecture as an art are: "Tradition" as the refuge of the incompetent. Academic sentimentality. "Art" in quotation marks. Unqualified wealth. A government, the helpless creature of the majority.

The immediate future of architecture in America will probably consist of a superficial emulation of the work of certain protestants. Eventually, we may have an organic architecture.

The revolt in architecture has little if anything to do with the general revolt in the arts, except as life in general insists upon itself and birth in some form is inevitable. Not much can be accomplished of a revolutionary character except in, and as, architecture because architecture is the synthesis of all arts.

Form is determined by function and modified by use when the forms are living-forms. "Renaissance" is impossible. Real forms, even once "re-born," are put on or taken off like garments. The machine ruined even these vestiges or vestments of the old order. New forms became imperative. They must be created.

Of course, all arts are subject to the same law. Principle in one is principle in all. Only technique changes, although, strangely enough, few artists knew anything about architecture. Anatole France was only annoyed by music.

Perhaps this is a good time to interrupt Wright's narrative in order to make a point about a problem common to many artists professing modernity: the dichotomous practice of their beliefs. A personal example should clarify the problem generally. I can vividly recall an experience as an undergraduate in an architectural school dedicated to modernism. One of the studio critics invited a few students to help with the drawings for a competition he had entered. As we worked we talked about modern architecture and architects, the need for honesty to the ideas of modernism, and so forth. We were speaking over seventeenth-century baroque music selected from the critic's record collection! Wright's love of classical music and especially of Bach, Handel, and Beethoven is well known: horror of horrors, all Old Europeans. Only once in his writing did he include a modern composer, Stravinsky, and only once did he speak of enjoying American modern music and that was jazz ("sometimes") and negro spirituals ("sometimes"). He did not otherwise support modern American composers or music. Anyway, his piece of 1929 for Sayler's book continued.

We in America have no outstanding modern achievements as "architecture" except as Europe accepted the early work of Sullivan and myself and some few of our architects subsequently learned from Europe to accept their acceptance. (This is frankly immodest. But if I must answer—it is at least true.)

There is no leadership in American architecture at the moment, at least, none that is sound and honest. A timely confusion may be seen everywhere.

The old leadership, if it can be called leadership, included: the Schools; the medievalists; the pseudo-classicists and their plan-factories. Last, but not least, the "modern" modistes themselves, may be seen as falsely assuming the role.

Public appreciation may be enlisted in the interests of better architecture by letting the people actually see some of it. Photographs can not show it nor advertising "tell" it. Nor does the propaganda of the half-baked architect and snapshot critic do more than harm.

The economic obstacles in the way of better architecture include: the natural timidity of vested "Interests"; the women paging Culture; the frailty of the architects themselves.

The American Business Man, unintimidated by "candy"-culture or "rocking-chair" esthetics, should be an asset to architecture. He has been the only asset, so far.

There is no trouble in the relations between client and builder. It is the architect who is in difficulties,—in that triangle.

Cooperation with the architect is the only real opportunity either painter or sculptor will ever have—or ever had, for that matter.

The work of the architect does not yet in any way correspond to mass-production. In a period of revolt, no leader of the Old can guide the New or should do so. Youth is a quality— in art as in life. The New is simply Youth—with all that is thereby implied. The Old is Old—that is all, and the Old may be found with a *"new-esthetic"* in modern architecture. The only possible analogy at the present time with "machine-made" and "hand-made" in industry is the "machine-made" structure itself and the "hand-made" ideals of "Exterior or Interior." Result: Architecture as a bad form of surface-decoration.[2]

"Youth is a quality." Indeed, it is a tidy outline.

Of course the more controversial of Wright's promotions in the late thirties were the object of comment and reaction, much of it rather severe in its criticism. His sincere belief in his own genius; his sincere friendship with the Soviet Union; his sincere hatred of colonialism, cultural especially but not musical: these combined with careless and extrovertish explosions championing his works and beliefs could not pass unchallenged, or at least unnoticed. The implications of his straightforward if not so plain talk were many. Some have been noted in the essays above; others can be found in the following. They reveal that it was not architectural productivity that closed the second most important decade of Wright's career.

25 Talent and Work

Undoubtedly there was a connection between Wright's patent talent, his architectural genius, and the way he employed his personality, or rather certain traits of his personality. At various moments in his career, both during the 1930s and after, there were peculiar outbursts about such issues as the folly of perpetuating colonial architecture, or damning aspects of American society, or insulting listeners or readers (as in his invitation to the skeptical English to laugh at his proposal and be bombed). Further, there was the perplexed observer or participant such as Elizabeth Kassler who spoke of her experiences at menial, almost trivial tasks and who, it should be recalled, noticed Wright's distrust of intellectuals. Many other examples may be cited of his bombastic and irreverent outbursts usually against tradition, authority, or the intelligentsia.

At first glance a reading of these episodes would seem to support the generally held belief that they were exhibitions of a pompous and arrogant man. To some extent they were, for Wright had displayed his conceit on many occasions throughout his professional life. It began in about 1900 and thereafter he exhibited not only an arrogance about his talent but a willingness to challenge anyone who held beliefs contrary to his. After he met and won Olgivanna his general outward demeanor altered marginally while the content of his verbal presentations changed mark-edly under the influence of the teachings of Gurdjieff. These were relayed to Wright by Olgivanna in the first instance and during the mid-1930s at odd moments by Gurdjieff himself. Nothing even hints of such influences or parallel thoughts intruding on Wright's writings before meeting Olgi-vanna. On the other hand, prior to 1925 there were no precipitating causes pressing for an exami-nation of new philosophies, and there was little time for such an impractical extravagance before 1922.

The first indication of these influences was contained in a letter of December 1928 to the Chicago landscape architect Jens Jensen, an old and trusted friend (see Appendix F). It is the most lengthy exposition by Wright on the subjects of work, creativity, and education, which also link to Gurdjieff. Later notes by Wright are just that, limited to a line or two in other contexts. In the same letter Wright included one of Olgivanna's thoughts and compared it with his own. Through muddled phrases it can be seen that there is in fact little difference between husband and wife. It should be remembered that the letter was composed at a critical transitional moment in Wright's life and career.

Wright described Olgivanna's belief "that the creative instinct is the original birthright of mankind and in some of them it lies dead—in any case paralysed and that by proper treatment it may be revived." The last six words are important. Wright also believed that the "creative-faculty is the birthright of Man" but that man has betrayed himself by playing tricks upon himself by application of his intelligence, "by means of his arrogant assumptions, abstractions" and bad education. He goes on to say that because of laziness and inactivity over generations the faculty of creative ability probably has been genetically sterilized. Wright also believed that a treatment was possible that would rekindle and effect a rebirth of "the creative instinct in Man" by—and this is interesting—"getting himself born into everything that he does." The force or chief "tool" by which this might be effected was *imagination,* which he saw as a positive and active opposition to the overemphasis in civilized worlds on selfish rationalism, on the "false premium upon will and intellect," on science. The mechanism was participatory education, a "little experimentation station" to woo and win humankind's lost creative instinct. But it was not a school of book learning but of "work." This outline of his contemplations can be favorably compared to the ideas of Gurdjieff and his acolyte Olgivanna.

Gurdjieff was born and raised in the Armenian town of Alexandropol, now called Lenin-akan, in the southern Caucasian mountains about 125 miles inland from Batumi. It was a land of ever-changing political borders—Turk, Kurd, Russian, Azerbaijani, but mainly Armenian throughout history. Gurdjieff's parents were Greek but perhaps of Russian nationality. Their name was Gordiades and his father was a "bard," an *ashokh,* perhaps in the tradition of Homer. Gurdjieff was brought up in the Orthodox church, a brilliant student at the nearby Kars monastery (which shared a site with a Russian fort to help protect the newly conquered lands taken from the Armenians.) Why he took the name Gurdjieff is not clear. Perhaps it was a slight russification of his father's name, or related to the Arabic or Semitic word *gurj* or *goorj,* meaning a person guided by personal interest. More than likely it came from the Sanskrit *guru,* more particularly *guruji,* which is a name of respect given by students to a teacher. With the suffix "eff" or "ov" it would mean belonging to a revered teacher.

In any event, at an early age Gurdjieff became intrigued by man's fears of evil spirits, by the supernatural, by magic and wizardry, by the occult. He traveled widely and made friends with Orthodox priests who believed in the supernatural, with *fakhrs,* dervishes, yogi, a group called "Seekers of Truth" in Turkestan, and many Muslim ascetics and/or magicians. In short, as a young man he was, through his varied practical experiences, in training to be a sophist. While Gurdjieff now rates only a mention in occult or parapsychology or psychic literature, he was for some people, especially from around 1922 to the late 1930s, a teacher and mystic of great importance. One follower contended that he was "so profound as to be ultimately unknowable," a contention held by many.[1] When Olgivanna met him he was at the height of his "powers."

Crucial to Gurdjieff's teaching is the proposition that for most people it is unrealistic to speak of themselves as "I." I breathe, I move, I laugh, I converse; the fact of the matter is that "it" (Nature, external forces) does these things. "It" breathes me, "it" moves me, etc. We *think* we do these things and that they are performed by a definable, consistent, purposive "I." But we can do none of these things because, according to Gurdjieff, there is no unity in us. There is no permanent "I"—only a multiplicity of little "I's"—jealous, competitive, conflicting, and changing places every minute as external influences vary. We don't notice this chaos because we are asleep, and so have no knowledge of what is really going on.

When Gurdjieff said that sleep is the chief feature of our being he was not speaking entirely metaphorically, nor was he talking chiefly about the human tendency to daydream and fantasize. He meant that nearly everything we do is done "on automatic." The most striking example of this is driving over a familiar route and "awaking" at our destination with no recollection of the journey, which must have included hundreds of observations and relevant adjustments to our driving. But our whole lives are like that, in fact. We are slaves of circumstance. Whatever we do we can't help doing and we do it unknowingly.

Gurdjieff sometimes called his system of spiritual teaching the "way of the sly man" who exploited the three ancient teachings of the fakir, the monk, and the yogi without renouncing the world as they did. The fakir tries to attain a state of bliss by physical denial and mortification; the monk seeks the love of God by the way of religious emotion, faith, humility, and service; the yogi desires enlightenment or union with a Supreme Being by mental concentration. In Gurdjieff's system the student worked simultaneously in these three directions of control over bodily, emotional, and intellectual functions. The only renunciation was not a material but an existential one. It required a denial of the fundamental human conviction that, at least in our ordinary daily existence, we possess the power to direct our lives. To make decisions and act on them; in short to will, to act, and to do.

All this, said Gurdjieff, is *illusion.* Man is an automaton, a mere machine activated by external stimuli, like a typewriter, a record player, or a gun. *Things happen to* machines; forces act upon them. Machines can do nothing of themselves; nor can people. To those who indignantly reject the charge that they are composed of such volatile, inconstant, and chaotic stuff it is necessary only to ask them to concentrate on themselves for the space of a single minute. It is doubtful that anybody can manage this without practice. But even if they can, it is certain that they will be unable to entertain *any other thought* at the same time, which makes self-remembering (a core of Gurdjieff's method) useless as far as pursuing the business of daily life is concerned.

If we could self-remember it would be uncomfortable because we should become aware that we tell lies incessantly. These are the product of an automatic control system that "buffers" us from the force of the shock we should experience if we were not shielded from full consciousness of the contradictions of words and actions of the various competing false personalities that all bear our name. To be truly master of oneself, to create the foundations of a permanent and consistent "I," one must stop telling lies to oneself and to others; one must cease being a machine.

The first requirement for achieving this was to renounce the illusion that anyone had free will to do anything. Without awareness of our sleeping state we remain almost indistinguishable from the great majority of human beings who are going nowhere and don't know where to go, who hate to think about themselves, have no wish to change *themselves,* but only to change others, in the sense of making others do their bidding. Such people, Gurdjieff thought, were *walking dead* and there was no hope for them since they couldn't recognize their sleeping condition. To wake up it was necessary to study oneself; but before that it was necessary to *learn* how to study; and then how to do work on oneself. This was the Institute's raison d'être. Study and work had to be carried out in a group, selected and organized by a teacher. All work consisted in obeying the teacher's directions absolutely and uncritically. People came to Gurdjieff because they felt themselves to be handicapped or imprisoned in some way (the image varies; tunnel, maze, darkness) and had a compulsive desire to escape without knowing how to begin.

Theoretical knowledge was ancillary to self-study; not psychological self-analysis but self-recording of the activities of the "centers" of the human machine: motor, instinctive, sensational, emotional, and intellectual. Thus the Institute's program included breathing and rhythm exercises, gymnastics and dervish dances, mental exercises, and others to strengthen memory, attention, and

25.1 Photograph of G. Gurdjieff in the 1930s.

will power: all this under unsparing direction. Those who persisted in such extraordinarily strenuous and distressing work proved the sincerity of their belief that, in Gurdjieff's words, it is better to die making efforts to awaken than to live sleeping.[2]

The methodology of Gurdjieff's teaching focused on work. It should be recalled that when Gurdjieff first spoke to Olgivanna in Tiflis, he said, "You do nothing, and you wish for immortality!" He went on to say that it did not come "by wishing but by a special kind of work. You must work, make effort, for immortality. Now I will show you how to work. First, tell servants to go and begin by doing everything yourself."[3] The practical reality of work was one thing, the people another. "What Gurdjieff did at his institute was to turn bored, egotistic, confused people into well-balanced machines, too busy to think about themselves." The plan was to "allow" his students' "natural capacities to operate again." Therefore Olgivanna could argue that through proper treatment certain instincts, including the "creative," could be *revived*. Wright could argue that even if it was lost over centuries of genetic desensitization, a proper education could restore creativity to mankind.

Further, work at Avon was bound to dance. Various aspects of Gurdjieff's teaching were also part of the public shows he put on, very much like performance exhibitions. One observer present at the New York "display" of 1924 (in which Olgivanna participated) said that what excited and interested him "was the amazing, brilliant, automaton-like, inhuman, almost incredible docility and robot-like obedience of the disciples, in the parts of the demonstration that had to do with 'movement.' They were like a group of perfectly trained zombies.... They did things, without suffering any apparent hurt, almost as dangerous as dropping off a cliff, and certainly more dangerous than leaping through fiery hoops." The observer went on to say that what he felt "the demonstration showed, even more than their control over themselves, was the terrific domination of Gurdjieff, the Master." At another point in the description of the event, the observer felt Gurdjieff was "a slave-master or wild-animal tamer, with an invisible bull-whip swishing inaudibly through the air." Gurdjieff was described as a "calm, bull-like man, with muscles in those days as hard as steel, in immaculate dinner clothes, head shaven like a Prussian officer's, with black luxuriant handlebar moustaches, and generally smoking expensive Egyptian cigarettes."[4] As noted in an earlier essay, music was for Wright, dance or movement was for Olgivanna. In Wright's first press release about the Fellowship in 1932 he mentioned that "drama and rhythm" were to be "collateral" studies.[5] Dance for Gurdjieff took many forms, but always it was related to conscious mental control of the body's musculature as well as dervish rhythms and induced ecstasy.

How was this theory applied at Taliesin? Contrary to what most descriptions of the regime suggest, the complete set, as it were, of teachings were not attempted. Yet it is worth remembering that as early as 1933 Wright had said, if ambiguously, that the human soul can only be free again if "able and willing to work," that work was the "first condition of true gentility. Taliesin sees work itself where there is something growing and living in it as not only the salt and savor of existence but as the opportunity for bringing 'heaven' decently back to Earth where it really belongs." Work was a vital routine and it was composed of a great variety of activities often too menial for many people. Olgivanna and Wright made no demands of their Fellows to participate in yoga or tricks or exercises for body control, or for that matter meditation or divination, at least in the 1930s. There was field, kitchen, servant, and construction work. For the Fellows Wright selected only the less contentious aspects of Olgivanna's teachings. He seemed to adopt a paternalistic tone and attitude toward his youngish student entourage. The reasons may be many: the principal work of the Fellowship was to assist Wright in his architectural office, so time elsewhere was not helpful; he wished the Fellows to have practice in construction, so they built buildings for Wright's school and later at Taliesin West; most Fellows were mature people and dedicated to a profession and not initially prepared for work other than as it might be directed toward fulfilling architectural ambitions; and there may be other inhibiting factors including a belief that all that mystic nonsense was not going to help create architects who would spread the gospel according to Wright.

However, as Gurdjieff's influence decreased in England and Europe and after he closed his Institute at Avon to take an apartment in Paris, his influence became more obvious on Olgivanna and her daughter in the 1930s, finally culminating with great activity in music and movement in the late 1940s and the 1950s. The growth of that influence can be measured in the many ways already described or alluded to. Further evidence is found in a short passage in Wright's 1932 autobiography where he wrote of a minor domestic routine: the 6:30 "ante-breakfast" rang, then everyone got up and went to the living room where they turned on recorded music and had "the morning frolic." There the description ends. In 1940–41, however, in revising that portion of the book, he made significant clarifications and additions: that in the living room they played their "favorite dance music" and had a "morning frolic" that they called "setting-up exercises, but really they are more like dancing"; the dances Olgivanna had learned at the "Institute at Fountainbleau and taught them to us."[6] This rewriting occurred after a visit to Taliesin by Gurdjieff in 1939 and a summer visit by Gurdjieff acolyte Stanley Nott in 1940.

Thus it seems that by c. 1930 Wright and Olgivanna practiced her teachings privately. By the late 1930s if not earlier Wright was more willing to admit an association with the occultist, perhaps because he was more secure professionally and in his social life. His willingness can be measured, for he continued his autobiographical rewriting in 1940–41 with new additions that suggest he thought himself familiar and knowledgeable in the subject. Instead he exposed ignorance and used Olgivanna as a disclaimer. "The Institute Gurdjieff," he said, "I had already heard about"; apparently that was before meeting Olgivanna in 1924. "The Asiatic savant had brought his group to New York the summer before [sic] and performed remarkable studies in human correlation at Carnegie Hall. She herself had been in the group and I now [in the 1920s] learned from her more of that remarkable training. The Institute took unrhythmical"—he wrote—"neurotic human beings in all the social stratas, took them apart, and put them together again better correlated, happier, more alive and useful to themselves and others." This was followed by the disclaimer: "I am putting here what Olgivanna said. . . . It seems that Ouspensky, Orage, Lady Rothermere, Katherine Mansfield, and many others were Gurdjieff beneficiaries and disciples. Olgivanna, Jean Zartsman, Lili Galounian, the Hartmans, and Schoenvalls were all star leaders in the teachings Gurdjieff." The strange language and misspelling of names aside, that was his offering on the subject.[7]

In 1949 Ouspensky was in New York City, and the Wrights attended his lectures and encouraged others to do so.[8] By then his understanding of Gurdjieff seems to have matured; at least he was attempting to better understand "Gurdovanich," as he once called the mystic. Wright believed that "everybody in America" should know about Gurdjieff and read his new book *In Search of the Miraculous,* for America must cease its "arrogance and become a little more understanding," especially of the Orient, its people and philosophies. Gurdjieff "pursued" those ancient cultures and to Wright's reckoning "came out" of his search "with the most profound analysis of an organic relationship to the cosmos." As far as Wright was concerned Gurdjieff's illuminations might assist Americans not to misjudge other peoples.[9] The iron curtain, cold war, and "red menace" were realities in 1949 and they troubled Wright as much as anyone else.[10]

There is a tale, not necessarily apocryphal, about an episode when Gurdjieff was trying to make a point to students gathered about him at the Institute. So that they would forever remember the point, he squatted and defecated on the dance floor. A kind of shock treatment no doubt, but effective, or at least effective enough to be remembered as a peculiar act. Routine, norm, prejudice, commonplace, the automaton, the machine, or whatever, need to be constantly and actively challenged, eventually altered. Wright understood this when he said that Gurdjieff would take people "by the scruff of the neck and fling them in. If they couldn't swim, he would listen to their shrieks with delight."[11]

So, Wright might have reasoned that this was true singly or collectively; at least his conduct of the Fellowship and public actions through words strongly suggest such a reasoning.

It is not implausible to suggest that Wright believed there was *cultural* apathy, machine conditioning, daydreaming, fantasizing—automatic responses—and that there were corporate bodily, emotional, and intellectual functions blinded by routine and indifference. Perhaps there was a cultural "self" or a collective "I." In a manner like Gurdjieff, therefore, he applied a verbal shock, a SLAP as it were, so his audience might not just hear but listen more carefully; that they should see, think, concentrate—on Wright's words and equally importantly his architectural works. Examples of the application of the method applied are many. In a bastion that prided itself on perpetuating the history and traditions—and myths—of English-colonial America, the state of Virginia, Wright said colonial America was the worst thing that happened to the USA, and he denounced the Rockefellers' restoration of British Williamsburg. At another time he said he favored the relocation of the nation's capital to Mississippi, away from the hidebound center of the northeastern states. But why not the geographic center, Kansas? Simply because that was too reasonable.

Two points should be made. First, this manner of presentation was not used by Wright before 1925. It might be suggested that he presented similar challenges much earlier, say in 1908 in his famous essay "In the Cause of Architecture" for *The Architectural Record.* But the parts of that essay that concern the point here were more like lamentations about historical eclecticism and a severe chastisement to those who would mimic his architecture. Moreover, he claimed authority and creative originality—always about architecture and his contribution—as a genius. Louis Sullivan had provided the words but Wright had *created* the architecture and his readers must never doubt that truth. The second point may seem obvious: the world had honored him as a talented and innovative architect and the *creator* of a new architecture that evolved to become a potent artistic expression of the twentieth century. This acknowledgment heightened his arrogance and urged his conceit to an extent that he believed he had a license, almost a sanction, to lecture America and England, even the Soviet Union. A simple understanding of Gurdjieff's teachings provided a method. And so his personality was allowed free rein and he acted out on unsuspecting audiences the lessons he learned from Olgivanna. It seems fair to say that he believed his method in support of his organic philosophy would see humanity transcend cultural impedimenta.

Was his and Olgivanna's method successful in shaking the apathy, so to speak, out of his audience? In brief, no. Note that Wright wanted to change people and therefore he was, in Gurdjieff's reckoning, one of the walking dead. Wright's shock treatments, as mild or as extreme as they may have been, together with his strangely constructed verbal logic, *appeared* to his audiences as naive or as merely extensions of an inflated, narcissistic ego. He may have assumed that he did not need to undertake fundamental self-study because he was the teaching Master, was not like "most people" and above such needs. However, he was ill-prepared to undertake the program he set for himself as philosopher and curator of cultural ills. His audiences did not see him as a sage but as a strangely hapless eccentric; and there were times when he seemed rather content in that role.

Yet Wright's elemental philosophy remained virtually unaltered from his earliest days in Chicago in the 1880s: a Whitmanesque Americanism and an Emersonian agrarianism. "Work" and a collective "I" fitted—perhaps in Wright's mind they enhanced—the idea of returning to the land, to a rebirth of agrarian America, to forms of small or subsistence farms, "little farms" beside a democratized Broadacre City. The inherent correctness and pleasurable morality of providing one's own living through labor—work—applied to the land was always central to Wright's at times seemingly disparate actions. Thus Olgivanna's teaching reinforced Wright's fundamental outlook on life. Indeed, she said that "he taught me to see into the great visible world, and I taught him to see into the invisible world."[12] Do these notions of work and self fit Jaeger's *paideia*? The wholesomeness of mind and body developing in concert is an obvious connection. But Jaeger was describing a historical precedent established in ancient Greek culture, and therefore his work was an *explanation*. It was not clear how practice would be effected, especially in modern society. Nonetheless the Wrights found much intellectual sustenance in *paideia*.

The following must be made plain: politics, economics, autobiography, and philosophy *dominated* Wright's utterances during the 1930s. He seldom talked about architecture except as it might relate to those dominant themes; and even more seldom about the stuff of architecture—materials, proportion, plan, scale, construction techniques, order, and such—the very foundations of his writing from 1900 to 1910 that architects worldwide found so attractive.

26 The Soviets

With knowledge of the practical aspects of Wright's relations with the Soviets, and parallel activities, philosophic hypotheses can be more easily established as well as the reasons for his actions after appearing at the All-Union Congress. Nothing could have been more persuasive for the Soviets in inviting Wright to Moscow than their admiration of American technical excellence and their love of probing the innermost workings of a theoretical proposition, especially when elevated to seeking the riddle of human aspirations or foibles.

Technical expertise had always been an issue in the Soviets' relations with foreign architects. In 1925 Erich Mendelsohn was invited to prepare designs for a factory for the Leningrad Textile Trust. Construction took two years but Mendelsohn was dismayed by the interference of local authoritarians, lack of materials, and the abysmal quality of workmanship. He refused to allow photographs to be published of the buildings and nearly disclaimed any association. Mendelsohn was one of the few Europeans or outsiders we know of who was allowed commissions in the Soviet Union in the 1920s. Then, with the first Five-Year Plan announced in 1929 a few architects from around the world offered their labor and ideas to see the plan to fruition. Most arrived in the early 1930s only to leave disillusioned soon thereafter. A few Central Europeans were involved, though usually with theoretical matters rather than with more practical endeavors. An even smaller number of those Europeans were employed for more than a few months, Hans Schmidt and André Lurçat being well-known examples. The usefulness of all these architects to the Soviet Union was limited because the great majority were too idealistic, perhaps dreamers. Gropius returned from a visit to the USSR in 1932 a bitterly disillusioned man, shaken by what he had experienced. While in Russia Hannes Meyer found essentials such as glass, nails, and steel "worth their weight in gold," and the foreign architects were treated as "precious precision instruments."[1] However, two American architects invited to the Soviet Union in 1929 were the most practical of men, Albert and Moritz Kahn. No precious theoretical stuff for them.

Between 1929 and late 1932 the Kahns designed an amazing 521 factories throughout the Soviet Union's colonial empire, from Kiev in the Ukraine to Yakutsk in eastern Siberia. Their association began with a $40,000,000 automobile plant built outside a new town called Stalingrad. This was followed by a plant at Moscow to house production systems for cars and Fordson tractors. A second Ford plant was simultaneously built at the new town of Gorky (then Nizhni) by the Austin Company of Cleveland, Ohio. (By 1927 when negotiations for the plant began, eighty-five percent of *all* tractors and trucks in the Soviet Union were "Ford built."[2] The major problem was servicing those vehicles: there was no expertise or systematic training.)

But why seek the assistance of Henry Ford? A short but instructive history of Ford's relationship with the Soviets in 1920–35 has been written by Allan Nevins and Frank E. Hill. Their answer is clear. Ford was a revolutionary; he had radically changed production and manufacturing systems and thereby provided inexpensive transport for the proletariat and farmer. Further, **while Henry Ford was alternately denounced as a slave-driver and lauded as a mighty innovator, [his] ideas were thirstily accepted as promising the regeneration of Russia. . . . Ford's name [was] emblazoned on banners in workers' processions, as emblematic of a new era; long articles appeared on Ford methods; and the Communists eagerly devoured translations of Ford's *My Life and Work* and *Today and Tomorrow*.**[3]

In his 1922 *My Life and Work* Ford spoke at great length against Communism and more generally socialism for all the reasons one can imagine; most of them many times over proved correct. He also spoke clearly about the need to decentralize urban and industrial centers. A major part of the Soviets' first Five-Year Plan was to reach extraordinary extremes in the dispersal of manufacturing and creation of new towns. Forced migration and labor "camps" policed by secret police were one of the social consequences. Anyway, on the 1929 contract Ford lost considerable money. But as Nevins and Hill have said, "To give his ideas a practical illustration on the world stage, Henry Ford would gladly have sacrificed twice that sum."[4]

The decision of Albert Kahn to take on the initial commission was difficult for the Jewish emigrant from Germany. The United States did not recognize the Soviet government in 1929. Kahn believed the people with whom he did business in America had strong feelings against Communists and further, the enemies of "his people" were taking the Nazi line that accused the Jews of fostering Communism. But the challenge "fascinated" him. More importantly he believed that people in the Soviet Union, "regardless of their form of government—were entitled to help after all their generations of suffering under the czars." He soon became convinced that to accept the challenge was, as he said, "the right thing to do."[5] Once in the USSR and faced with rural peasants in his labor force (who were actually forced laborers living in camps always under guard), the Kahns did not become dismayed or retreat. Moritz supervised in Russia and it was he who offered a solution to the Soviets; they allowed the Kahns to train the peasants to be builders, to become craftsmen in the construction industry, to convert peasant to "worker."[6] The Kahns applied American technical and management expertise directly, practically, and materially and thereby made a significant contribution to the reconstruction of the various Soviet societies. One result of the Kahns' efforts was remarkable: over 1,000 people were trained in industrial architecture. As previously noted, many if not most of the new towns and many of the industrial buildings were built by contractors from the United States. Why go to the most powerful capitalistic nation in the world? Who else could they go to for the expertise they needed? As well, no other nation had the capacity to respond not only to the enormous size of the building programs throughout the USSR but to the urgency demanded by the schedule of the first Five-Year Plan.

Wright knew Albert Kahn and his industrial architecture well, and visited him on occasion. Apparently Kahn was offered Wright's job in the office of Adler and Sullivan when Wright left—or rather was fired—in 1893. While the two men were at opposite poles of the strange profession of architecture they nonetheless held each other in respect. Kahn thought Wright well-intentioned if misguided, and therefore a noble champion.[7] Wright was once asked, "Who do you regard as the best architect in the country?" He replied without hesitation, Albert Kahn.[8] After visiting a Ford plant designed by Kahn he said it was "a beautiful building," that it "was a fine thing."[9]

Kahn satisfied the Soviets' admiration of American technical know-how and excellence; so too, it must be added, their need for willing cooperation. Yet while Wright applied technology differently and in often dramatic ways, he more satisfactorily responded to the Russians' love of things theoretical and philosophical. While one was more rational, both Americans had offered means to ends. Further, Wright was a founder of the new-age architecture, of modernism. Part of the Russian love of philosophy was a trust of the venerable in history, in those who in some way nurtured the Russian soul or in the 1930s the Soviet presence. It was almost natural for the Russians, or more exactly the Soviet Communist Party, to invite Wright and certainly it was appropriate for them to ask him to offer his "impression of USSR" even if they suspected his response might be slightly incomprehensible.

This he did at the end of June 1937 in a short article for the *Moscow Daily News* (see Appendix E) in which he praised Soviet expertise in the 1930s and criticized those who would criticize it. The article ended with an attempt to marry America and the USSR in a communion dedicated to freedom. "Yes—the world has at least two great hopes for a better life struggling forward—the USSR and the USA. Two different roads to the same place—a free life for a free people."[10] This theme, together with an attempt to link the two nations by invoking historical similarities, often erroneously conceived, were contained in writings offered to the press immediately after his Russian adventure.

Almost his first act on returning to American soil was to write an essay that was subsequently published in both *The Architectural Record* and the pro-Soviet magazine *Soviet Russia Today*.[11] The essay was close to an apologist's view on all issues touching the USSR—even architecture. That view of Russia's Communism was held by Wright and Olgivanna until the American

Congress's House Un-American Activities Committee became active again in the late 1940s, preceding the rise of McCarthyism in the early 1950s.

Wright's position was fundamentally genuine, almost ingenuous in its unsophisticated presentation. He admired the Soviet experiment. He acknowledged there were problems but there were problems with America too. The Soviet desire to begin anew and eliminate the shackles of the old aristocracy had, in Wright's mind, an affinity with America's casting off of British colonialism. He ignored the repression exerted by Soviet colonialism on independent nations. He deplored, he noted elsewhere, the continuing hereditary aristocracy in Britain. Connected with this was his contention that there existed a new dual aristocracy in America: big business and big government. The Soviet *desire* was therefore central to his admiration. With honest conviction he believed that "if Comrade Stalin, as disconcerted outsiders are saying, is betraying the revolution, then, in the light of what I have seen in Moscow, I say he is betraying it into the hands of the Russian people."[12]

The American architect was not totally naive: he was hopeful. He sensed very strongly and with some intellectual insight, not only the folly but the danger of failing to at least attempt to understand the Soviets in Russia. Against the odds—and of course he enjoyed the position of underdog—he defended their cause. To many people, the narrow-minded and bigoted in Wright's estimation, it was a cause possessing horrific ingredients, one therefore to be approached with grave suspicion. Undaunted, Wright wanted to participate, to counsel, even to enter a new competition that he proposed for a future Palace of Soviets.

"Iofan! What do you say?" said Wright, "Let's declare it off with the Palace of Soviets. Let's have another competition. I will gladly enter myself and we shall see how much you have grown."[13]

In making such an offer—and with such paternal arrogance—he could not have understood the pain many architects suffered in seeing the competition through its bureaucratic morass to a pathetic result.

His attitude can be summed up positively by reissuing his frankly spoken words to the Association of Federal Architects in Washington, D.C., in October 1938, shortly after returning from Moscow. America today, he said, lacks

what we properly call culture. The same lack of culture—the "cultural lag"—is here that exists in Russia today—which does not flatter us. Russia—a great nation, 90% illiterate (mostly serfs who had far less than nothing) is now free. Eating, during their life time, of the hand of a superior class—seeing what culture the upper classes had—their tall ceilings, glittering glass

chandeliers, sensual paintings, statues, with fountains playing on wide terraces: utter magnif-icence—now what? Can you talk to these freed serfs of simplicity? Can you talk to them of the things of the spirit and mind? You cannot. They want that which they did not have and were subject to when they were slaves—only now they want all of it twice as tall, want twice as many glittering chandeliers, more sensuality, more and bigger statues: more "magnificence," in short.[14]

Wright understood the observation that the Soviet Union was governed by people who had been peasants, that the former serfs were now powerful rulers. As to his own profession, perhaps he really understood the Soviets' need for architectural revivalism. Not that he believed they were correct, just that he understood. Conceding that his words might have sounded "like socialism, communism or what-not," he emphasized that

I am no student of socialism, but I *am* a student of organic structure; and in search for it in the bases of our civilization today I could not find it. I have read Henry George, Kropotkin, Gesell, Prudhomme, Marx, Mazzini, Whitman, Thoreau, Veblen and many other advocates of freedom; and most of the things that applied in those great minds in the direction of freedom[,] as conditions exist for us today[,] point to a great breakdown. Before the long depression we, as architects, did not think much of this—but this is no "depression." It is certainly a breakdown. One that cannot be "fixed" by tinkering.[15]

Wright saw for the Soviet Union a glimmer of hope; in America he felt the tinkering of Roosevelt's New Deal offered little help. The Washington speech was similar to much of what he had written before visiting Moscow and it did indeed read as a socialist document, albeit rather befuddled. Was Wright aware of the fragility of democracy, of its inward nature, of its loathing of threats to its existence yet its reluctance to counter them, of its weakness in defense—internal especially—against enemies who might seek its annihilation, indeed of its inherent character of tolerance even toward those who would work against it legally? Probably not. Otherwise he would not suggest dramatic interference and alterations regardless of the nobility of his intentions. And further, for those who might have sympathized with him there was a paradox: if you cannot control one anarchist, how do you structure what might be called socialist anarchy?

The Communist Party branch at the University of Wisconsin challenged his interpretations of Communism and published an open letter to him in the Madison, Wisconsin, *Capital Times* rhetorically charging that he committed a "serious slur on the Communist Party of the United States."[16] Their letter and his replies were equally vague. He prominently included this parochial issue in his 1943 autobiography in order that he might air his views generally, not specifically. He also unashamedly altered relevant texts in his autobiography of 1943—even those that had been previously published—to elaborate and further promote his views.

There is yet another paradox. He often appeared more on the right, more conservative than he might have believed, or wished. The "great breakdown," as he would have it, of the American system, of the American dream was, he surmised, also linked to the coming war. He disliked the thought of America's possible entry into the war, for he feared it would prejudice elemental freedoms and individualism; that there would be increased centralization of government bureaucracy, even more than the Roosevelt administration had centralized it in the 1930s. Further, he believed that private capital would reap excessive profits from the war. But fundamentally he believed as his preacher uncle Jenkin Lloyd Jones believed: "War is the culmination of wickedness, the sum of all the villanies!" Uncle Jenkin has been described as an "intense, earnest, zealous man, a big man physically as well as mentally." Around the turn of the century he established All Souls Church and soon thereafter Lincoln Center, both in Chicago, and "eloquence in his sermons caused him to loom large" in Chicago's and Wisconsin's history.[17] He was outspokenly against America's participation in World War I and acted in consort with the likes of Zona Gale, Robert La Follette, Henry Ford, and Jane Addams. Uncle Jenkin was a powerful influence on Wright. In the months before December 1941 Wright endorsed Charles A. Lindbergh's "isolationist sentiments." During the war Wright encouraged conscientious objection; a few from his Fellowship became COs, as they were called. The farm he inherited from his mother's parents and on which he built Taliesin was then about six hundred acres. During the war it expanded and diversified its agricultural output. In 1943 Wright estimated the role of the Fellows in the war effort: "We have 27 boys in armed services, 3 in jail as C.O.s, 2 in concentration camps—about twelve still here, several on agricultural deferment."[18] Wright blasted away as late as 1944–45 when in his book *When Democracy Builds* he exclaimed that "conscription is the ultimate form of rent." He was deeply concerned for the welfare of those on deferment and the COs. The support he and others outside the Taliesin family, so to speak, gave to those men, including the three in a federal prison, is revealed in part in a recent book of *Letters to Apprentices* which contains some of Wright's wartime correspondence.

There was little contact between Soviets and Wright after 1943. In 1949 he confided that as soon as Russia "found out what I was all about she has had no use whatever for me. I am an individualist—democratic in thought and action—opposed to her methods in every sense."[19] In view of his words in Moscow and immediately after, that was proven to be only partially true. Beginning in the 1950s Olgivanna wrote a few comments about Soviet Russia and Communism in a Madison, Wisconsin, newspaper and here and there in books such as *Our Home* (1959), *The Shining Brow: Frank Lloyd Wright* (1960), and *The Roots of Life* (1963). As an interesting footnote to all of this it should be mentioned that Wright's trusted right-hand man at Taliesin, William Wesley Peters, married Stalin's mercurial daughter Svetlana in 1970; however, they were soon divorced, she denouncing the Fellowship. With great publicity she returned to Moscow in 1984 and then, after a brief respite and with little publicity, she returned in 1986 to, of all places, Taliesin, if only briefly.

Beginning with his return from Moscow, Wright received many books, pamphlets, or plain propaganda from the USSR Society for Cultural Relations with Foreign Countries (or VOKS), principally during 1938 through 1940. Also he received requests for statements in support of Soviet policies and later their war against the Nazis. Included were requests from the American Russian Institute and the magazine *Soviet Russia Today*. In October 1937 he was invited by *Izvestia* to write a short piece about "culture and fascism," which he did but which apparently did not make a deadline and therefore was not published.[20] In March 1938 Samuel Sillen, literary editor of the magazine *New Masses,* asked Wright to review Mumford's book *Culture of Cities,*[21] and in that same month Wright's former client Elizabeth Noble wrote a sympathetic survey about "Architecture in the U.S.S.R." for the same magazine.[22] But Wright resisted all overtures to be officially tied to a domestic faction.[23] Rather, he elected to remain an outsider and support issues or people selectively, more or less as each occasion presented itself. Alfred Kazin may well have been right when in the late 1930s he said that Louis Sullivan and Wright were really not socialists, but merely "social-minded architects" and perhaps as such "children of John Ruskin."[24]

Wright did not become the authority on Soviet affairs that he might have wished, not even on its architecture and city planning. Nonetheless two speculations emerge from this study. First, he wanted to test his peculiar holistic ideas and ideals by presenting them to people in conversation and to the public via his Moscow talk and its subsequent publication. Soviet Russia was a place remote and different to the point of appearing hostile to the West. If his holism, his organic philosophy could prevail in such a place then it should sustain itself anywhere. The Soviets proved unreceptive. And there is no evidence that Wright's architectural philosophy offered any sustainable stylistic influence on Russian architects—or anyone else in Europe—beyond that initially exerted just after the turn of the century and so well remembered four decades later. His architecture of the 1930s was known and discussed but rather dismissively for it was believed too idiomatic, too idiosyncratic especially for the dominant Central European proponents and Soviet regulators. His

Broadacre City concept was less an individuated idea and therefore of more polemical value to the practical Soviets.

The second thought suggests that Wright wanted to test his intellectual liberality. A proper individualism must not, he might have argued, exclude things and ideas, there must be no predeterminism; *his* pragmatism must be inclusive. Ideas and things he did reject were those that insisted on exclusiveness and its allies of artistic and cultural devolution. Therefore, with a preponderant general intolerance in America of and about Soviet Communism it was his duty to defend what he saw as the liberalism of Soviet Communism with his own liberalism. The test was to face it personally, on it own soil, so he might share, understand, and evoke responses—theirs and his.

Concomitant with his investigation and a second part of his test was the need to defend his actions and views on his return; actions and views that had been exercised or offered before and during his visit to Russia. His defense was a verbal offense, often pugnacious: this was a means to conceal the weakness of his position vis-à-vis Stalin's tyranny and the nature and extent of Soviet artistic suppression. If he did not realize the nature of his offense then it was a subconscious act and for good reason. To reveal that either weakness could be interpreted as acceptable to him would be to renounce his own individualism and his sense of propriety. His intellectual liberality, then, would be a sham and devalued as a hoax. On the other hand he made statements that were naive and others that were intended to be intelligently suave but were only clever; statements such as that the more you analyze Soviet Communism along with "German Fascism, Italian Fascism, British Democracy and American Democracy, the less you will be able to see any substantial differences between them in practice."[25] Do we not, he generously supposed, desire the same things? Not even clever.

It turns out that Kazin was at least partially right. In the end Wright was more socialist than not, but he discovered he could not be fully committed. The individual and society could not be engineered: people and their society were much more than a science or the sciences. Simply and ultimately he did not believe that the individual could *assign* his personal conscience to the collective conscience, including a political party or a state. That would be blasphemous. So by definition he could not practice his individualism under the strictures of a total—or even a quasi—socialist state. Its proven tendency for a central authority was abhorrent to him. This was consistent. As early as 1914 he said that a "socialist might shut out the sunlight from a free and developing people with his own shadow" but an "artist is too true an individualist to suffer such an imposition, much less perpetrate it."[26]

His form of schizophrenia was clear. To some the dichotomy between his words and architecture was patent. The Hollander J. J. P. Oud once remarked that "Wright the artist renounces what Wright the prophet proclaims." This was true. Moreover, Broadacres spoke the language of a moderately reformed socialism: his architecture spoke the language of artistic libertarianism practiced only as a *result* of basic freedoms such as the practice of speech, artistic will, and individualism. This too was consistent. Through all of his mature life the highest, most precious realm was what he called "the Sovereignty of the Individual."

27 The U.S. Government

In 1935, before architectural commissions returned to Wright, he sent a letter to Mrs. Franklin D. Roosevelt at the White House, addressed incorrectly to "My Dear Madame President." He told her that in Washington's Corcoran Gallery across "the lawn from your home" was an exhibition of Broadacre City. He noted that the exhibition was about an idea that, through models, etc., "seeks merely to sensibly interpret certain changes taking place in us and around us to find for them some way out of chaos." The hopelessness of the present situation demanded action, and he had the wherewithal. He asked that the President visit the Corcoran and he mentioned—not wholly in error—that he and his ideas had been accepted overseas but not in America: "'no prophet is with honor in his own country'—(you see how modest I am)."[1] The letter implied that Wright wanted to influence government bureaucracies through the President's office and was, of course, hoping to obtain some work.

There was good reason for Wright to approach Eleanor and Franklin Roosevelt.

I want to destroy all [these urban slums] . . . this is no way for people to live. I want to get them out on the ground with clean sunshine and air around them, and a garden to dig in. Spread out the cities, space the factories out, give people a chance to live.

[Take] industry from crowded urban centers to airy villages, and [give] scrawny kids from the slums opportunity for sun and growth in the country.[2]

That was not Wright or Henry Ford speaking but Roosevelt. He was expressing a heartfelt yearning for a solution to two problems: slums in the city and rural displacement. Rexford Tugwell was an agricultural economist and one of Roosevelt's "brain trust." In 1935 he presented the President with an idea he called resettlement. Tugwell believed that because of agricultural technology, rural demographic decline was inevitable and therefore pressures on city housing with the possibility of slums were always a real threat. Resettlement was meant to rehouse both distressed population groups in new towns dispersed away from large cities. As Wright proposed in Broadacre City, none were to have an employment center such as industry or manufacturing. To this end, in 1935 Roosevelt created the Resettlement Administration within the Department of Agriculture with Tugwell as director under Secretary Henry C. Wallace. The philosophical and practical reasons supporting Tugwell's concept can be gleaned from a series of statements.

• "What the Resettlement Administration is trying to do is to put houses and land and people together in such a way that props under our economic and social structure will be permanently strengthened" (Tugwell).

• "Tugwell maintained that effective social policies had to be dictated by contemporary resources, techniques, and circumstances: that they had to be tuned to the times rather than to an imaginary environment in some Utopia" (historian Bernard Sternsher).

• "New towns would house the displaced farm family while the father, or head of the household, could obtain employment in nearby industry" (historian David Myhra).

• "I am inclined to believe that such ["back to the land"] settlements will function merely as small eddies of retreat for exceptional persons and that the greater part of our population will prefer to live and work in the more active and vigorous mainstream of a highly complex civilization" (Tugwell). "Utopia still presented itself to him [Roosevelt] in the cherished image of Hyde Park . . . tranquility in the midst of rich meadows and farmlands, deep forests, and a splendid flowing river" (historian Arthur Schlesinger).

• "My idea is to go just outside centers of population, pick up cheap land, build a whole community and entice people into it. Then go back into cities and tear down slums and make parks of them" (Tugwell).

• *I am sick of the nation's stenches*
  I am sick of propertied czars . . .
  I have dreamed my great dream of their passing.
  I have gathered my tools and my charts;
  My plans are fashioned and practical;
  I shall roll up my sleeves . . . make America over.
(Lines from a poem by Tugwell, who should have thanked Whitman, while a university student.)

• "Tugwell felt that people were generally opposed to planning; that there were strong emotional and physical investments in the status quo; that the effectuation of planning required change in institutions, a realignment of vested interests, and the displacement of people; and that planning involved conclusions and commitments with respect to an indefinite future" (historian David Myhra).

• "I grew up in an American small town and I've never forgotten it" (Tugwell).

• "Greenbelt towns program. Automotive transportation makes it possible for men to live a considerable distance from their work; pure air, rural surroundings, and contact with the ground, are physically and psychically good; life is better in a small town where social cooperation is possible; by eliminating inflated land values, by appropriate planning, by large-scale construction, and by taking advantage of very reasonable means for reducing living costs" (Elbert Peets, a planner for Greendale).[3]

Much of it all sounds so familiar, and with good reason. The ideas, pragmatism, and means—of some form of central authority—were similar to Wright's and Henry Ford's. While at no time has it been stated that Broadacre City was influential on the Tugwell concept as presented by himself and others, Wright proposed his model of decentralization verbally beginning in 1931 and its suggested physical form in 1935–36. Those putting the case for decentralization also supported Wright's idea: for instance Mumford, Albert Mayer, Howard Wright, Clarence Stein, and the Regional Planning Association (more or less). It was an uphill struggle for all, not just Wright. Whereas something lake a Garden City was acceptable to socialists around 1930, by the mid to late 1930s such acceptability had been weakened, discredited by a large part of the intelligentsia. As Mumford noted, the period was "deeply colored by communist thought" and Garden Cities were dismissed as either bourgeois or a "left deviation."[4]

Three Greenbelt towns were built: Greenhill outside Cincinnati; Greendale outside Milwaukee; and Greenbelt outside Washington, D.C., in Maryland. A fourth was planned but it along with the Resettlement Administration were killed by courts and Congress, and by 1937 it was all history. An extraordinary bureaucratic success for Tugwell, Wallace, and Roosevelt but too demagogic for Congress and its influential constituencies who feared the encroachment of centralized power.

Finally in 1941 Wright did obtain U.S. government work, or almost.

There is a story about Wright and the Division of Defense Planning of the Federal Works Agency told by the Chief of Planning Section that exposes something of the Wright personality and ego (the "Great American Genius," as characterized by Reyner Banham), something of the politicians' and bureaucrats' burden. It goes something like this.

In 1941 Wright received a long-distance phone call from Clark Foreman, Director, Division of Defense Housing of the Federal Works Agency.

"I don't see your name anywhere on our roster. Why don't you contribute something?" said Foreman.

"I'd like to, but I've never been asked," replied a modest Wright.

"Well, I guess I understand that oversight but I think we ought to end it. Will you do a project for us?"

"I will."[5]

And the story continues as recorded by the government's architect Talbot Wegg. It is ten o'clock of a stifling, humid morning typical of Washington summertime in August 1941. In Foreman's unairconditioned office the director and the chief of the division's Planning Section are awaiting the arrival of an important visitor.[6] A buzz and over the intercom a metallic female voice: "Mr. Wright is here for his 10 o'clock appointment; shall I send him in?" "Please do," replies the debonair Foreman with the faintest trace of a Georgia accent.

Enters Wright, striding, quite oblivious to the steaming cauldron of the Foreman office. He carries a cane and wears a jaunty porkpie hat, gloves, an Inverness cape, pepper and salt tweed suit, Hoover-style starched collar and Windsor tie. Approaching the offered chair he slips off his cape, doffs the hat, strips the gloves, and settles down, resting his chin on the top of the cane. An entrance that only a Barrymore could have matched.

After introductions and the customary amenities Wright comes quickly to the point. "What is it you wish for me, Dr. Foreman? I am seventy-four years old and do not have much time left. I have much to do and no time to waste." Foreman explains the division's determination to make its housing program not merely a contribution to the nation's defense but also to its architecture. He cites the mediocrity of most existing public housing and his conviction that, by employing the nation's leading architects and giving them maximum freedom within cost limitations, the stigma on government housing may be eliminated.

Wright is less guarded and shows a flicker of warmth. "My country has never before called on me. If you are serious and want me to work for you, I will do it and you will be proud of the results." The broad outlines of the proposed project are quickly sketched: 100 dwelling units for workers at an ordnance plant producing rifles, situated in the rolling Berkshire Hills at Pittsfield, Massachusetts. Most defense housing projects were, of necessity, located in such drab surroundings as Allegheny County, Pennsylvania, Hudson County, New Jersey, or Detroit, and opportunities to achieve a harmonious environment were severely limited.

By the end of the meeting Wright has shed the armor of skepticism and positively exudes enthusiasm for the new venture. Once the basic premise and promise had been accepted, the meeting with Foreman was closed on a note of happy anticipation and Wright was turned over to the Chief of the Planning Section, architect Talbot Wegg, for consideration of the nuts and bolts requirements, contract, working schedule, cost limitations, travel regulations, etc., the bureaucratic minutiae toward which Wright exhibited an utter and abiding indifference that was to cause future problems of no little complexity.

Almost without reading it, he signed a contract that bound him to practices and behavior completely foreign to his customary professional operations. Wegg, somewhat knowledgeable of the master's past and fully aware of the incipient booby traps, begged him to ponder the obligations spelled out in small print before committing himself, but caution was not Wright's way. He had a contract with the United States of America; his country had, at last, seen fit to recognize him and he was on his way!

While the general location of the projected development was Pittsfield, the specific site had not yet been selected, and it was decided (as an unusual departure from normal procedure) to have Wright participate in the site selection. Preliminary reconnaissance had been made and four potential sites had been lined up.

As the brilliant New England fall burgeoned, Wright and Wegg met in New York and rode a dirty day coach to Pittsfield, a trip that would have been miserable without the master's lively reminiscences and opinions, occasionally prompted by questions but more often poured out without reserve. Naturally, the conversation revolved about architects and architecture, like this:

Wegg: "Whom do you regard as the best architect in the country today?"

Wright without hesitation: "Albert Kahn."

Wegg: "Do you think there are any other good men?"

Wright: "Yes, my son John has learned something from me. He's pretty good."

Wegg: "Who are some of the good, younger men coming on?"

Wright: "Don't know of any, and why bother with them while I'm still working?"

He believed American architects and the public to have little understanding of architecture. Witness the failure of the American Institute of Architects to recognize him while so many foreign countries, France, Germany, the USSR, and now Britain had given him official honors. Almost without changing pace he turned to glum observations on the meager financial returns of his own professional life. He cited, with envy, the cushy berths occupied by Eliel Saarinen and Gropius at Cranbrook and Harvard, which they had gained primarily because they were foreigners favored by snobbery. To Wegg's misgivings Wright stated his hopes that the government contract would pay enough to discharge disturbing fiscal obligations.

These mournful reflections were terminated by their arrival in Pittsfield, where there had been arranged a veritable red-carpet reception by the mayor and local dignitaries. Wright, responding to adulation with grace, benevolence, and almost papal condescension, charmed the Irish mayor with compliments on the beauty of his city and elated the Chamber of Commerce with a promise to confer national distinction on Pittsfield with the project.

A small cavalcade of cars was provided to tour the sites. The first, generally level and verdant, had once been farmed and the open fields would insure a pleasant environment as well as reasonable development costs. Wright was not impressed. While the troupe examined it on foot, he remained in the car, restlessly. The second site was on rough ground with great rock outcroppings. Wright's eyes lit up.

"Stop!" he cried and fairly leaped from the car. Moving with the grace and vigor of a youth, he roamed the hills and dales, clearly enraptured by the austere crags.

"This is it," he exclaimed. "This is it; this is New England."

"But, Mr. Wright, there are two other sites we should see," said Wegg, whose bureau-cratic mind was tottering at the thought of the probable site preparation costs.

"No need to look further," replied Wright. "This is where we shall build our project."

In abject retreat Wegg asked, "This site will need a good deal of landscaping; what would you propose?"

"We'll bring in trees. Mature, beautiful pines and dogwood and evergreens. We'll make it the showplace of the Berkshires."

Well aware that he had already surrendered, Wegg numbly reckoned with the stark realities of justifying the site selection and costs to a hard-boiled General Accounting Office. With several years exposure to the GAO, he had no hope of stretching the rules to sanction the master's normal *modus operandi*. The only hope was to persuade him to change his ways and accept federal dictum word for word. As an opening gambit in this campaign, Wegg wrote Wright a carefully worded letter, expressing pleasure at the progress to date and suggesting that perhaps, occasionally, personal preferences might have to be tempered somewhat to the (obviously) unreasonable require-ments of fiscal regulations, etc. Replied Wright on November 8:

My dear Wegg:

     Your good letter is reassuring and in turn I want to assure you all . . . of my very best. It is high time I took a hand in governmental building in my own country and co-operation with Dr. Foreman and yourself will be only the beginning, I foresee, of a real pleasure to me.

     My education as an architect has proceeded to the point where I should be a great strength to you in your endeavor, and the liberality and intelligence of that endeavor I respect. So don't worry about results. You will be gratified.

     The personal idiosyncracy (whatever it may be) shall not get in the way, too much, and only serve to make work a little livelier and more interesting.[7]

An inveterate optimist, Wegg preferred to believe from this letter that Wright had got the message and all would be well, after all. During some weeks of silence from Taliesin he preserved equanimity, but in early December the exigencies of a production schedule calling for submission of preliminary sketches and cost estimates within one month of the contract date began to intrude. On a cold December morning shortly after Pearl Harbor, he picked up his phone to hear: "This is Frank Lloyd Wright and I have sketches of Cloverleaf for Pittsfield. How about lunch at the Carlton about noon?"

Wegg approached the meeting with mixed feelings: personal affection on the one hand, uneasiness on the other. He was greeted by an effulgent Wright who had reserved a table in the plush dining room, crowded with Army and Navy brass. He ordered a sumptuous repast garnished with cocktails and wine and then, apparently more interested in the war than Cloverleaf, launched into a eulogy of the Japanese, drawing on his Tokyo years.

"They're a wonderful people," he said in what seemed to be unnecessarily loud tones, "Artistic, industrious, peaceful. They don't want to fight us. It's the British," he continued, "they sucked us into it, just as they did in 1917. They've been making fools of us ever since 1812." Having established the duplicity of our allies and the nobility of our enemies, he turned to more personally pertinent matters.

"I've just had a book published," he said, "and I want you to buy it. I won't give it to you because I cannot afford it, but I'll autograph it." A copy of *In the Nature of Materials* was purchased and cordially autographed. With half the afternoon gone they headed to the Planning Section office where a dozen mounted sketches of Cloverleaf were on display.

One look at these drawings was enough to affirm that Wright was ever young, fresh, inventive, and skillful enough to design dwellings that resembled no housing project on record. Here would be a project to honor Pittsfield and the USA. On that day of apparent felicity, however, ominous clouds portending trouble for the whole housing program began to build up. A phone call from John W. McCormack, at that time Majority Leader of the House with clout second only to that of the Speaker and a fierce, parochial concern for his Massachusetts constituents.

"Dr. Foreman, how come you've hired a Wisconsin architect for a Massachusetts project?" he asked.

"Mr. McCormack," Foreman replied, "I don't think Mr. Wright would be considered as a Wisconsin architect. He has a worldwide reputation and may be the greatest architect in this century."

"He comes from Wisconsin, doesn't he? And he's keeping Massachusetts architects from making a living, isn't he?"

Foreman attempted to explain the division's policy of fostering excellence in design but the Majority Leader paid no attention.

"What's more, you've been hiring New Jersey architects for Connecticut projects and New York architects for Pennsylvania projects and Republican architects all over the country. The House is likely to take a pretty hard look at your operations before we appropriate any more money for defense housing."

Appropriations for housing, schools, utilities, and other public facilities made necessary by the proliferating defense program were generated in a House Committee dominated by Southern Democrats; the chairman was Fritz Lanham of Texas and the vice chairman Frank Boykin of Alabama. The interest of committee members in social and design aspects of the housing program had seemed to Foreman and his associates less marked than their interest in the selection of specific sites and the employment of specific individuals as surveyors, appraisers, housing managers, etc. Where Foreman suspected that the prospective site was owned by, or the prospective employee was a relative of, the committee member, he refused to go along. Foreman acted properly but hardly endeared himself.

The committee's mounting aversion was directed not only at Foreman but also at Nathan Straus, administrator of the U.S. Housing Authority, which played a major role in the Defense Housing program. The torrents of loathing spilled over shortly after Pearl Harbor when the committee (orally and off the record) demanded the scalps of Foreman and Straus as a prerequisite to further appropriations for housing. On the record they specified that future defense housing would be designed and constructed by the Public Buildings Administration, which had a huge staff of architects and engineers; and that no more projects would be assigned to the Division of Defense Housing or the U.S. Housing Authority (the agencies that employed private architects).

When the battle smoke cleared, it was seen that Foreman and Straus were not the only victims. Wegg and his immediate staff reported for work on the morrow of the massacre to find their furniture in the hall and their offices occupied by henchmen of the chief of construction, who had emerged as the new leader. Had Wright known something—anything—of the internal machinations of local or national bureaucracies he might have revised some vital aspects of his Broadacres idea.

In ignorance, Wright was left like a forlorn orphan, utterly helpless. He was informed in writing that his contract was terminated, that he would be paid for preliminary sketches but not for travel from Phoenix to Washington. The letter was signed by Baird Snyder, acting administrator of the Federal Works Agency.

And then a note in reply to a Christmas photograph of Wegg's family by their lakeside home, a melancholy epilogue: "My dear Wegg: I am glad to see all you Weggs' so beautifully situated . . . and it is good that all are so far away from Washington. As for me, I expect less than nothing from Washington at any time—past, present or future."[8]

So ended Wegg's story. And a postscript: in 1942 Wright designed a house for Clark Foreman but it was not built.

Exactly how often or when Wright was considered for government work is of course unknown. But he recalled one incident in the late 1930s when federal agency chief Rex Tugwell approached the aging architect and said, "Wright, why are you such a controversial item? We would like to employ you, but we don't dare." Probably a wariness shared by most bureaucrats faced with such decisions. Wright conceded he was controversial "and that was that."[9] The dare was not taken.

Wright's isolationist position and oft-spoken admiration for the USSR were probably not influential in decisions about Pittsfield. Composition of relevant American congressional committees and bureaucratic agencies and authorities were too diverse. The "leading architects" commissioned by the Federal Works Agency before Wright's engagement were also diversely opinioned in matters political and no doubt about the war: Gropius, Breuer, Eliel Saarinen, Louis Kahn, Neutra, Antonin Raymond, Victor Gruen—notice the number of immigrants and emigrés—and William Wurster, Hugh Stubbins, Edward Stone, and the planner Clarence Stein. Was Wright a victim of the varieties of bureaucratic incest and inefficiencies of sectionalism within government? Or what?

Wegg's description of the Pittsfield debacle did not mention the source of Wright's "Cloverleaf," which was designed to place twenty Cloverleaf units and two half units on a relatively flat site.[10] It was, of course, an enlargement of his Suntop homes for suburban Ardmore near Philadelphia. Suntop homes were first designed for Otto Tod Mallery's Tod company in early—probably February—1938 and not in 1939 as often stated. Mallery believed Wright was as much an inventor as an architect and looked to Wright to improve what Mallery believed was an industry "most backward" and a "jumble of anarchy and convention." Wright did include some ideas like heating coils in concrete floor slabs. Only one Suntop unit was constructed and that was after a year's delay. Some local citizen had concerns—some of which were actually relayed to and printed in the *Architectural Forum*—that were soon allayed, and the Suntop opened in July 1939.[11] Mallery was vindicated and Wright's scoffers were floored. Construction costs were below average ($16,000 total or $4,000 per home) and this was passed on in the form of low rent. However, people on a waiting list were disappointed. An interesting parenthetical note: a report in the *Architectural Forum* about the Suntop building contained the descriptive phrase "a four-leaf clover," which predated Wright's term for the Pittsfield units by three years.

The differences between the 1938 Mallery scheme and the 1942 Cloverleaf proposal were subtle. The tall masonry walls remained as did the general disposition of functions. But what had been a rather simple plan for Mallery became complex, no doubt to satisfy government (perhaps FHA) requirements. The masonry walls were no longer party walls, thereby diluting the concept. What had been a carport/garage at the junction of each unit became a "yard" (for clotheslines?), and the carport/garage was placed under a bedroom! A stair system next to the carport/garage was moved to the exterior edge which blocked garden views and natural light; and other changes were evident including rather pinched rooms. Generically "The Ardmore Experiment," to use Wright's title, and the Pittsfield design should be called "Quadruple Homes."[12] As a housing and land use scheme there is much to commend the idea.

He also prepared very preliminary sketches for an ambiguously defined defense plant, perhaps related to the Cloverleaf scheme, for a site near Pittsfield. It was to be a very large building almost wholly devoted to large spaces cluttered with Wright's "dendriform" columns. What was to have been processed or fabricated is unknown.

In his letter canceling Wright's Pittsfield contract, government bureaucrat Baird Snyder said that "while we cannot use this design in Pittsfield, it is hoped that it can serve as a guide for project design in other localities." Wright refused to sell his design to the government. (Snyder also

27.1 Four floor plans of one Suntop unit of The Ardmore Experiment, Pennsylvania, 1938, as published in *Architectural Forum*, August 1939.

27.2 Site plan number two for The Ardmore Experiment, Pennsylvania, 1938, showing ground-floor plans for each Suntop unit. Courtesy and © 1986 the Frank Lloyd Wright Foundation.

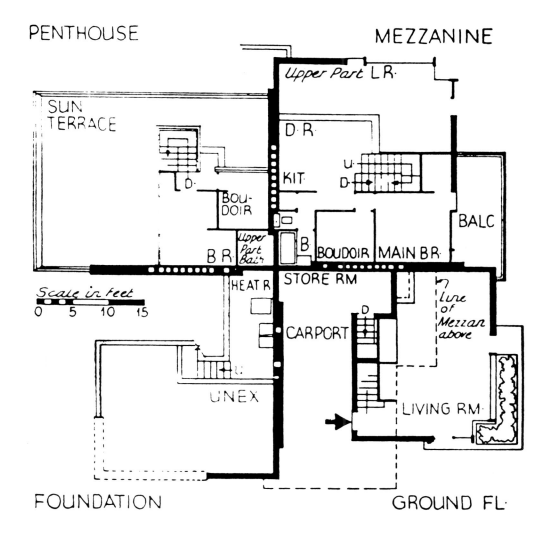

PENTHOUSE

MEZZANINE

Upper Part L·R·

SUN TERRACE

D·R·

D·

KIT·

BOU-DOIR

U·
D·

BALC

Upper Part Bath

B·R·

B·

BOUDOIR

MAIN B·R·

HEAT R·

STORE RM·

line of Mezzan above

Scale in feet
0   5   10   15

D·

CARPORT

U·

LIVING RM·

UNEX

FOUNDATION

GROUND FL·

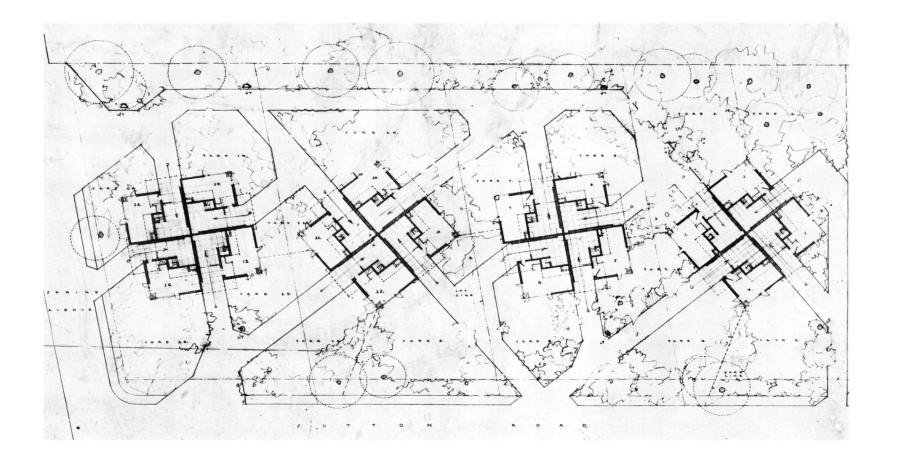

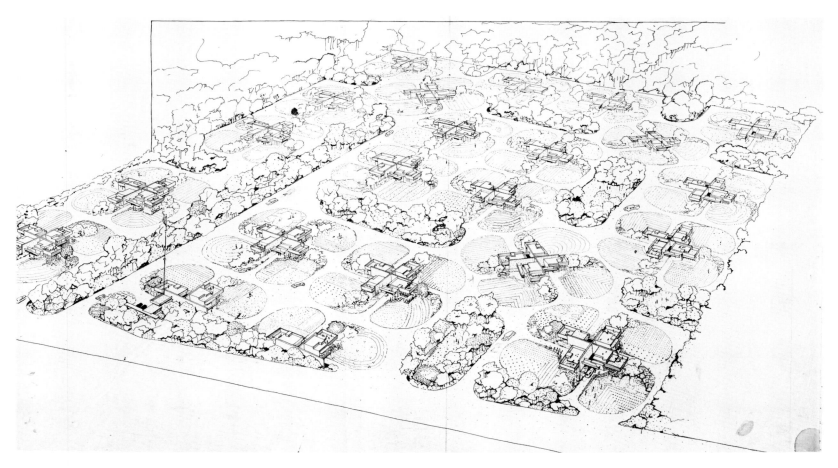

**27.3 Aerial perspective of proposed Clo-
verleaf units for Pittsfield, Massachusetts,
site, 1941. Courtesy and © 1990 the Frank
Lloyd Wright Foundation.**

**27.4 Perspective of a proposed Cloverleaf
unit, Pittsfield, Massachusetts, 1941.
Courtesy and © 1962 the Frank Lloyd
Wright Foundation.**

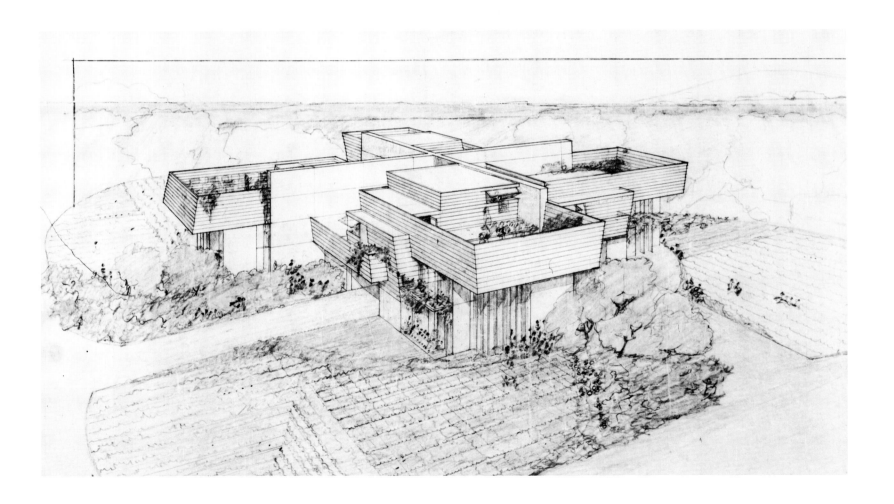

said that his agency "hoped" it could "commission you [Wright] to design a prototype" demountable house, a commission apparently never offered.) But Suntop had *already* become "a guide." The U.S. Housing Authority's "research" produced a trite, staid lookalike "quatrefoil" plan in early 1940 that was coupled with a variety of site plans (with only on-street parking) deftly linking the quatrefoils. A perspective showed the typical government defense-housing appearance.[13]

According to the recollections of Carleton Smith, apparently a musicologist and seeker of the famous and infamous, Wright finally met President Roosevelt and in a professional capacity. He was invited to the White House Oval Office to discuss the possibility of designing housing for workers at Oak Ridge, Tennessee. Being close to power supplied by the Tennessee Valley Authority, the town was chosen in 1942 as the site for development of the atomic bomb. Smith recorded that Wright walked in and shook hands with Roosevelt, saying, "Frank, you ought to get up out of that chair and look around at what they're doing to your city here, miles and miles of Ionic and Corinthian columns!"[14] Perhaps a meeting took place and words similar to that were said, but surely in a different context. There is no record of what else might have occurred in the Oval Office and no record of Wright-designed projects for Oak Ridge. Suffice it to say, though, that Wright and federal government functionaries at all levels did not get along and for good reason: they were meant to administer the acceptable and preferred, while Wright was interested in innovation and change.

In 1943 Wright organized a petition apparently signed by sixty-four sympathizers, a "non-political list" was Wright's phrase, which included financiers ("capitalists") Sterling and Nelson Rockefeller, poet Archibald MacLeish, philosopher John Dewey, scientist Albert Einstein, architects Edward D. Stone, Albert Kahn, Gropius, and Mies van der Rohe, author and playwright Marc Connelly, playwright Thornton Wilder, painter Georgia O'Keeffe, "mechanical engineer" Buckminster Fuller, and, curiously, museum curator Alfred Barr, Jr.[15] It urged the Roosevelt administration to authorize architect Wright to develop and plan "a true capitalist society now known as Broadacre City." Presumably authorization would have been coupled to government money, as it had been with Tugwell's greenbelt towns nine years earlier. If there was a response it must have been negative.

The word "apparently" was used immediately above because it is not clear that all seventy-five people Wright listed did support the petition. For instance, in Wright's words seven signatures had "not yet" been obtained, other people were asked but refused, and at least one was listed as a signer but had said no. Wright had used the good offices of his friend Mendelsohn to ask Albert Einstein if he would support the petition. Einstein replied that he did "not believe in the possibility of a decentralized production at least if it is based on private enterprise." Therefore, "in all conscience" he could "not support" Wright's plan.[16] It seems clear that Wright selected people he had never met or casual acquaintances or friends with the intention of impressing Roosevelt with the "well-known," as he put it. Others unwilling to sign were Orson Welles and John Ford in Hollywood. Letters forwarding the petition, to those he wanted to sign implied Wright's dread of war and belief in a proper democracy. Coupled with words in the petition there was a further implication that the prevention of future wars was possible by the institution of the philosophy supporting Broadacre City. For instance, when he wrote to Walter Gropius he thanked him for a pleasant visit in Cambridge of a few years before and then included the short paragraph he sent to all potential petitioners that concluded with, "I choose my own weapons and fight for Democracy and true capitalist system my way."[17]

The petition was the last attempt by anyone, including Wright, to see Broadacres realized beyond the various individual buildings Wright designed from time to time after 1935 for his model city, or the occasional cooperative.

Suntop signaled the beginning of a few schemes that had titles often including the word Usonian but were more plainly subdivision schemes or cooperatives in the strictest sense of the word. There was to be a cooperative of sorts for a small group of large houses in Lansing, Michigan, in 1939; it was not realized for lack of financing. In 1942 Wright designed "Cooperative Homesteads" for auto workers on a site outside Detroit, Michigan, with some innovative berm and rammed-earth houses, but these were not realized. Then the Cloverleafs in 1942–43. Then in 1946–47 two cooperative communities—Parkwyn and Galesburg—were planned near Kalamazoo, Michigan, where a couple of clients built their own houses to Wright designs plus a few by other architects. Little else was achieved at the Michigan suburbs. And another scheme was developed privately and cooperatively by David Henken, an engineer who spent 1942 to 1944 at Taliesin as a Fellow before embarking on his venture at Pleasantville, New York, in 1947. Three houses were built to Wright's designs, who during eight years visited the site fourteen times, and by 1953 there were houses by nine other architects.[18]

The site plans for the two Michigan and Pleasantville suburban cooperatives contained circular one-acre lots that tangentially touched each other or adjacent roadways. The reason for these site shapes has never been fully explained by Wright or anyone else except to say there were aesthetic considerations relevant to the landscape. Since a house seldom was centered in a circle the rationale seems less than relevant. The Pleasantville—or Usonian Homes Inc.—cooperative was registered as such. At times the suburb, now forty-seven houses, has been referred to as a modest attempt to see Broadacre City realized, but one small cooperative housing scheme does not a city or village make.

At about the same time as the Pittsfield project was being tossed about, Wright had been commissioned to design a hotel and office complex for Washington, D.C., not for the government but for a private syndicate headed by Roy Thurman. The scheme included a large five-story parking complex with a landscaped terrace. Thurman and Wright included a hotel, private apartments, movie theater, and retail shops. The capital city's planning commission, however, was dominated by conservatives and the planners preferred Beaux-Arts classicism. But that was not the whole of the problem. The complex was dominated by a wall of linked high-rise buildings each based on Wright's St. Mark's Apartment Towers for the Bowerie, New York, a project of 1929. The plans and elevations for St. Mark's did not function properly in 1929 or in 1940 at Crystal Heights: improper exit stairs, tiny almost unusable rooms, and solar heat build-up, for instance. The problems exposed themselves in 1956 when the Price Tower was built in Bartlesville, Oklahoma, only to be quickly altered and recently abandoned to become dead storage for records. Variances for Thurman's tower were refused in December 1940.[19]

The general concept of a high concentration of parking with a community of services above or on the periphery was theoretically challenging for the year 1939. It was also influential on Wright's design of a Self-Service Garage for Edgar Kaufmann in 1949. More importantly, together with the aborted Monona Terrace of 1938 for Madison, Wisconsin, a direct lineage can be detected as follows: Wright's Pittsburgh Point Park Civic Center (with mass transit termini) of 1947–48; Louis I. Kahn's brilliant theoretical plan for Philadelphia of 1952–53 and soon thereafter Victor Gruen's similar study for Dallas; and all subsequent similar schemes including the megastructure proposals that arose in the late 1950s worldwide.

28 Rededication

At no time did American critics or architects dwell on the fact that the Central Europeans were promoting a socialist or Marxist architecture. In America the International Style was viewed throughout the 1930s and 1940s as simply a new style and not as having a political base. As a notable example, architect and historian Vincent Scully, Jr., has said, "I never saw the International Style as socialist," adding that this allowed his "intense social convictions . . . to remain free of stylistic predeterminism.[1] If so, then Scully was not typical of the style's promoters. Nor was Wright typical in opposition. He was one of few architects or critics in the early 1930s to publicly challenge the architecture of Central Europe for its narrow political bias and equally restricted aesthetic. As such,

27.5 Aerial perspective of the Crystal Heights project, Washington, D.C., 1939–40. Courtesy and © 1942 the Frank Lloyd Wright Foundation.

he argued, it was ipso facto full of dangerous predeterminants and caught in the sweeping current of an intransigent positivism. For him it had frightening consequences that he found difficult to adequately express. Perhaps the words of philosopher Susanne Langer would have been the kind of alarm Wright wanted to issue. "Any miscarriage of the symbolic process is an abrogation of human freedom," she has said, and

the most disastrous hindrance is disorientation, the failure or destruction of life symbols and loss or repression of votive acts. A life that does not incorporate some degree of ritual, of gesture and attitude, has no mental anchorage. It is prosaic to the point of total indifference, purely casual, devoid of that structure of intellect and feeling which we call personality.[2]

Indeed, it would erase cultural identities, in fact nearly did so east of Bavaria in the 1920s and 1930s.

Alberto Pérez-Gómez has outlined the debilitating effect of positivism. While humans may say they search for order (formal, syntactic, symmetrical correspondence), their *action* is always to the contrary, toward reverence, history, poetry, tradition, symbols, even the irrationality of violence, and therefore to the transcendental. The "invariance" of mathematics, if one believed the propagandists, provided the structure that enabled the search, and then it became the functionalist's foundation. Its supposed immutable neutrality was perceived as the ultimate of orderliness. But as a human contrivance it could not reconcile, for example, the "conception of architecture as an art rather than a science." Indeed, the assumption that architecture "can derive its meaning from functionalism . . . [this algebraization] of architectural theory as a whole, the reduction of architecture to a rational theory," assumed importance in mid-seventeenth century to culminate with Durand. His functionalized theory was "already a theory of architecture in the contemporary [mid-twentieth-century] sense; replete with the modern architect's obsessions, thoroughly specialized, and composed of laws of an exclusively prescriptive character that purposely avoid all reference to philosophy or cosmology." Only economy and technology were relevant.

The main concern became "how to build in an efficient and economical manner, while avoiding questions related to why one builds and whether such activity is justified. . . . The inception of functionalism coincided, not surprisingly, with the rise of positivism in the physical and human sciences." Around 1800 developments in mathematics "augured the possibility that the external world of man could be effectively controlled and dominated by a functionalized theory subsumed by technology." Understandably, at its socially political extreme it became integral with the materialistic rationalism of Communism, but it infected all Western thought. One result of the crisis created by technological dominance "has been an unprecedented inversion of priorities: Truth—demonstrable through the laws of science—constitutes the fundamental which is always ambiguous and accessible only through the realm of 'poetics.'" Theory became methodology, process replaced "ultimate objectives."

Applying this to architecture, Pérez-Gómez observes that

because positivistic thought has made it a point to exclude mystery and poetry, contemporary man lives with the illusion of the infinite power of reason. He has forgotten his fragility and his capacity for wonder, generally assuming that all the phenomena of his world, from water or fire to perception or human behavior, have been "explained" [or will be explained].

And further, no matter how much

architecture may resist, it cannot renounce its origin in intuition. While construction as a technological process is prosaic—deriving directly from a mathematical equation, a functional diagram, or a rule of formal combinations—architecture is poetic, necessarily an abstract order but in itself a metaphor emerging from a vision of the world and Being.

Wright may not have been consciously aware of the historical implications of the devolution of what has been described as the human condition, but as a disciple of Sullivan he, if in the beginning less than Sullivan, saw the threat. He was soon committed to the restoration of intuition, which is a responsibility that resides only within the individual. He challenged the persisting trend first by proclaiming the beauty of transcendentalism by example (something Sullivan was unable to do), then fighting for that beauty. (Beauty, of course, can not exist in a functionalist, *quantitative* world.) First, therefore, by his productivity around the turn of the century when he constantly reaffirmed the fundamentals of nature as a perceived phenomenon. Perception can be described as "our primary form of knowing and does not exist apart from the a priori of the body's structure and its engagement in the world. . . . The body has a dimension. Through motion it polarizes external reality and becomes our instrument of meaning."[3]

Second, after much personal suffering, Wright reiterated his deep concern about what he believed was the sterilizing effect of the materialization of life. For example, he was not being cute when he asked, "Does it thrill you to know the heart is a suction pump?" He fought against the subtraction of human engagement and cultural symbolization, and for his firmly held beliefs, by word and by a reinvigorated architecture and rededicated lifestyle. By example he hoped to be persuasive. It is difficult to find another architect so deeply and openly committed. He laid bare his personal commitment for all to see and savor and belittle as it turned, for he could not effectively communicate his beliefs. Except through architecture; and there his intellectuality was *almost* universally misunderstood.

That is not wholly correct. He could and did display his beliefs by example. The activity that united Wright's philosophy and its varied practices was the Fellowship as it supported both his lifestyle and profession. And the spirituality of the philosophy and the manner of life in its practice—not for the apprentices, though—was attractive to many as was Wright's apparently quixotic personality. During the turmoil generated by Germany in Poland, Czechoslovakia, and elsewhere in Europe, and by Japan in the Far East (or Far West when viewed from Chicago), Wright was occupied with revising his autobiography. Out of context and much as a reverie about the 1930s he inserted the following:

Young people had come from all over the world. . . . to learn I suppose what message the indigenous United States had for Europe. And, evenings, after good work done, the piano, violin and cello spoke there the religion of Bach, Beethoven and Handel. William Blake, Samuel Butler, Walt Whitman and Shelley often presided. Carl Sandburg, Edna Millay and Ring Lardner, too, had something to say or sing. And life in the hills revived for the little cosmopolitan group eager to know this "America," for Taliesin was at work quietly Americanizing Europe while American architects Europeanized America.[4]

The impending war bothered him; the good *old* musicians and painters thrilled him; good like-minded friends, mainly in the letter arts, sustained him. However, the current hegemony of the Central European architectural aesthetic did not just rankle, it made him mad.

There were, of course, other architects opposed to the new European architecture but they were more often than not critical of its aesthetic qualities, so to speak. Most were against it because it challenged tradition and the safety of historical continuity. They may have determined that its source was, as architect Cass Gilbert noted, Weimar Germany and the Soviet Union, but such a discovery did not necessarily mean a distaste for or even a recognition of the extremes of the political left, or more importantly, of the materialistic and positivistic symbolism patent in the European styles. To better understand Wright's position, a brief look at a notable reactionary should be instructive.

Along with other individuals of the political right and left, including historian Charles A. Beard and Wright's crony Philip A. La Follette, architect Gilbert was somewhat infatuated with the "bold energies" of Benito Mussolini. It was not surprising then that around 1930 he referred to architecture's modernist malady, to paraphrase Gilbert, spreading out of the USSR and Central

Europe as a threat to the status quo Gilbert himself represented. Moreover, in support of his artistic beliefs he linked radical art with radical politics. Gilbert belonged to and actively participated in a number of august organizations including the American Academy of Arts and Letters, the Society of Arts and Sciences, the Architectural League, and the National Academy of Design. As early as the late 1920s he warned that there was "generally a tendency of such organizations to drift into the extreme Bohemian or vulgar form of association and thereafter to become radical or 'Bolshevik' in art, manners and point of view." He thought it a "danger to be avoided." As for the imported architecture, he stated with emphasis in 1933 that "crude and ill-drawn forms and strident inharmonious colors is *not* progress," that there were people leading the United States "back to barbarism" and the American Academy of Arts and Letters should—must—"guide public taste toward the paths that lead to the higher realms of Arts and Letters and warn them against perversion."[5]

Gilbert was a model of typicality of his time who, for his last commission, redesigned the Roman temple to house the U.S. Supreme Court, for which construction began in *1932*. Note the difference: Gilbert was at all times defending historicism and the status quo while Wright sought new symbols identifiable as American. Wright's arguments against the imported architecture and its political bias were always in a realm much distant from the more narrow protestations of those people typified by the ultraconservative Gilbert.

29 A Sad Ending

The content and outline of Wright's article for the London *News-Chronicle* sustained Wright on occasions when he needed to further his—and only coincidentally the isolationist—cause in the United States. The isolationists' popular if not titular head was Charles Lindbergh, who around 1930–40 was almost more famed for his outspoken ultra-antiwar position than as a long-distance pilot. As early as May 1940 Wright wrote to Lindbergh a private communication of three short lines, praising the aviation hero and ending by saying that talk is "cheap and unreliable—you are brave enough to talk straight. I respect your integrity."[1] Obviously Lindbergh and like-minded people were one resistance to intervention in the war, a thorn that irritated and effectively restrained Roosevelt. The position of neutrality as argued by the isolationists was a mighty force affecting America's international diplomacy and measured its participation. Its influence ceased immediately with the attack on Pearl Harbor.

Again Wright played out his role not within the group but as one aligned with their purpose. One cannot help but hold a strong impression that Wright was for maintaining appeasement, that as far as he was concerned Prime Minister Neville Chamberlain was not necessarily strategically correct but certainly morally so when he obtained a written assurance from Hitler that there would be only peace in his time.

From 1931 on Wright periodically published magazines, pamphlets, and broadsides. Through 1939 their subject matter was devoted to the Fellowship or to architectural matters or to promoting Broadacre City and his "Usonian" houses. During 1940 Wright asked his summer visitor Stanley Nott to produce a new magazine entitled *Taliesin*.[2] Nott prepared two issues with that title during the summer. The editor was Wright and the issues carried short articles not only about Taliesin and the Fellowship and architecture but antiwar pieces; one was by Nott on "A Way to Beat Hitler." The second issue was released in about February 1941 and was much like the first in content, including an antiwar piece by one Burton Goodrich and another by Nott, "An Englishman Looks at Taliesin."

Beginning in 1941 almost all Wright's magazines were called *A Taliesin Square-Paper: A Nonpolitical Voice from Our Democratic Minority.* With few exceptions their content was, of course, quite political. The titles of some of the articles paraphrased their subjects: e.g., of what use a great navy with no place to hide, and how to beat the enemy. Some were altered reprints of previous publications. After the war Wright published on subjects such as the price of peace, building democracy, and "harum-scarum" (about Communism). In one issue Wright wrote one of his more notable pieces of illogical ambiguity: that democracy is "of such sense and courage; the highest form of Aristocracy the world has ever known because it is integral. In the nature of materials. Who would want to fight a nation built that way? Certainly not Hitler."[3] That was in a *Square-Paper* distributed in July 1941. The first issue of *A Taliesin Square-Paper* in March 1941 was in a square format and, supposedly, was a square-shooting broadside.[4] In it Wright reprinted (almost correctly) the *News-Chronicle* cablegram requesting his views; this was joined by a dramatically edited version of the article he had sent to London.

Handed out or distributed through the mails, Taliesin publications were sent to many people but held the attention of few; one recipient was Lewis Mumford, in particular the May antiwar *Square-Paper.* On 30 May 1941 he sent Wright a letter that was subsequently published as an open letter to Wright in *The Leader* newspaper. Mumford said that he was astonished by Wright's "crassness," blindness, and "shameless defeatism." He was amazed that Wright would reproach the British Empire and say not a word against the "Slave Empire" of Germany. Mumford continued his attack and then offered concluding remarks: "You shrink into your selfish ego and urge America to follow you," and "like Lindbergh, [you] have already freely given the fruits of victory" to "those

Nazi overlords."[5] Wright responded ineffectually, defending his position and attempting to counter each of Mumford's points. Wright ended with: "Goodbye, Lewis, . . . your real opinion is worthless whatever you may write."[6]

There were other opportunities for Wright to express himself, each eagerly grasped with equal vigor; that was until the bombing of Pearl Harbor. There followed needed—if not respectful—silence. It was a sad ending to Wright's second golden age . . . but what an age!

**Life demands that we go
forward with wisdom and
understanding. To remain
dependent upon the personality
that the person himself
transcended through struggle,
rather than upon the ideal,
is to stagnate.**

John Lloyd Wright, 1960

Appendix A   "Frank Lloyd Wright and the New Pioneers," by Lewis Mumford[1]

This monograph[2] on Frank Lloyd Wright has the honor of being the first of a series on the masters of contemporary architecture; and, as everyone knows who is familiar with the history of modern architecture in America and Europe, the honor is well-deserved. The writer, however, is not a Frenchman, but an American, Mr. Henry-Russell Hitchcock—a fact which possibly testifies to the unfamiliarity of the French with Mr. Wright's work, since his influence in France has been negligible, and his method and point of view are foreign both to the official architecture of the past and to that of the contemporary classicists of the machine.

Mr. Hitchcock's introduction occupies only four pages of this monograph, the rest consisting chiefly of photographs of Mr. Wright's buildings, together with a few obscurely reproduced plans, yet in these four pages Mr. Hitchcock manages to raise, by statement or implication, many of the important issues that must be faced in modern architecture. I find myself a little puzzled by Mr. Hitchcock's summary of Mr. Wright's career, for the critic's admiration is so thoroughly counterbalanced by his disapproval of the central motives in Mr. Wright's work that one is driven to conclude that either Mr. Wright is not the great master Mr. Hitchcock says he is, or the critic's feelings do not square with his abstract principles.[3]

Let us try to clear up this confusion. To begin at the beginning, Mr. Hitchcock places Mr. Wright at the head of the movement which is represented by Berlage in Holland and by Hoffmann in Austria. This manner of placing Mr. Wright puts him definitely with the past generation, and it serves to bring out Mr. Hitchcock's underlying thesis of a cleavage in form between the generation of Wright and the generation of Le Corbusier and Oud, but it ignores the fact that America has gone through a different architectural and social development from Europe, and that the contemporaries of Berlage and Hoffmann, architecturally speaking, are Richardson and Sullivan. The worship of industrialism, which has become the keynote of the modern movement in Europe today, belongs to an earlier generation in America, that which actually built the grain elevators and the primitive skyscrapers of Chicago. There is, of course, a difference in technical methods between a stone construction like the Monadnock Building [Chicago] and a house by Le Corbusier but the philosophy and method of approach are exactly the same.

This limitation of architectural design to its technical elements was native in America; but it was none the less thoroughgoing; and the buildings that it produced are still, in their rigorous line and bold mass, among the best we can show: if they lack much that architecture can give, everything they do possess is a clean gain. When Mr. Hitchcock observes that Mr. Wright has learned less from the "lesson of Ford" than the European has, he neglects the fact that the Chicago of Mr. Wright's youth was wholly conceived in the image of Ford; business success and mechanical efficiency were the only factors that entered into the architectural problem; and Mr. Wright's development, instead of being toward the goal of the "building-machine" had this conception, rather, as a starting point.

Had the Chicago architects of the eighties been as intellectually conscious as Le Corbusier, and had they had an intelligent public, ready to apply in the home the successes they could boast of in the office building, there would have been dwelling houses which reflected all the virtues that the "new pioneers" seek to enthrone. The victory of the new pioneers in Chicago was incomplete, partly because, in the hands of Sullivan and Wright, their architecture began to go through a natural and inevitable process of development. With his fundamental education as an engineer, and with that solid acquaintance with utilitarian necessities which the very being of Chicago gives, to a philosopher like Dewey or to a poet like Sandburg quite as much as to the business man or industrialist, Mr. Wright took the next step. This step consisted in the modification of mechanical forms in harmony with the regional environment and with human desires and feelings.

Here is the point where Mr. Hitchcock's admiration suddenly wilts. He sees in Mr. Wright's use of ornament partly the pressure of rich clients, partly the "bad influence" of Sullivan, and partly Mr. Wright's own concern for the picturesque. Instead of becoming harder and harder in line, starker and starker, and bleaker and bleaker, Mr. Wright's art became more rich and warm. In the Imperial Hotel in Tokyo Mr. Wright forced to design for a people with habits of work other than those of the West even embraced handicraft and permitted the building to take on the complicated forms of craftsmanship, the result being a monument far less European and mechanical than the painful sub-European specimens of architecture which the native architects scatter over the East. There is more ornament in the Imperial Hotel, 1916, or the Millard Residence in Pasadena, 1923, than in the Willett's [sic] House, 1901. If Mr. Hitchcock is right, this phase of Mr. Wright's development is an unfortunate atavism, and it makes more and more pronounced the breach between his work and that which will be produced during the coming generation.

That is one view of the case, but my own belief is just the opposite of this. The glorification of the machine by people who are just becoming acquainted with its possibilities and are learning to use it is "modern" in Europe today precisely because it is forty years behind our American experience. While for Europe the lesson of Ford is increasing standardization and mass-production, because few of the economies in design so introduced have been practised there, for us the lesson of Ford which he learned at a price that would have bankrupted an ordinary manufacturer is the pathetic insufficiency of our old-fashioned industrial design, with its contempt for problems of pure form and its disregard for other human interests than efficiency. If this be true, Mr. Wright is not the forerunner of Le Corbusier but, in a real sense, his successor. He has passed that painful step in learning when one is conscious of one's movements and one's instruments, and has reached that period in pure mechanical design when he can play with it, in short, the engineer has given way to the artist, and despite a hundred efforts to prove either that the engineer is the artist, or that engineering is the only possible type of art in the modern world, Mr. Wright's work exists as a living refutation of this notion. He had achieved Cubism in architecture before the Cubists, and he has gone on to an integral architecture which creates its own forms with, not for, the machine.

Mr. Hitchcock's aesthetic and social philosophy keep him, I think, from recognizing this as a valid development, hence his disparagement of Mr. Wright's art at the very moment he is seeking to praise it. For me, on the contrary, Mr. Wright's architectural development justifies itself, and not the less so, certainly, because I am more interested in humanity and its needs and desires than I am in the abstract perfection of the machine, or in the pragmatic justification of Spengler's historical dogmas.

In failing to grasp the inevitability of this humanization of the machine, this addition of feeling to form, or of poetry to mathematics as we become more and more the master of it, Mr. Hitchcock has, it seems to me, lost the central clue in Mr. Wright's career. This becomes apparent in the final apostrophe, in which he compares him with Wren and repeats the phrase so true of Wren in the city of London: "si monumentum requiris circumspice." The comparison does not hold at any point, but it falls down chiefly on the mere historical detail that one cannot find Wright's work by looking around in Chicago; on the contrary, one must search and pry and go on long motor rides, only to find, as in the Midway Gardens built but fifteen years ago, that vandals have already ruined the building. Up to recently Mr. Wright had built no skyscrapers, and with all the vast volume of industrial and semi-industrial building he has had little to do. His architecture is not in the current of the present regime any more than Walt Whitman's writings were in the current of the Gilded Age: hence his value is not that he has dominated the scene and made it over in his image, but that he has kept the way open for a type of architecture which can come into existence only in a much more humanized and socially adept generation than our own.

Mr. Wright's art is prophetic: it does not simply conform and adjust itself to existing conditions, it reacts and makes demands, demands that the builder of speculative houses or rent-barracks has no intention of complying with. Success under present conditions demands unhesitating conformity on the part of the engineer to the terms laid down by the banker and investor, the result is sometimes good design and economy, and quite as often it is poor design and deformity and inadequacy to perform the function that the building is supposed to perform. This is not the milieu in which good architecture can become the rule, and if modern architecture flourishes in Europe and lags here, it is because the Europeans have far better conditions under which to work, as a result of the socialized activity of European municipalities, with their comprehensive and financially unremunerative housing programs.

The truth is that Mr. Wright's capital qualities alienate him both from the architects who do not acknowledge a handicap in conforming to the present demands and from the society that ignores the higher values of life if they happen to conflict with the principle of a quick turnover and a maximum profit. Chief among these qualities is Mr. Wright's sense of the natural environment; and here again, I think, Mr. Hitchcock's principles keep him from grasping Mr. Wright's significance. Mr. Hitchcock refers to the "absurdity and the provincialism of the term prairie architecture" to characterize Mr. Wright's early Chicago work. On the contrary, the phrase is not absurd but accurate. Mr. Wright is, definitely, our greatest regional architect, his Chicago houses *are* prairie houses, as his Pasadena homes are "mediterranean" ones, to harmonize with that climate and milieu. Even machines, as some of our new pioneers forget, differ in design according to the region they are used in: steamers designed for tropical trade have larger ventilating units than the usual North Atlantic liners, and automobiles in England are designed for low power because of the relatively easy contours of the country. The essential form of architecture is of course largely conditioned by the method of construction, but this again is not independent of regional qualifications, as the use of the concrete form instead of the steel frame in Chicago testifies.

Now, these qualities are largely ignored by the older classical architecture, with its concern for a single method of construction and a single mode of design. Wherever a building was placed or whatever its purpose, the problem of the architect was to make it resemble, as far as possible, a Greek or Roman temple. The neo-classicists of the machine have revamped this formula, but the spirit behind it is the same, the chief difference being that the archetypal form is no longer a temple but a factory, and the principal offense against taste consists, not in the use of free or "barbarous" ornament but in the use of any ornament at all, however integral, however intimately a part of the design and necessary for its completion. Mr. Wright's great virtue consists in the fact that he uses to the full modern methods of construction and boldly invents new forms without losing his great sense of tact, the tact of the artist with his materials, of the lover of nature with the earth, and of a man with other men. Hence the importance of the garden which surrounds and completes almost all of his buildings: it is a true symbol of his entire work the picture of life, warm, earthy, insurgent, breaking in waves of foliage over the stony masses of the building, and showing the power and logic of the form at the very moment of departing from it and counterbalancing it. This is an art which cannot be contained in a narrow classical formula, and if the new pioneers have as yet no place for it in their philosophy, so much the worse for their philosophy. Mr. Wright's architecture is an early witness of what may generally come to happen when our regional cultures absorb the lesson of the machine without losing their roots or renouncing all those elements which give landscapes and men their individualities. The formula which would exclude such a manifestation belongs as little to the future as the five orders.

Notes

1. First published in *Architectural Record,* 65 (April 1929), pp. 414–416.

2. In this article Mumford was reviewing Henry-Russell Hitchcock, *Frank Lloyd Wright* (Paris: Editions Cahiers d'Art, 1928), a pamphlet whose authorship should be shared with André Lurçat, a French architect who ventured to Russia in the early 1930s. It was Lurçat who selected the illustrations that occupy 30 of the book's 34 pages. Presumably he also wrote the captions. The plan of the Dana house was incorrectly captioned as the Coonley house, and the Isabel Roberts house was called the "Maison Isabey," while the Coonleys' kindergarten building was referred to as their home. Hitchcock incorrectly aligned Wright with a European "movement" represented by Berlage, Hoffman, Garnier, and Perret; stated that Wright received a "diploma" in civil engineering in 1889 (he did not study civil engineering and did not receive a diploma or degree); called the term "prairie architecture" absurd and provincial; said that in residential design Wright's "exteriors" were never really "sound" (whatever that meant) and his ornamentation only interesting; said that the Imperial Hotel contained "mediocre reception rooms," and regretted that it survived "various earth tremors"; and believed that Wright's California block houses displayed "excessive taste" and that his work during the mid-twenties contained "nostalgia" for the Orient and, with Strzygowski, a nostalgia for ancient Nordic art (how strange). Yet Hitchcock believed Wright's architecture greater than any of his contemporaries', calling him a brilliant engineer and the greatest American of the first quarter of the twentieth century. Hitchcock also referred to Mumford as a distinguished critic. In spite of the accolade it is no wonder that Mumford responded so emphatically to Hitchcock's tendentious, delicate, and art historically naive essay.

3. Mumford's puzzlement was not only resolved with utmost clarity in his 1929 review but again much later, in his 1952 *Roots of Contemporary American Architecture,* when he was more concise. "That a real break in the American tradition had taken place between 1910 and 1925 . . . is proved by the fact that the new doctrines of architecture, derived from the Machine and from Cubism, came *back* [my emphasis] to America in the mid-twenties without most people noting that they were only returning to the country of their origin. Even such a good historical student as Henry-Russell Hitchcock could treat Wright's early work, which was aesthetically far more developed than Le Corbusier's, as if it were by then a back-number; a fact that made his early (1929 [sic]) monograph on Wright's work irritatingly patronizing. . . . From the perspective of a whole generation one can now see that Le Corbusier, in his historical innocence, sought to substitute a mannerism for the genuine organic style, visible in our grain elevators and our factories, that was in fact still in existence in America."

In 1929 and 1952 Mumford refrained from stating the obvious: that in the late 1920s and 1930s Hitchcock—and Alfred Barr—were mainly interested in architecture promoted by the political left, therefore out of necessity the Central Europeans' style. Americans were of interest to them only in as much as they emulated or adopted that style.

Appendix B   Wright's Writing

Wright changed what had already been published not to correct the earlier writing nor to alleviate what might have been a misunderstanding—except in odd cases. Rather, he was interested in carrying on a polemical battle that confronted him more or less at the moment of writing or editing. This does not infer he was thematically inconsistent. On the contrary, he was true to fundamental themes such as individualism, European cultural hegemony, or his interpretation of holism. Issues that were contrary and engaged him at a given moment or over time, seemed enlarged in his own mind; perhaps in fear that they might diminish his philosophy, generally or specifically.

To most readers Wright's literary style is imprecise yet evocative, lacks concision, is contradictory, railing, negative, grammatically incomparable, desperate, at times confusing or barely intelligible. Now and then he approached literary brilliance, but only the odd moment. Some readers have tried to read Wright aloud, speaking a variety of inflections or emphases; usually to no avail. One person, Baker Brownell, tried to analyze Wright's style, if briefly, in that part of his book about The Human Community *where he analyzed "The Philosophy of the Community.*[1]

In this incidental work of a great artist [Wright] can be seen at once the energy and integration of his impulse and the surface disorder of materials to which he is able to give no linear pattern. His impulse breaks through in his prose as if from a deeper level of integration. It erupts with all the power and consistency of a volcano, but its deposits on the surface of the earth are disorderly. Although an impressive number of books and articles have come from the great architect's pen, they have aroused, because of this lack of clarity, only minor interest in the reading public.

Wright has confined himself in his prose to insights and explosions. He makes magnificent love to the blue domes of Persia but vast denunciations of Michaelangelo. The broken-nosed Italian as an architect was a good painter, who felt no thrust or tension in materials or the muscular distribution of forces. Wright turns away from St. Peter's to write with tenderness of stones, lava, tile, wood, glass, steel, canvas. He is not a commentator noting this and that in an orderly fashion. He is a poet identifying himself with these materials. He climbs into this concrete block. He becomes the brick. His words grunt and struggle with the unaccustomed effort.

Or he writes his hates of cramping institutions with pompous contempt. It is scattered anathema strewn across the pages amid anecdotes and communiques of personal and philosophic life. To most readers it seems disordered and sudden, very different from his buildings. His prose is angry, sometimes vituperative, and noisy. His buildings never are, for buildings express dislike only by silence. Wright deprecates his prose style and has called himself a "dub" as a writer. For so confident a spirit this is a remarkable admission.

His prose indeed is not consecutive. It lacks flow. It lacks linear order. To the reader it seems disorganized, flashing forth abruptly with a cosmic utterance, then sinking back into formless superlatives and mumblings until the time for eruption comes round again. To the reader it lacks the mystic grace of his buildings. His prose never gets itself said, while his buildings are the utterances of a great spirit. They, not his words, are his poems.

All this may be said of Frank Lloyd Wright's prose; still I believe him to be a great writer. His prose may not be subtle, but it has power. It may lack craft, but it flows all from one source. It may not have linear continuity, but it has spiritual coherence and a proud though harsh integrity. His prose is not sensitive to the materials that the writer must use. Wright sees those materials; he walks among them with eyes open; but I am not sure that he hears them or feels them. He can find more poetry in a brick than in a word and more sensuous delight in his lyrics of glass and stone than in the niceties of language. But his language is direct. And if he is blank sometimes to verbal distinction, quality, and sound, he is also blank to the worn dance routines, the times kicks and fillips of the professional word masters of our day.

On the background of the thousands of fully written books and articles, raised like a screen to filter the sun, produced with endless competence in all the professionally tested modes, Wright's prose is somehow naked and revelatory. It is direct, whole, abruptly real. Though it is not always professional or fluid, nor even competent, his prose has the sting and substance, not of a book, but of a man.

It is integral rather than linear. It lacks the marching rhythms and proximate coherence of style that goes, as it were, from one place to the next. His words shift and run like quicksilver under his hands. They bulge beyond his control, and their damned plasticity makes fixation of meaning for him, or definition, impossible. But his style has the kind of spherical continuity, wholeness, the mystical or spiritual coherence, that often mark great work.

Wright, indeed, is never mainly linear in his thinking but integral. Because his thinking lacks connectives, it seems saltatory. Because it is not a line or a linkage of one thing related to the next thing in terms only of those two things, his conversation seems to be a series of pounces. The things that he writes emerge abruptly like divers from under the water. They come up like bubbles. They have radial organization rather than surface continuity. Because his thought is integrated on other levels, the visible bubbles seem to have little continuity with one another.

This lack of continuity in his prose style may be related to the fact that architecture, his chosen field, is involved more in the rhythms of space and matter than in the time and movement of words. That may or may not be true. Beyond that however is the fact that things in an integrated situation are deeply and wholly related in terms not of one line of functions or causes but of many. Wright's prose, for all its literary faults and incapacities, or because of them, reveals this deeper integration. Structurally it is a body, not a line. Each item of it refers not merely to its proximate predecessor and successor but in a multitude of imitations to all the members of the group.

His recent book, *Genius and the Mobocracy,* is an appreciation of the master, or *liebermeister,* Louis H. Sullivan. The book does indeed uncover, as it drifts like sand across the years, brilliant bits and memories of Sullivan as well as searching insights into his meaning as an artist. But these seem incidental. The drifts seem incidental. Each comment and wise saying, each person uncovered anecdotally, and even Wright himself as told in the scattered events of many years, all seem incidental to a great storm, hidden and brooding, pressing on the barriers of events. This storm is not in the book; still it conditions the items in it. It is implicit, passionate, a half-frustrated giant, that would overturn our culture, blow through the lies and greed and the massed towns, and restore human life to what is right. This angry power generates Wright's prose. In his architecture, because of the nature of the art, it finds little or no expression.

Note

1. Reprinted from Baker Brownell, *The Human Community* (New York, 1950), pp. 235–237, with the kind permission of Harper & Row. The rather romanticized overtones to Brownell's analysis resulted, in one case, in his asking, "Did not Wordsworth commune with Nature, and Frank Lloyd Wright with his beloved bricks and stones?" And later, with pseudo-Oriental insight, Brownell observed that "the brick in its simple way may experience Frank Lloyd Wright, even as Wright on his part experiences the brick" (p. 241).

Appendix C   "To the young Man in Architecture—a Challenge," by Frank Lloyd Wright[1]

I have taken over the writing and editing of the January ARCHITECTURAL FORUM.

I turned editor partly because Howard Myers came to Taliesin and asked me to—partly because I felt the time had come to restate a few fundamentals which are strangely missing from the contemporary scene.

The days and nights and the long hours I have put into the making of this issue are important only to me. But important to you are the months and years that went into the making of these buildings whose plans and photographs this issue brings you for the first time with critical text.

This ARCHITECTURAL FORUM is the first and only record in print of what we have come to call the modern movement, from its inception to its present interpretation. Some of the buildings shown as examples were built more than forty years ago. Some were recently completed. They were produced under a wide variety of circumstances—both social and economic, and for clients from West to East.

Together they show the basic principles which give vitality and integrity to such architecture as we have. Here in some 100-odd pages of plates, text and plans, you will see architecture as indigenous to America as the earth from which it springs, just as here you will see the futility and dishonesty of trying to transplant to America an architectural veneer which finds its roots in God knows where or what.

*   *   *

It is a sense of the whole that is lacking in the "modern" buildings I have seen, and in this issue we are concerned with that sense of the whole which alone is radical. There is more beauty in a fine ground plan itself than in almost any of its consequences. So plot plans and structural plans have been given due place in this issue as of first importance.

Many of the houses demonstrate the folly of imagining that a true and beautiful house must employ synthetics or steel to be "modern" or go to the factory to be economical. Glass? Yes, the modern house must use glass liberally. Otherwise it may be a simple wood house under a sheet of copper.

*   *   *

I would rather solve the small house problem than build anything else I can think of (except the modern theatre). But where is a better small house to come from while Government housing itself is only perpetuating the old stupidities? I do not believe it will come from current education, from big business or by way of smart advertising experts. It must come from common sense—a pattern for more simple and at the same time more gracious living.

To give the little Jacobs family a sensible house with benefit of the industrial advantages of our era, we must do more than plant for them another little imitation of a mansion.

And so in the January FORUM I have shown a $5500 house—a house with a new sense of space and light and freedom. And this house has no visible roof; no plague-spot of an old-fashioned basement (a steam-warmed concrete mat four inches thick laid directly on the ground over gravel filling is better); no radiators or light fixtures, no painting, no interior trim, no plastering, no gutters, no down-spout, no garage (a carport will do as cars are made today).

In the January FORUM I have also shown a plan for a skyscraper with each floor proceeding outward as a cantilever slab from a concrete core to an enclosing shell of glass and copper—the only urban skyscraper fit for human habitation.

I have shown an office building designed to be as inspiring a place to work in as any cathedral ever was in which to worship—a building which becomes, by way of long glass tubing, crystal, where crystal (either translucent or transparent) is most appropriate.

I have shown my own Taliesin, a house of the North. I have shown a house designed for living down in a glen of a mountain stream. I have shown a house for the rolling prairie, and a home for Texas (Texas needs a Texas house). I have shown a house for California, a house for the desert.

*   *   *

My purpose and hope in presenting this material in the ARCHITECTURAL FORUM is to promote discussion and rekindle enthusiasm for an honest American architecture. After months of work on this January issue I am more convinced than ever that this work should prove of value, particularly to the younger architects, who are America's last line of defense.

Here is a challenge; may I see it answered in three dimensions across the country.

Faithfully,
[signed] Frank Lloyd Wright
Frank Lloyd Wright
TALIESIN: SPRING GREEN: WISCONSIN: January 10th, 1938

Note

1. A two-page broadsheet probably published and distributed by *Architectural Forum,* reprinted here from a copy in the Willcox papers, University of Oregon. The need for concision heightened the critical, architectural, and design sense and character of his verbal presentation perhaps better than the contents of the magazine itself. The last line begs commissions. It should be noted that the splendid 1938 and 1948 issues of *Architectural Forum* devoted to Wright's work were, as put by Bruce Brooks Pfeiffer, part of editor Howard Myers's "effort, work, and constant campaigning" presumably to place Wright's work before the architectural public. Pfeiffer says that Wright and Myers often visited and the "deep bond that arose between the two men strengthened with the passing of time" (F. L. Wright 1984, p. 153).

Appendix D Observations by Leonard Reissman

The Visionary   The disenchantment with industrial society emerged in one of three ways, depending upon the value placed on industrialism and the social change thought to be needed. (1) Reaction against it all by which industrialism was entirely, if naively, discredited. The machine, the factory, and the city were considered to be beyond salvation in that they could not add anything worthwhile to society. In a reaction against industrialism the tightly comforting security of medievalism was sought through its image of a rediscovered rural utopia. This philosophy has continued, in one form or another, up to the present, where it has become centered around the small community as the alternative to the metropolis. (2) Reform of some features of industrial society to keep such advantages as labor-saving machinery, release from monotonous tasks, and the comforts that machines could fashion. The reformers championed what Mannheim has called a "spatial wish," the projection of utopia into space. By controlling industrialism for the benefit of all in a new social environment, the reformer argued, man could once again progress. Applied to the city, this view became the basis for the "Garden City" and its variations. (3) Revolt was yet a third alternative. The revolutionary accepted industrialism as a necessary historical phase; history neither could be set back to some earlier epoch nor could it be stopped. Industrial society could not be preserved as it was, nor could it be remodeled, even in part. Instead, a massive reconstitution was required, by which all existing institutions, values, and social mechanisms would be replaced by a new social order forging into reality the unfulfilled promises of industrialism. Mannheim, once again, has called these wish fulfillments "chiliasms," projections of dreams into time, the social utopias.

The visionary at one time or another has been identified with all three of these disenchanted responses to industrialism. Ebenezer Howard set forth one such spatial utopia in some detail. Later visionaries, such as Frank Lloyd Wright, perceived that tampering with the urban pattern necessarily involved changing economic mechanisms, political administration, and social philosophy. And throughout much of the writing by visionaries, the simple desire to return to a rural civilization is obvious again and again.[1]

Frank Lloyd Wright: Broadacre City Wright was more than simply the American counterpart to Ebenezer Howard and his Broadacre City more than just the American version of Garden City. Howard, as a true Victorian, after carefully adding up the economic costs and arguing for the feasibility of the garden city, had accepted much of the prevailing ideology. An overcrowded and congested London was bad business whereas a planned garden city was good business. Wright, on the contrary, never entered the market place to sell his plans. He much preferred to be the prophet on the mount shouting "Doom!" to the multitudes below. Wright felt the city and the industrial civilization that produced it must perish. They were the consequences of diseased values, and to achieve health, new values had to be established in a new environment. Wright was more consciously a social revolutionary than was Howard. He was prepared to recognize social mechanisms and willing to alter them. Howard's aim was to build a few garden cities to prove they were feasible, and by this publicity to have the revolt against the city initiated by society itself. Wright was more impatient. He wanted the wholesale decentralization of cities carried on simultaneously with the creation of Broadacre City. He had no patience with businesslike arguments to support his plan. Perhaps one could not blame him for his impatience and his loftiness, since he was so convinced that human civilization would be strangled by its industrial creation unless decisive and total action was taken. Any less drastic plan would have been hypocritical.

As the citizen stands, powerful modern resources, naturally his own by uses of modern machinery, are (owing to their very nature) turning against him, although the system he lives under is one he himself helped build. Such centralizations of men and capital as he must now serve are no longer wise or humane. Long ago—having done all it could for humanity—the centralization we call the big city became a centripetal force grown beyond our control; agitated by rent to continually additional, vicarious powers.

The city, according to Wright, has perverted our values and has become the environment of false democracy, false individualism, and false capitalism. We have, by our inaction, allowed ourselves to be overwhelmed and dominated by falsity. "The citizen," Wright argued, "is now trained to see life as a cliche." He must be trained to see life as natural for "only then can the democratic spirit of man, individual, rise out of the ground. We are calling that civilization of man and ground . . . democracy." As for capitalism: "Out of America 'rugged individualism' captained by rugged captains of our rugged industrial enterprises we have gradually evolved a crude, vain power: plutocratic 'Capitalism.' Not true capitalism. I believe this is entirely foreign to our own original idea of Democracy."

The cause of these perversions of our basic social values in the city is industrial civilization, where most of the visionaries locate the blame. Wright's contribution was to specify the causes more precisely. First, among these is *land rent,* and Henry George is resurrected as a guide to salvation. The rent for land has contributed to the "overgrowth of cities, resulting in poverty and unhappiness." Land values are artificial monsters that have taken over the destiny of the city, thereby removing us further from the natural state of mankind. Second, *money,* "a commodity for sale, so made as to come alive as something in itself—to go on continuously working in order to make all work useless. . . . The modern city is its stronghold and chief defender." Here the Puritan and Jeffersonian in Wright emerges, berating man to go back to the land and to honest labor. Third, *profit.* "By the triumph of conscienceless but 'rugged individualism' the machine profits of human ingenuity or inspiration in getting the work of the world done are almost all funneled into pockets of fewer and more 'rugged' captains-of-industry. Only in a small measure . . . and these profits . . . where they belong; that is to say, with the man whose life is actually modified, given, or sacrificed to this new common agency for doing the work of the world. This agency we call 'the machine.'" In these few words, Wright has fairly condensed the Marxian theory of surplus value. Fourth, *government and bureaucracy.* "In order to keep the peace and some show of equity between the lower passions so busily begotten in begetting, the complicated forms of super-money-increase-money-making and holding are legitimatized by government. Government, too, thus becomes monstrosity. Again enormous armies of white-collarites arise." These are Wright's beliefs on the state of industrial civilization. The need for revolt is clear; the means are at hand.

Infinite possibilities exist to make of the city a place suitable for the free man in which freedom can thrive and the soul of man grow, a City of cities that democracy would approve and so desperately needs. . . . Yes, and in that vision of decentralization and reintegration lies our natural twentieth century dawn. Of such is the nature of the democracy free men may honestly call the new freedom.

How emphatically this point of view, so characteristic of the visionary, separates him from the mundane practicality of the practitioner. For Wright, the city in its present form cannot be saved, nor is it worth saving. A new environment must be envisioned and built. It must be one that is developed out of our technology, but one that excises the diseased growth that has infected our basic and still sound values. The plan is Broadacre City, realized by "organic architecture" or "the architecture of democracy."

Broadacre City was a more detailed utopia than Garden City. Wright had drawn not only the ground pattern (one acre to the individual) but also planned homes, buildings, farms, and automobiles. He also clearly specified the activities that would be permitted. Wright held definite views, to say the least, not only about architecture, but music, education, religion, and medicine as well. He was an authoritarian, some would say a messianic figure, as sure of the true and the good and the beautiful as were Christ and the early Christian prophets, along with Lao-tse and Mohammed, whom he sought to emulate.

Wright's plans for the physical setting and social order of Broadacre City were comprehensive. They contained small factories because the newer technology has made the centralized large factory obsolete, wasteful, and constricting. Office buildings housing the financial, professional, distributive and administrative services necessary for business, would be organized as a unit. Professional services would be decentralized and made readily accessible to the clients. Banks, as we know them, would be abolished and in their place there would be a "non-political, non-profit institution in charge of the medium of exchange." Money no longer would have the power it now has; therefore, the need for its "glamorization" would be removed. Markets and shopping centers would be designed as spacious pavilions to make shopping itself a pleasant aesthetic experience. There would be apartments, motels, and community centers. Radio would carry great music to the people. "The chamber music concert would *naturally* become a common feature at home" [my italics]. Churches would be built, but the "old idea" of religion would be replaced by a more liberal and nonsectarian religion. There would be less concern with the hereafter, with superstition, with prejudice, and with deference to authority. With this new religion man, though still humble, would be made more understanding of himself and more democratic towards others.

Wright also had plans for education and the material to be taught in the schools and university of Broadacre City. He would replace the specialized, mass product of the universities of his day with a student who would obtain a deeper understanding of nature's laws governing the human spirit. Education would be a total and continuous process for the resident of Broadacre. Aside from the schools, this would be accomplished by "style centers," and "television and radio, owned by the people [which would] broadcast cultural programs illustrating pertinent phases of government, of city life, of art work, and [would have] programs devoted to landscape and study and planting or the practice of soil and timber conservation; and, as a matter of course, to *town planning* for better houses."

This long discourse . . . is a sincere attempt to take apart and show . . . the radical simplicities of fate to which our own machine skills have now laid us wide open and [to] try to show how radical eliminations are now essential to our spiritual health, and to the culture, if not the countenance, of democratic civilization itself. These are all changes valid by now if we are to have indigenous culture at all and are not to remain a bastardized civilization with no culture of our own, going all the way down the backstairs of time to the usual untimely end civilization have hitherto met.

With Frank Lloyd Wright, the visionary's argument found its most dramatic and radical expression, and its most completely detailed one. Wright magnified Howard's plan and spelled out more specifically the visionary's discontent and rebellion against the industrial city. In Wright's words, the planned utopia became a loud protest against the evils of industrialism. His architectural philosophy was, at the same time, a radical social ideology. Wright recognized this and did not hesitate to make the connection clear. His principle contribution to the study of the city, if one does not care to accept his dream or his philosophy, was in the repeated insistence on the relationship between the city and the society that produced it. The contemporary city, for Wright, was a product of industrial civilization. One could not understand all of its institutions: the political system, social stratification and the economic order, religion and education. Wright might be excused for his authoritarianism, for his failure to consider the motivations of individuals, for his brash structuring of existing social relationships into something he wanted. For he did grasp something of the underlying complexity that sustained the city as a social environment. That he refused to consider what others wanted, or what others thought, was due to his conviction that he was absolutely right. Can the prophet, after all, have any doubts?[2]

Notes

1. Excerpts require the following acknowledgment: "Reprint with the permission of the Free Press, a division of Macmillan, Inc. from THE URBAN PROCESS: Cities in Industrial Societies by Leonard Reissman. Copyright © 1964, 1970 by the Free Press." The relevant pages are 42–43.

2. Ibid., pp. 57–62. Does the sociologist see the city as people who have physical things and the architect see the city as a physical phenomenon fulfilling people's needs?

Appendix E "Wright, American Architect, Gives His Impressions of Moscow and of Soviet People"[1]

As my visit to Moscow extends one impression grows concerning the foreign newspaper correspondents: either most of them are blind or vipers. The best of them seem busy drinking the tub of dye to find out what color it is. The notable exceptions are perhaps the "Manchester Guardian" and the "New York Times," whatever their political creed may be. Can any man with a heart and a head see the liberation of a whole people actually working out a new life, without rejoicing with them?

The great nations should gladly stand by, "hands off," to protect the growth of this struggling democracy instead of standing by to see the great effort compelled to waste, on getting ready to fight, resources needed to make better living conditions.

But the human fiber of the ultimate Russia will only be stronger because of this needless difficulty added to inevitable ones.

Yesterday at the Moscow building exhibit [in the House of Unions] I saw a splendid exposition of plans and models for the buildings, towns and cities in the Soviet Union. That exhibit could not be equalled in the world today.

I do not say that all the buildings were what they should be—many were infected by the old grandomania, many were yearning for luxury of the old pastry cook elegance—but I say enough were better than good to show how much better all will be soon. The exhibit stands far above the level of anything America could show, America, the country toward which these lovable people look with such pathetic appeal. So much in the architecture of our own country is bad for the Soviet Union at this critical time.

These are the impressions of a sentimentalist, you may say. But first impressions are usually best impressions and it has never been necessary for me to drink a tub of dye to know its color. The other day I spoke at the All-Union Congress of Architects in the hall of the former Nobles Club [sic] the great room filled with Soviet architects. Although my remarks were critical, the amazing honor they heaped upon me until they broke me down showed that it is not praise they value most.

I believe the Russian people to be naturally sensitive to beauty, kind at heart, generous by nature—strong and, in the long run, hardest of all people to fool by superficial pretense.

When we remember the birth of the Soviet Union, we must realize not only how young the nation is but how many unfortunate inheritances entered into its composition and even now course in its blood stream.

If they worship heroes—well, the heroes now belong to them—to the people.

If they are proud of their achievements, those achievements are the work of their own heads and hands. Achievements, too, belong to the people.

If they are suspicious of the world surrounding them, seeing sinister shadows moving within and without their gates, who can blame them?

The sinister is there.

Like some pregnant mother going carefully, unfortunately this one must go fearful, too.

Yes—the world has at least two great hopes for a better life struggling forward—the USSR and the USA. Two different roads to the same place—a free life for a free people. The breaking of the new polar route between the two countries by Russian enterprise will place both nations in a central position among the nations of this Northern Hemisphere. A trade and passenger route 35 hours long from the center of the USSR to the center of the USA!

Prejudices will fade to show the world changed in its center of power.

I might almost say its political center of gravity—changed.

So here's to Russia's America and to America's Russia.

May both live long and grow together.

[signed] Frank Lloyd Wright

Note

1. As published in the *Moscow Daily News,* 28 June 1937, p. 4; reprint as "An American Architect's Impression of USSR," *Moscow News,* Sunday, 7 July 1937, p. 4. In the adjacent column was the following, which was condensed from "Eminent Foreign Architects . . .," *Moscow Daily News,* 30 June 1937, p. 3.

Architects Vote Congress Huge Success

The First All-Union Congress of Architects, which ended in Moscow last week, was voted a huge success not only by the Soviet architects but by the many distinguished foreigners who had been invited to attend the sessions.

"I had assumed that it would be the sort of narrowly professional gathering that we are accustomed to in the West," the British architect C. Williams Ellis said. "I was therefore astonished at the alert interest displayed apparently by the entire public in the congress and even in its long and often highly technical debates. If an architect in my country were to speak not merely as a specialist, but also as a severe critic, mentioning the names of colleagues whom he considered had made grave mistakes—well, I really don't know what would happen!"

Mr. Ellis felt that the congress should be repeated on an international scale, similar to an olympiad, with architects of all democratic countries participating. He expressed his admiration for the advances made since his last visit to the Soviet Union, five years ago, evidences of which he found on every hand. A similar statement was made by F. Jourdain, French architect, who last visited Moscow 10 years ago.

"The first thing that strikes one on arriving in Moscow," he said, "are the new buildings, wide streets, cleanliness, new appearance of people who do not seem to experience need; and large shops filled with goods and buyers, bookstores which cannot keep pace with the tremendous demand for literature. The love for books and thirst for knowledge seem to me most characteristic of the Moscovites and apparently of the Soviet people in general. This great cultural rise is naturally reflected also in architecture."

Appendix F   Education of the Architect: A Letter from Frank Lloyd Wright to Jens Jensen[1]

It is never possible to bring out the meaning of any subjective matter without being rehearsed in the language—in being sure that all are speaking the same language. The only difference between Olgivanna and myself is that she believes that the creative instinct is the original birthright of mankind and in most of them it lies dead—in any case paralysed and that by proper treatment it may be revived. I too believe that creative-faculty is the birthright of Man—the quality which enabled him to distinguish himself from the brute, but that owing to his betrayal of himself, the tricks which he has played upon himself with his brain, what he calls his intellect—and by means of his arrogant assumptions, abstractions, all turned into a system of so called education, he has sterilized himself. And I believe that now not only is this creative-instinct dead in most, but it has ceased to exist at all, to such an extent that perhaps three fifths of humanity lacks any power of that kind. Now I believe the creative instinct in Man is that quality or faculty in him of getting himself reborn and born again—of getting himself born into everything that he does, everything that he really works with. By means of it he has got the gods if not God. It is his imagination that is chiefly the tool with which this force or faculty in him works. By putting a false premium upon will and intellect he has done this injury upon himself—he has worked this injury upon himself.

Now how to get it back—this quality of Man—back again to men. How to preserve what little there is glimmering of it in whatever human being it may be glimmering in. Our first concern about that should be the first thought of every thinking man in our country today.

And that Jens, is why I am interested in this proposed school. I should like to be one to initiate steps that would put a little experimentation station at work where this thing might be wooed and won, if only to a small extent. I know it cannot be taught.

No doubt what you mean by "dried-up" and being "hooked" is what you imagine to be the exhorbitant egotism of the man who arrogates to himself creative power and denies it to most. Very well. Hypocrisy has many good and desirable features—modesty is among them, chivalry too. Where people live much together, these things are essential. But men "dry up" from the inhibition which imposes these things upon the ego. Those who allow the ego a natural scope and insist on the privileges and rights due to the equality of man he may feel working in him are wiser—Walt Whitman foremost among these. Of course Jens, that man will be most beloved who concedes most to his fellow man, who will make the grandest gestures and say the things he knows his fellow man likes to see and hear about himself. But there is a wholesome candor more valuable in any final analysis, conspicuously lacking in any such democracy as ours and while I have no less faith in man than any or all of my opponents in this long-lasting argument of ours, I have less faith in men. And I am for taking steps—constructive steps—*now,* not sometimes, to save the precious quality which is the soul of man himself, from further atrophy, from greater degradation at his own hands. So I am no singer from this false sentimentalized American democracy. I see the evil consequence all too plainly of this making of gods of Demos—of this patting of the common-denominator on the back and ascribing to it the virtues of deity.

Note

1. Excerpts from a letter from Wright to Jens Jensen, Chicago landscape architect, 8 December 1928, reprinted in whole in F. L. Wright (1984), pp. 71–72; quoted with kind permission of the Frank Lloyd Wright Foundation. These excerpts should be compared with F. L. Wright (1936b).

Appendix G Centennial Gold   Wright's individualism, so often gone wrong in public displays, got him little from colleagues in the profession. His derogations and, some believed, the insults uttered in the 1930s alienated him from most of his fellow professionals. Such damaging pronouncements date back to 1914 in an article in the *Architectural Record* where he attacked those who mimicked him and then the profession generally for architectural eclecticism. His harsh words and invective persisted into the 1940s and greatly affected attitudes when he was considered for the AIA Gold Medal. He said he "didn't want to accept" the medal but he did so because he "didn't want to be a cad," a statement difficult to believe.[1] His abuse continued well into the 1950s.

The AIA medal of 1949 was won through great effort not by a majority but by a coaxing minority, and a minority was again involved in promoting Wright for the AIA's Centennial Medal of Honor. Deliberations over that medal not only reflected Wright's image but highlighted a reaction to European influence in America that had begun in the 1930s. An outline of the affair should illumine aspects of Wright's career and philosophy in the 1930s.

In 1951 Ralph Walker, then president of the AIA and winner of the institute's Gold Medal in 1946, wrote in the *AIA Journal* in oblique but obvious terms censuring his colleagues for allowing the immigrants and emigés, the European "prophets" and their architecture, to be so persuasive. As far as Walker was concerned the problem facing architects at midcentury was how to "release the potentialities of the civilization developing" in America. "We cannot look to Europe," said Walker, "as it means looking to a civilization which for the last 75 years has been bent upon destroying itself, and the prophets it has sent to the United States are wholly negative in philosophy—stripping down culture to unattractive minima or in twisting neurosis into Nihilism. We must ourselves and in our own way, find the architectural answer to our needs," continued Walker, "and in the very beginning cease imitating despair and negation to find a positive way toward an architectural form. Imitation of a universal form is fatal and indicates laziness, for if truly creative men are developed by our schools, there will be little unanimity [uniformity]. We, as Americans must beware of the *Schleiermachers,* i.e., veilmakers."[2]

This measured statement, influenced as much by jealousy as by the impress of the U.S. Congress's House Un-American Activities Committee did not indicate a desire to return to tradition but was representative of a latent hostility to the immigrants' successes (especially with university appointments) and of reactionary attitudes within the design profession. Reactions were soon revealed architecturally in a sensuality contrary to the International Style: e.g., thin-shell concrete domes, hyperbolic paraboloids, organic shapes, a new emphasis on natural materials and on an identifiable regionalism (therefore in opposition to internationalism).

Walker's words, although appearing to be kin to Wright's, did not represent the latter's general view; Wright did not offer opinions similar to Walker's narrowly conceived nationalism. Gropius was right to challenge Walker and to wonder why Walker could seriously question the contributions made to the profession "by men like Mies van der Rohe, Neutra, Chermayeff, Breuer" and himself.[3]

However, we can now more clearly appreciate why Walker supported Wright for the 1949 Gold Medal. Although Wright wryly told Walker he always counted him as a "friend for some reason—probably yourself,"[4] Wright seems not to have warmed to him. This in spite of the fact that in 1955 Walker helped raise funds at a testimonial dinner to help Wright pay his taxes; he was again in debt![5]

Perhaps in the view of some people Walker and Wright had similar views and indeed similar personalities, for Walker has been described as a man "whose ego knew no bounds." Obviously their *social* standing in the profession was poles apart. When it came to the Centennial Medal of Honor both men were serious contenders: Walker, the consummate New York professional, versus Wright, the consummate architect as artist. The 1957 Centennial award, offered in the year of the one hundredth anniversary of the Institute, was to be given only once to honor "the architect of the century." The fact that again the AIA's board alone made the decision was strangely elitist for an American organization.

In recognizing sentiment in favor of Wright the AIA's executive director Edmund R. Purves provided arguments very similar to those used in support of Wright for the 1949 Gold Medal: "It would be the worst kind of public relations for us to ignore the existence of the greatest architect the world has ever seen at the Centennial Celebration." But they did ignore and Walker won. His citation read in part: "In this year when the Institute feels entitled, through reaching an established maturity, to express unashamedly its affection for a favorite and gifted son, this token of its pride needs no further warrant." Walker's words against the European immigrants (regardless of why they emigrated) and for a myopic nationalism were reinforced in the AIA government's citation: "unashamedly" they expressed their "affection for a favorite and gifted son." Ironically, it was Purves's private opinion that Wright's influence was "largely synthetic" and would "not be lasting."[6] Who now remembers Walker and if so for what reasons?

Notes

1. Pfeiffer (1988), p. 22.

2. As quoted in Hines (1982), p. 289.

3. Quoted in ibid.; letter in possession of Hines.

4. FLW to R. Walker, 27 May 1949, FLW Archives.

5. Actually that is not quite correct. Wright and his accountants created the Frank Lloyd Wright Foundation, which was incorporated in Wisconsin in 1940. As far as he was concerned he was penniless; his income went to the Foundation from which he received expenses. This was his reckoning: the Foundation was a "non-profit accredited cultural-education establishment," and it belonged to "the Nation." Of course as president he ran the Foundation (Twombly 1979, pp. 377–379; Frank Lloyd Wright Foundation to Headquarters, Continental Air Command, 21 July 1941, in F. L. Wright 1982; and FLW to G. Loeb, 23 December 1944). When in 1944 he sent letters to some of his wealthier clients requesting donations, as far as he was concerned the money was not to be for him personally but for the Foundation, to run the Fellowship during lean war years. He asked Edgar Kaufman for $25,000, Herbert Johnson for $10,000, and Gerald Loeb and John Nesbitt for $10,000 each, and apparently he received some assistance (see, e.g., FLW to J. Nesbitt, 27 December 1944; also discussed in my "Frank Lloyd Wright versus Hollywood," manuscript in preparation). When in 1955 he accepted money at the testimonial dinner attended by three hundred and seventy well-wishers and chaired by Walker, it was for back taxes (Twombly, p. 379).

6. The description and quotations are taken from Wilson (1984), pp. 30, 31.

Notes

THEME / **Precedents**

1 Olga Milan Lazovich

1. F. L. Wright (1943), p. 509.

2. Ingraham (1980), p. 10; Twombly (1979), p. 186. It is assumed that Olgivanna would have proofread her own marriage announcement even if she did not correct later books by Wright or herself:

> **Married**
>> **August 25**
>> **Rancho Santa**
>> **Fe California**
>
> **Olga Ivanovna**
> **Daughter of**
> **Ivan Lazovich and**
> **Militze Milan of**
> **Cettinje Montenegro**
> **To Frank Lloyd Wright**
> **Son of Anna Lloyd-Jones**
> **and William Cary Wright**
> **Taliesin Wisconsin. 1928**

The closed spacing of "Milanof" caused some historians to believe that her maiden name was Milanof or Milanov. Note that Wright's mother is named first whereas Olgivanna's father precedes her mother, the more common form. Hand-lettered announcement, W. R. Heath papers, Library of Congress, as reproduced in Fishman (1977).

3. As quoted in Pfeiffer (1987), plate 1 description.

4. This marriage (and its issue, Svetlana) was ignored by compiler Ingraham (1980), p. 10. There are other problems with the compilation. For an outline of the often-forgotten side of Frank Lloyd Wright's family—the Wrights—see Johnson (1980), which is being updated.

5. Nott (1961), p. 84.

6. Olgivanna's life prior to joining Wright in February 1925 is reconstructed from conflicting evidence found in O. L. Wright (1959), pp. 31–36, 274–275; Nott (1961), pp. 32–41, 62, 84–85; Twombly (1979), pp. 186–187 (which is more or less the traditional view of biographers and historians); *Who's Who in America,* 1980–81; Gurdjieff (1969), pp. 252–253, 284–287; Gill (1987), pp. 290–291, 326–327; Hartmann (1983), pp. xix, 98, 106–130; P. D. Ouspensky, *In Search of the Miraculous* (London, 1950), chapters 1 and 2; *Current Biography 1952,* p. 654;

Barbara Jelavich, *History of the Balkans* (Cambridge, 1983), pp. 34–37, 108–121; F. L. Wright (1932a), pp. 274–275; F. L. Wright (1943), pp. 508–514; and Pfeiffer (1985a), pp. viii–ix. There are few publications about only Montenegro but see the illustrated article by Bryan Hodgson, "Montenegro: Yugoslavia's 'Black Mountain,'" *National Geographic,* November 1977, pp. 663–682. On Miriam Noel see J. L. Wright (1946), chapter 14.

7. F. L. Wright (1943), p. 303; not in the 1932 edition of the autobiography. Biographers differ on the number and names of incorporators.

8. Twombly (1979), pp. 189–192; see also Einbinder (1986), pp. 222–248.

9. List dated 12 December 1932, sent to A. Kroch, Chicago, copy in FLW Archives.

10. FLW to C. Morgan, 12 December 1929, in F. L. Wright (1984), pp. 79–80.

11. FLW to Raymond Hood, 2 June 1930, in ibid., pp. 80–81.

2 Ocotillo Camp

1. Green (1983), p. 5.

2. F. L. Wright (1932a), pp. 302–303.

3. Wright spelled it Ocatilla, Ocatillo, and seldom Ocotillo. Since he specifically mentioned that the name was taken from the plant, all spellings herein are Ocotillo.

4. F. L. Wright (1932a), p. 303.

5. Ibid., p. 305; further described in de Fries (1930), pp. 342–343, with excellent illustrations on pp. 344–347.

6. Mentioned to de Fries; noted in ibid., p. 342.

7. FLW to R. L. Jones, 10 October 1929, in F. L. Wright (1986b), p. 48; Hanks (1979), p. 223; de Fries (1930), p. 342; and Twombly (1979), p. 238. Hitchcock (1940), p. 13, stated that de Fries's writings on Wright, especially de Fries (1926), could be "largely ignored"; obviously they can not.

8. F. L. Wright (1932a), p. 306.

9. Ibid., p. 307.

10. Green (1983), p. 7.

11. F. L. Wright (1932a), p. 308.

12. This discussion is based on Johnson (1987b).

13. Cf. George M. White, *Living in Montana* (Ronan, Montana, 1982), p. 97.

14. Clay Lancaster, *The American Bungalow 1880–1930* (New York, 1985), pp. 181–184.

15. Pfeiffer (1985a), plate 71. Previously Wright had done a preliminary design for a "desert dwelling" (1921?) of uncertain construction. See Neil Levine, "FLW's Own Houses . . . ," in Bolon et al. (1988).

16. I discuss this more fully in "Frank Lloyd Wright versus the City: Architectural and City Planning Theory" (manuscript in preparation).

17. Cf. Banham (1969), p. 516, who described Ocotillo as one of the great statements of twentieth-century architecture.

18. Green (1983), p. 11.

19. Izzo and Gubitosi (1981), items 78–85; and Pfeiffer (1985a), photos 90–120. Strangely, in Hitchcock (1942) Ocotillo was dismissed (p. 78 and plate 277).

20. FLW to R. L. Jones, 10 October 1929, in F. L. Wright (1986b), p. 47, and Green (1983), p. 15.

21. F. L. Wright (1932a), p. 306; see de Fries (1930); and cf. K. Loenberg-Holm, "The Week-end House," *Architectural Record,* 68 (August 1930), pp. 188–191, and the incomplete views of Ciucci (1978). Wright acknowledged and presumably favored de Fries's publication (Wright 1932a, p. 306). It was in a letter to a former employee, Werner Moser, that Wright first coined the name "Taliesin in the great Desert" (FLW to Moser, 25 July 1929, in F. L. Wright 1984, p. 75).

22. F. L. Wright (1932a), p. 308.

23. De Fries (1930), p. 344. The last line provided the title for daughter Iovanna Lloyd Wright's *Man in Possession of His Earth* (New York, 1962; London, 1963), a biography of Wright of sorts with some personal ideas of influences on design.

24. F. L. Wright (1932a), p. 306. There are seven draftsmen in a photograph held by the FLW Archives.

25. Twombly (1979), p. 220.

3 Trilogy: Wright, Gutheim, Hitchcock

1. Dust jacket of the 1957 printing of the second (1943) edition.

2. FLW to F. L. Jones, 16 December 1929, in F. L. Wright (1986b), p. 59.

3. FLW to Cheney, 26 December 1930, FLW Archives.

4. Letter of 21 June 1979 from Dr. J. A. Edwards, Archivist, University of Reading (where the Longmans papers are held) to Mr. David Lea, Longmans Group, in response to a request of the author.

5. FLW to N. Gutherie, 9 February 1931, in F. L. Wright (1986b), p. 290.

6. Edwards to Lea, 21 June 1979.

7. "Copyright Window Displays," *Publishers Weekly,* no. 1212 (2 April 1932), p. 1563.

8. Duell to FLW, 28 September 1939, FLW Archives.

9. Duell to FLW, 10 November 1939, FLW Archives.

10. FLW to Duell, 27 January 1940, FLW Archives.

11. Gutheim to FLW, 7 March 1940, FLW Archives.

12. FLW to Gutheim, 15 March 1940, FLW Archives.

13. FLW to Duell, 2 April 1940, FLW Archives.

14. Gutheim to FLW, 16 July 1940 and 8 August 1940, FLW Archives.

15. Telegram, FLW to Duell, 11 February 1941, FLW Archives.

16. Letter, FLW to Duell, 11 February 1941, FLW Archives.

17. Kimball (1928), pp. 192 and 200.

18. FLW to Mumford, 30 April 1928, in F. L. Wright (1984).

19. Hitchcock (1928b), p. 341, which precedes Wright's "In the Cause of Architecture. II. The Meaning of Materials—Stone," in the same issue.

20. Barr et al. (1932), p. 37.

21. See Holger Cahill and Alfred H. Barr, Jr., *Art in America* (New York, 1934), p. 72.

22. Mumford (1931), p. 167. There were other observers who followed Mumford's lead. For instance Ralph T. Walker perceptively remarked in 1930 that "the European architect took over the American factory and the ideas of Frank Lloyd Wright" (address of Ralph T. Walker, in the AIA pamphlet "A Symposium on Contemporary Architecture" [Washington, D.C., 1931], p. 21).

23. FLW to Hitchcock, 15 September 1937, p. 2, FLW Archives, also in F. L. Wright (1984).

24. FLW to Hitchcock, 15 June 1938, FLW Archives.

25. FLW to Hitchcock, 12 July 1938, in F. L. Wright (1984). In all, seven letters from Wright to Hitchcock, from 1928 to 1958, are published in *Letters to Architects,* pp. 133–140.

26. FLW to Duell, 1 June 1941, FLW Archives.

27. FLW to Hitchcock, 1 April 1941, FLW Archives.

28. Tafel (1979), pp. 144–145.

29. FLW to Duell, 7 June 1941, FLW Archives.

30. FLW to Hitchcock, 13 June 1941, FLW Archives.

31. FLW to Duell, 22 December 1941, FLW Archives.

32. H.-R. Hitchcock, "Frank Lloyd Wright at the Museum of Modern Art," *Art Bulletin,* 23 (March 1941), pp. 72–76. Compare Bruce Blevin, Jr., "Frank Lloyd Wright," *New Republic,* 103 (9 December 1940), pp. 790–791; and Talbot Hamlin, "Frank Lloyd Wright," *Nation,* 51 (30 November 1940), pp. 541–542, where Hamlin attempted an academic put-down and stated that the show contained "strange lacunae," that it lacked coherence and a "progress or subject pattern," and that the "decorative side" seemed "overweighted." A more balanced view if not praiseworthy or wholly correct was in T. Hamlin, "A Pot Pourri for an Architect," *Pencil Points,* 22 (January 1941), pp. 55–56. But then Hamlin was writing for a very different audience. The exhibition was called "Two Great Americans" and the other artist was filmmaker David W. Griffith.

33. *Saturday Review of Literature,* 8 (23 April 1932), pp. 677–678.

34. Information on Faber imprint is in a letter of C. M. Whittaker (Faber and Faber) to the author, 7 September 1981. A third edition of the autobiography was first planned in 1951, at which time Wright edited some text. He thought Duell, Sloan and Pearce were to publish it (see letter, FLW to Bruno Zevi, 19 September 1951, in F. L. Wright 1984, p. 189), and similarly a second edition of *In the Nature of Materials* (see letter, Hitchcock to FLW, 19 September 1952, in ibid.

35. FLW to B. Zevi, 19 September 1951, and FLW to Hitchcock, 19 September 1952, in F. L. Wright (1984).

4 Fellowship

1. FLW to P. M. Cochius, 5 December 1928, and P. M. Cochius to FLW, 4 February 1929, in Johan Ambaum, "Outwerpen van Frank Lloyd Wright voor de glasfabriek Leerdam," *Jong Holland,* no. 1 (1987), pp. 45–46.

2. See the letters of FLW to Jens Jensen, 8 December 1929, FLW to Moser, 25 July 1929, and FLW to Lewis Mumford, 7 January 1929, in F. L. Wright (1984), pp. 71–72, 76.

3. FLW to Wijdeveld, 6 August 1930, as outlined in Meehan (1983), pp. 233–234, and information kindly supplied by Dr. Donald Langmead; and cf. R. Neutra to FLW, 6 July 1929, FLW Archives. The "students" were described as Okami from Tokyo and Laubi from Zurich.

4. FLW to Wijdeveld, n.d. [c. October 1930], Wijdeveld Papers.

5. Wijdeveld to FLW, 3 January 1931, FLW Archives.

6. FLW to Wijdeveld, 6 April 1931, Wijdeveld Papers.

7. Cable, FLW to Wijdeveld, 17 April 1931, FLW Archives.

8. Cable, Wijdeveld to FLW, 16 April 1931; and cable, Wijdeveld to FLW, 18 April 1931, FLW Archives.

9. Wijdeveld to FLW, 11 April 1931, copy in Wijdeveld Papers.

10. Wijdeveld to FLW, 10 June 1931, FLW Archives.

11. Jensen to Wijdeveld, 15 June 1931, FLW Archives.

12. FLW to Wijdeveld, 13 August 1931, Wijdeveld Papers.

13. Contract draft, date added, November 1931, FLW Archives.

14. Wijdeveld to FLW, 1 January 1932, FLW Archives.

15. FLW to Wijdeveld, 13 February 1932, Wijdeveld Papers. The copy in the FLW Archives is not that of the letter received by Wijdeveld. On the Académie Européenne Méditeranée, see H. Th. Wijdeveld, *Naar een internationale werkgemeenschap* (Santpoort, 1931).

16. Wijdeveld to FLW, 13 October 1947, Wijdeveld Papers, and discussions with Dr. Langmead.

17. Drafts, FLW to Wijdeveld, 21 October 1947, FLW Archives, and in F. L. Wright (1984), pp. 106–108, which is *not* the letter received by Wijdeveld. Wijdeveld did visit in 1947 and obtained a visiting professorship at the University of Southern California. See various letters in the Wijdeveld Papers and FLW Archives, 1947–49, for Wright's role.

18. Wijdeveld to FLW, 1 January 1932, copy in Wijdeveld Papers.

5 Apprenticeship

1. F. L. Wright (1932a), p. 236. Oddly, these and other observations on education of c. 1931 were not significantly altered in the 1943 edition of the autobiography, although Taliesin was then ten years old. Wright seemed intrigued by the idea of education rather than the actual process of educating, a thought strengthened by his confession "I am no teacher."

2. Smith (1979), p. 136.

3. Tafel (1979), p. 137.

4. J. L. Wright (1946), pp. 32–33.

5. Shay (1926), pp. 129, 425; and Champney (1983), p. 189. On Hubbard see also the entry in *Dictionary of American Biography* (New York, 1932); William Alfred Hines, *American Communities and Co-operative Colonies* (Philadelphia, 1908; reprint 1975), pp. 513–521; and Charles F. Hamilton, *Roycroft Collectables* (San Diego, 1980).

6. William Marion Reedy, *A Little Journey to East Aurora* (East Aurora, N.Y., 1912), p. 33. See also Champney (1983), p. 190, and Smith (1979), p. 136.

7. Andrews (1955), p. 248.

8. On Ashbee see Crawford (1985).

9. Cf. Hanks (1979).

10. Borsodi (1972), pp. xxvii–xxviii.

11. The discussion of *paideia* is in O. L. Wright (1963), pp. 204–206. It is not clear if Olgivanna obtained the book independently of Gurdjieff; it was first published in Germany in 1933 and two volumes followed. It was published in English in three volumes in 1939–46 after expatriate Jaeger had been established at Harvard University. Jaeger states that *paideia*

like other broad comprehensive concepts (*Philosophy,* for instance, or culture) refuses to be confined within an abstract formula. . . . It is impossible to avoid bringing in modern expressions like *civilization, culture, tradition, literature,* or *education.* But none of them really covers what the Greeks meant by paideia. . . . The ancients were persuaded that education and culture are not a formal art or an abstract theory, distinct from the objective historical structure of a nation's spiritual life. (Jaeger 1965, p. v; his emphases)

The description of *paideia* as education through the development of mind and body may appear a trite simplification, yet the concept was popularly described as such. Jaeger's notion that only the nobility had access to *areté* is patent and distinct—"ordinary men have no *areté* . . . it was impossible to dissociate leadership and *areté*" (p. 5).

12. Smith (1979), p. 140.

13. Cf. the "Work Song" in F. L. Wright (1943), before p. 379; also Ulrich Conrads, ed., *Programmes and Manifestoes on 20th-century Architecture* (London, 1970), frontispiece.

14. F. L. Wright (1932a), p. 236, and F. L. Wright (1943), p. 236. Wright saw all employees as potentially traitorous; see, e.g., Johnson (1977), pp. 22ff. Loyalty by the fellows took many forms; among other duties Tafel acted as chauffeur for most of his nine years at Taliesin. Or there was this publicized incident in 1932:

On a street in Madison, Wis., Architect Frank Lloyd Wright met one C. R. Sechrest, one time farm laborer at Taliesin, [who] . . . demanded $282 which he said was owing his wife for cooking at Taliesin. They scuffled, fell in the gutter, Sechrest's knee broke Wright's nose. Two nights later five of Wright's students called on Sechrest with a blacksnake whip shouting "Kill the s-o-b!" Sechrest drove them out with a butcher knife, had them arrested. The judge thought $100 fine and 60 days in jail "inadequate." (*Time,*** 20 November 1932, p. 52)**

Tafel (1981), p. 62, denies the episode took place.

15. F. L. Wright (1936a), p. 210.

16. O. L. Wright (1963), pp. 206–207.

17. Smith (1979), p. 135.

18. F. L. Wright (1932a), p. 238, abridged in the 1943 autobiography and slightly altered in the 1977 edition.

19. In 1932 Wright said the charge was $675 per annum; Pfeiffer (interview 1982) said it was $650 and then became $1100 per annum in 1933, $1500 in 1945, and was raised again in 1959. See also FLW to E. Bauer, 4 June 1932, and comment on p. 58, in F. L. Wright (1982).

20. J. L. Wright (1946), p. 33; and Kassler (1975), p. 11.

21. Olgivanna L. Wright (given as "Mrs. Frank Lloyd Wright" in the author line), "The Last Days of Katherine Mansfield," *The Bookman,* 23 (March 1931), pp. 6, 12. Perhaps thinking about Gurdjieff's Institute and its relation to the proposed Fellowship revived her memories of Mansfield's death. It is one of Olgivanna's best pieces of writing.

      When Mansfield entered the Institute in October 1922, it had begun operations at Fontainebleau; forty "mostly Russian" people were still cleaning and clearing and constructing (see John Middleton Murry, *Katherine Mansfield's Letters to John Middleton Murry 1913–1922* [London, 1951], p. 676.). Mansfield has described her first meeting with Olgivanna: "Presently steps came up and a woman appeared, very simply dressed, with her head bound in a white handkerchief. She had her arms full of logs. I spoke in French, but she didn't understand. English—no good. But her glance was so lovely—laughing and gentle, absolutely unlike people as I have known people" (Murry, p. 678). By November Mansfield and Olgivanna were "old friends." Mansfield died of tuberculosis in January 1923.

22. A remarkability not agreed to by Mrs. Wright (see the letter of FLW to Gutheim, 14 February 1941, FLW Archives).

23. As quoted in Twombly (1979), p. 147. Over the years words have been written in praise of or damning institutes like Gurdjieff's. His was known falsely, for instance, as the place that killed Mansfield. There are two carefully considered views that are less journalistic than Lewis's. The latest is by a long-alert biographer of Mansfield, Anthony Alpers, whose recent book *The Life of Katherine Mansfield* (London, 1980) held that Gurdjieff's teachings were

either too naive or too well worn, and were mainly suitable for persons not well read. Of moral content they had none. His "know thyself" was hardly modern Greek; his notion of "balancing the centres" came from the sort of man who could make a good firm milking stool, but would hardly depose the Trinity. Yet he comes out of all the literature as a kindly decent friend to Katherine Mansfield in her last and most desperate endeavour to locate her "self." . . .

      He was not a fraud. A man who lays bricks and planes wood, cuts out dress materials and printing stencils, designs all the decorations of a "holy place," mends Oriental carpets, and picks up a little shredded cabbage in the kitchen, is something else. (Pp. 378–379)

A view that might have been shared by the apprentices at Taliesin and perhaps by Wright. Another view is that of Olgivanna, that "one of the most humane acts Gurdjieff ever did was to accept her [Mansfield] into the Institute" ("Last Days," p. 6). The opinion of everyone including her doctors was that Mansfield was dying when she entered the Institute. John Middleton Murry, Mansfield's husband, referred to the Institute as "a kind of spiritual brotherhood . . . to help its members to achieve a spiritual regeneration" (*Journal of Katherine Mansfield* [New York, 1946], p. 255).

24. Twombly (1979), p. 147.

25. FLW to Kenneth Bayes, London, 17 July 1939, copy in FLW Archives; and F. L. Wright (1943), p. 510. For the character and kind of restrictions imposed by the Wrights see Tafel (1979), pp. 128ff.; Twombly (1979), pp. 173ff.; and compare Alpers, *Life of Katherine Mansfield,* pp. 367–369. Also see Sidney K. Robinson, "Composed Places: Taliesin and Alden Dow's Studio," Ph.D. dissertation, University of Michigan, 1974, esp. chapters 7–9, and S. K. Robinson, *The Architecture of Alden B. Dow* (Detroit, 1983). On Gale and Gurdjieff, see Derleth (1940), pp. 176–193.

26. Tafel (1979), p. 138.

27. Ibid., p. 139. The Wrights' daughter Iovanna studied with Gurdjieff (ibid., p. 135). The regimen at Taliesin can be found also in these letters and notes, all in F. L. Wright (1982): a list of rules of 4 January 1934 (pp. 63–64); FLW to W.B. Fyfe, 21 October 1933 (pp. 82–83); FLW to E. Bauer, 4 June 1932 (pp. 14–16); and a statement of December 1933 (pp. 205–207). See also the reflections of Dankmar Adler's daughter in Saltzstein (1969); and comments here and there in Meehan (1984).

28. Tafel (1979), p. 139; see also Saltzstein (1969), and Meyer Levin, "Master-Builder," *Coronet,* 3 (December 1937), pp. 171–184.

29. Tafel (1981), p. 62.

30. FLW to Willcox, 7 February 1934, Willcox Papers; Albert Kahn to FLW, 9 September 1932, FLW Archives; and letters to/from E. Kahn, 21 April 1932 to 30 August 1932, FLW Archives.

31. FLW to E. J. Kahn, 21 April 1932, FLW Archives.

32. Kassler (1975), p. 8. Cf. F. L. Wright (1936b) and Kassler (1981).

33. Klumb to Wijdeveld, 11 April 1933, Wijdeveld Papers.

34. Kaufmann (1986), pp. 36–39.

35. See various testimonials in F. L. Wright (1982), pp. 193–205; and also Bernard M. Boyle, "Taliesin, Then and Now," *Architecture,* 73 (March 1988), pp. 129–132.

36. Branden (1986), pp. 190–191. I also discuss Rand's reactions to Taliesin in "Frank Lloyd Wright versus Hollywood" (manuscript in preparation).

37. Branden (1986), p. 191.

38. Quotations selected from Nott (1969), pp. 146–155.

39. Anne Baxter (daughter of Wright's daughter Catherine), *Intermission: A True Tale* (London, 1977), p. 19. See also the short remembrances of 12 former apprentices in Mervyn Kaufmann, "Frank Lloyd Wright Remembered," *House Beautiful,* 126 (August 1984), pp. 30, 111.

40. F. L. Wright (1943), p. 291, slightly altered in F. L. Wright (1977), p. 419.

THEME / **Architectural Issues: National versus International**

6 Architecture

1. Cf. Johnson (1977).

2. Johnson (1987c), pp. 105–106.

3. Mumford (1952), p. 398.

4. Behrendt (1952), pp. 398–399.

5. I discuss comparable uses of steel in "Frank Lloyd Wright versus Hollywood" (manuscript in preparation); and see Hines (1982), pp. 120–127.

6. E. Masselink to G. Nelson, 14 April 1938 and 25 April 1938, copies in FLW Archives.

7. Behrendt (1952), p. 399.

8. Andrews (1955), p. 172; and cf. Hines (1982) and David Gebhard, *The Architecture of Gregory Ain* (Santa Barbara, 1980). The unbuilt Sussman house (1955) was used for the 1988–1990 "In the Realm of Ideas" exhibition. It has a Davidson plan.

9. See also Pommer (1983), pp. 158–169.

10. Donald Langmead and I present this research and discuss the relevant issues in our "Frank Lloyd Wright: The View From Holland" (manuscript in preparation).

11. FLW to E. Noble (daughter), 11 March 1930, copy in FLW Archives.

12. E. Noble (mother) to FLW, c. May 1930, FLW Archives.

13. Frank Lloyd Wright, "Principles of Design," *Annual of American Design,* 1931, pp. 101–104.

14. FLW to Hitchcock, 8 March 1958, in F. L. Wright (1984); and cf. Muschamp (1983) here and there (no index was provided, a worrisome discourtesy).

15. See Schulze, (1985), pp. 237ff; and cf. Pfeiffer (1985a).

16. Frank Lloyd Wright, "Living in the Desert," *Arizona Highways,* 25 (October 1949), p. 2.

17. Banham (1969), p. 516.

18. FLW to Alden Dow, 11 September 1934, F. L. Wright (1982), p. 26.

19. Tafel (1979), pp. 194–200.

20. This is discussed in my "Frank Lloyd Wright versus Holywood" (manuscript in preparation).

21. If as generally agreed *Taliesin* no. 1, in which the zoned houses appeared, was published in 1934 then the date of 1935 in Pfeiffer (1985a) is in error. The "suburban" zoned house was also illustrated in that publication. Wright stated that his zoned designs were a direct response to a suggestion contained in a letter (published in *Taliesin*) from Dorothy Johnson Field. Her ideas about the zoned house were eventually published as *The Human House* (New York, 1939) where Wright's zoned house project and Willey house were illustrated. That book in turn influenced Robert Woods Kennedy's very fine study, *The House and the Art of Its Design* (New York, 1953), where Field and Wright are quoted (pp. 127–130) and H. H. Harris and Wright are illustrated.

7 Prejudices Old and New

Epigraph, Matthew Nowicki, "Function and Form," in Mumford (1952), p. 417.

1. Dwight Janes Baum, "This Modernism," *Pencil Points,* 13 (September 1932), p. 600. See also the AIA pamphlet "A symposium on contemporary architects" (Washington, D.C., 1931).

2. John F. Harbeson, "Design in Modern Architecture, 3—The City of Tomorrow," *Pencil Points,* 9 (March 1930), pp. 165–172. Cf. "Frank Lloyd Wright and Hugh Ferriss Discuss This Modern Architecture," *Architectural Forum,*

63 (November 1930), pp. 535–538 (taken from the text of a radio broadcast).

3. See, for instance, Dora Landau, "An American Architect Exhibits in Berlin," *The American Magazine of Art,* 23 (July 1931), p. 165; W. L[eotze], "Unter der Lupe, Frank Lloyd Wright und die Kritik," *Die Form,* 6 (September 1931), pp. 356–358; Bull (1931), p. 54; and "Wright in Berlin," *The Art Digest,* 5 (July 1931), p. 12.

4. From my review of the evidence; see also Sweeney (1978).

5. Cf. Leonard K. Eaton, *American Architecture Comes of Age: European Reaction to H. H. Richardson and Louis Sullivan* (Cambridge, Mass., 1972).

6. Tselos (1931), p. 42. In Tselos's view the Bauhaus exhibit was also wanting.

7. Klumb to Hoffman, 5 September 1980, in Donald Hoffman, *Frank Lloyd Wright's Robie House* (New York, 1984), p. 27.

8. Announced in, e.g., "Exhibition of Modern Architecture," *Architectural Record,* 71 (January 1932), p. 29. Of the better-known German architects, only Mies van der Rohe and Mendelsohn drew Wright praise. When Gropius and Le Corbusier visited the University of Wisconsin in the 1930s (at different times) they asked to visit Taliesin; Wright refused (see Tafel 1979). On Mendelsohn, see, e.g., "Frank Lloyd Wright and Hugh Ferriss Discuss This Modern Architecture," p. 536, and "Wright in Berlin," p. 12, where Mandelsohn described Wright as "a great artist whom we love as the father of new times." See also Mandelsohn, "Frank Lloyd Wright," *Wasmuth's Monatshefte für Baukunst,* 10 (1926), pp. 244–246; Mendelsohn, "Frank Lloyd Wright und siene historische Belentung," *Das neue Berlin* (September 1929), pp. 180–181; and Tafel (1979), p. 151. On Mies see, e.g., Tafel (1979), pp. 69ff, and Schulze (1985), esp. pp. 178–183.

9. New York, 1932; reprint edition 1966.

10. F. L. Wright (1932c), p. 10.

11. Ibid., p. 11. On Le Corbusier's 1925 letter see Turner (1983), pp. 351–352; Donald Langmead and I discuss it in our "Frank Lloyd Wright: The View from Holland" (manuscript in preparation).

12. FLW to P. Johnson, 11 February 1932, in F. L. Wright (1984), pp. 90–91.

13. FLW to J. Nesbitt, 4 October 1954, FLW Archives.

14. Vincent Scully, "Frank Lloyd Wright and Philip Johnson at Yale," *Architectural Digest,* 43 (March 1986), p. 91.

15. Stanley Tigerman, "Mies van der Rohe: A Moral Modernist Model," *Perspecta 22* (New York, 1986), p. 115.

16. Statement in F. L. Wright (1982), p. 205.

17. Reyner Banham, "A Set of Actual Monuments," *Architectural Review,* 175 (April 1989), p. 90.

18. Frank Lloyd Wright, "To the students of the Beaux-Arts Institute of Design, all departments," *Architecture,* 66 (October 1932), p. 230.

19. E. J. Kahn to FLW, 1 September 1932, FLW Archives.

20. F. L. Wright (1934b), pp. 55–60.

21. F. L. Wright (1943), p. 560. In the 1977 autobiography the words, "in our own country," were added (p. 589).

22. Alexander (1935), p. 28; letter of reply, *New Masses,* 23 July 1935, pp. 23–24.

23. Wright's attitude toward the skyscraper shifted over the years. Before c. 1932 he saw the tall building as an architectural problem to be solved. He said of Louis Sullivan's Wainwright Building, "The skyscraper is a new thing beneath the sun, an entity imperfect, but with virtue, individuality, beauty all of its own—was born. Until Louis Sullivan showed the way tall buildings never had unity, the tall building's its height triumphant" (F. L. Wright 1932a, p. 267, slightly altered in F. L. Wright 1943, p. 270). After c. 1932 his view of the skyscraper was aimed not at the architectural problem, like the Soviets, but at its social and economic implications. (Other passages in the 1932 autobiography mark the turning point; some of these correspond with parts of his 1930 lectures at Princeton University and with parts of his antiurbanism arguments in regard to Broadacre City. In any event the Princeton lectures are the predecessor of most of his writings 1931–c. 1945.) Of course Wright proposed many skyscrapers before and after 1932.

24. I am presently completing a study of Wright's architectural and city planning theories to c. 1913 for the University of Washington Press.

8 Broadacre City

1. Curtis (1982), p. 210. Johnson (1988) contains an outline of the essay herein.

2. The varieties of analysis of Broadacres are rather extensive. Some of the more cogent are by Lionel March, who gave three broadcasts about Wright on BBC radio; two were published and the relevant one is March (1981); see also relevant sections of Goodman and Goodman (1960); Grabow (1977); Reiner (1963); Sergeant (1976); Fishman (1977); Reissman (1964); Scully (1969); Schapiro (1938); Alofsin (1989); Lewis Mumford, *The Urban Prospect* (New York, 1956); Smith (1979); Creese (1985); and Collins (1963). Of less value are Ciucci (1978); Twombly (1979); and Speck (1989).

3. F. L. Wright (1958a), p. 60. *The Disappearing City* was reprinted in F. L. Wright (1969).

4. F. L. Wright (1932d). For the sources of some comments between 1931 and 1935 see entries in Alofsin (1989), pp. 41–43, and Sweeney (1978), pp. 51–56.

5. *New York Times,* 20 March 1932, pp. 8–9. See also "Frank Lloyd Wright Tells of the Broadacre City," City Club of Chicago *Bulletin,* 25 (15 February 1932), pp. 27, 29, which reports that an amazing 300 people attended the lecture, an event unparalleled since the Club's progressive days prior to U.S. entry into World War I.

6. FLW to E. Tafel, 12 November 1934, F. L. Wright (1982), p. 88; and Sergeant (1976), p. 123.

7. These were first published in O. L. Wright (1970), p. 111.

8. Curtis (1982), p. 210.

9. There are a few examples of buildings that evolve from or were incorporated into the plan, including the Automobile Inn. The Ras-el-Bar beach cabins, for instance, were modified to become the San Marcos Water Gardens project and with further revisions became a "tent-town for weekends" project of 1931. Later, the same design was used as the Automobile Inn in the 1935 Broadacres plan and remained there through 1958 (see quadrant G of Figure 3). This is best illustrated in Wright's article "Die Machanisierung und die Materialien," *Die Form,* 6 (September 1931), pp. 346–347, and Pfeiffer (1985a), various plates.

10. The plan and model were published to coincide with the exhibit (see F. L. Wright 1935b, 1935c; Sergeant 1976, p. 123). Changes after 1935 can be seen in F. L. Wright (1945), called a "second edition" (presumably to

The Disappearing City; see esp. p. 52); and in F. L. Wright (1958b), a large color liftout.

11. Based on Gallion (1950), p. 392. The Frank Lloyd Wright Archives does not possess the original drawings but does possess those used for *The Living City* (F. L. Wright 1958b).

12. Alofsin (1989), pp. 10, 22. Alofsin neatly brings together the 1934–35 published visual presentations on pp. 19–27.

13. Edgar Tafel and Frank Lloyd Wright, "The architect's many enemies: A Taliesin script, 1934," *Architectural Association Quarterly,* 13 (December 1982), pp. 65–67. Cf. Kopp (1970), pp. 164–186.

14. Wright suggested 5.0 people per family (F. L. Wright 1935b), but in 1935 the average was closer to 3.5.

15. Few authors have presented visual information for their speculations of a regional plan for Broadacres, but see Sergeant (1976), p. 169.

16. As identified in the FLW Archives.

17. F. L. Wright (1943), p. 349. Ludwig Hilberseimer's ascetic decentralized and regional pattern is very similar to Wright's; see esp. Hilberseimer, *The Nature of Cities* (Chicago, 1955), pp. 225ff.

18. Fein (1968), introduction.

19. McKelvey (1973), p. 143.

20. Fein (1968), introduction. On Olmsted's development of Riverside, Illinois, see Creese (1985), pp. 219–239.

21. Material in FLW Archives. On the Larkin Company see Quinan (1987). Walter V. Davidson should not be confused with Alexander Davidson, for whom Wright designed a house in Buffalo in 1908.

22. Tafel (1979), pp. 83–84; the model is illustrated in Hitchcock (1942), plate 312.

23. The entire plan is on a 5 × 9 inch sheet, in the FLW Archives; and see Creese (1985), p. 273.

24. As quoted in Pfeiffer (1985a), plate 158. Coincidentally in 1931 Los Angeles architect J. R. Davidson proposed a "Driv-in Curb Market" that was to be located on a city street corner with curbside and on-site parking; see Wilson et al. (1986), p. 165.

25. Illustrated in Pfeiffer (1985a), plates 188–189. The caption says construction was to be "pre-fabricated sheet steel," but the drawings say reinforced concrete. Pfeiffer (1985a) refers to "Exhibition Markets" for Davidson in 1928, but the FLW Archives, reexamining the drawings (November 1987), deemed a 1932 date correct.

26. Brooks (1972), p. 150. Marion Mahony married Walter Burley Griffin in 1911 and in 1912 she, no doubt with Walter, designed a house for Ford. Foundations were laid when Ford, the contractor, and perhaps the architect quarreled. Ford switched to architect W. H. Van Tine, who prepared plans for a new house that was built more or less on the foundations of Marion Griffin's design. Ford called the manor Fair Lane and it was complete in December 1915 as a rather Gothic "plain, oblong structure, broken by a few abortive irregularities." (See David T. Van Zanten, "The Early Work of Marion Mahony Griffin," *Prairie School Review*, 3, no. 2 [1966], pp. 18–22; Brooks [1972], p. 163; and Nevins and Hill [1957], p. 21.)

Ford reiterated his thesis of decentralization in Anne O'Hare McCormick, "Ford Seeks a New Balance for Industry," *The New York Times Magazine,* 29 May 1932, pp. 4–5. It followed Wright's article in the same magazine by only five weeks. Wright's secretary Karl Jensen wrote to Ford noting the similarity of theses and suggested the two men meet. There was no reply. Jensen to Henry Ford, 10 June 1932, copy in FLW Archives.)

27. Nevins and Hill (1957), pp. 36ff.

28. F. L. Wright (1943), p. 501.

29. Quoted in Nevins and Hill (1957), p. 226; Henry Ford, *Ford Ideals* (Dearborn, 1922), as quoted in Gallion (1950).

30. Quoted in Nevins and Hill (1957), p. 227.

31. Ibid., p. 229.

32. Quoted in ibid.

33. See Wik (1972), chapters 6 and 7.

34. Wik (1972), pp. 106–108; Nevins and Hill (1957), chapter 12; Ciucci et al. (1978), pp. 333ff.; Sergeant (1976), pp. 133–134; Scott (1964), pp. 301ff.; Henry Ford, *My Life and Work* (London, 1922), chapter 13.

35. Gutheim (1941), p. 144.

36. F. L. Wright (1931), pp. 108–109. See also Ciucci (1978).

37. Henry Ford, *Moving Forward* (New York, 1931).

38. Nevins and Hill (1957), p. 317. See also ibid., chapter 12, and Wik (1972), chapter 7.

39. Stein (1956), p. 19.

40. See esp. Michael Simpson, *Thomas Adams and the Modern Planning Movement* (London, 1985).

41. Cf. Anne Whiston Spirn, *The Granite Garden* (New York, 1984). See also Creese (1985), pp. 241–278.

42. Lipman (1986), pp. 9, 13.

43. Barney (1965), p. 155.

44. Lipman (1986), p. 15.

9 Bitter Root

1. Information about the Montana projects is taken from Johnson (1987b), which was based on research in the FLW Archives, University of Montana Archives, and Bitter Root Valley Archives, Hamilton, and site visits in 1985.

2. I discuss this in "Frank Lloyd Wright versus the City: Architectural and City Planning Theory to 1913" (manuscript in preparation).

10 And Le Corbusier?

1. William H. Jordy, "'I Am Alone': Le Corbusier, Bathrooms, and Airplanes," in Hilton Kramer, ed., *The New Criterion Reader* (New York, 1988), p. 176.

2. Cf., e.g., Lampugnani (1982), pp. 66ff.

3. Barnett (1986), p. 115.

4. Ibid., pp. 115ff.

5. Pfeiffer (1985b), plate 64b.

6. Collins (1963), p. 74.

7. Sargent (1979), p. xvi.

8. J. L. Wright (1946), pp. 33–34; freely selected from section 5, lines 109–134. Parenthetically the comments of

Harold W. Blodgett and Scully Bradley are relevant. To Whitman "the broad-axe is an emblem of a 'long varied train' which is the poem itself, powerfully setting forth the attributes and shapes which the great instrument, both builder and destroyer, symbolizes—the creative strength of man deriving from the confident, independent masculinity and femininity which the poem celebrates" (Walt Whitman, *Leaves of Grass,* ed. Blodgett and Bradley (New York, 1965), pp. 184–185.

In eight locations of the January 1938 *Architectural Forum* Wright placed extracts of Whitman's poetry, again freely selected and joined, including the following:

Beware what precedes the decay of the ruggedness of states and men.

Beware of civilization.

Charles Ashbee wrote a book he entitled *Where the Great City Stands.*

9. F. L. Wright (1933), p. 4.

10. [Statement], December 1933, in F. L. Wright (1982), pp. 206–207.

11 Lectures and Exhibitions: Willcox

1. Smith (1971), p. 5. The following discussion is based on Johnson (1987c).

2. Telegram, Willcox to White, 5[?] April 1929, and reply telegram from White, 6 April 1929, copies in Willcox Papers. Apparently Bock stayed with Willcox for only three years; in 1932 he returned to Illinois and then retired to California. (See Donald P. Hallmark, "Richard W. Bock, Sculptor. Part II: The Mature Collaborations," *Prairie School Review,* 8, no. 2. [1971], p. 29. See also Hanks 1979, pp. 77, 88, 122–123, 170.) Many of the White-Willcox letters are retained in the Willcox Papers (see Smith 1971), and four were republished in part in Brooks (1981), pp. 83–92, where Willcox is not even identified.

3. Willcox to FLW, 18 October 1930, copy in Willcox Papers. See also Don Genasci and David Shelman, "W. R. B. Willcox (1869–1947): His Architecture and Educational Theory," pamphlet, Department of Architecture, University of Oregon, 1980, in University of Oregon, Special Collections.

4. FLW to Willcox, 17 [or 27?] October 1930, Willcox Papers.

5. FLW to Willcox, 12 November 1930, Willcox Papers.

6. Weatherhead to Willcox, 16 January 1931, Willcox Papers.

7. Marginal notes in ink by FLW on a letter from the Western Association of Art Museum Directors to FLW, 12 June 1930, FLW Archives. See also the letter of FLW to Pauline Schindler, n.d. [1931], in F. L. Wright (1984).

8. Hitchcock (1942), p. 85; see also Barr et al. (1932); Hines (1982), pp. 100–105; and David Gebhard, *Schindler* (London, 1971), pp. 114–116.

9. FLW to Willcox, 21 January 1931, Willcox Papers, much of it handwritten afterthoughts ("Audac" refers to AUDAC, the American Union of Decorative Artists and Craftsmen); and FLW to R. L. Jones, 4 March 1931, in F. L. Wright (1986b), p. 65. Lloyd Wright's contact in Seattle is unknown.

10. FLW to Willcox, 21 January 1931.

11. David Shelman, "Freedom and Responsibility . . . ," in Genasci and Shelman, "W. R. B. Willcox," p. 26.

12. Clifford to FLW, 10 January 1932, FLW Archives.

13. Clifford to FLW, 8 March 1931, copy in Willcox Papers, and "Foremost U.S. Architect to Speak Here," *The Oregon Statesman,* 8 March 1931, pp. 1, 2.

14. FLW to Willcox, 2 April 1931, Willcox Papers, a portion in FLW Archives.

15. Ibid.

16. "Seattle-Made Daylight Lamp Excites Visitor," *The Seattle Times,* 15 March 1931, p. 1.

17. Robert E. Burton, *Democrats of Oregon: The Pattern of Minority Politics, 1900–1956* (Eugene, 1970), p. 74; and Arthur H. Bone, ed., *Oregon Cattleman/Governor Congressman: Memoirs and Times of Walter M. Peirce* (Portland, 1981), p. 337. See also Gordon B. Dodds, *The American Northwest* (Arlington Heights, 1986), pp. 228–232.

18. Clifford to FLW, 10 January 1932, FLW Archives.

19. FLW to Clifford, 15 February 1932, FLW Archives.

20. Putnam to FLW, 24 March 1932, FLW Archives.

21. Lipman (1986), pp. 176, 178.

22. See Johnson (1987b).

23. Donald Leslie Johnson, "Frank Lloyd Wright's Contribution to Wenatchee's Riverfront Park," *Confluence* (North Central Washington Museum), 3 (Summer 1986), pp. 92–94.

24. Belluschi to FLW, 2 July 1931, quoted in Gideon Bosker and Lena Lencek, *Frozen Music: A History of Portland Architecture* (Portland, 1983), pp. 105–107, where a drawing is illustrated.

25. F. L. Wright (1943), p. 364. Sequences of events in the section of the autobiography on the years 1930–32 are often wrong. The March trip is not in F. L. Wright (1932a) and appears slightly altered in F. L. Wright (1977), p. 390.

26. FLW to A. Barnsdall, 28 September 1934, in F. L. Wright (1982), p. 84.

27. FLW to N. Gutherie, 9 February 1931, in F. L. Wright (1986b), p. 190.

28. The show's European itinerary is discussed in Donald Langmead and my "Frank Lloyd Wright: The View from Holland" (manuscript in preparation).

29. Surely he meant "wolken kratzer"—skyscraper. FLW to Willcox, 31 July 1931, Willcox Papers. Little is known of the trip to Rio; it is not mentioned in Twombly (1979) or Hitchcock (1942), briefly and impressionistically in F. L. Wright (1943), pp. 515–519, and not in F. L. Wright (1932a), perhaps because the book was then in production. Wright was informed of his selection to the jury on 24 July 1931 (K. Jensen to FLW, 24 July 1931, FLW Archives).

30. FLW to N. Gutherie, 20 November 1928, in F. L. Wright (1986b), p. 282.

31. Based on my records, which are more complete than Sweeney (1978).

12 Lectures and Exhibitions: Brownell

1. FLW to Brownell, 2 May 1933, 1 December 1933, 6 December 1933, as described in Meehan (1983), pp. 271, 275, 276.

2. Gutheim (1941), pp. 3–4, 23–24.

3. FLW to Brownell, 5 February 1934, as described in Meehan (1983), p. 278.

4. Brownell class lecture program for May 1935, FLW Archives.

5. Brownell to FLW, 10 February 1937, FLW Archives.

6. Brownell to FLW, 11 February 1935, FLW Archives.

7. Ibid.

8. FLW to Brownell, 10 October 1936, as described in Meehan (1983), p. 310.

9. Brownell to FLW, 1 February 1937, FLW Archives.

10. FLW to Brownell, 22 May 1937, as described in Meehan (1983), p. 329.

11. Telegram, FLW to Brownell, 11 August 1937 (?), FLW Archives.

12. Brownell to FLW, 10 February 1937, FLW Archives.

13. Ibid., p. 2.

14. *Twentieth Century Authors* (New York, 1955), p. 134.

15. B. Brownell, *Art Is Action: A Discussion of Nine Arts in the Modern World* (New York, 1939; rpt. 1972), pp. 56–57.

16. Schapiro (1938), p. 42. Also compare Smith (1979), p. 171.

17. Brownell and Wright (1937), p. 87.

18. Ibid., p. 167.

19. Ibid., p. 243.

20. There are many studies of Fabianism but one of balanced and detailed value remains Margaret Cole, *The Story of Fabian Socialism* (London, 1961).

21. A personal conversation with Schulze, paraphrased in Schulze (1985), p. 211.

22. Schulze (1985), p. 211; on Mies and Wright see Tafel (1979), pp. 69–80, and Schulze (1985), pp. 209–211; Mies's relation to Wright while still in Europe is discussed in Donald Langmead and my "Frank Lloyd Wright: The View from Holland (manuscript in preparation).

THEME / **Moscow**

1. The Congress has usually been called something similar to an international or world conference, which of course it was not; see, e.g., F. L. Wright (1943), p. 541; O. L. Wright (1959), p. 37; Twombly (1979), p. 292; and Ciucci (1976). "All-Union" congresses were common in the USSR in the 1930s.

2. For example, Gill (1987) makes no mention of Moscow, Russia, or the USSR and Einbinder (1986) mentions the subject in passing.

3. See Johnson (1987a).

13 The 1920s

1. Cooke (1983), p. 356.

2. Lubetkin (1956), p. 262.

3. Taylor (1961), p. 9.

4. Ibid., p. 122. Cf. Lance Marinetti Barbi, "Marinetti and Futurism," *The Structurist,* 12 (1972–73), pp. 51–55.

5. Hahl-Koch (1980), pp. 87–88; see illustrations in Lissitzky (1970).

6. Zygas (1980), esp. pp. 112–114; Gray (1962); Starr (1978), pp. 21–22; see also Kopp (1985).

7. Zygas (1980), p. 117.

8. *Encyclopédie des arts décoratifs et industriels modernes au XXème siècle* (Paris, 1925; rpt., New York, 1977), No. 2, p. 77 and plate XLIV.

9. *L'Architecture vivante* (Paris: Morance, 1925), [part 2], plate 47; plan, section, elevation in 1927 [part 1], plate 21. For discussion of the building see Starr (1978), chapter 5; and of the Russian context see Kopp (1985), pp. 132ff.

10. Cooke (1983), p. 36; and see Szymon Bojko, "Vkhutemas," in Barron and Tuchman (1980), pp. 78–80, and Khan-Magomedov (1981), pp. 66–150.

11. Cf. Zevi (1949), chapter 2.

12. *Architectural Design* (1970), pp. 71ff.

13. Lubetkin (1956), pp. 262–263; quotation cited by Frampton (1980), p. 167.

14 Prelude to the 1937 Congress

1. Shatz (1980), p. 84; cf. Tolstoy (1981).

2. Cf. Carmichael (1976); Conquest (1968), pp. 26–32ff.; and Tolstoy (1981).

3. Fainsod (1964), pp. 195–196.

4. Deutscher (1949), p. 425.

5. Barron and Tuchman (1980), p. 13.

6. Among the Australians was Henry Pynor; see Johnson (1980a), pp. 111–112.

7. Starr (1978), p. 220; and Conquest (1968), p. 443.

8. F. L. Wright (1943), pp. 541ff.

9. O. L. Wright (1959), p. 41.

10. *Architecture of the USSR,* July–August 1937, p. 5.

11. *Pravda,* 19 June 1937, p. 4.

12. Starr (1978), p. 221.

13. Cf., e.,g, Cooke (1983); Kopp (1970); Shvidkovsky (1971); Barron and Tuchman (1980); Kopp (1985); Lubetkin (1956); the 1925 *Encyclopédie des arts décoratifs;* Voyce (1948); Berton (1977); Bliznakov (1971); and "Constructivist Architecture in the U.S.S.R.," *Architectural Design,* 2 (February 1970) the issue under the guest editorship of O. A. Shvidkovsky. Its successor was Shvidkovsky (1971).

14. Shvidkovsky (1971), p. 18; on the April 1932 decree see Bowlt (1976), esp. pp. 288ff.

15. Bliznakov (1971), pp. 3, 209.

16. As spoken to Clara Zetkin, published in *The Studio* (London), Autumn 1935, p. 8.

17. Starr (1978), p. 221.

18. As outlined in Zevi (1949); and see Arkin (1935), p. 17.

19. As reported in *Moscow Daily News,* 27 May 1937, p. 2.

20. Voyce (1948), p. 149.

21. Willen (1953), p. 30.

22. Bliznakov (1971), pp. 203–204.

23. "Soviet Congress of Architecture," *Pravda,* 15 June 1937, p. 1. The Congress was also announced in *Architectural Review,* May 1937, pp. 2–6.

24. Berton (1977), p. 222; and see also "Molotov Points Out Tasks of Architecture," *Moscow News,* 30 June 1937, p. 8.

25. *Moscow Daily News,* 23 April 1937, p. 4; and A. Shchusev, "Soviet Architecture Offers Wide Scope to Creative Talents," *Moscow Daily News,* 12 June 1937, p. 3.

15 Wright, Architecture, and the Soviets prior to 1937

1. See the George Howe and William Lescaze project for the Museum of Modern Art of 1930 in Alison Slay and Michelle Stone, *Unbuilt America* (New York, 1976), plates 195–197. Lescaze was Swiss and studied in Zurich under Karl Moser, whose son was later employed by Wright.

2. Lucio Costa was associated and Le Corbusier was a consultant; see Hitchcock (1969), pp. 519–521.

3. Starr (1978), p. 242. Cf. F. L. Wright (1910, 1911); Bliznakov (1971), pp. 142–143, 212–213; and Moisei Ginzburg, *Style and Epoch,* intro. and trans. A. Senkevitch (Cambridge, Mass., 1982).

4. Cooke (1983), p. 37, with illustration of blocks.

5. Hines (1982), p. 64; Starr (1978), p. 23.

6. MS copy, FLW Archives, original in Library of Congress, Manuscript Division. The letter promoting FLW's response is not extant.

7. MS copy, FLW Archives. The 1932 response to *Pravda* should be dated about October. The second manuscript is a letter, FLW to M. Olgin (*Pravda,* New York office), dated October 1933. FLW and Gutheim misunderstood the manuscripts when they combined and only partially quoted them in Gutheim (1941), p. 171, where the correct dates should be, as noted above, 1932 and 1933.

8. Letter, D. Arkin to FLW, no date (but referring to events that date it sometime in 1933), FLW Archives.

9. Ibid.; and Starr (1978), p. 242.

10. Typescript dated December 1933, FLW Archives. Incorrectly dated 1937 in Gutheim (1941), pp. 216–218, which differs slightly from the typescript.

11. Starr (1978), pp. 242–243, emphasis Starr's and probably Melnikov's.

12. See F. L. Wright (1934a), pp. 70–71, the date of which helps confirm the date of Arkin's letter cited in note 8; and D. Arkin, "Notes on American Architecture," *Architecture of the USSR,* March 1934, pp. 47, 48, 51.

13. Cable, FLW to CULTSWIAZ, no date but text suggests late 1935. The head of the requesting letter is cut off, so the sender is assumed to be the Society; copy in FLW Archives.

14. The paucity of information is revealed by Parkins (1953) and Senkevitch (1974).

15. Galantay (1975), pp. 42–45; Parkins (1953), pp. 16–29; Noble (1938), p. 29.

16. Berton (1977), pp. 220–221; Tafuri and Dal Co (1979), chapter 12.

17. French (1984), pp. 365–368.

18. Hall (1984), p. 53; Simon et al. (1937), p. 201; Berton (1977), p. 232.

19. Berton (1977), p. 220. See Ernst May, "Moscow: City Building in the U.S.S.R.," in Lissitzky (1970), pp. 188–203.

20. Parkins (1953), p. 33; Simon et al. (1937), p. 201. Simon's book was adequately reviewed in *Architectural Record,* 67 (August 1937), p. 28.

21. As quoted in Parkins (1953), p. 36. Cf. Kopp (1985), chapter 7.

22. French (1984); Berton (1977), pp. 232–234.

23. Both are displayed in Evenson (1984).

24. Starr (1978), p. 10.

25. Turner (1983); and Doremus (1985), but Doremus should be read cautiously.

26. Sweeney (1978), entries for 1911 and 1915.

27. *American Architect,* 138 (December 1930), pp. 48ff.

28. *The Studio* (London), Autumn 1935, p. 17. The relationship between theater set design and architecture is made explicit.

29. *Decorative Art: The Studio Year Book* (London, 1933), p. 29, fully illustrated.

30. FLW to Michael A. Kostanecki in Krakow, Poland, copy in FLW Archives, dated 2 Jan. without year. Wright asked Kostanecki to "oversee the setting up" of Wright's proposed exhibits at the Milan Triennale of August–September 1933; therefore a date for the letter of 1933 seems reasonable. (In the end Wright did not exhibit.) Further, Wright stated that "the translated piece from the Soviet you have probably seen in Shelter. I think Lescaze sent it to them." See S. T. Woznicki, "USSR—On the Problems of Architecture," *Shelter,* 2, no. 5 (1932), p. 82. Also cf., e.g., "Milan 1933," *Architectural Review,* 74 (September 1933), pp. 111–114.

31. See various articles in *Shelter,* 2, no. 5 (1932), pp. 80–93.

32. Bliznakov (1971), p. 194.

33. Ibid., pp. 195–196.

34. Noble (1938), p. 30.

35. Peter Davey, "Arts and Crafts Gardens," *Architectural Review,* 176 (September 1985), p. 35.

36. Williams-Ellis (1960), p. 266.

37. "Architects in the U.S.S.R. Meet to Consider Architecture," *Architectural Record,* 83 (October 1937), p. 59.

16 Why Attend?

1. Wright's health during 1936–37 was interpolated from the following information: letters from E. Masselink to Carl Sandburg, 21 October 1936 and 17 December 1936, Sandburg Archives; Hanna and Hanna (1981), esp. chapter 3; letter, Brownell to FLW, 10 February 1937, FLW Archives; telegram, FLW to Paul Hanna, 26 January 1937, in Hanna and Hanna (1981), p. 48; letter, FLW to Hanna, 27 January 1937, in ibid., pp. 50–51 (and in F. L. Wright [1986b], p. 126).

2. As observed by Twombly (1979), pp. 216–217.

3. FLW to D. Arkin (Moscow), 20 January 1943, copy in FLW Archives, also published in F. L. Wright (1984), p. 103, where it was also addressed to Alabian.

4. Cf. letter, Amkino to FLW, 4 September 1935, FLW Archives.

5. F. L. Wright (1937a), p. 50.

6. F. L. Wright (1937b), p. 15.

7. Letter, FLW to U.S.S.R. Consul General, New York, 22 May 1937, copy in FLW Archives.

8. A comprehensive illustrated list and map is contained in Catherine Cooke, "Moscow Map Guide 1900–1930," *Architectural Design,* 53, nos. 5/6 (1983), pp. 81–96.

17 To Moscow and the Congress

1. FLW to M. A. Kostanecki, 2 Jan [1933], p. 1, copy in FLW Archives. Kostanecki's letter to Wright is not available but see Kostanecki, "Tworczosc arch. Frank Lloyd Wright A," *Architecktura i Budownictwo,* 9, no. 6 (1933), pp. 179–187.

2. FLW to M. J. Olgin, 17 March 1934, copy in FLW Archives.

3. FLW to Alden Dow, 11 September 1934, in F. L. Wright (1982), p. 26; and FLW to B. A. Verdernikov, 10 May 1935, copy in FLW Archives. Verdernikov's letter to FLW is not available.

4. Telegram, FLW to Soviet Consul General (Boroway?), 21 May 1937, copy FLW Archives; and "City Architects Prepare for Congress," *Moscow Daily News,* 1 June 1937, p. 3.

5. Chaitkin (1973), p. 55.

6. F. L. Wright (1937b), p. 18.

7. F. L. Wright (1943), p. 541.

8. Williams-Ellis (1960), p. 266. Apparently Williams-Ellis did not give a paper, but see his views outlined in "Eminent Foreign Architects . . . ," *Moscow Daily News,* 30 June 1937, p. 3; and "Architects Vote Congress High Success," *Moscow News,* 7 July 1937, p. 10. English architect W. Townsend may have attended the Congress; see "British Architects Call Moscow's Development a Dream Come True," *Moscow News,* 7 July 1937, p. 10.

9. F. L. Wright (1943), p. 541; O. L. Wright (1959), pp. 37–38.

10. O. L. Wright (1959), pp. 39, 41 (her emphasis).

11. Berton (1977), p. 222. Berton's quotations of Wright's speech are not taken from *Pravda,* as implied, but from Wright's 1943 autobiography.

12. F. L. Wright (1943), p. 542, an interesting slip for FLW's father attended Madison University before it was renamed Colgate University. The slip was corrected in the 1977 edition to University of Wisconsin "boy" (F. L. Wright 1977, p. 568). See Johnson (1980b). Davies's "Mission to Moscow" and his role as an apologist are well known.

13. F. L. Wright (1943), p. 542.

14. F. L. Wright (1937b), p. 18.

15. "Soviet Art Notes," *Moscow News,* 23 June 1937, p. 7; *Moscow Daily News,* 16 May 1937, p. 3, 1 June 1937, p. 3, and 17 June 1937, p. 1.

16. F. L. Wright (1943), p. 543. It is not certain what "similar architects" meant, and it was not clarified in the 1977 edition of the autobiography.

17. F. L. Wright (1943), p. 543.

18. *Architecture of the USSR,* May 1937, p. 2.

19. Tafuri and Dal Co (1979), p. 174. Lurçat arrived in Russia in 1934.

20. Breines (1937), p. 63; and "Architects Begin Union Congress Today," *Moscow Daily News,* 16 June 1937, p. 1. See also *Architectural Design,* 1970, p. 107; "Foreign Guests . . . ," *Moscow News,* 16 June 1937, p. 5; and "A noted guest to architects' congress," *Moscow Daily News,* 14 June 1937, p. 4.

Breines said Heiberg was from Denmark but he was a Norwegian who taught at the Dessau Bauhaus up to 1930 and then worked in Copenhagen. Enticed by the second Five-Year Plan, Heiberg traveled with Hannes Meyer to Russia in the mid-1930s. Meyer became director of the Bauhaus on the resignation of Walter Gropius in 1928 but his outspoken support of the extreme political left forced his replacement in 1930.

21. S. Breines, "Paper Architecture," *American Architect,* 139 (March 1931), pp. 24–25, 82, 86. See also "Frank Lloyd Wright and Hugh Ferris Discuss This Modern Architecture," *Architectural Record,* 43 (November 1930), pp. 535–538.

22. S. Breines, "The Federation of Architects, Engineers, Chemists and Technicians," *Architectural Record,* July 1934, pp. 59–60, and October 1934, p. 18.

23. Breines (1937); and see, e.g., "Swimming Pool on Estate in Cos Cob, Conn.," *Architectural Forum,* January 1938, pp. 493–496 (a piece of Germanic modernism); and articles in *Architectural Record,* 82 (October 1937), p. 5; *Architectural Forum,* 70 (June 1939), p. 459; and *Architectural Review,* 86 (August 1939), pp. 64, 70.

24. *Architecture of the USSR,* May 1937, p. 2.

25. Senkevitch (1974), p. xxi.

26. "Serving the People Is Guiding Principle of Soviet Architecture," *Moscow Daily News,* 17 June 1937, p. 5; and Breines (1937), p. 64.

27. Breines (1937), p. 64.

28. *Pravda,* 18 June 1937, p. 4. See also "First Congress of Architects Opens," *Moscow News,* 23 June 1937, p. 3.

29. *Pravda,* 18 June 1937, p. 4. See also S. O. Khan-Mahomedov, "M. Ya. Ginsburg 1892–1946," in Shvidkovsky (1971), pp. 90–96.

30. See relevant sections of *Pravda* from 15 to 27 June 1937, *Moscow Daily News* from 17 to 26 June, and *Architecture of the USSR,* July–August 1937, double issue devoted to the Congress.

31. Breines (1937), p. 65. Viktor Vesnin attempted a difficult path between classical eclecticism and some form of modernism; see, e.g., V. A. Vesnin, "Working Out Style Worthy of Socialist Epoch . . . ," *Moscow Daily News,* 16 June 1937, p. 5.

32. *Pravda,* 26 June 1937, p. 51. There were three brothers, all architects; see *Who Was Who in the U.S.S.R.,* ed. Heinrich E. Schulz and Paul K. Urban (Metuchen, N.J., 1972), pp. 569–580.

33. Some confessions were painful. The composer Dmitrii Shostakovich went through a kind of hell in 1936 and finally subtitled his 1938 Fifth Symphony, "A Soviet Artist Replies to Just Criticism" (Starr 1978, p. 227). After the censure of constructivism, Aleksandr Vesnin severely restricted his architectural and artistic activity.

34. See "Architects End First All-Union Congress," *Moscow Daily News,* 27 June 1937, p. 1; and "All-Union Congress of Architects," *Moscow Daily News,* 28 June 1937, p. 2.

18 Wright's Paper

1. *Pravda,* 26 June 1937, p. 4. Translation by Donald Leslie Johnson and Sonya Hasselberg-Johnson.

2. Speech by architect Karo Alabian, *Pravda,* 20 June 1937, p. 4.

3. F. L. Wright (1943), p. 544. Perhaps architect David E. Arkin did the translation. Wright believed Arkin was the "editor of Pravda," but he was in fact an academic and architectural critic who may have written for *Pravda* but was founding editor of *Architecture of the USSR.*

4. See, e.g., F. L. Wright (1943), p. 437.

5. Wright's closest friend in Moscow according to Starr (1978), p. 223, and his personal interpreter according to F. L. Wright (1943), p. 544.

6. Ibid., last paragraph. The number of errors in just part of the paragraph about his speech is amazing; for a sample see Johnson (1987a), p. 70.

7. F. L. Wright (1937a); translation by Donald Leslie Johnson and Sonya Hasselberg-Johnson. There is a typescript in the Library of Congress as well as some edited typescripts in the FLW Archives. Wright's prose is difficult at best, with vague allusions and esoteric terminology as well as imprecise grammar. Russian prose is active yet repetitive and, in the 1930s, replete with pet Soviet terms like "social order." Translation from Wright to Soviet Russian then back to English is dicey business. H. de Fries published a similar apology when he translated Wright's words into German for his 1926 book.

8. F. L. Wright (1943), p. 544.

9. "Manuel Sanches-Arcas (Spain)," *Architecture of the USSR,* July–August 1937, pp. 45–56. Wright was not mentioned in the brief preliminary program contained in the May issue of this journal (pp. 2–4), probably because he first refused to travel and then accepted in late May.

10. For a literal comparison of the two texts see Johnson (1987a), p. 71.

THEME / **London**

1. Mabel Moran (secretary at Taliesin) to G. Nelson, 8 July 1937, and E. Masselink to Nelson, 12 July 1937, copies in FLW Archives.

2. Discussed in my "Frank Lloyd Wright versus Hollywood" (manuscript in preparation).

3. H. Myers to FLW, 27 November 1936, in F. L. Wright (1984); Nelson to FLW, 17 February 1937, and Nelson to Masselink, 26 April 1937, FLW Archives.

4. Nelson to Masselink, 11 May 1937, FLW Archives.

5. Myers to FLW, 28 July 1937, and FLW to Myers, 31 July 1937, both in F. L. Wright (1984).

6. The issue was ready to distribute on about 10 January 1938: Myers to FLW, 11 January 1938, in F. L. Wright (1984); FLW to Nelson, 7 June 1937; and correspondence of April 1937 through March 1938 passim, FLW Archives.

7. Myers to FLW, 23 January 1940, in F. L. Wright (1984).

19 Interest and Preparation

1. Angela Mace, Archivist, RIBA Archives, to Donald Leslie Johnson, 22 April 1982.

2. R. C. Lindsay, British Embassy, Washington, D.C., to FLW, 19 March 1938; Wright accepted by return mail on 29 March (FLW Archives). Wright stated incorrectly that the invitation came "by way of the British Ambassador to the United States" in April 1939 (F. L. Wright 1943, p. 534; repeated in F. L. Wright 1977, p. 561).

3. F. L. Wright (1943), p. 534. This part of his autobiography about relations with the Sulgrave Manor is probably correct.

4. Wright confirmed the fee of $US 2500 (F. L. Wright 1943, p. 353).

5. Letter, "Spencer" (whoever that may have been at Sulgrave) to FLW, 10 June 1938, FLW Archives; and F. L. Wright (1943), p. 535. See also Margaret Richardson, "The RIBA Building," *Architectural Design,* 49, nos. 10–11 (1979), pp. 60–69.

6. Seckel (1938), pp. 61–63, written for a general audience.

7. Elizabeth Kassler (who had been researching Fellowship membership) to Donald Leslie Johnson, 29 October 1980; and Sergeant (1976), Appendix E. Marya Lilien was sponsored by Wright when she needed to leave Poland in front of the Nazi armies; see note preceeding the letter from FLW to the Consul General, Warsaw, 11 October 1938, in F. L. Wright (1982), p. 40.

8. See, e.g., Bruce Brooks Pfeiffer, "Frank Lloyd Wright: His Life, His Work, His Words," in Izzo and Gubitosi (1981); Storrer (1978); and Zevi (1980).

9. Gloag (1935a), p. 16.

10. As recalled in a letter, Gloag to FLW, 18 April 1956 (FLW Archives), at a time when Gloag's son lived in Prairie View, Illinois.

11. The essay was first published as an article in *The New Yorker,* 6 (29 July 1930), pp. 22–25.

12. Gloag (1935b), p. 1.

13. Ibid., p. 2.

14. Gloag (1935c), p. 202.

15. Hastings (1929), p. v.

16. Williams-Ellis (1934), p. 179. Williams-Ellis's unhappiness also reflected his concern for the English environment, first raised in a book of 1927, *England and the Octopus,* which helped inspire a renewed conservation movement.

17. Gloag (1934), p. 187.

18. Gropius to Tomás Maldonado as quoted in Naylor (1986), p. 174; Loos as translated in "Basic Principles," *Architectural Review,* 76 (October 1934), p. 151. See also Jackson (1970), pp. 54–56. For a sampling of what was actually built, see "Britain in the Thirties," *Architectural Design,* 49, nos. 10–11 (1979), pp. 296ff.

19. *The Studio* (London), 105 (April 1933), pp. 249–256.

20. Hitchcock (1928a), introduction; and see Lewis Mumford's review of the pamphlet (reprinted here as Appendix A).

21. P. Morton Shand, "Scenario for a Human Drama. VI. La Machine-a-Habiter to the House of Character," *Architectural Review,* 77 (February 1935), p. 62. For Oud's views see J. J. P. Oud, "Der einfluss von Frank Lloyd Wright auf die architektur Europas," *Bauhausbücher,* 10 (1926), pp. 77–83; and cf. J. J. P. Oud, "Wp-yw Franka Wright's na architektura Europejska," (FLW's Influence on European Architecture), *Architektura i Budownictwo* (Warsaw), 9, no. 6 (1933), pp. 188–189. On Shand see Jackson (1970), pp. 29ff; and John Betjemen, "P. Morton Shand," *Architectural Review,* 128 (November 1968), pp. 325–328. Some of Shand's articles from the series were reprinted with slight alterations in *Architectural Association Journal,* 75 (January 1959), pp. 158–183. See also John R. H. McDonald, *Modern Housing* (London 1931).

22. Willett (1978), p. 127.

23. Graeff (1975). Nineteen architects were invited by Mies, who was chosen to lead the Werkbund in 1926; the exhibition had been proposed in 1925. See Campbell (1978), esp. chapter 7; Schulze (1985), pp. 131–134; and the contemporary observation of Kurt Schwitters, "Stuttgart, 'The Dwelling, Werkbund,'" as translated by S. Frank, *Oppositions,* Winter 1976, pp. 80–83. On Graeff see Schulze (1985), pp. 106ff; and Wingler (1968), pp. 284, 375.

24. Graeff (1975), p. 153.

25. Willett (1978), p. 124.

26. Frampton (1980), p. 169; see also Searing (1983) pp. 170–177; and cf. Donald Langmead, "English Language Sources on Dutch Modern Architecture 1900–1940: Monographs Not by Dutch Authors," *Vance Bibliographies, Architecture Series £A1671* (Monticello, Ill., 1986), introduction.

27. Graeff (1975), p. 153.

28. Herbert (1969), p. 14, quoted with his kind permission.

29. Fishman (1977), p. 160. For later conscriptive schemes see Mary McLeod, "Le Corbusier and Algiers," *Oppositions,* 19–20 (Winter 1980), pp. 54–85. McLeod points to the "naive deception" that aesthetic good equals social good, naively assuming, one supposes, that the reverse is correct. Cf. Reiner (1963), pp. 71ff.

30. Fishman (1977), p. 160. See also Brian Hoonigan's review of Fishman in the *Journal of the Society of Architectural Historians,* 37 (December 1978), pp. 299–300.

31. F. L. Wright (1932e), pp. 348–349.

32. F. L. Wright (1935a), p. 116; and letter, Masselink to Hastings, 10 January 1935, FLW Archives.

33. *Architectural Review,* 81 (March 1937), pp. 99–100, written before Wright left for Moscow.

34. Cf. F. L. Wright (1932a), pp. 334–344; altered in F. L. Wright (1943), pp. 353–357. In F. L. Wright (1977), the AIA is implicated against Wright (pp. 377–379).

35. Frank Lloyd Wright, "The Chicago World Fair," *Architect's Journal*, 81 (13 July 1933), pp. 45–47.

36. Robertson (1931), p. 62. See also Robertson's book *Modern Architectural Design* (London, 1931); one "W. G." (perhaps) said that Robertson "does not dart off into rhapsody, epigrams, or daring theories as so many continental architects are apt to do, but sticks calmly to the practical facts of the present day and recalls or suggests the principles by which the material difficulties of our period may be overcome. He finds the essence of modern architecture in a revived sense of orderliness, and as one of the first pronouncements of a practising English architect on new development, his book has a special interest" (*Studio*, 105 [January 1933], p. 59). The book and review are indicative of the response by a majority of British architects (and their clients) to the vigor of European proselytizing.

37. Bull (1931), p. 540; and F. L. Wright (1943), pp. 357, 363.

38. Hitchcock (1937), p. 2.

39. *Architectural Review,* 87 (September 1937), p. 144.

40. Ibid, p. 222. See also "Correspondence," *Architectural Review,* 87 (November 1937), p. 221.

41. Robertson (1931), p. 63.

42. Cf. Hastings (1929); he was the newly appointed editor of *The Architectural Review.*

43. Johnson (1980b).

44. O. L. Wright (1966), p. 16; and cf. Barney (1965).

45. "A Summer School of Town Planning," *Architects' Journal*, 78 (13 July 1933), p. 36.

46. Harrison (1981), p. 252.

47. Stuart Samuels, "The Left Book Club," in Walter Laqueur and George L. Mosse, ed., *The Left-Wing Intellectuals Between the Wars 1919–1939* (New York, 1966).

20 To London

1. *RIBA Journal* (1938), p. 1.

2. Cable, FLW to Sulgrave, 16 October 1938, FLW Archives, where FLW states that "unexpected delays on three buildings" forced him to cancel or postpone his engagement. On 17 October 1938 FLW agreed by cable (FLW Archives) to early May 1939. Cf. cable, Sulgrave to FLW, 20 July 1938 and subsequent letters, FLW Archives.

3. FLW to L. Spivey, 18 April 1939; Eugene Masselink to Sulgrave, 1 May 1939; FLW Archives.

4. Gloag to FLW, 10 March 1939, FLW Archives. Various letters of invitation and response are in FLW Archives along with an annotated proposed schedule.

5. "Mr. Frank Lloyd Wright at the A.A.," *Architectural Association Journal,* 54 (May 1939), pp. 268–269.

6. "Frank Lloyd Wright," *The Builder,* 156 (28 April 1939), p. 789.

7. F. L. Wright (1943), p. 537; F. L. Wright (1977), p. 564.

8. F. L. Wright (1943), pp. 536–537, his emphasis; altered in F. L. Wright (1977), pp. 563–564.

9. *The Times,* 8 May 1939, p. 20. It should be mentioned that the TECTON architecture group had just published their *Planned, A.R.P.* (London 1939), i.e., air raid precaution.

10. *Spectator,* May 1939, p. 738.

11. "American Architect Looks at England," *The Observer,* 7 May 1939, p. 11.

12. Pevsner (1939); Fry (1939).

13. *Architectural Association Journal,* 54 (May 1939), p. 269.

14. "Exhibition at Building Centre," *The Builder,* 156 (8 May 1939), p. 858; and "Mr. Frank Lloyd Wright's Drawings at the A.A.," *The Builder,* 156 (26 May 1939), p. 953; and exhibit catalogue in FLW Archives.

15. E.g., George Herrick, "A Functional Office Building, U.S.A.," *The Builder,* 156 (8 May 1939), pp. 857–858; and the proposal of Johnson Wax Building was contained in "Office Building in Wisconsin," *Architects' Journal,* 85 (18 February 1937), p. 289; and "Administration Building. . .," *Architectural Design and Construction,* 9 (June 1939), pp. 232–233; and many of the articles noted here for 1937–39, all in England.

The best contemporary publication was a small pamphlet, "A new house on Bear Run, Pennsylvania," prepared by John McAndrew for his exhibition of the Fallingwater House at the Museum of Modern Art in 1938. Some of its illustrations are reprinted together with many other contemporary and new photographs and drawings in Hoffman (1978); and see also Zevi and Kaufmann (1962).

16. "Frank Lloyd Wright Architecture Club dinner," *The Builder,* 156 (5 May 1939), p. 855; and cf. *Builder* (1939).

17. "Frank Lloyd Wright," *Architects' Journal,* 84 (11 May 1939), p. 757 (their emphasis).

18. "Murus," "Frank and Free," *The Builder,* 156 (12 May 1939), p. 890.

19. F. L. Wright (1943), p. 352.

20. Discussed in my "Frank Lloyd Wright versus Hollywood" (manuscript in preparation); see also F. L. Wright (1943), pp. 260ff.; Twombly (1979), pp. 191–192; Gill (1987), p. 131; Sergeant (1976), Appendixes E and F; and Ben Hecht, *Charlie* (New York, 1957).

21. "Frank Lloyd Wright," *RIBA Journal,* 46 (22 May 1939), p. 700.

22. "Frank Lloyd Wright," *Architects' Journal,* 84 (11 May 1939), p. 757.

23. Edward J. Carter, foreword to F. L. Wright (1939b).

24. "Tributes to Bobby Carter from his friends," *Architectural Association Quarterly,* 4 (1982), pp. 68–69.

25. Reginald Isaacs, "Gropius at/in Harvard," *bauhaus archive* (Berlin, 1983), p. 12.

26. *Architects' Journal,* 84 (11 May 1939), p. 757.

27. Nott (1969), p. 138.

28. Lionel Brett, "Influence in This Country," *The Listener,* 36 (12 December 1946), p. 838, part 2 of "Work and Theories of Frank Lloyd Wright" in the same issue.

21 Reaction

1. *The Builder,* v. 156. "Organic Architecture. Mr. Lloyd Wright's First Watson Lecture. 1.—The Philosophy of That Architecture" (5 May 1939, p. 586); ". . . 2.—Organic Architecture—The Movement" (12 May 1939, pp. 907–909; ". . . 3.—The Practical Applications To-Date" (19 May 1939, pp. 951–954); and ". . . 4.—Exemplars and

Technique" (19 May 1939, p. 954). Not all questions at the lectures and their answers were published. See also F. L. Wright (1939b), where the illustrations are probably those from the U.I.A./London Building Centre exhibition; they are Taliesin, the Kaufman house, the Ardmore four-family house (1939), the Jacobs house 1937), the Johnson building, and Taliesin West. For an example of autobiographical license about the book and events in London see (and compare) F. L. Wright (1943), pp. 535–537, with alterations in F. L. Wright (1977), pp. 561–564.

2. "Frank Lloyd Wright," *Focus,* Summer 1939, p. 49; my emphasis.

3. *RIBA Journal,* 47 (20 November 1939), p. 17.

4. *RIBA Journal,* 47 (11 December 1939), p. 44.

5. *RIBA Journal,* 47 (15 January 1940), p. 65.

6. *RIBA Journal,* 46 (16 October 1939), p. 1005; *Architectural Review,* 86 (November 1939), pp. 228–229.

7. F. L. Wright (1939b), p. vii.

8. Gutheim (1941), p. 265. It is difficult to know for certain if this was a prewritten lecture or a text prepared from notes taken at a lecture. It does wander to many subjects. In October 1939 Wright accepted the chairmanship of the Advisory Committee to the Art Department of Hull House; see letter from Hull House to FLW, 24 October 1939, FLW archives.

9. See the excellent book by Coe and Reading (1981).

10. F. L. Wright (1943), p. 364.

11. Ibid., p. 414.

12. *Time,* 32 (November 1938), p. 37.

13. FLW to Spivey, 16 June 1939, FLW Archives.

14. Gutheim (1941), p. 265.

15. See "Frank . . . ," *Architectural Forum,* 67 (August 1937), p. 10, probably extracted from the same Taliesin press release published in *Architectural Record* and *Soviet Russia Today* of the same year.

16. Nott (1969), p. 139.

17. Pevsner (1939), p. 731.

18. Cf. letters between FLW and Gloag, 1940–41, FLW Archives.

19. FLW to Ashbee, 11 May 1939, in Alan Crawford, "Ten Letters from Frank Lloyd Wright to Charles Robert Ashbee," *Architectural History,* 13 (1970), p. 71.

20. Giedion to FLW, 23 September 1938, FLW Archives.

21. Giedion (1956), p. 421.

22. Ibid., pp. 424, 492.

THEME / **Gold**

1. R. C. Lindsay (probably associated with Sulgrave Manor) to FLW, 4 April 1938, FLW Archives.

2. R. C. Lindsay to FLW, 17 May 1938, FLW Archives.

22 Royal Gold

1. Information in the form of a contemporary note, no date, supplied by RIBA Archive for this and the previous paragraph.

2. Minute, RIBA Royal Gold Medal Committee, 17 October 1940, RIBA Archive.

3. "The RIBA Council 1940–41," *RIBA Journal,* 47 (15 July 1940), p. 222.

4. Lionel Esher, *A Broken Wave* (London, 1981), pp. 20–21.

5. Minute, RIBA Royal Gold Medal Committee, 17 October 1940, RIBA Archive.

6. *The Observer,* 7 May 1939, pp. 15ff for route and expectations as relayed to the British public.

7. Cf. "Architecture in the U.S.S.R.," *RIBA Journal,* 48 (September 1941), pp. 150, 155–158.

8. As quoted in Jackson (1970), p. 54.

9. Coe and Reading (1981), p. 12.

10. Dannatt (1959), p. 17.

11. Esher, *A Broken Wave,* pp. 16–25.

12. Howard Robertson, "Domestic Architecture and the Second Great War," *Decorative Art,* 1940, p. 17.

13. Minute, RIBA Royal Gold Medal Committee, 17 October 1940, RIBA Archive.

14. Letter, Secretary of RIBA to The Keeper, 19 December 1940, copy in RIBA Archive.

15. Edward R. Murrow, "Introducing America," *The Listener,* 25 (16 January 1941), pp. 71ff.

16. Charles H. Reilly, "Modern Movements in Architecture," *The Listener,* 25 (20 March 1941), pp. 399–401.

17. His autobiographical account of the 1939 London trip and later RIBA award is riddled with confusion and error (F. L. Wright 1943, pp. 534–538). Some of the errors are noted elsewhere; others are: the book of the Watson lectures was not titled *Frank Lloyd Wright;* a copy of his book did not take more than a year to reach him after its release; "Carter" was not secretary of the RIBA; Wright did not become an "honorary member" of the RIBA, nor was his honorary corresponding membership conferred before he went to London in 1939. Gill (1987), p. 405, uses the autobiography in his few notes.

18. Ian MacAlister (Secretary, RIBA) to FLW, 4 November 1940, copy in RIBA Archive. A copy in the FLW Archives is not original but a typed transcription.

19. Cablegram, FLW to MacAlister, RIBA, 17 December 1940, RIBA Archive. Mysteriously that sentence is not reproduced in the version in F. L. Wright (1943), p. 536, or in F. L. Wright (1977), p. 563. The FLW Archives copy is a typescript and the last sentence reads differently: ". . . such a culture can never lose."

20. "Elections: February 1941," *RIBA Journal,* 48 (18 November 1940), p. 17; and "Membership Lists," *RIBA Journal,* 48 (10 February 1941), p. 71.

21. His election was confirmed in a letter, RIBA to FLW, 6 February 1941, FLW Archives.

22. Secretary, RIBA, to FLW, 31 December 1940, copy in RIBA Archive.

23. Secretary, RIBA, to Minister of Information, 31 December 1940, copy in RIBA Archive. Wright may have been advised to listen to the traditional New Year broadcast of honors, or Royal favors. On learning of the award, John Gloag sat down that evening and wrote a note of congratulations (1 January 1941, in F. L. Wright 1984, p. 208).

24. The reply is extant: H. V. Johnson (American Embassy) to MacAlister, RIBA, 2 January 1941, RIBA Archive.

25. Letter, Windsor Castle (sic) to FLW, 20 December 1940, as reported in F. L. Wright (1984), p. 204.

26. MacAlister, RIBA, to FLW, 17 June 1941, copy in RIBA Archive, original in FLW Archives.

27. D. Colles (Secretary of the Privy Purse) to Secretary, RIBA, 21 July 1941, RIBA Archive.

28. As reported in a RIBA Executive Committee minute, 30 December 1946, RIBA Archive.

29. "The Royal Gold Medal," *RIBA Journal,* 54 (February 1947), p. 217.

30. "The Royal Gold Medal 1945," *RIBA Journal,* 52 (January 1945), p. 81; see also "Academician Victor Vesnin," ibid., 51 (December 1944), p. 29.

31. "Royal Gold Medal," *RIBA Journal,* 52 (July 1945), p. 277.

32. "Building Problems in the U.S.S.R.," *RIBA Journal,* 52 (June 1945), p. 24.

33. "Presentation of Royal Gold Medals," *RIBA Journal,* 54 (March 1947), p. 245.

34. FLW to C. D. Sprigg (at RIBA), 21 July 1947, in F. L. Wright (1984), p. 209.

35. J. L. Wright (1960), p. 4. See Twombly (1979) for other awards that Wright began to receive in the 1930s.

36. "Mr FLW," *RIBA Journal,* 57 (August 1950), p. 373.

23 A Touching Affair

1. F. L. Wright (1943), pp. 537–538.

2. FLW to Gloag, 1 October 1938, copy in FLW Archives.

3. "From Frank Lloyd Wright," *Christian Century,* 13 November 1940, p. 1420.

4. See Twombly (1979), pp. 218–221.

5. Telegram, Robert Waithman (New York correspondent, *News-Chronicle*), to FLW, 21 January 1941, and telegram collect, FLW to Robert Waithman, 22 January 1941; FLW Archives. Both F. L. Wright (1943), p. 538, and F. L. Wright (1977), p. 565, erroneously state that he was asked in 1942.

6. Letter, E. Masselink to Waithman, 25 January 1941, copy in FLW Archives. On the same day Wright sent copies of the cable (slightly altered) and his article to Gutheim asking him to include it in the new book, but entries in the book ended with 1939. Letter, FLW to Gutheim, 25 January 1941, copy in FLW Archives.

7. F. L. Wright (1941a); F. L. Wright (1941b); F. L. Wright (1943), pp. 538–539; F. L. Wright (1977), pp. 565–567. The *Square-Paper* version mentions a cable from London reporting on the article's reception, implying that the first *Square-Paper* was not published until early March.

8. F. L. Wright (1941b), p. 4.

9. F. L. Wright (1941a), p. 4.

10. MS copy prepared by the Tax Relief Association of California, Willcox Papers.

11. E.g. especially March (1981) and Sergeant (1976).

12. As reported in "Wright over London," *Architectural Forum,* 75 (August 1941), suppl. p. 68. *Architectural Forum* also reported that Wright's article was received with "waspish criticism," its information presumably coming from Wright.

13. F. L. Wright (1941b).

14. Waithman to FLW, 31 March 1941, FLW Archives.

15. *News-Chronicle,* 25 February 1941, p. 4.

16. Ibid. (letter from B. A. Gross).

17. Letter to Editor, copy in FLW Archives.

18. "Architects' Chief Wants Colourful New London," *News-Chronicle,* 31 March 1941, p. 5.

19. F. L. Wright (1943), p. 539. Altered in F. L. Wright (1977), p. 567, to read as a question: "a touching affair— that check?"; and a new sentence immediately followed: "And how involved and far beyond in its significance anything I had to offer." Again, anyone's guess for a meaning.

24 AIA Gold

1. FLW to T. A. Hughes, 22 January 1945, in F. L. Wright (1984), pp. 208–209.

2. This and the previous paragraph paraphrased and quoted from Wilson (1984), pp. 28–29.

3. FLW to D. W. Orr, 15 January 1949, in F. L. Wright (1984), p. 217.

4. Wilson (1984), p. 29; see also Henry H. Saylor, *The A.I.A.'s First Hundred Years* (Washington, D.C., 1957), p. 155; and Meehan (1987), pp. 219–229.

THEME / **The Closing**

1. Sayler (1930), introduction.

2. Ibid., pp. 327–329.

25 Talent and Work

1. As paraphrased in Wilson (1971), p. 403.

2. The outline of Gurdjieff's philosophy and methodology was kindly prepared by Alan Flashtig.

3. Nott (1961), p. 84.

4. This paragraph paraphrased and quoted from Wilson (1971), pp. 393–394; see also Gurdjieff (1969).

5. F. L. Wright (1932e), p. 349.

6. F. L. Wright (1932a), p. 366; F. L. Wright (1943), p. 370.

7. F. L. Wright (1943), p. 510.

8. G. Loeb to FLW, 3 May 1949, FLW Archives.

9. Meehan (1987), pp. 17–19.

10. The "red menace" in relation to Wright is outlined in my "Frank Lloyd Wright versus Hollywood" (manuscript in preparation).

11. Pfeiffer (1988), p. 45, part of a story of how Gurdjieff cured Wright's gall bladder trouble.

12. Pfeiffer and Nordland (1988), p. 175; cf. p. 171 re Cornelia Schneider.

26 The Soviets

1. Whittick (1956), pp. 71–72; and Saint (1983), pp. 132–136.

2. Nevins and Hill (1957), p. 673.

3. Ibid.

4. Ibid., p. 683.

5. Hildebrand (1974), p. 129.

6. Ibid., pp. 128ff; Nelson (1939); Handlin (1985), pp. 207–211; and *Macmillan Encyclopedia of Architects* (New York, 1982), pp. 535–537.

7. Hildebrand (1974), p. 128.

8. Wegg (1970), p. 50.

9. Gutheim (1941), p. 143.

10. "Wright, American Architect, Gives His Impressions . . . ," *Moscow Daily News,* 28 June 1937, p. 4; and "An American Architect's Impression of USSR," *Moscow News,* 7 July 1937, p. 10. On 29 June 1937 Wright attended a final reception; see "Visiting Architects Given Reception," *Moscow Daily News,* 20 June 1937, p. 1.

11. F. L. Wright (1937c), p. 59.

12. F. L. Wright (1937b), p. 15; and compare F. L. Wright (1939b), pp. 29–31 and FLW to Thomas Creighton, 10 January 1953. Also see FLW to Hitchcock, 18 February 1953, in F. L. Wright (1984).

13. F. L. Wright (1937b), p. 18.

14. F. L. Wright (1939a), p. 21. The question and answer part of the article is also in "Frank Lloyd Wright Again," *Architect and Engineer,* March 1939, p. 4. See also F. L. Wright (1939b), pp. 29–31.

15. F. L. Wright (1939a), p. 23. For other views from 1937–39, always in the same vein, see Twombly (1979), pp. 293–296.

16. As quoted in Twombly (1979), pp. 216–220.

17. August Derleth, *The Wisconsin* (New York, 1942), pp. 208–209, and Derleth (1940), pp. 221–222.

18. FLW to G. Loeb, 22 December 1943, FLW Archives. See also Twombly (1979), pp. 294–298.

19. FLW to Hilla Rebay, 28 February 1949, in F. L. Wright (1986a), p. 120.

20. Telegram, Verlinsky (also head of Amkino Corp.) to FLW, 12 October 1937, and related correspondence, FLW Archives.

21. Sillen to FLW, 9 March 1938, FLW Archives.

22. *New Masses*, 26 (15 March 1938), pp. 28–31.

23. This outline of post-Moscow events is based on a study of pertinent documents in FLW Archives; see also Twombly (1979), pp. 292–293.

24. Kazin (1943), p. 173.

25. In Wright's London lectures and reprinted in part in "Excerpt from London Lectures," *New Directions in Prose and Poetry* (New York, 1940), p. 266, one editor of which was Edgar Kaufmann, Jr.

26. F. L. Wright (1914), p. 408.

27 The U.S. Government

1. FLW To Mrs. Roosevelt, 12 July 1935, copy in FLW Archives.

2. As quoted in Myhra (1974), p. 177.

3. All statements taken from ibid., pp. 177–187.

4. Cady (1970), p. 313 and chapter 11. See also Christensen (1977), chapter 6; Grabow (1977), p. 118; Sergeant (1976), p. 136.

5. F. L. Wright (1948), p. 80.

6. Perhaps October 1941 rather than August. Wright's long response to Foreman's invitation is dated 17 October 1941 (copy in FLW Archives).

7. Letter, FLW to Wegg, 8 November 1941, copy in FLW Archives.

8. The story is digested from Wegg (1970), with many thanks to the AIA and BPI Communications Inc., for permission to quote. Wright's brief recollection is quoted in Pfeiffer (1985b), plate 28a.

9. Pfeiffer (1988), p. 22.

10. Cf. F. L. Wright (1948), pp. 80–81; and cf. description plate 28a in Pfeiffer (1985b). On Ardmore problems see the letter to the editor from J. V. Esposito (Chair, Neighbor's Committee), *Architectural Forum,* 71 (December 1939), p. 26; and from Vernon Harrison, ibid., 71 (November 1939), p. 82.

11. Wegg (1970), p. 52. See also Pfeiffer (1986), plates 128–134, which are dated 1938 or 1939 or 1940.

12. The history of Wright's Quadruple Homes and Quadruple Block Plan is complex, covering sixty years; I am studying it for a book manuscript in preparation. See "Usonia comes to Ardmore," *Architectural Forum,* 71 (August 1939), pp. 36, 142–143; and Sergeant (1976), pp. 72–75.

13. "USHA's Research Produces . . . ," *Architectural Forum,* 72 (May 1940), pp. 372–373. Cf. Harwell Hamilton Harris, "The Highway Hotel," ibid., 72 (October 1940), p. 248.

14. As recorded in Gill (1987), pp. 416–417, based on unpublished memoirs of Carleton Smith.

15. See Sergeant (1976), p. 201, for petition and signatories.

16. Einstein to E. Mendelsohn, March 1943, as translated by Mendelsohn, FLW Archives.

17. FLW to Gropius, 6 February 1943, copy in FLW Archives.

18. F. L. Wright (1948), pp. 79–84; Sergeant (1976), pp. 72–81; Priscilla J. Henken, "A 'Broad-acre' Project," *Town and County Planning* (London), June 1954, pp. 294–300; and David and Priscilla Henken, *Realizations of Usonia* (Westchester, 1985).

19. Gill (1987), pp. 413–414. See also David Guise, "Preservation: Price Tower Vacant," *Progressive Architecture,* April 1989, pp. 21, 26. To Gill's charge that Wright was numerically incompetent (p. 414), 2,100 cars end to end equals a length of eight miles, and of course it would take only twenty minutes to inject or eject those cars from a properly designed garage. Gill's credentials for competency in architectural matters remain unspecified.

28 Rededication

1. "Vincent Scully," interview, *Domus,* 665 (October 1985), p. 22.

2. As quoted in Art Peterson, "Architecture and the Tradition of Symbolism in Northwest Art: The View from

Cold Mountain," *Column,* 5 (1988), p. 16.

3. These last three paragraphs are based on Pérez-Gómez (1983), especially pp. 5–7, 263, but the entire book is commended.

4. F. L. Wright (1943), p. 260.

5. Blodgett (1985), esp. pp. 626–629.

29 A Sad Ending

1. Letter, FLW to Lindbergh, 24 May 1940, copy in FLW Archives; and see Gill (1987), pp. 402–405.

2. Nott (1969), p. 155; and cf. Sweeney (1978), pp. 248–249.

3. F. L. Wright (1941c), p. 4.

4. I explore Wright's use of the square in "Frank Lloyd Wright versus the City: Architectural and City Planning Theory to 1913" (manuscript in preparation).

5. Letter, Mumford to FLW, 30 May 1941, copy in FLW Archives along with a copy of Mumford's newspaper article (penciled date of "6.14.41").

6. Letter, FLW to Mumford, 3 June 1941, FLW Archives, draft copy only; a copy is reprinted in F. L. Wright (1984), pp. 146–148.

The parting of ways for Mumford and Wright was a sad turn indeed. It is not known if Wright's response to the open letter of 1941 reached Mumford, but one must assume so. Publicly Wright got a parthian shot. In a review of Mumford's Dancy Lectures for Alabama College published as *The South in Architecture* (New York, 1941), Wright found Mumford wrong on most counts and ended on a most inappropriate note: "With Lewis we are indeed back to . . . the imperative need of throwing the lives of American boys at Hitler—at once. Blood, sweat, and tears have been promised to the British lads by Churchill. He is keeping his promise. Lewis Mumford now promises all these to us" (Wright, "Mumford Lectures," *The Saturday Review,* 24 [23 August 1941], p. 16). Mumford's son Geddes died during the course of the war. There was an awkward reconciliation after the war, as revealed in letters of 1951–58 (see FLW Archives and F. L. Wright 1984, pp. 148–152).

References

Archives

The Frank Lloyd Wright Foundation Archives, Taliesin West, Arizona.

Royal Institute of British Architects, London, RIBA Archive, British Archtectural Library.

Carl Sandburg Archives, University of Illinois, Champaign.

Dutch Institute for Architecture and Town Planning, Rotterdam, Wijdeveld Archives, and Rijksdienst voor de Monumentenzorg Nederlands, Documentatiencetrum voor de Bounwbunst (cited as Wijdeveld Papers; material seen by Dr. Donald Langmead).

The Walter R. B. Willcox papers, Special Collections, University of Oregon Library, Eugene.

University of Oregon, Special Collections.

University of Washington, Seattle, Archives and Special Collections.

Principal Published Works

In my opinion the third edition of Wright's autobiography is the least reliable. Since he died in 1959 many readers will assume that Wright did not rewrite the text and was not its editor. I have assumed that he was not the only editor and that other people participated in rewriting.

Alexander, Stephen (1935). "Frank Lloyd Wright's Utopia." *New Masses,* 15 (June), pp. 28–29.

Alofsin, Anthony A. (1989). "Broadacre City: The Reception of a Modernist Vision, 1932–1988." *Center,* 5, pp. 8–43.

Andrews, Wayne (1955). *Architecture, Ambition and Americans.* New York.

Arkin, David (1935). "Architecture." *The Studio* (London), Autumn, pp. 12–26.

Banham, Reyner (1960). *Theory and Design in the First Machine Age.* London.

Banham, Reyner (1969). "The Wilderness Years of Frank Lloyd Wright." *RIBA Journal,* 76 (December 1969), pp. 512–519.

Barnett, Jonathan (1986). *The Elusive City.* New York.

Barney, Maginel Wright (1965). *The Valley of the God-Almighty Joneses.* New York.

Barr, Alfred H., Jr., et al. (1932). *Modern Architects.* New York.

Barron, Stephanie, and Maurice Tuchman, eds. (1980). *The Avant Garde in Russia 1910–1930: New Perspectives.* Los Angeles.

Behrendt, Walter Curt (1952). "The Example of Frank Lloyd Wright." In Mumford (1952), pp. 396–403.

Berton, Kathleen (1977). *Moscow: An Architectural History.* London.

Bliznakov, Milka Tchernova (1971). "The Search for a Style: Russian Modern Architecture in the U.S.S.R." Ph.D. dissertation, Columbia University.

Blodgett, Geoffrey (1985). "Cass Gilbert, Architect: Conservative at Bay." *The Journal of American History,* 72 (December), pp. 615–636.

Bolon, Carol R., et al., eds. (1988). *The Nature of Frank Lloyd Wright.* Chicago.

Borsodi, Ralph (1972). *Flight from the City.* New York. First published 1933.

Bowlt, John R., ed. (1976). *Russian Art of the Avant-garde: Theory and Criticism 1902–1934.* New York.

Branden, Barbara (1986). *The Passion of Ayn Rand.* New York.

Breines, Simon (1937). "First Congress of Soviet Architects." *Architectural Record,* 82 (October), pp. 63–65.

Brooks, H. Allen (1972). *The Prairie School: Frank Lloyd Wright and His Midwest Contemporaries.* Toronto. Reprinted New York, 1976.

Brooks, H. Allen, ed. (1981). *Writings on Wright.* Cambridge, Mass.

Brown, Theodore M. (1956). "Greenough, Paine, Emerson, and the Organic Aesthetic." *Journal of Aesthetics and Art Criticism,* 14 (March), pp. 304–317.

Brownell, Baker, and Frank Lloyd Wright (1937). *Architecture and Modern Life.* New York.

Bull, Harry Adsit (1931). ["Wright."] *International Studio,* August, p. 54.

Cady, David Barry (1970). "The Influence of the Garden City Ideal. . . ." Ph.D. dissertation, University of Wisconsin.

Campbell, Joan (1978). *The German Werkbund.* Princeton.

Carmichael, Joel (1976). *Stalin's Masterpiece: The Show Trials and Purges. . . .* New York.

Chaitkin, William (1973). "Frank Lloyd Wright in Russia." *Architectural Association Quarterly,* 5 (April), pp. 45–55.

Champney, Freeman (1983). *Art and Glory.* Kent, Ohio.

Christensen, Carol Ann (1977). "The American Garden City: Concepts and Assumptions." Ph.D. dissertation, University of Minnesota.

Ciucci, Giorgio (1978). "The City in Agrarian Ideology and Frank Lloyd Wright." In Ciucci et al. (1978).

Ciucci, Giorgio, et al., eds. (1978). *The American City from the Civil War to the New Deal.* Cambridge, Mass.

Coe, Peter, and Michael Reading (1981). *Lubetkin on Tecton.* London.

Collins, George R. (1963). "Broadacre City: Wright's Utopia Reconsidered." In *Four Great Makers of Modern Architecture.* New York. Reprinted 1970.

Conquest, Robert (1968). *The Great Terror,* rev. ed. London.

Cooke, Catherine (1983). "Form Is a Function X: The Development of the Constructivist Architect's Design Method." *Architectural Design,* 53 (5/6), pp. 34–49.

Cowles, Linn (1976). *An Index and Guide to An Autobiography: The 1943 Edition by Frank Lloyd Wright.* Hopkins, Minn.

Crawford, Alan (1985). *C. R. Ashbee.* London and New Haven.

Creese, Walter L. (1985). *The Crowning of the American Landscape.* Princeton.

Curtis, William J. R. (1982). *Modern Architecture since 1900.* Oxford.

Dannatt, Trevor (1959). *Modern Architecture in Britain.* London.

Davies, Merfyn (1982). "The Embodiment of the Concept of Organic Expression: Frank Lloyd Wright." *Architectural History,* 25, pp. 120–130.

de Fries, H. (1926). *Frank Lloyd Wright: Ans dem Lebenswerke eines Architekten.* Berlin.

de Fries, H. (1930). "Neue pläne von Frank Lloyd Wright." *Die Form* (Berlin), 5 (July), pp. 342–349.

Derleth, August (1940). *Still Small Voice: The Biography of Zona Gale.* New York.

Deutscher, I[saac] (1949). *Stalin, a Political Biography.* Oxford.

Doremus, Thomas (1985). *Frank Lloyd Wright and Le Corbusier: The Great Dialogue.* New York.

Einbinder, Harvey (1986). *An American Genius: Frank Lloyd Wright.* New York.

Evenson, Norma (1984). "Paris, 1890–1940." In Sutcliffe (1984).

Fainsod, Merle (1964). *How Russia Is Ruled*, 2d ed. Cambridge, Mass.

Fein, Albert, ed. (1968). *Landscape into Cityscape.* Ithaca.

Fishman, Robert. (1977). *Urban Utopias in the Twentieth Century: Ebenezer Howard, Frank Lloyd Wright and Le Corbusier.* New York.

Ford, Henry (1926). *Today and Tomorrow.* New York.

Frampton, Kenneth (1980). *Modern Architecture.* Oxford.

French, R. A. (1984). "Moscow, the Socialist Metropolis." In Sutcliffe (1984).

Fry, E. Maxwell (1939). "Frank Lloyd Wright." *The Listener,* 218 (18 May), pp. 1050–1052.

Galantay, Ervin Y. (1975). *New Towns: Antiquity to the Present.* New York.

Gallion, Arthur B. (1950). *The Urban Pattern.* New York.

Geselbracht, Raymond H. (1975). "Transcendental Renaissance in the Arts: 1890–1920." *New England Quarterly,* 48 (December), pp. 463–487.

Giedion, Sigfried (1956). *Space, Time and Architecture.* 3d ed. Cambridge, Mass.

Gill, Brendan (1987). *Many Masks.* New York.

Gloag, John (1934). "The Next Third." *Architectural Review,* 75 (May), pp. 186–187.

Gloag, John (1935a). "Design in America, VII. Frank Lloyd Wright." *Architects' Journal* (London), 81 (January), p. 16.

Gloag, John (1935b). "Frank Lloyd Wright and the Significance of The Taliesin Fellowship." *Architectural Review,* 72 (January), pp. 1–2.

Gloag, John (1935c). "Frank Lloyd Wright." *Architects' Journal* (London), 81 (31 January), p. 202.

Goodman, Paul, and Percival Goodman (1960). *Communitas.* New York.

Grabow, Stephan (1977). "Frank Lloyd Wright and the American City: The Broadacres Debate." *Journal of the American Institute of Planners,* 93 (April), pp. 115–124.

Graeff, Werner (1975). "The Dwelling." Translated in Tim and Charlotte Benton and Denis Sharp, *Architecture and Design,* (New York, 1975), pp. 152–153. Originally published in *Die Form,* 2 (1927), pp. 259–260.

Gray, Camilla (1962). *The Great Russian Experiment: Russian Art 1863–1922.* New York.

Green, Margerie (1983). "A National Register Evaluation of Camp Ocotillo and Pima Ranch." Archaeological Consulting Services, Tempe.

Gurdjieff, G. I. (1969). *Meetings with Remarkable Men.* New York.

Gutheim, Frederick, ed. (1941). *Frank Lloyd Wright on Architecture.* New York.

Hahl-Koch, Jelena (1980). "Kandinsky's Role in the Russian Avant-Garde." In Barron and Tuchman (1980), pp. 84–90.

Hall, Peter (1984). "Metropolis 1890–1940: Challenges and Responses." In Sutcliffe (1984).

Handlin, David P. (1985). *American Architecture.* London.

Hanks, David A. (1979). *The Decorative Designs of Frank Lloyd Wright.* New York.

Hanna, Paul R., and Jean S. Hanna (1981). *Frank Lloyd Wright's Hanna House.* New York.

Harrison, Charles (1981). *English Art and Modernism 1902–1939.* London.

Hartmann, Thomas de (1983). *Our Life with Mr. Gurdjieff,* rev. ed. San Francisco.

Haskell, Douglas (1928). "Organic Architecture: Frank Lloyd Wright." *Creative Art,* 3 (November).

Hastings, Hubert deC., ed. (1929). *Recent English Domestic Architecture, 1929.* London.

Herbert, Gilbert (1969). *Frank Lloyd Wright, the Architect of His Era.* Haifa.

Hildebrand, Grant (1974). *The Architecture of Albert Kahn.* Cambridge, Mass.

Hines, Thomas S. (1982). *Richard Neutra and the Search for Modern Architecture.* Oxford.

Hitchcock, Henry-Russell (1928a). *Frank Lloyd Wright.* Paris.

Hitchcock, Henry-Russell (1928b). "Modern Architecture." *Architectural Record,* 63 (April).

Hitchcock, Henry-Russell (1937). "The Architectural Future in America." *Architectural Review,* 87 (July).

Hitchcock, Henry-Russell (1940). "Wright's Influence Abroad." *Parnassus,* 12 (December), pp. 11–15.

Hitchcock, Henry-Russell (1942). *In the Nature of Materials.* New York. Reprinted 1975.

Hitchcock, Henry-Russell (1969). *Architecture: Nineteenth and Twentieth Centuries,* 3d ed. Harmondsworth.

Hoffmann, Donald (1978). *Frank Lloyd Wright's Fallingwater: The House and Its History.* New York.

Hoffman, Donald (1986). *Frank Lloyd Wright: Architecture and Nature.* New York.

Ingraham, Elizabeth Wright, comp. (1980). "Descendants of Anna Lloyd-Jones." *Frank Lloyd Wright Newsletter,* 3, no. 2.

Izzo, Alberto, and Camillo Gubitosi (1981). *Frank Lloyd Wright: Three Quarters of a Century of Drawings.* London and Florence.

Jackson, Anthony (1970). *The Politics of Architecture: A History of Modern Architecture in Britain.* Toronto.

Jaeger, Werner (1965). *Paideia: The Ideal of Greek Culture,* 2d ed., vol. 1. Oxford.

Johnson, Donald Leslie (1977). *The Architecture of Walter Burley Griffin.* Melbourne.

Johnson, Donald Leslie (1980a). *Australian Architecture 1901–51: Sources of Modernism.* Sydney.

Johson, Donald Leslie (1980b). "Notes on Frank Lloyd Wright's Paternal Family." *Frank Lloyd Wright Newsletter,* 3, no. 2, pp. 5–7. Presently being revised.

Johnson, Donald Leslie (1987a). "Frank Lloyd Wright in Moscow: June 1937." *Journal of the Society of Architectural Historians,* 46 (March), pp. 65–79.

Johnson, Donald Leslie (1987b). "Frank Lloyd Wright's Architectural Projects in the Bitter Root Valley, 1909–1910." *Montana: The Magazine of Western History,* 37 (Summer), pp. 12–25.

Johnson, Donald Leslie (1987c). "Frank Lloyd Wright in the Northwest: The Show, 1931." *Pacific Northwest Quarterly,* 78 (July), pp. 100–106.

Johnson, Donald Leslie (1988). "Broadacres Geometry: 1934–35." *Journal of Architectural and Planning Research,* 5 (Summer), pp. 129–144.

Kassler, Elizabeth B. (1975). "The Whole Man." In Frederick Gutheim, ed., *In the Cause of Architecture: Essays by Frank Lloyd Wright for Architectural Record* (New York, 1975).

Kassler, Elizabeth B. (1981). "1932–1982 The Taliesin Fellowship Directory of Members." Published by the author. Also Supplement, 1982.

Kaufmann, Edgar, Jr., (1982). "Frank Lloyd Wright at the Metropolitan Museum of Art." *Metropolitan Museum of Art Bulletin,* 60, no. 2.

Kaufmann, Edgar, Jr. (1986). *Fallingwater: A Frank Lloyd Wright Country House.* New York.

Kazin, Alfred (1943). *On Native Grounds.* London.

Khan-Magomedov, Selim O. (1981). Pioneers of Soviet Architecture. London.

Kimball, Fiske (1928). *American Architecture.* New York.

Kopp, Anatole (1970). *Town and Revolution.* New York.

Kopp, Anatole (1985). *Constructivist Architecture in the U.S.S.R.* London.

Lampugnani, Vittorio Magnago (1982). *Visionary Architecture of the 20th Century.* London.

Lipman, Jonathan (1986). *Frank Lloyd Wright and the Johnson Wax Buildings.* New York.

Lissitzky, El (1970). *Russian: An Architecture for World Revolution.* Cambridge, Mass. (reprint).

Lubetkin, B[erthold] (1956). "Soviet Architecture: Notes on Development from 1917–1932." *Architectural Association Journal,* 71 (May), pp. 260–264.

McKelvey, Blake (1973). *American Urbanization: A Comparative History.* Glenview, Ill.

March, Lionel (1981). "An Architect in Search of Democracy: Broadacre City." In Brooks (1981), pp. 195–206.

Meehan, Patrick J. (1983). *Frank Lloyd Wright: A Research Guide to Archival Sources.* New York.

Meehan, Patrick J. (1984). *The Master Architect: Conversations with Frank Lloyd Wright.* New York.

Meehan, Patrick J. (1987). *Truth Against the World.* New York.

Mendelsohn, Erich (1929). *Russland, Europa, Amerika.* Berlin.

Mumford, Lewis (1929). "Frank Lloyd Wright and the New Pioneers." Review of Hitchcock (1928). *Architectural Record,* 65 (April), pp. 414–416.

Mumford, Lewis (1931). *The Brown Decades.* New York.

Mumford, Lewis, ed. (1952). *Roots of Contemporary American Architecture.* New York.

Muschamp, Herbert (1983). *Man about Town.* Cambridge, Mass.

Myhra, David (1974). "Rexford Guy Tugwell: Initiator of America's Greenbelt New Towns, 1935–1936." *Journal of the American Institute of Planners,* 40 (May), pp. 176–188.

Naylor, Gillian (1986). *The Bauhaus Reassessed.* New York.

Nelson, George (1939). *Industrial Architecture of Albert Kahn, Inc.* New York.

Neutra, Dione, comp. (1986). *Richard Neutra: Promise and Fulfillment, 1919–1932.* Carbondale.

Nevins, Allan, and Frank Ernest Hill (1957). *Ford: Expansion and Challenge 1915–1933.* New York.

Noble, Elizabeth (1938). "Architecture in the U.S.S.R." *New Masses,* 26 (15 March), pp. 28–31.

Nott, C. S. [Charles Stanley] (1961). *Teachings of Gurdjieff: A Pupil's Journal.* London.

Nott, C. S. [Charles Stanley] (1969). *Journey through This World: The Second Journal of a Pupil.* London.

Parkins, Maurice Frank (1953). *City Planning in Soviet Russia.* Chicago.

Pérez-Gómez, Alberto (1983). *Architecture and the Crisis of Modern Science.* Cambridge, Mass.

Pevsner, Nikolaus (1939). "Frank Lloyd Wright's Peaceful Penetration of Europe." *Architects' Journal* (London), 84 (May), pp. 731–734.

Pfeiffer, Bruce Brooks, ed. (1985a). *Frank Lloyd Wright Monograph 1924–1936*. Tokyo.

Pfeiffer, Bruce Brooks, ed. (1985b). *Treasures of Taliesin: Seventy-six Unbuilt Designs*. Carbondale.

Pfeiffer, Bruce Brooks, ed. (1986). *Frank Lloyd Wright Monograph 1937–1941*. Tokyo.

Pfeiffer, Bruce Brooks, ed. (1987). *Frank Lloyd Wright: Preliminary Studies 1933–1959*. Tokyo.

Pfeiffer, Bruce Brooks, ed. (1988). *Frank Lloyd Wright: His Living Voice*. Fresno.

Pfeiffer, Bruce Brooks, and Gerald Nordland, eds. (1988). *Frank Lloyd Wright in the Realm of Ideas*. Carbondale.

Pommer, Richard (1983). "The Flat Roof: A Modernist Controversy in Germany." *Art Journal*, 43 (Summer), pp. 158–169.

Quinan, Jack (1987). *Frank Lloyd Wright's Larkin Building: Myth and Fact*. Cambridge, Mass.

Reiner, Thomas A. (1963). *The Place of the Ideal Community in Urban Planning*. Philadelphia.

Reissman, Leonard. *The Urban Process*. New York.

Robertson, Howard (1931). "Frank Lloyd Wright Lectures at the Art Institute of Chicago." *Architect & Building News*, 128 (16 October), pp. 62–63.

Saint, Andrew (1983). *The Image of the Architect*. New Haven.

Saltzstein, Joan W. (1969). "Taliesin through the Years." *Wisconsin Architect*, 40 (October), pp. 14–18.

Sargent, Lyman Tower (1979). *British and American Utopian Literature, 1916–1975*. Boston.

Sayler, Oliver M., ed. (1930). *Revolt in the Arts*. New York.

Schapiro, Meyer (1938). "Architect's Utopia." *Partisan Review*, 4 (March), pp. 42–47.

Schulze, Franz (1985). *Mies van der Rohe: A Critical Biography*. Chicago.

Scott, Mel (1964). *American City Planning since 1890*. Berkeley.

Scully, Vincent, Jr. (1969). *Frank Lloyd Wright*. New York.

Searing, Helen (1983). "The Dutch Scene: Black and White and Red All Over." *Art Journal*, 43, no. 2, pp. 170–177.

Seckel, Harry (1938). "Frank Lloyd Wright." *The North American Review*, 246 (Autumn), pp. 61–63.

Senkevitch, Anatole, Jr. (1974). *Soviet Architecture, 1917–1962: A Bibliographic Guide to Source Material*. Charlottesville.

Sergeant, John (1976). *Frank Lloyd Wright's Usonian Houses: The Case for Organic Architecture*. New York.

Shatz, Marshall S. (1980). *Soviet Dissent in Historical Perspective*. Cambridge.

Shay, Felix (1926). *Elbert Hubbard of East Aurora*. New York.

Shvidkovsky, O. A., ed. (1971). *Building in the U.S.S.R.* London.

Simon, E. D., et al. (1937). *Moscow in the Making*. London.

Smith, Nancy K. (1968). "W. R. B. Willcox: A Study." Typescript, dated 12 March 1968, copy in Willcox papers, based on typescript autobiography in Willcox papers.

Smith, Nancy K. Morris, [ed.] (1971). "Letters, 1903–1906, by Charles E. White, Jr. from the Studio of Frank Lloyd Wright." *Journal of Architectural Education*, 25 (Fall), pp. 104–116.

Smith, Norris Kelly (1979). *Frank Lloyd Wright: A Study of Architectural Content,* 2d ed. New York.

Speck, Lawrence W. (1989). "The Individual and the City." *Center,* 5, pp. 105–116.

Starr, S. Frederick (1978). *Melnikov: Solo Architect in a Mass Society.* Princeton.

Stein, Clarence (1956). *Towards New Towns for America.* New York.

Storrer, William Allin (1978). *The Architecture of Frank Lloyd Wright: A Complete Catalog,* 2d ed. Cambridge, Mass.

Sutcliffe, Anthony, ed. (1984). *Metropolis, 1890–1940.* Chicago.

Sweeney, Robert L. (1978). *Frank Lloyd Wright: An Annotated Bibliography.* Los Angeles.

Tafel, Edgar (1979). *Apprentice to Genius: Years with Frank Lloyd Wright.* New York.

Tafel, Edgar (1981). "Wrights and Wrong." *Architectural Association Quarterly,* 13 (October), p. 62.

Tafuri, Manfredo, and Francesco Dal Co (1979). *Modern Architecture.* New York.

Taylor, Joshua C. (1961). *Futurism.* New York.

Tolstoy, Nikolai (1981). *Stalin's Secret War.* London.

Tselos, Dimitris (1931). "Frank Lloyd Wright." *Art in America,* 29 (January), p. 42.

Turner, Paul Venable (1983). "Frank Lloyd Wright and the Young Le Corbusier." *Journal of the Society of Architectural Historians,* 42 (December), pp. 350–359.

Twombly, Robert C. (1979). *Frank Lloyd Wright: His Life and His Architecture,* 2d ed. New York.

Vickery, Robert (1978). "The Transcendental Dream: Frank Lloyd Wright and Suburbia." *Architectural Design,* September, pp. 512–515.

Voyce, Arthur (1948). *Russian Architecture.* New York.

Wegg, Talbot (1970). "Frank Lloyd Wright versus the USA." *AIA Journal,* 53 (February), pp 48–52.

Whittick, Arnold (1956). *Eric Mendelsohn.* New York.

Wik, Reynold M. (1972). *Henry Ford and Grass-Roots America.* Ann Arbor.

Willen, Paul (1953). "Soviet Architecture: Progress and Reaction." *Problems of Communism,* 2, no. 6, pp. 24–33.

Willett, John (1978). *The New Sobriety.* London.

Williams-Ellis, Clough (1934). "Periods and Patrons." *Architectural Review,* 75 (May), pp. 179–180.

Williams-Ellis, Clough (1960). "A Retrospect." *Town Planning Review,* 30 (January), pp. 263–272.

Wilson, Colin (1971). *The Occult: A History.* New York.

Wilson, Richard Guy (1984). *The AIA Gold Medal.* New York.

Wilson, Richard Guy, et al. (1986). *The Machine Age in America, 1918–1941.* Brooklyn and New York.

Wingler, Hans M. (1968). *The Bauhaus,* 2d ed. Cambridge, Mass.

Wright, Frank Lloyd (1910). *Studies and Executed Buildings by Frank Lloyd Wright.* Chicago. Reprinted Chicago, 1975. German ed. as *Ausgeführte Bauten und Entwürfe von Frank Lloyd Wright.* Berlin, 1910.

Wright, Frank Lloyd (1911). *Ausgeführte Bauten.* Berlin.

Wright, Frank Lloyd (1914). "In the Cause of Architecture, Second Paper." *Architectural Record,* 35 (May).

Wright, Frank Lloyd (1931). *Modern Architecture: Being the Kahn Lectures for 1930.* Princeton and Oxford.

Wright, Frank Lloyd (1932a). *An Autobiography.* New York.

Wright, Frank Lloyd (1932b). *The Disappearing City.* Chicago.

Wright, Frank Lloyd (1932c). "Of Thee I Sing." *Shelter,* 2 (April), pp. 10–11.

Wright, Frank Lloyd (1932d). "Today . . . Tomorrow, American Tomorrow." *American Architect,* 141 (May), pp. 14–17, 76.

Wright, Frank Lloyd (1932e). "The Taliesin Fellowship: A Modern Artists Guild." *The Studio,* 4 (December), pp. 348–349.

Wright, Frank Lloyd (1933). "The City of Tomorrow." *Pictorial Review,* 34 (March), pp. 4, 61.

Wright, Frank Lloyd (1934a). "How I Work." *Architecture of the U.S.S.R.,* February, pp. 70–71.

Wright, Frank Lloyd (1934b). "Opinion in American Architecture. 1—Architecture of Individualism." *Trend,* 2 (March), pp. 55–60.

Wright, Frank Lloyd (1935a). "Louis Sullivan Words & Works." *Architectural Review,* 77 (March), p. 116.

Wright, Frank Lloyd (1935b). "Broadacre City: A New Community Plan." *Architectural Record,* 77 (April), pp. 242–254.

Wright, Frank Lloyd (1935c). "Broadacre City." *American Architect,* 146 (May), pp. 55–62.

Wright, Frank Lloyd (1936a). "Apprenticeship-Training for the Architect." *Architectural Record,* 80 (September), pp. 179, 208–210.

Wright, Frank Lloyd (1936b). "Taliesin: Our Cause." *Professional Art Quarterly,* 2 (March), pp. 6–7, 24, and 2 (June), pp. 39–41.

Wright, Frank Lloyd (1937a). "Frank Lloyd Wright (USA)." *Architecture of the U.S.S.R.,* July–August, pp. 49–50.

Wright, Frank Lloyd (1937b). "Architecture and Life in the U.S.S.R." *Soviet Russia Today,* 6 (October), pp. 14–19, cover.

Wright, Frank Lloyd (1937c). "Architecture and Life in the U.S.S.R." *Architectural Record,* 82 (October), pp. 58–63.

Wright, Frank Lloyd (1938). *Architectural Forum,* 68 (January), the issue, pp. 1–102.

Wright, Frank Lloyd (1939a). "Speech to the AFA" *The Federal Architect,* 9 (January), pp. 20–23.

Wright, Frank Lloyd (1939b). *An Organic Architecture.* London. Reprinted London and Cambridge, Mass., 1970.

Wright, Frank Lloyd (1941a). "How I Would Do It." London *News-Chronicle,* 17 February 1941, p. 4.

Wright, Frank Lloyd (1941b). *A Taliesin Square-Paper,* no. [1], March(?).

Wright, Frank Lloyd (1941c). *A Taliesin Square-Paper,* no. 4, July(?).

Wright, Frank Lloyd (1943). *An Autobiography,* [2d ed.]. New York.

Wright, Frank Lloyd (1945). *When Democracy Builds.* New York.

Wright, Frank Lloyd (1948). "Frank Lloyd Wright." *Architectural Forum,* 88 (January), the issue, pp. 54, 65–156.

Wright, Frank Lloyd (1958a). *A Testament.* New York.

Wright, Frank Lloyd (1958b). *The Living City.* New York.

Wright, Frank Lloyd (1969). *The Industrial Revolution Runs Away.* New York.

Wright, Frank Lloyd (1977). *An Autobiography,* [3d ed.]. New York.

Wright, Frank Lloyd (1982). *Letters to Apprentices.* Ed. Bruce Brooks Pfeiffer. Fresno.

Wright, Frank Lloyd (1984). *Letters to Architects.* Ed. Bruce Brooks Pfeiffer. Fresno.

Wright, Frank Lloyd (1986a). *The Guggenheim Correspondence.* Comp. Bruce Brooks Pfeiffer. Fresno and Carbondale.

Wright, Frank Lloyd (1986b). *Letters to Clients.* Ed. Bruce Brooks Pfeiffer. Fresno.

Wright, John Lloyd (1946). *My Father Who Is on Earth.* New York.

Wright, John Lloyd (1960). "An Appreciation of Frank Lloyd Wright." *Architectural Design,* 30 (January), pp. 1–34.

Wright, Olgivanna Lloyd (1959). *Our House.* New York.

Wright, Olgivanna Lloyd (1963). *Roots of Life.* New York.

Wright, Olgivanna Lloyd (1966). *Frank Lloyd Wright: His Life, His Work, His Words.* New York.

Zevi, Bruno (1949). *Towards an Organic Architecture.* London.

Zevi, Bruno (1980). *Frank Lloyd Wright.* Zurich.

Zevi, Bruno, and Edgar Kaufmann, Jr. (1962). *La Casa sulla Cascata di F. Ll. Wright* (FLW's House Fallingwater). Milan.

Zygas, K. Paul (1980). "Cubo-Futurism and Vesnins' Palace of Labor." In Barron and Tuchman (1980), pp. 110–117.

Acknowledgments

Research for this book began with my studies of the Chicago and Prairie School architect Walter Burley Griffin. It is not unreasonable to again say thank you to the people acknowledged in my books and articles about Griffin, the Prairie School, and the sources of modernism in Australia. The Flinders University Research Committee financially supported my investigations of Wright, the Prairie School, and Griffin over many years and Washington State University, Pullman, helped financially support work in Montana and earlier on Griffin.

Some people kindly read portions of the manuscript and offered valuable comments, assistance, or encouragement. More generally there were David Gebhard at the University of California, Santa Barbara; Gilbert Herbert at the Technion University, Haifa; Philip Lockwood at Flinders University, Adelaide; Steve Harfield at the New South Wales Institute of Technology, Sydney; and the late Edgar Kaufmann, Jr., at New York University. Some people generously offered advice on particular aspects of the research and/or manuscript. On Soviet Russia it was my wife Sonya and Frederick Zuckerman at the University of Adelaide; Alan Flashtig at Flinders University on Gurdjieff; Carol Zabilsky in Seattle on the Pacific Northwest material and text; Donald Langmead at the South Australian Institute of Technology, Adelaide, on the 1920s, Wijdeveld, and the Dutch; Kenneth Frampton at Columbia University, New York, on European modernism and on the first third of the manuscript; Catherine Cooke at the Open University, England, on people in Moscow. Bridget Jolly at Flinders University shared her research on Buckminster Fuller and *Shelter* magazine; Marianne Keddington gave editorial help with Montana material and text; and Samuel Wayne Williams at Washington State University, Pullman, assisted with the Montana project. Thank you to Mary Banham, wife of the late Reyner Banham, for the contact.

Six people assisted with translations: Margaret Chong, Edmund K. Jettinger, Irena Pavlovs, Donald and Coby Langmead, and Sonya Johnson. During the past twelve years research assistants patiently applied their time and knowledge: Chris Gaunaut, Elizabeth Beck, Anton Johnson, Chris Finnimore, K. D. Pederson, Mary Gunn, and Bridget Jolly as early as 1977.

Staff in libraries in Europe, North America, and Australia assisted invariably kindly and promptly, especially: *libraries*: Flinders University, which for many years and with great efficiency obtained necessary books, processed troublesome interlibrary loans, and through the photographic section provided excellent service; the Library of Congress; Alvin Boyarski and Andrew Higgett at the Architectural Association, London; *libraries and archives*: University of Washington; University of Oregon; Royal Institute of British Architects; *archivists and archives*: Dr. Dale Johnson at the University of Montana, Missoula; Hilary Cummings at the University of Oregon, Eugene; Erma Owings of the Bitter Root Valley Historical Society, Hamilton; Bruce Brooks Pfeiffer, Indira Berndtson, and Oscar Munoz at the Frank Lloyd Wright Foundation, Taliesin West; Angela Mace at the RIBA Library, London; David Lea with the Longman Group, London; C. M. Whittacker (Miss) at Faber and Faber, London; J. A. Edwards at the University of Reading; Pamela Louise Johnston at the Archives of the History of Art in the Getty Center, Los Angeles; and architect Eric Lloyd Wright, Malibu.

Over the years short articles on aspects of this study have been published in *Montana: The Magazine of Western History* (Helena), *Journal of the Society of Architectural Historians* (Philadelphia), *Pacific Northwest Quarterly* (Seattle), *Journal of Architectural and Planning Research* (College Station and London), and *Confluence* (Wenatchee), and I thank their editors for permission to quote relevant parts. The Frank Lloyd Foundation gave its kind permission to quote letters and selections from the first and second editions of *An Autobiography*. The RIBA Archive, Royal Gold Medal Committee, British Architecture Library, London, gave its kind permission to publish certain material. The Dutch Institute for Architecture and Town Planning, Rotterdam, Wijdeveld Archives, gave its kind permission to publish letters. I thank all who assisted with other quotations and illustrative material as mentioned in notes and captions.

At MIT Press a special thank-you to Roger Conover who had faith in this work, and Matthew Abbate, a dedicated line editor who also guided the book through production.

It is important to know what attempts were made for information or service but were unsuccessful. The Sulgrave Manor Board, England, refused to answer a number of enquiries by mail and those made in person when I was in London in 1987. The United States Embassy, London, would not assist in 1987; staff even refused to leave their upper-floor cubicles. The Marine sergeant at the reception desk was, however, most pleasant during my four-hour wait. Horizon Press, publishers of the peculiar third edition of *An Autobiography*, refused to answer all enquiries as did the Meredith Corporation (who succeeded Duell, Sloan and Pearce) and David McKay Co. (who took over the American house of Longmans, Green). And another sour note. Of the many requests for permission to quote material the only publisher to demand a fee was Macmillan.

Ros O'Neill typed and retyped (*ad nauseam*) the manuscript with care and always in good spirit. When she departed for greener pastures, Joan Stephenson continued with equal dedication and Pat Davies helped.

To Sonya, thank you for everything worthwhile.

Index